CONTENTS

Theoretical Issues in Psychology

Theoretical Issues in Psychology

An Introduction

second edition

Sacha Bem and Huib Looren de Jong

SAGE Publications

London ● Thousand Oaks ● New Delhi

Second edition first published 2006

First edition published 1997, reprinted 2002, 2003, 2004, 2005, 2006

SAGE Publications Ltd
1 Oliver's Yard
55 City Road
London EC1Y 1SP

SAGE Publications Inc.
2455 Teller Road
Thousand Oaks, California 91320

SAGE Publications India Pvt Ltd
B-42, Panchsheel Enclave
Post Box 4109
New Delhi 110 017

British Library Cataloguing in Publication data

A catalogue record for this book is available from
the British Library

ISBN -10 0-8039-7826-X   ISBN-13 978-0-8039-7826-3
ISBN -10 0-8039-7827-8 (pbk)   ISBN-13 978-0-8039-7827-0 (pbk)

Library of Congress Control Number: 2005926012

Typeset by C&M Digitals (P) Ltd., Chennai, India
Printed on paper from sustainable resources.
Printed in Great Britain by The Alden Press, Oxfordshire

PREFACE

Like its first edition, this book is about theoretical and philosophical issues in psychology. Two questions stand out: what is *science* in general, and the science of the mind or psychology in particular; and what is *mind*, one of the most important objects of psychology?

Twentieth-century philosophy of science has passed through a tumultuous development. It came into being by the light of the Vienna Circle of logical positivist philosophers, scientists and mathematicians, who thought it was high time to stop metaphysics and its boundless speculative discussions, and 'to set philosophy upon the sure path of a science' (Ayer, 1959: 9). This new ideal for philosophy brought along a kindred ideal for science. Prescriptions for meaningful statements turned into rules for scientific theories. Empirical observation had to be the solid anchor for the logical justification of theories. And so the first, positivist, phase in the twentieth-century philosophy of science was characterized by the search for a demarcation criterion to distinguish science from mere speculative thought.

Though it is fair to say that the second phase of the philosophy of science started in 1962 with Kuhn's seminal *The Structure of Scientific Revolutions* (1970), the ensuing debate about the positivist law and order, and what is and what is not scientific, had already been anticipated by Wittgensteinian analytic philosophers – not to mention the continental philosophers who, educated mainly in an idealist context, were anti-positivists and anti-empiricists by nature. The bone of contention was the empirical doctrine of given, objective, sense data as the foundation for objective science; this was replaced by the notion of the theory-ladenness of observation. It turned out, then, that science had its subjective side; though at the same time the rationality and objectivity of science were at stake. Alongside this philosophical debate, Kuhn's work gave rise to a wealth of studies on the historical and social context of scientific theories, merging with studies from the continental, partly Marxist, side which started from what was seen as the ideological nature of science and technology.

Attention to the subjective, social origins of science divided into studies of broad socio-economic or cultural influences on the development of theories and scientists, and into work which focused on social and psychological constraints on epistemological issues, such as the construction of facts, theories and scientific culture. In these empirical studies on what scientists really do, we can also discern a turn towards psychological, in particular cognitive issues: research on observation, thinking, problem-solving, creativity, etc. So, alongside sociological interests, psychological interests for science came to the fore.

This cognitive turn in science studies interbred with cognitive psychology in general. The contribution of philosophy of mind to studies of cognition is impressive. Mind, intentionality, representation, consciousness are issues of hot debate and are among the most important theoretical issues in psychology. The so-called 'cognitive revolution' started as a rather abstract, grammar-inspired and linguistically modelled study of cognition. This mechanistic, logical view of mind was accompanied by research in artificial intelligence. Some decades ago, however, the shortcomings of this abstraction became obvious: neuroscience, evolutionism and pragmatism influenced ideas about the interaction between mental or brain functions and (social) environment, though not one but many different theories and models – mechanistic, biologically plausible, anti-mechanistic – issued from the debate.

The second edition has been rewritten. The material is now spread over ten chapters, and we have reworked, expanded, and thoroughly updated the text. The two main theoretical issues in psychology, on science (the nature of scientific psychology) and mind, and its all-over structure, though, have been maintained – theoretical concepts of science (Chapters 1 and 2); the classical philosophy of science in a light historical presentation, that is, positivism and its critics (Chapter 3); the ensuing discussion about the reliability of science in terms of the realism–relativism debate (Chapter 4); and the social and psychological context of science (Chapter 5). This concludes the first half of the book.

The second part starts with an introductory chapter on philosophy of cognition and mind (Chapter 6). Cognitive psychology started as a linguistic and logic-centred venture – mind as an abstract system of so-called 'mental language' (Chapter 7). In the next chapter (Chapter 8) brain-centred approaches to mind questioning the biological plausibility of the linguistic approach are examined. From the beginning the cognitive approach was criticized for its general confinement of mind to internal processes; in the next chapter (Chapter 9), therefore, the main proposals for extending mind beyond the individual are reviewed. In the last chapter (Chapter 10) some central concepts of mind and science are revisited.

How to use this book

Each chapter starts with a *Preview* that briefly lists its main subject and some of the issues involved. *Boxes* in the text highlight important concepts and definitions, or enumerate in a list-wise fashion viewpoints and theoretical constructs. The boxes should be helpful in identifying the key notions in the text, and provide a framework for ordering, comparing and contrasting the various approaches and viewpoints. Definitions of recurring technical terms and philosophical concepts are listed in the *Glossary* at the end of the book; a note in the margin of the main body of text signals a Glossary term, which the reader is invited to look up. The *Conclusion* of each chapter summarizes the main issues, and tries to wind up the problematic of the chapter and draw a few general lessons. To verify whether she has picked up the substance of the chapter, the reader may want to check the Preview after reading a chapter, review the boxes and have a second look at the Conclusion.

We thank anonymous reviewers of this edition for their useful suggestions and remarks. We are also indebted to Dingmar van Eck, Yrrah Stol, and Frank van der Velde for their comments and suggestions.

1. SCIENCE: WHY, AND HOW?

Some Basic Ideas in Scientific Method

PREVIEW: In the first two chapters we will present some central concepts in the philosophy of science. We discuss what knowledge is, and how knowledge claims might be justified. Almost every concept in the field has been the subject of intense debate and, though we cannot introduce them without some philosophical discussion, here we will try to present the consensus with respect to fundamental concepts in the theory of science. Chapter 3 deals with different and sometimes conflicting philosophical views and ideals of science.

After a first primer on the nature of science (1.1), the second section (1.2) introduces two extreme views on the nature of scientific knowledge and the scope of truth: realism and idealism. These epistemological positions bear upon the question of how much objectivity science can claim. The present authors' answer is an intermediate position, pragmatism. A further question is how scientific knowledge may be different from common sense.

In section 1.3 a number of epistemological concepts, that is concepts we use in our knowledge claims – such as deductive and inductive arguments; laws, theories and facts; justification and discovery of theories – will be discussed. The nature of causal laws is the subject of section 1.4. We explore some aspects of typically scientific knowledge, such as explanations, laws, observations, and causes.

1.1 Introduction: Why Science?

Demarcating science

In modern societies, trust of and esteem for science seems almost unconditional. Laboratory tests count as a guarantee of the quality of drugs, food and cosmetics. Logic and mathematics are the hallmark of certainty and objectivity. No one seems to question the almost magical ability of scientists to estimate the safety of a new nuclear plant in terms of the probability of an accident, per million years. Apparently, science is seen as the epitome of rationality. Most people believe that science and technology have led us on the way to more welfare, health, freedom and prosperity (Toulmin, 1990). In our society common sense yields to scientific knowledge: psychological testing takes the place of empathy, evidence-based medicine replaces lore and intuition. Briefly, over the past four hundred years (or so), scientific thinking and research have been a huge success. 'Unscientific' and 'pseudo-science' are (almost) terms of abuse.

Strangely enough, philosophers of science have as yet failed to find out exactly what defines science and its methods, what accounts for its success, and how to make an airtight demarcation between science and pseudo-science. Even more surprising, in the light of the omnipresence of science nowadays, some reject the idea of a difference in principle between science and other social activities: its alleged objectivity is just the self-congratulation of the establishment – whatever is accepted as truth is determined by power and propaganda. These philosophers consider the practice of scientific inquiry the subject matter of sociology (see Chapter 5), to be explained in the same way as one might study primitive tribes or groups like Hell's Angels: acceptance of theories is governed by 'mob psychology' rather than by objective 'scientific' criteria (see Chapters 4.3 and 4.5). These social and anarchistic approaches tend towards **relativism**; one theory is as good as the next one, and preferences for any scientific approach are due to arbitrary, irrational factors.

We will defend the view that scientific practice is *not* arbitrary and that scientific knowledge has a legitimate claim to **truth**; that it, in a way, corresponds to an external reality, while at the same time we recognize that it is subject to a host of social, pragmatic and sometimes irrational influences, and that scientific truth is not something separate from human concerns.

Unification and underlying causes

An impressive feature of science is that it can explain disconnected phenomena as the effects of underlying causal structures. A bewildering variety of chemical reactions, for instance, can elegantly and parsimoniously be explained within the framework of

Mendeleyev's table of elements, which in turn is explained by the composition of chemical elements (atoms, consisting of electrons, neutrons and protons) governing binding and so on. A good example in psychology (although a controversial theory) would be psychoanalysis, which shows how underlying traumas produce neurotic behaviour. Theories unify and systematize knowledge. Everyday phenomena are *reduced* to something more basic; they can be fitted into a comprehensive theory, and in that way can be explained and predicted (and manipulated in laboratories). That, of course, is a major triumph of science. Reduction also has the somewhat disturbing consequence that these everyday phenomena are 'really' nothing but atoms and molecules, that thoughts are nothing but physiological mechanisms, etc. Explaining, for instance, the physiological mechanisms of consciousness or memory seems tantamount to eliminating the interesting aspects of mental life, and reducing real people like you and me to drab machines (for the problem of reduction, see Chapter 2.5).

'Criticism': keeping an open mind

Another meeting point of science and culture is that science has been associated with a critical attitude, open-mindedness, and Western liberal democracy (e.g. Popper, 1966). Historically, the rise of empirical critical investigation and the rejection of authority have gone together on several occasions. It was characteristic of Protestantism and the associated New Learning movement in England in the middle of the seventeenth century, which combined a politically progressive (if not subversive) demand for freedom of speech and press with the development of science, mathematics and medicine (see Schafer, 1983). It could be argued that science is a characteristic of modern society: rejection of dogma, a critical attitude towards authority, the feeling that in thinking for oneself an individual can find the truth. Others, however, see science as the stronghold of political oppression: it has been identified (especially in psychology and the human sciences) by, among others, Marxists and feminists with repressing human concerns in a methodological straitjacket, providing the establishment with ideological legitimations and/or the technological means for maintaining the status quo of capitalist exploitation and unthinking technocratic dominance (Marcuse, 1964; Weizenbaum, 1976; see Chapter 5).

More generally, science has been part of the project of modernity (e.g. Toulmin, 1990), seeking rational criteria for conduct in a wide range of human activities. Thus, it has received its share of postmodernist criticism, which rejects the idea of universal criteria for rationality (Rorty, 1979; Feyerabend, 1975).

This kind of debate on the proper place of science, its limitations and strengths, may be elucidated (if not decided) against the background of a principled account of the nature and limitations of knowledge, and of scientific knowledge in particular. Philosophers call the special branch of their trade that deals with evaluating the claims of knowledge: **epistemology**.

glossary

1.2 Knowledge: Realism and Idealism (Relativism), Common Sense and Science

Realism

Knowledge is, according to most authors, justified true belief. Of course, one may ask how to fixate beliefs, and what constitutes justification. In broad outline, two possible grounds for justification have been proposed: one, idealism, focusing on the knower, the individual or social processes leading to knowledge claims; the other, realism, focusing on the known, the object of knowledge.

glossary   **Realism** says that knowledge corresponds to reality; more precisely, that terms of our theories refer to, 'correspond' with, real things in the world. Scientific realism is probably the (largely implicit) image most working scientists have of what empirical investigation really is (see Chapter 3). It is sometimes assumed that reality consists of elementary atomic facts, which are reflected in observation statements, plus the logical connections between them. Such observation statements thus represent elementary states of affairs ('facts') in the world, and they are connected by tautological logical rules, so that the build-up of knowledge makes a kind of mental blueprint of the world,
glossary   a **theory**. Language reflects reality in a mirror-like fashion, like a picture, or perhaps more accurately, like a blueprint (see Chapter 3.3 for the early Wittgenstein's picture
glossary   theory of truth). The common view of **truth** in realism is **correspondence**: theories are true if they correspond with nature. The unsolved (and unsolvable) problem, however, is that there is no measure for agreement between language and reality – if only because it would have to be put in language, in the form of a theory. Hence, objectivity in the sense of letting the world speak for itself, and objective knowledge as gathering its reflections in the mirror of our theoretical representations, is an illusion. When we ask whether some theoretical term is objectively real, for example, whether personality traits really exist, we can only give the answer in the form of a statement.

Idealism and relativism

glossary   The alternative, **idealism**, holds that the world as we know it is somehow a creation of the mind. Our knowledge is a subjective product, and does not necessarily correspond to an outside world; it is not even clear what the concept of an outside world exactly means, if it is construed as independent of a knowing subject. Idealism tends
glossary   to **relativism**; if knowledge is a subjective construction, then every subject or every group, every historical period, or socio-economic class may have its own truth.

Idealism is the classical alternative to realism. If all knowledge is a subjective construction, there is no rational, objective way to choose between different points of view. If theories are completely in the eye of the beholder, and have no relation with reality, then anything goes. Idealists like Berkeley, Kant and Descartes were forced to introduce God or Universal Human Nature to arrange for some correspondence between representations in individual minds and the represented things in the world.

The common view of **truth** in idealism is **coherence**: theories are true if they are consistent with the rest of our knowledge. The idea has some plausibility in, for example, mathematics: mathematical proofs are true when derived from a theorem's axioms. Mathematics is a self-contained construction of the mind: its truth cannot be checked by empirical means – it makes no sense to start to measure actual triangles in the world to see whether their angles always add up to 180 degrees. Rather, we deduce this result from a web of other internally cohering statements.

Relativism is a more modern term that emphasizes the collective nature and social determinants of ideas, and the impossibility of universal, objective knowledge. A position close to idealism and relativism is social constructionism: it is believed that much of science is a human construction, a reflection of social interactions in a collective of researchers and society at large, more than a reflection of the world. In Chapter 4 relativism (anti-realism) is discussed, and Chapter 5 is about the social and psychological influences on theory choice.

The dilemma: the impossibility of 'objective' knowledge

So, we seem to have two equally unattractive options: *idealism* – the mind makes up the world, perhaps entirely confabulates it; or *realism* – assuming that the world, as it is in itself, independent of human exploration and theorizing, is accessible to us. The latter option, which assumes that there is some criterion for matching a 'God's eye point of view' (Putnam, 1981) with our own view, is of course paradoxical. As Rorty (1979: 298) puts it, it involves the notion 'that we are successfully representing according to Nature's own conventions of representation', rather than 'that we are successfully representing according to our own'. In other words, there is no criterion for comparing our theories directly with the world, since any such comparison must be, it seems, a theory, so that there is no way of getting beyond, or stepping out of theory. Thus, realism in the epistemological literal sense is impossible.

Indirect support for *scientific realism* is sometimes sought in the empirical success of empirical investigations, especially in physics (Boyd, 1984). If new findings fit with and extend existing theories, and our world image seems to converge towards a final theory, then these theoretical terms (atoms, quarks, etc.) will probably correspond to something real; hence the name for this position, *convergent realism*. However, patently wrong theories can be quite successful predictors (Laudan, 1991). It seems that a theory's empirical success is no guarantee for truth-as-correspondence-with-the-world. But, of course, success is important, as the pragmatic view emphasizes. We postpone a more elaborate discussion of realism and relativism until Chapter 4, but let us offer you a preview of our own position.

The pragmatic view: functional knowledge

Our position in the realism–idealism dichotomy is that knowledge is interactive, is the product of actively exploring the world, revealing reality by acting on it. This is in a sense an intermediate position between realism and idealism or relativism (Bem, 1989), between **objectivism** and subjectivism. The idea is that 'the mind and the world jointly make up the mind and the world' (Putnam, 1981: xi). The product of this conjunction is subject-relative but not subjective or relativistic in the sense of arbitrary. We call this a functional view of knowledge. It holds that knowledge is a kind of interaction of subject and object, rather than being either passive picturing or subjective constructing. Knowledge is a methodologically regulated, constrained form of human action (praxis), and therefore is evaluative and value laden. In Rorty's (1979) words, knowing is coping with the world rather than mirroring it. Therefore, we should expect that the meaning of theoretical terms derives from their practical use, and that manipulation is a determinant in the structure of knowledge.

To sum up, the notion of functional knowledge designates an interactional view of the nature of knowledge, which avoids the extremes of realism and idealism or relativism, of focusing exclusively either on the objective, or on the subjective pole.

BOX 1.1   Realism, idealism and pragmatism

Realism: Knowledge pictures the objective world.
               Truth is correspondence between knowledge and world.
Idealism: Knowledge is a subjective (or social) construction.
               Truth is coherence with the rest of knowledge.
Pragmatism: Knowledge is functional and interactive, coping with the world.
               Truth is success.

Everyday knowledge and scientific knowledge

The difference between everyday knowledge and scientific knowledge is loosely related to questions concerning the nature of scientific methodology and scientific explanation, to the tension between methodological reduction and phenomenological experience, and to the relation between explanation and understanding. These questions we will set out later in this chapter.

The philosopher Wilfred Sellars (1963) made the classic distinction between the manifest and the scientific image. 'Image' refers to the concept of man in the world, the framework in terms of which man views himself. The manifest image is the world of objects and persons of sophisticated common sense, including traditional philosophical systems which are reflections on and refinements of primitive self-consciousness. The scientific image is the world of particles and forces posited by advanced science. Thus, the difference is 'not that between an unscientific conception of man-in-the-world and a scientific one, but between that conception which limits itself to what correlational techniques can tell us about perceptible and introspectible events, and that which postulates imperceptible objects and events for the purpose of explaining correlations between perceptibles' (Sellars, 1963: 19).

So, on the one hand, there is the image of refined categories of common sense and, on the other hand, the image in terms of postulated underlying reality; and these often seem in conflict, each claiming to be the true and complete account of man in the world. The scientific image aims at replacing the manifest one; it holds that water, for instance, is really H_2O; that only the scientific table as described in physical terms is real, the common-sense table is an illusion; that a person and her or his thoughts and feelings are really neurophysiological processes.

Three ways of confronting both images suggest themselves: (1) we may assume that they are identical – this is obviously wrong, since, strictly speaking, molecules are not wet or coloured; (2) the manifest image is real, and the scientific image is only an abstract or condensed way of describing it; (3) the scientific image is real, and the manifest image is only an appearance. Sellars assumes that the scientific image is in principle adequate and true.

Sellars goes for a fourth option: (4) – both are real. He wants to unite two images in 'stereoscopic' vision; we should realize that science is not finished, but might progress and recreate in its own terms the concepts of the manifest image. A fine example of this approach is Dennett's (1991a) theory of consciousness, which tries to incorporate consciousness in a state-of-the-art cognitive-neurophysiological theory (see Chapters 6 and 10). However, Sellars has also a more utopian view of integrating science with the goals of a community, appropriating the world as conceived by science into a rational and meaningful way of life.

To sum up, the relation of science and common sense is often conceived as a border dispute, with science in the role of the invader. The view taken in this book is that the relation between science and common sense is a continuum, in the sense that scientific methods are a restricted and regimented outgrowth of human praxis. In our view science can be best understood against the background of practice. A large part of Chapter 4 will be devoted to a discussion of a pragmatic view in the philosophy of science, as contrasted with the theory-centred view.

Some characteristics of scientific knowledge

Historically, science is no doubt continuous with the knowledge and concerns of daily life. In Western society practical problems, such as optimizing fertility in agriculture, measuring land, traditional healthcare, etc., have more or less smoothly merged into chemistry, geometry, biochemistry. There is apparently no sharp division between pre-scientific and scientific knowledge. Science is organized common sense (Nagel, 1961).

The methodically definite form of science as we know it began at the end of the Middle Ages. Later, in seventeenth-century England and the Netherlands, the demand for practical knowledge in artillery, fortress building, irrigation, and canalization boosted the study of mathematics and physics. What distinguishes this new scientific method from previous common-sense solutions is its systematic nature, and its endeavour to provide explanations for the phenomena observed. In a nutshell, science is systematic in the sense that it tries to formulate laws that apply everywhere, not just in traditionally established habits, and is explanatory in the sense that it tries to answer 'why' questions, providing an answer to the question of why the phenomena are as observed. Such explanations are both systematic and controllable by factual evidence. As Nagel (1961: 4) puts it: '[I]t is the organisation and classification of knowledge on the basis of explanatory principles that is the distinctive goal of the sciences.'

The following list of characteristics may be used to get the gist of scientific method (Nagel, 1961; Sanders et al., 1976):

1   *Systematicity.* Theories must be applicable across the board, the theoretical edifice must be coherent and if possible hierarchical; the domain of application is specified at the outset, and no ad hoc exceptions are allowed.

2   *Well-defined methods* (Kuhn, 1962). Methods also specify what count as legitimate subject matter, facts and explananda. Psychologists, for instance, will be reluctant to investigate 'poltergeists' as phenomena in their own right; chemists disown the philosopher's stone: they fall outside the framework, do not count as observation.

3   *Reduction,* both in the sense of ignoring certain aspects of reality (which are supposedly accidental) at the descriptive level, and in the sense of reducing phenomena to underlying principles at the explanatory level. As a simple example of the latter: water, steam and ice are explained as the same chemical substance under different conditions. A more complex example is that all matter may ultimately be explained by the final laws of a (future) complete physical theory in terms of elementary particles or fields.

4   *Objectivity,* in the sense of being controllable, reliable and intersubjectively observable. For instance, so-called slow schizophrenia, which could only be observed in Soviet dissidents by Soviet psychiatrists trained by Professor Snezjnevskij in KGB clinics, and nowhere and by nobody else (Joravski, 1989), is not a scientific concept: it is not replicable by others.

5   *Clarity.* Scientific statements are phrased unambiguously, in principle addressed to the public domain.

6   *Revisable.* Scientific knowledge is open, is at all times revisable and never definitive.

From this list, it will be clear that the distinction between scientific and commonsense thinking is a matter of degree, not of principle: science is just more systematic, general, methodical, open, etc. than common sense. So the dictum that science is organized common sense is reasonable, but something remains to be said about the specifics of the mode of organization. *Reduction* is the most distinguishing feature of science – more than in common sense, the aim is to find the hidden springs behind the phenomena. We devote Chapter 3.5 to this issue.

Notions of *classification* and taxonomy play an important role in reflections on scientific method. 'Cutting nature at the joints' is essential for the organization of knowledge in a systematic way. The suggestion that some term is 'merely' descriptive, and therefore unimportant and arbitrary, is certainly wrong. In biology the choice of taxonomy (mammals, reptiles, fish, insects) is a *sine qua non* for a viable science; the classification of whales as mammals, rather than fish, is no trivial or linguistic matter, but an essential feature of the systematic nature of science.

Classical accounts emphasize **explanation** as the hallmark of science (e.g. Nagel, 1961; Rosenberg, 1999; see Chapter 2), describing the underlying mechanisms that account for or cause surface phenomena. The explanatory aspect of science can be seen in its extensive use of unobservables, underlying explanatory entities (like atoms, or the Freudian unconscious) that try to explain the observed phenomena. This may sometimes have the unpleasant consequence of parting with the layman's view, as discussed above. Furthermore, systematicity implies that phenomena are isolated into small and unambiguously observable units, with the aim of subsequently integrating them in a larger system of facts. Science attempts to provide a logically unified body of knowledge, ideally in the form of a closed, axiomatic, deductive system (see Chapter 3 for the logical positivists, who pioneered this view of theories) in which propositions can be derived from theories describing empirical facts. A nice example would be Mendeleyev's system (the table of chemical elements).

glossary

In its *testability* science also goes beyond common-sense knowledge; common sense employs broad and relatively fuzzy concepts, whereas science refines these into precise notions. The greater determinacy of scientific concepts contrasts with the loose generalizations elsewhere, and allows more rigorous testing. It makes knowledge claims more vulnerable, but also provides more opportunities for neatly fitting them into a larger clearly articulated coherent theory. Thus, previously unconnected facts can be related and systematized. Common sense is relatively dependent upon unchanging conditions and a number of unarticulated background assumptions, whereas science is explicit as to its assumptions. Scientific knowledge is systematic and coherent in the way that everyday knowledge is not and, unlike common sense, it is explicit about the range of application of its concepts. Science avoids the inconsistencies common sense is not concerned about and tries to build a homogeneous network of concepts.

In our view, then, science is to be considered from a pragmatic perspective. Its methods are to be evaluated with respect to its central aim, producing knowledge about the world, and finding generalizations ('laws') that apply to the world (Chalmers, 1990). Thus we can circumvent, at least for practical purposes, the unsettling problems of relativism. Briefly, the view that pragmatism is relativist and irrationalist, and cannot distinguish between accidental success and genuine scientific rationality, only follows from the hidden assumption that a philosophical account of how knowledge is anchored in some form of contact with the world is the only defence against absurdity and fraud. We think that there is no need for a single, fixed ahistorical canon of scientific method. Knowledge about the world comes in many varieties, and should be evaluated pragmatically, in the light of practice.

1.3 Arguments: Deduction, Induction, Abduction

The objective of knowledge is to understand (parts of) the world in order to get on in it. Science is a special branch of knowledge; it is usually not content with the immediate environment, and probes deeper than common, everyday knowledge; and most important, science is a controlled enterprise. Scientists want to comprehend *why* things happen, what are the mechanisms or processes *behind* the phenomena. To form their opinions, to convince others, to provide evidence and to predict events they use different means – assumptions, observations, arguments, explanations, predictions, descriptions, theories, models. In this and the following sections we will discuss some of these basic scientific concepts.

Deductive arguments

Arguments are sets of statements (the premises) connected in such a way that a conclusion follows from them. In some arguments, the conclusion is definitively supported. An example is:

> Men are bigger than mice
> Mice are bigger than ants
> _____
> Thus: Men are bigger than ants

Because the premises 'contain', so to say, the conclusion, or the conclusion can be 'extracted' or deduced from the premises, these conclusive arguments or inferences are also called *deductive*. If you accept the premises of a deductive argument then you also must buy the conclusion; otherwise you produce a contradiction. The soundness of conclusive arguments is a consequence of the meaning of the relations (in the example, 'are bigger than') and the arrangement of the terms (the names which stand for the subjects). This pattern can be abstracted from inferences about specific states of affairs, and can be *formalized* as follows:

> $x\ R_t\ y$
> $y\ R_t\ z$
> _____
> Thus: $x\ R_t\ z$

where R_t stands for a transitive relation, such as 'bigger than', 'smaller than', 'older than'. So, we have here a valid inference-pattern which can be interpreted by any transitive relation between two different entities. This is what logicians do (among other things): they abstract from or generalize about specific arguments and study under what conditions arguments are valid, in what respect they are similar or different, etc. Unlike other scientists and people in their everyday discourse, a formal logician is not interested in the subject matter or content of arguments, only in the formal structure.

Among conclusive arguments *syllogisms* are well known. Here is an example:

> All politicians are liars
> All members of parliament are politicians
> _____
> Thus: All members of parliament are liars

In this example it is easy to see that a conclusive (deductive) argument that is perfectly valid can be doubtful or even false, because the first of the premises is. The truth has something to do with the content of the inference; the soundness with the pattern or form. So, the conclusion of a deductive inference is true on two conditions: (1) the argument must be valid or sound; and (2) the premises must be true. In other words, if an argument is deductively valid, it is impossible for the premises to be true while the conclusion is false.

This promise of absolute certainty constitutes the appeal of the deductive method. Ideally, one could start with a few unquestionable truths or axioms and then deduce other statements or theorems from them. The geometry devised by Euclid, the Greek geometer who lived in the third century BC, was such an *axiomatic system*. Very much impressed by the elegance of this system, the French philosopher René Descartes (1596–1650) thought it possible to deduce all scientific statements from some axioms, which were put into us as innate ideas by God. Many other scientists in the sixteenth and seventeenth centuries also thought that nature was mathematically structured, that the world was a machine, or clockwork, working according to precise mathematical laws, that the human mind was designed in accordance with that system and could comprehend it, and that knowledge reflected that system. In our century the behaviourist Clark Hull (1884–1952) had a similar ideal in mind for psychology. Psychology, he thought, is a natural science and since nature is a mathematical and mechanical system the mental is nothing but physical and behavioural, and psychology can be formalized into one single deductive system. In the end behaviour is the complex result of basic physical entities like electrons and protons. Since psychology is a chapter of the whole scientific system, theories and predictions about behaviour can be deduced from clearly stated principles (Leahey, 2001).

However, Hull's system didn't work out. Apparently, we cannot put our knowledge so rigorously and absolutely into a comprehensive, unified and fixed system. Scientific theories happen to be fallible and changeable. As we said before, science is never closed.

Inductive arguments

We cannot rely on deductive arguments exclusively; in science as well as in everyday discourse we mostly apply non-conclusive arguments. While the premises of a conclusive argument logically already 'contain' the conclusion, which therefore must be accepted, the conclusion of a non-conclusive argument is only, more or less, supported by the premises. If you do accept the premises, but still doubt the conclusion, you could be reproached for being stubborn or an arch-sceptic but you cannot be reproached for contradicting yourself. Among the non-conclusive arguments are *inductive* arguments which are generalizations from statements of lesser scope: what is true of a number of members of a class is likely to be true of all members. Here is an example:

> I know five psychologists and, boy, are they arrogant!
>
> Therefore, I think that all psychologists are arrogant.

If someone said this he had perhaps not been very fortunate in his meetings with psychologists, and was rather hasty in drawing this general conclusion from the poor sample, because there are thousands of psychologists. Suppose, however, that the sample of arrogant psychologists is not five but 100, or 1,000: wouldn't we be moving from less to more evidential support? Thus, inductive support for the conclusion comes in degrees; it depends on the amount of evidence in relation to the extent of the conclusion, and it varies with different types of subject matter. It is reasonable therefore that people who are confronted with inductive conclusions should want to know the weight of the evidence. In order to accept, for instance, the assertion that frequent use of marijuana or hashish every day will impair your memory, one wants to know how the study which constitutes the evidence has been done, how many subjects have been examined (the sample), what data have been gathered, etc. A subclass of inductive arguments are *statistical* arguments in which the degree of probability is given in numbers or percentages; often you will find non-numerical terms such as 'many', 'nearly all', or 'never' in the conclusion.

The 'problem' of induction

In an inductively strong argument, then, if the premises are true, it is only probable that the conclusion is true. Some logicians think it better to speak of a successful induction not as a valid but as a strong argument; they reserve the notion of validity for deductive arguments. No matter how strong the inductive reasoning, it will always be an inconclusive argument: the conclusion will always go beyond the evidence. For this reason philosophers of science have had a love–hate relationship with induction. On the one hand, it is acknowledged that inductive arguments provide new empirical knowledge, that is, knowledge that is not already contained in the premises as with deduction. Science is to a great extent empirical and inductive; it generalizes from observed instances and it predicts by inferring what will happen from what has happened. This, one could say, has contributed to scientific successes. But on the other hand, it does not provide the ardently desired certainty, one cannot anticipate future cases or predict with certainty; and one has seldom witnessed all the cases in the past. There is always room for *scepticism*, as the empiricist David Hume wrote:

> *That the sun will not rise tomorrow* is no less intelligible a proposition, and implies no more contradiction than the affirmation, *that it will rise.* (1748/1963: section iv, 25–6, original emphasis)

On reflection you would perhaps point to the general presupposition upon which expectations of natural events are based: that the course of nature is uniform and continuous. This means that, other things being equal, if nothing interferes, nature will operate in the same way. But, replies Hume, that again gives you an inductive inference: up till now nature behaved … etc. And then you realize that you are merely begging the question; you are going in circles.

Hume's conclusion of his discussion of induction is sceptical and negative: inductive arguments cannot be justified by (logical) reasoning; there is no rational foundation for them. There is no cogent line of reasoning that leads from premises to conclusion, no absolute certainty in the manner of deduction. We arrive at inductive conclusions by a non-rational process: by habit. The process of inference is not logical thinking but a psychological step. We are used to the fact that the sun rises every morning, and the prediction that it will rise tomorrow is not the conclusion of a rational – read: logical – argument but a psychologically understandable expectation. For Hume 'rational' is deductive certainty and, except in mathematics, most scientific reasoning is 'merely' inductive.

This lack of certainty or, more precisely, the suspicion that scientific inference is not justifiable, and consequently that science is unfounded, has been called *the problem of induction*. Philosophers have been trying to find a logic of inductive justification. A classic example illustrates why this never worked out: the 'Raven paradox'. If we are to inductively confirm the hypothesis that all ravens are black, we list all ravens and check whether these are all black. However, logically (x) $(rx \Rightarrow bx)$ (for every x, if it is a raven, it is black) is equivalent with (x) $(-bx \Rightarrow -rx)$ (for every x, if it is not a raven, it is not black). So, observing non-black things that are not ravens confirms that ravens are black; seeing a pair of white sneakers corroborates the blackness of ravens. That result is bizarre of course, but logically impeccable, and the conclusion must be that the logic is not working for induction – induction cannot be logically justified in the way deduction can.

There is an even deeper problem with induction: one has to start with concepts and criteria to gather observations – in particular, criteria for similarity. In order to generalize, you have to know what counts as instances of the same and what not: one should be able to tell a swan from a flamingo, and a mammal from a fish. Whether a flamingo is a pink swan or a separate species, and whether a whale is a fish or a mammal depends on one's starting assumptions. And where could these come from? If from observation, then we get stuck in a circle. In addition, you have to know in advance what is relevant: just listing everything you see (the colour of the clouds, the balance on your bank account) won't do. On the other hand, in principle anything might bear upon anything (maybe details about cell biology help decide whether there is life on Mars); unfortunately there seems to be no rule for deciding in advance what does (Quine, 1969b).

Some scientists think the problem can be ignored, saying that only if you think that science has to search for absolute certainty, only if you think that truth has to be absolute, do you have a problem because you ask too much; it is enough that science scores its successes without strong logical justification. This is the pragmatic response (see Quine, 1969b). Others also deny that there is a problem, saying that not only science but also life would be impossible if the zillion everyday expectations stood in need of strong foundation, such as: if I collide with that tree my car gets smashed up. Some philosophers of science, however, are not satisfied with the idea that the factual success of science and scientific reasoning lacks justification, and hence is simply fortuitous.

Inference to the best explanation

Inconclusive reasonings are often used in explanations. Coming home you find the fridge open. Since your partner, the only other inhabitant, has lately developed the bad habit of showing some negligence in this matter, you conclude that he, again, has left open the door of the refrigerator. Of all the possible other explanations this is the best. But is the conclusion more logically legitimate than others? What you did was arrive at a hypothesis. The question is: how do we do that, and on what basis?

glossary   This kind of probably reliable explanation, **inference to the best explanation** as it is called today, the pragmatist C.S. Peirce once christened **abduction**. It is a kind of reasoning in which an explanatory hypothesis is derived from a set of facts and has the following structure:

> If S is the case then R
>
> R is the case
> _____
> Therefore, it is possible that S was the case
>
> (If it has rained, the streets are wet
>
> The streets are wet
> _____
> It may have rained)

Note that this is not a logical certainty, just a possibility (a water pipe may have burst). Peirce was very much interested in the testing of these hypotheses and he tried to construct a logic of it. How do we arrive at hypotheses? And what criteria can we legitimately use for testing them? This logic of testing and of finding rules and criteria for hypotheses is also called the *logic of discovery*.

BOX 1.2   Induction, deduction and abduction

Induction: from individual observations to general statements.
  No logical certainty, but new knowledge.
  Example: Lots of swans were observed, all were white
        Maybe all swans are white

Deduction: from general statements to individual observations.
  Logical certainty, because conclusion contained in premises: no new knowledge.
  Example: All humans are mortal
        Socrates is human
        Therefore, Socrates is mortal

Abduction: inference to the best explanation.
  No logical certainty, new hypothetical knowledge about causes.
  Example: All CJD patients ate beef
        Beef may be the cause of CJD

Context of justification and context of discovery

Some philosophers, however, denied that there can be a logic of discovery because discoveries are too different and complex to be captured in logical and methodological rules. There is no algorithm for discovery, or a recipe that inevitably and mechanically leads to new facts and generalizations – as the induction problem shows. And they contended that the acquisition of scientific facts or theories is not the business of philosophy but of psychology. All kinds of extrascientific factors induce discoveries, such as Archimedes sitting in his bath and discovering the way to calculate the volume of solid objects; and Newton guessing the law of gravitation by observing an apple falling from a tree. These philosophers consider it the task of the philosophy and methodology of science to guard the rationality of science and to analyse whether the scientific products, the finished theories, can be justified, abstracting from the messy ways in which scientists arrive at their conjectures: What is the argumentative basis? What are the empirical data? How strong are the logical connections between the statements? What are the norms for good theories? Romantic flashes of insight and other personal histories are non-rational or irrational and irrelevant to the task of justification.

This led to the distinction between the **context of justification** and the **context of** `glossary` **discovery**, introduced by traditional empiricist philosophers to demarcate the domain of scientific rationality (for which only the context of justification is relevant). Others, in direct opposition, demonstrate the importance of the historical, social and psychological contexts of scientific discoveries (Thomas Kuhn, 1970, see Chapter 3.7; see also Chapters 4 and 5). Apart from the question of whether there is a discovery algorithm, they argue that:

> to ignore discovery, innovation, and problem solving in general is to ignore most of the scientists' activities and concerns, in many cases not only the most interesting phases of scientific research but also (more importantly) phases highly relevant to epistemology, e.g., to the theory of rationality and the understanding of conceptual change and progress in science. (Nickles, 1980: 2)

In fact, sociologists and psychologists took over segments of the epistemological domain that philosophers traditionally claimed for themselves – guarding rationality and setting the rules for scientific method. This takeover is part of what has been called *naturalistic epistemology*. In this project, initiated by the philosopher W.V.O. Quine, epistemology is seen as a part of natural science because it 'simply falls into place as a chapter of psychology' (Quine, 1969a: 82). It can be contested whether psychology is entirely a natural science, but if one takes 'naturalistic' in a broader sense, meaning 'continuous with science', one might perhaps agree with our suggestion that the sociology of science, psychology of science and/or psychology of cognition are legitimate chapters in the programme of naturalizing epistemology. We consider this project as an inquiry into the processes by which scientists tend to arrive at their scientific beliefs. In various chapters we will pursue this line of thinking.

BOX 1.3 Context of discovery and context of justification

Context of discovery

In this context the focus is on a *description* of the historical, social and psychological circumstances and influences that were relevant to the invention or *discovery* of scientific theories. Historians and sociologists of science try to find out under what conditions science works.

Context of justification

In this context the focus is on *normative* criteria for holding a theory true, or acceptable, or *justified*. Philosophers of science try to develop general methodological requirements for a scientific theory, for example, the degree to which the conclusions are empirically or logically supported (induction, deduction).

In the traditional view, philosophy of science is only about justification, not about the social or psychological circumstances of the problem-solving situation.

1.4 Laws, Theories, Models and Causes

Empiricism: pure observation?

It is sometimes said that the job of science is to discover facts. This has to be qualified, however. The **empiricist** Francis Bacon (1561–1626) thought that collecting facts like a bee gathers honey is the right method of doing science: doing research is systematically collecting observations and compiling lists of data, and if the scientist does that carefully the scientific laws will be discovered automatically. However, it is highly implausible that science has ever been done in such a way because it is not an automatic process at all. One always departs from preconceived ideas when gathering data. You cannot do science without some power of imagination, without some idea what to look for. For Bacon, however, imagination and fantasy constitute dangers for science, which should eschew prejudices ('idols'), and he put all his money on 'pure' empirical facts.

So direct, 'pure' observations are a problem. There is a tension between observation and theory (meaning here, going beyond direct observations) that has always haunted philosophers of science. It is, of course, a major concern of science to understand what happens and what will happen. To this end scientists have to generalize about relations between different facts. We saw earlier that empiricists reached the view that inductive reasoning was highly problematic. The philosophers of science whose idea of science was strictly empirical (observation is the foundation of inquiry) had to think hard about these problems, and to accept a certain amount of uncertainty (see Chapter 3 on the Logical Positivists). Observations cannot be strictly objective but perhaps intersubjective agreement is possible, and the ideals of exact observation statements as the foundation of theories has remained.

Observation and unobservables

However, to comprehend underlying structures, to formulate 'laws' of nature, scientists have to venture beyond the mere inspection, enumeration and description of what can be observed. This very often makes them decide to conjecture *unobservable entities* and relations, such as protons, gravitation, energy, attitudes, motives, personality traits, or the cognitive map – none of these is directly observable.

You can imagine that the empiricists' focus on observable facts made them suspicious about theoretical imagination. Strict empiricists do not want to have anything to do with unobservables. However, criticism of strict empiricism has become so loud since the 1950s and 1960s that almost nobody thinks any more that science can be exciting, or can be done at all, without conjectures about unobservables. A philosopher who calls himself an 'empiricist' (Van Fraassen, 2002) now just advocates a critical attitude towards speculation about a world 'behind' the phenomena, and urges us to 'save the phenomena', and to be wary of **metaphysics**. Van Fraassen has, however, abandoned the attempt to lay a firm foundation for science in objective empirical observation.

glossary

Theory-ladenness

The notion of theory-neutral data to be 'read off' from the world has been severely attacked and has given way to the notion of the **'theory-ladenness'** of observations: observation is always partly determined by one's theoretical assumptions (see Chapter 2). Observations are not neutral; facts are not directly given events in the world – facts are statements about those events one holds to be true. A fact is a conviction or a belief that something is the case and is never independent of other notions one happens to believe.

glossary

Hence, the one-time demand that every scientific statement should be reducible to (an) observation statement(s) has been replaced by the notion that theories can be 'underdetermined by data' (see Chapter 3.5): several different theories may be compatible with the same dataset; or you may have simply not enough data. Cognitive science, for instance, would be impossible if we had to stick to direct observations.

This is not to say that empirical tests can be dismissed. On the contrary, to use your imagination in order to construct bold theories is one thing; to stay open-minded and to revise and even refute your theory in the light of evidence to the contrary is another. This is a far cry from mere speculation, superstitious explanation and prejudice. Unscientific explanations, like these, tend to be final and dogmatic, invoking revelation or authority, without giving reasons and seeking evidence. Science, on the contrary, should be open to tests and arguments and sensitive to evidence, including empirical evidence. For this reason, the logician Irving Copi wrote: 'The vocabulary of "hypothesis", "theory", and "law" is unfortunate, since it obscures the important fact that *all* of the general propositions of science are regarded as hypotheses, never as dogmas' (1961: 423, original emphasis).

As we said before, scientific knowledge is at all times revisable and never definitive. Though scientists may have good reasons and may have good evidence for thinking that their theories are true, they can never be certain in an absolute sense.

Theories

glossary Informally speaking, a **theory** is a set of statements that organizes, predicts and explains observations; it tells you how phenomena relate to each other, and what you can expect under still unknown conditions. De Groot gives the following more formal definition:

> [A theory is] a system of logically interrelated, specifically non-contradictory, statements, ideas, and concepts relating to an area of reality, formulated in such a way that testable hypotheses can be derived from them. (1969: 40)

A theory, to some extent, fixes the vocabulary in which observations are phrased. A feature of natural science is that its vocabulary consists of a limited set of unambiguously defined terms; mathematical symbols are the most telling example, but also in physics the description of what is observed is limited to what can be expressed in terms of force, mass, velocity, etc.

From a theory predictions can be derived, and predicting is tantamount to explaining. When your theory predicts the position of the planets, that is, when a prediction can be derived in an unambiguous way from the theory, you can be said to have a model that explains (a relevant part of) the movement of the planets.

What 'deriving' predictions exactly means is tricky. As discussed elsewhere (Chapter 3), the original idea (with the logical positivists) was that theories have a formal structure, like an abstract calculus, and deriving predictions is considered an exercise in formal logic. In physics, mathematical theories do indeed permit such quantitative predictions. In the history of psychology, however, Hull's attempt to build a formal deductive system for the prediction of behaviour was a failure (see above in section 3). In most cases we have to rely on informal but still reasonably uncontroversial ways of deriving predictions from a theory. Usually, additional assumptions are therefore required, and some kind of translation of theoretical terms in empirical phenomena is needed.

Laws and theories

A law can be defined as an empirical generalization. Ideally, it has the form: $(x)(Px > Qx)$ for all x at any time and place, if x is P, then it is Q – for example, frustration leads to aggression: all individuals, if frustrated (P), will exhibit aggression (Q). Of course, all kinds of exceptions and conditions will usually have to be specified.

Laws then are generalizations, but not all generalizations are laws. A nasty problem   `glossary`
in the theory of science is: how to distinguish between real laws and accidental generalizations. There is a genuine difference between the law that (all) copper (always) expands when heated, and the fact that all coins in my pocket are silver. The former is a law of nature, the latter is an accidental generalization. The difference is usually expressed in terms of necessity or of counterfactuals.

A law must necessarily hold, even in circumstances which do not now obtain – which is known as *counterfactual*. If we took a piece of copper to the moon and heated it, it would expand, but if I put a copper coin in my pocket, it would not turn into silver. The former generalization is counterfactual-supporting, and thus a real law; the latter is not.

Put slightly differently, we may require that theories exceed the known evidence for them, that is, tell us more than we already knew. A genuine theory is also a commitment about what might happen, under conditions as yet unobserved.

The philosopher of science Karl Popper made refutability (the possibility that future situations will prove a theory wrong) of predictions the hallmark of real science, as we will see in the next chapter.

Furthermore, being part of a network of theories and concepts, and being as strictly as possible (logically) connected to other laws, is a highly desirable property for laws in science. The system of classical mechanics is a case in point. Hooking up to good theories in other domains enhances the credibility of a theory. In psychology, for example, a good working relation with functional neurophysiology is an asset for a model in cognitive or clinical psychology.

Empirical/experimental and theoretical laws

A distinction can be made between empirical and theoretical laws (De Groot, 1969: 76–7; Nagel, 1961). Laws in which *observables* occur are *empirical* generalizations, laws with *unobservables* can be defined as *theoretical* laws. In genetics, Mendelian laws which capture regularities in the inheritance of certain traits (e.g. hair colour, eye colour) are empirical; in contrast, whenever genes or chromosomes are mentioned in a law, this assumes a theoretical character.

As you can imagine, reverting to abstract and/or unobservable parameters goes hand in glove with larger and more theoretical networks. This suggests that there is virtue in constructing theoretical laws. First, it enhances the scope and the anchoring of a theory; empirical laws are in danger of just enumerating familiar and trite facts. Second, theories ideally bring together qualitatively different phenomena in a single framework. Empirical laws capture commonalties at a phenomenal level, but theoretical laws suggest a deeper insight into underlying mechanisms and, consequently, the possibility of bringing together disparate observations under the same conceptual umbrella. Unification, the subsumption of many domains of empirical observation under a single conceptual framework, is an important goal of scientific inquiry. A classic example is Newtonian mechanics, which applies to falling apples as well as to the movement of the planets, and more recently to launching missiles, accelerating motorcycles and whatnot.

 The difference between empirical and theoretical laws is not absolute, but gradual: observations in empirical laws are **theory-laden** (the theory to some extent determines what counts as a phenomenon), and unobservables in theoretical laws must also be verified by observation – only indirectly (see the paragraph on operationalization, below, 1.4). Nevertheless, it is useful to be clear about the difference. An example in psychology where this tends to be ignored is Freud's psychoanalysis, where theoretical constructs are easily confused with clinical observations. Presumed 'observations' were only understandable and verifiable to trained observers who already subscribe to the whole theoretical framework.

Box 1.4 shows a classical way of ordering observations, laws and theories.

Models

A **model** is a kind of mini-theory: it provides a more or less visualizable representation of the theory, as in some kind of analogy. A classic example is the model of the atom as a collection of coloured balls (electrons) circling around a core composed of differently coloured balls (protons and neutrons).

The term 'model' is also used for a more or less abstract picture of a part of reality in a field of inquiry where no fully fledged theory is (yet) available. Psychology is rich in models: in any textbook of cognitive psychology you will find pictures of boxes and arrows that purport to model things like the working of memory (say, different kinds of storage from which information is retrieved), or attention (which may be modelled as a searchlight focusing on selected objects or a glue integrating features to objects). Sometimes, the model takes a mathematical form. Such models are, for example, used in economics to express relations between economic parameters (say, between average wage and unemployment) and can be used even if the underlying causes of such relationships are still unknown, that is, when a real theory is not available. In psychology, computer programs that simulate cognitive processes, like learning or problem-solving, can be regarded as models in the above sense. Whether such simulations qualify as a genuine *theory* of the domain they model is a moot point (De Groot, 1969: 335–42).

BOX 1.4   Theories, laws and data: a hierarchy of language levels

1   *Theories*: a deductive system of related statements, partly unobservable, connected with correspondence rules to observations (e.g. kinetic gas theory).
2   *Experimental laws*: single statements about invariant relations between concepts, inductive generalizations (e.g. Boyle's law $PV = cT$).
3   *Assigning numeric values to concepts* (e.g. $P = 1.4$, $V = 3.2$, where P is pressure, V is volume of a gas).
4   *Primary data* (observations, e.g. instrument readings).
    (after Losee, 2001: 159–160)

From bottom to top, as we move from observation to theory, predictive power increases. The lowers levels 'interpret' the higher levels, in the sense that they provide the connection between a theory and data, and they provide visualizable or conceptual models (Nagel, 1961: ch. 5). Correspondence rules connect theoretical notions with measurement operations (e.g. P is the reading of a manometer).

Causes

A notorious problem in philosophy is the notion of **causality**. Philosophers have spent considerable effort in investigating the metaphysical foundations for the notion of cause (see e.g. Bochenski, 1973; Sosa and Tooley, 1993): do causes really exist as a part of the furniture of the world? The answer to that question is still debated. We only want to remark here that, in practice, what counts as a cause depends on the context and the *explanatory interests* of the investigator. When you ask what caused the death of an assasinated politician, you may say that religious extremism was the cause; but also that it was sloppy security; and for a pathologist it would be the biomechanics of bullets and human tissue – it depends on whether your explanatory interests are in politics, physiology, or security tactics. Usually, phenomena are the products of a web of causes; what we single out as 'the' cause depends on what sort of 'why' question we like to be answered, and what counts as the most relevant or conspicuous factor depends on a point of view. One man's cause is another man's background assumption. To give just one very simplified example, in one context we can say that genes cause depression, in another context that neurotransmitter deficiency causes depression, or that maternal deprivation causes depression. All these are legitimate answers to the question why an individual is depressive.

We will ignore the metaphysical niceties, and focus on the notion of causal laws. If we take a law to be a generalization connecting several events (as in the example of Box 1.4, increasing the temperature and keeping volume constant will increase pressure), then there is, intuitively, a difference between mere contiguity of two events and a causal relation. One position is that to be really explanatory, laws must be causal. Recall the models and experimental generalizations: ideally, we want to know the universal causes of things, such as the laws of gravity that explain falling apples, and soaring rockets and planetary motion. A crucial distinction mentioned above is between real laws and accidental generalization: an infection is lawfully caused by germs, but the fact that the whole village caught the germs at the church fair and the vicar has blue eyes is immaterial. The difference is that causes distinguish real laws from accidental generalizations. The intuition is that cause determines or necessitates the effect, and that in the necessary connection underwrites the explanation. One might ask whether that solves the problem, since the question now becomes how to define causes. If physical necessity is part of that definition, we must admit that this is observable, and real empiricists must be wary of such metaphysic constructs.

Nagel (1961: 74) lists four conditions for causal laws. First, there must be an invariable relation between cause and effect; the cause must be both a necessary and a sufficient condition for the effect. Second, cause and effect must be in the same spatial domain, or there must be an intermediate chain of causes connecting them across space. Third, the cause must precede the effect and be temporally close to it. And fourth, the relation must be asymmetrical: sunlight causes shadows, but not vice versa. According to these criteria, many laws of nature are not causal: it is a law that water is H_2O, but this is not a causal relation. Boyle's law does not qualify as causal, since P and V change at the same time. Furthermore, very few if any interesting laws in psychology are necessary: frustration leads sometimes not to aggression. A partial solution is the notion of *ceteris paribus* laws: the effect follows only when the circumstances do not change. But even then, we must admit that many laws are only statistical: it is pretty sure, and very important to know that smoking causes cancer, but the latter does not always follow from the former, only more frequently.

It seems then that the notion of causal laws satisfies our intuition that, unlike accidental generalizations, real explanations show how the effect follows with physical necessity from the cause, but that it is unclear how to delineate causes and necessity.

Bringing induction, deduction, laws and observations together: the empirical cycle

The notion of an empirical cycle (De Groot, 1969) nicely captures the interplay of data and theory, deduction and induction, in the practice of science. It consists of the following stages: observation, **induction**, **deduction**, testing and evaluation (De Groot, 1969: 27ff.).

glossary

Observation is the stage where empirical material is collected and ordered. As a first approximation, it is systematic perception (recall that organized – or systematic – common sense was our 'quick and dirty' definition of science). Tentative or implicit hypothesis formation also occurs in this stage – if only because no perception is possible without (perhaps implicit) concepts and presuppositions, without some point of view. What is selected and observed reflects implicit hypotheses and theories; these are made explicit in the next stage.

Induction (including abduction) then is the phrasing of an explicit hypothesis. 'Explicit' means that the hypothesis yields specific, verifiable predictions that can be empirically tested.

Deduction refers to the derivation of predictions from hypotheses. The logical positivists demanded that all theories have a strictly logical or mathematical form, so that in their view deduction was an exercise in formal logic or mathematics. Such strictly formal theories, however, are very rare in psychology, if they exist at all, and as mentioned before, attempts by, for instance, Hull to force such an abstract calculus on psychology were unsuccessful – some would say, just silly. However, even in a less formalistic conception of hypothesis, the requirement that empirical consequences of a theory must be specified (and subsequently tested) remains. One of the ways to derive testable predictions from theoretical concepts is *operationalization*. This means that a concept is defined in terms of measurement operations. A good example is intelligence, defined as the score on an intelligence test. The choice of quantifiable behavioural indicators for psychological constructs is an important aspect of psychological experimentation.

The aim of the *deduction* stage is to formulate predictions, in such an explicit, precise and unambiguous way that they can be tested against empirical data.

The *testing* stage is about the confrontation of these predictions with empirical data. It must be emphasized that a hypothesis is a generalizing statement: it refers to a class of events, not to single facts (it is, possibly, a law that stress is conducive to premature ageing; it is not a law that John has grey hair). This implies that predictions must contain references to new situations, which are not already observed. For example, the law that frustration leads to aggression should be tested by comparing the prediction with the behaviour of a new population.

Finally, in the *evaluation* stage the results of the test are used as feedback for the more general theory from which the hypotheses are derived. Depending on the situation, one of two competing theories might have to be rejected in favour of the other, but more frequently, no such choice is available, and the theory will be expanded, qualified or amended; for instance, frustration leads to aggression only in certain circumstances, or in certain populations. There are no hard and fast rules for the interpretation of the results; the decision about what to change in one's theory will to some extent remain subjective, influenced by prejudices and opportunism. For example, the investigator may blame contradictory results on artefacts, or nuisance variables or whatever, or may invent ad hoc hypotheses to save his or her favourite theory. Alternatively, unexpected results may lead to new discoveries completely beyond the hypothesis tested (so-called serendipity). This stage then is at least partially to be situated in the context of discovery.

In any case, the new theory will again spawn new hypotheses, to be tested on new data, leading to new tests and interpretations: the empirical cycle starts all over again. Bad ideas will fade away when no empirical evidence for them is found. The empirical cycle is thus a never-ending circular process, where subjective decisions will always in principle be formulated in (at least partially) objectively testable form. Thus, the *context of discovery* and the *context of justification* are both in play. Induction is as indispensable as deduction.

BOX 1.5   **The empirical cycle**

1   *Observation*
2   *Induction, abduction* ⇒ Hypothesize theory/law
3   *Deduction of prediction from theory*
      (may require *operationalization*: define concepts as measuring
      operation, e.g. IQ)
4   *Testing hypothesis*
      observation, confirmation or disconfirmation
5   *Evaluation* ⇒ 2. hypothesize revised theory
Note that:

- Induction is to some extent guesswork; its results are not objectively certain.
- Explaining is equivalent with (successful) prediction; both consist in deducing from a theory.
- Observations are *inductively* collected into a theory, and then predictions/explanations are *deduced* from the theory.
- Testing and evaluation are theory-laden, and depend on interpretation and interest.

1.5 Conclusion

In this chapter we outlined the contours of scientific knowledge. Explanation and reduction, referring to underlying causes, are crucial for science. Causes are difficult to define, but intuitively causal explanation (or explanation by laws) marks an intuitive difference between deep necessary explanations and accidental generalizations.

Realism, idealism and pragmatism are different views on the origin and justification of knowledge. Pragmatism recognizes both the subjective component and the objective success of science.

Justification of knowledge should be distinguished from factors influencing discovery, but the distinction is fluid. Induction, deduction and abduction underpin knowledge claims. Induction and abduction generate (fallible) theories from which testable hypotheses are deduced, and after empirical testing new or amended theories are produced, and so on.

The difference between observations and theories is a matter of degree: observations are theory-laden, theories should be partly translatable into possible observations.

A convenient way to understand the relation between data, laws and theories is as a hierarchy of descriptions from more concrete observable to more abstract formalized statements.

FURTHER READING

Kukla, A. (2001) *Methods of Theoretical Psychology*. Cambridge, MA: MIT Press.
A textbook on theory construction in psychology.

Boyd, R., Gasper, P. and Trout, J.D. (eds) (1991) *The Philosophy of Science*. Cambridge, MA: MIT Press.
A collection of important readings.

2. KINDS OF EXPLANATIONS

Laws, Interpretations and Functions

PREVIEW: In this chapter, first, we discuss three different types of explanations that occur in psychology, and we try to show that each has its own domain and uses. None is (or should be) privileged a priori. Second, we discuss reduction, in particular the reduction of psychological processes to neuroscientific ones. Our conclusion is that all-out reduction, the replacement of psychology by neuroscience, is not a plausible option. These two points support pluralism in explanation.

2.1 Introduction: Modes of Explanation: Nomological, Hermeneutical, Functional

The ideas of explanation discussed in the previous chapter can be called classical: they aim to describe as adequately as possible the way science should work. Theories describe objective facts, and explanation is subsuming facts under general laws. Theories and facts should be tested and verified objectively and rigorously. This is nomological explanation (α (nomos) is ancient Greek for law). Not surprisingly, the main sources for this account of explanation were 'hard' sciences like physics.

It is, however, much more difficult to apply these criteria to other sciences, especially those that are closer to psychology, like biology and the humanities. Biologists often refer to functions or goals in explaining why organisms have certain traits: evolution presumably selects adapted organisms with traits that serve survival. Explaining complex systems, like organisms, but also computers, and perhaps mind, is also a kind of functional explanation: it shows how they work by identifying the functions of the parts. As we will see below, functional explanation in cognitive science, and adaptationist explanation in evolutionary biology, both invoke goals and designs, and do not seem to fit well in the nomological model. Yet another kind of non-nomological explanation can be seen in the humanities, which does not deal in laws, but in the interpretation of meanings. Since the nineteenth century, such understanding (*Verstehen*) has been contrasted with nomological explanation (*Erklären*).

This makes for three kinds of explanation which we will discuss in turn, starting with the explanation–understanding dichotomy. Next we will turn to reduction, which is closely related to explanation. The final sections defend a pluralism of several kinds of explanations. The focus here is on kinds of explanation and reduction. In Chapters 3 and 4 we will turn to the philosophical roots of the nomological and hermeneutical views.

2.2 Nomological Explanation: The Classical View

Deductive-nomological explanation

The job of science is to explain phenomena and events in the world. In the first half of the twentieth century, philosophers opted for a philosophy of science as a normative branch of philosophy, stating criteria for clearly demarcating science from nonscience, laying down strict conditions for theories, observations and explanations (e.g. Nagel, 1961; Klee, 1997). (See Chapter 3 for a more in-depth discussion of the philosophy behind these ideas.) For an explanation to be really scientific it had to satisfy certain logical norms. According to the orthodox theory of scientific explanation, explaining an event is subsuming it under a general **law** – showing how it can be [glossary] brought, as a specific instance, under a general law.

If we have to explain why a strip of copper expands in the sun, we have to search for a general theory that covers this event. This theory is formulated as a law of nature, let us say: 'All metal expands when heated.' The phenomenon or the event to be explained is shown to have occurred in accordance with a general regularity of nature. It is said to be a consequence of this general law of nature and some initial or specific conditions pertaining to the situation in question. This model of scientific explanation is called the *covering-law model* because the event to be explained, the *explanandum*, is subsumed under or covered by a law of nature, that is, is shown to be an instance of a general rule. The explanation is also called a *deductive-nomological* because the event can be logically deduced from the law of nature (or the theory) and some specific conditions. The law and conditions are called the *explanans* (meaning: that what explains) and the event or phenomenon deduced from (and explained by) it is called the *explanandum* (meaning: that what has to be explained).

The logical structure of the covering-law model of scientific explanation is a syllogism, a classical reasoning pattern (for example: All men are mortal, Socrates is a man, therefore: Socrates will die.). We can add more laws and conditions to this pattern. Normally, it is presented as follows:

$$\left.\begin{array}{l} L_1 \ldots, L_n \\ C_1 \ldots, C_m \end{array}\right\} \text{together the } explanans$$
$$\overline{\text{E} \qquad \text{the } explanandum}$$

The explanans consists of two premises: one about one or a set of general laws (L); and the other about one or a set of specific conditions (C) relevant to the event (E) to be explained. The explanation is a deductive argument in which the explanandum is a logical consequence of the explanans (Hempel and Oppenheim, 1948/1965; Losee, 2001, Chapter 12). For a complete explanation you not only need general laws, but you also have to specify the conditions under which the phenomenon occurs. For example, if you want to explain how much a balloon expands when heated, you not only need to know the gas law that the ratio of volume and temperature is constant, but also how much temperature increases, and the elasticity of the balloon, etc. (Losee, 2001: 163–64).

glossary According to the **deductive-nomological (D-N) model of explanation**, whenever you can deduce a statement that describes an event from a general law plus conditions you have *ipso facto* explained the event. Furthermore, an explanation is equivalent to a prediction: when you have the explanation of an event as an instance of a general law, you could have predicted it. In the examples below, if you can predict the behaviour of copper and football fans, you can claim that you have explained it.

For example:

L_1 : metal expands when heated
L_2 : copper is a metal
C_1 : this is a piece of copper
C_2 : it is heated
$\overline{\text{E: this copper expands}}$

Or:

L_1 : frustration leads to aggression
L_2 : football (soccer) supporters whose club loses are frustrated
C_1 : and these supporters' club just lost
$\overline{\text{E: these football supporters are aggressive}}$

Problems with the deductive-nomological model

The deductive-nomological (D-N) model is nice and clear, but its application brings about all kinds of problems (and in the above simple form probably no philosopher would subscribe to it – Losee, 2001).

One problem is that the most interesting aspect of science is left out: we are not told how to find general laws, and the induction problem is not solved (see Chapter 1.3). In addition, the D-N model cannot very well distinguish between real laws and accidental generalizations. It is presumably a real law of nature that metals expand when heated, and that serves to explain the behaviour of a strip of copper in the sun. However, even if it is true that all coins in my pocket are copper, that is accidental: it does not explain why a particular five-cent piece in my pocket is copper (presumably that was somehow a decision of the Central Bank, not a law of nature).

Another problem is that observations are not neutral. We arrange new observations in theories we already cherish. We apply categories and classifications we are already familiar with. We embed new concepts in networks of already existing concepts, and seldom concoct them out of the blue. Facts, observations, explanations, laws never just speak for themselves. That implies that the way the explanandum is described is not logically independent of the explanans, and that the theoretical framework in a sense creates its own phenomena – put simply, it is a bit like finding the Easter eggs where you hid them yourself in the first place. So, **theory-ladenness**, where the theory influences the observations, | glossary | is a serious problem for the D-N model. We will explore it in more detail in Chapter 3.

Further, what this deduction between explanans and explanandum exactly means in reality is not clear and has been an object of lively debate. Ideally, we would like that the conditions referred to in one of the premises may be called the **cause** of the | glossary | event and the explanation qualifies as causal. But it is not always the case that deductive explanations are causal. One example are *dispositions*: is the molecular structure of glass the cause of its brittleness, if we take, as usual, a cause to precede its effect, but the glass has not been broken yet? The disposition, its brittleness, is a tendency: only after the glass has fallen to the ground does it break.

A deeper problem is that deduction is a purely formal relation, and that not every deduction is an explanation. A notorious case is the following. The length of a shadow made by a flag pole can be deduced from its length and the position of the sun – so far so good, since there is an obvious causal relation. However, deduction the other way round is also possible, but we would not say that the shadow of the flag pole explains the position of the sun, let alone causes it. Obviously, deduction does not always amount to explanation. So, the deductive-nomological model must have got it wrong somewhere.

Prediction and probability

Besides explanation, prediction – saying what will happen or how somebody will behave – is an important objective of science. To strengthen the predictive power of a theory, and then to test it, is the royal road to strong *empirical support* for the theory. The standard most important criterion of a good theory is its *empirical content*, the amount of predictive information (Popper, 1974; Hyland, 1981), although more factors may contribute to theory evaluation (Kukla, 2001: ch. 4). Philosophers took it as a corollary of the covering-law argument that the same model for explanation could be used for prediction. There is symmetry between deductive-nomological explanation and prediction. If we know the laws of nature and control the conditions of an experiment, for instance, we can predict with certainty the outcome. This may be true in the ideal case.

However, universal laws are rare; and even in physical science we have to accept statistical probabilities. Some 'laws' of science are to our best knowledge no more than statistical. And predictions too are not always certain; sometimes only statistical predictions can be produced, when, for instance, one does not know, or cannot be sure of all the variables, as is mostly the case in psychology. Here is an example of a probabilistic generalization: the probability that persons with different sexual partners who do not have safe sex will become HIV-positive is x per cent.

Besides the deductive model which requires a universal law, philosophers of science had to accept a probabilistic model. The explanans of a probabilistic explanation contains a statistical 'law'. But, of course, the connection between a probabilistic explanans and the event to be explained or predicted is weaker than in a deductive-nomological explanation or prediction. It is possible that the explanans is a good one for most cases and that it nevertheless fails to explain or predict the event at hand. Thus, there is no airtight logical deductive relation between explanans and explanandum in these cases. Some orthodox philosophers who could not accept the resultant ambiguity attempted to assimilate statistical explanation as closely as possible to deductive explanation, and considered this latter model as the ideal against which all forms of explanation are to be measured. To conclude, the deductive-nomological model seems to capture our intuitions of what an ideal explanation would be like, but on closer scrutiny explanation in science is not so neat as the ideal.

Certainty or reliability?

Behind this strict requirement for explanation lies an interpretation of science as the pursuit of certainty, the endeavour to establish scientific truth once and for all. It should provide us with a science that is universal in that it is ahistoric; a science that is not infected with local and temporary interests. This idea has inspired confidence in the deductive model because an explanation or a prediction according to this model will work without flaw only if the explaining general theory and observations, that is, the premises, are true. However, the problem is, we never can be absolutely sure. History teaches us that human knowledge is fallible, and until now, all theories in science have been wrong to some extent – so our current knowledge will be fallible as well.

Nevertheless, we have to trust our scientific efforts and results. After all, that we could be wrong about features of the world does not preclude the possibility that we could be right and that we should trust our theories when they fit the best (practical) evidence we can get. Moreover, if we could not trust in principle our knowledge we would not survive. So, it seems best to balance a realistic picture of science against some relativism; that is, we should assume that science gives some kind of grip on the real world, but nevertheless be modest and open-minded about (the faults of) our theories and models.

(Pseudo-) causal explanation in the social sciences

What we seek to explain in social science and psychology is (among other things) people's behaviour, or **actions**. For a deductive argument to work logically the explanandum must be defined independently of the explanans, the cause of the event. To explain the fact that, say, this lump of sugar has dissolved in your coffee by saying: 'because sugar is soluble', does not help very much. In this way we sometimes produce explanatory fictions, or pseudo-explanations. The famous example is Moliere's mock-explanation of the working of opium. 'Why does opium put people to sleep?' is the question put before the candidate doctor in Moliere's play *Le Malade imaginaire* (1673). And the man answers, to the enthusiastic cheers of the examiners: 'Because it has "Vis dormitiva"' – a power that puts you to sleep. It sounds professional, but it explains nothing; exactly what the French playwright had in mind, because he loathed the pedantry of doctors.

A related demand is that the meanings of the terms in the argument have to be unambiguous. These requirements seem to present a major problem when we have to define and explain someone's action. In describing an action we are already taking account of the attitudes, motives and intentions by which we would like to explain the act. Other than a mere movement, the description of an action is not in the least unequivocal. Consider the following descriptions: 'He raised his arm', 'He greeted someone', 'He called a halt', 'He saluted the "Führer"'. The same movement of the arm could be described in various ways and the descriptions are not independent of the very intentions or motives we would use in the explanation of the act. What is observed can be interpreted and described differently. The same behaviour can be seen and valued as heroic and patriotic by one observer, but macho and racist by another (just think of your favourite example of a western or a war movie).

The terms used in the social sciences are mostly derived from everyday discourse and carry their indeterminate interpretative and sometimes vague meanings into science. Take for instance attitude, role, belief, the unconscious, whatever. It is hardly possible to restrict the connotations these terms have in daily life, and give unambiguous scientific definitions, without loss of meaning or without changing them beyond recognition. Moreover, for many concepts, like 'ideology' or 'libido', definite descriptions are incomplete; they require the whole context of the theory. And this goes for natural scientific concepts as well, although perhaps to a lesser extent.

To sum up, applying the deductive-nomological model to the social sciences seems hopeless. Common-sense descriptions of social behaviour are coloured by context, are

glossary

theory-laden and evaluative; restricting them to objective facts, subsumed under laws, throws away the baby with the bath water. Some authors have argued that, in the human sciences, explanation has to be something completely different – it has to be hermeneutical (Winch, 1958). It is about understanding the meaning of action, not the nomological explanation of behaviour; it is about **reasons**, not causes (see Chapter 2.6).

BOX 2.1   **Nomological explanation**

- Explanation is subsuming a fact under a general law by deducing an explanandum (a statement describing a fact) from an explanans (a general law plus initial conditions).
- Starting from objective (intersubjective) observations, from individual facts expressed in observation statements.
- Causal, universal laws generalizing over many identical events.
- Prediction equals explanation.

- *Problem 1*: cannot account for motives, reasons, meaningful action in human behaviour.
- *Problem 2*: not every deduction is an explanation.

2.3 Hermeneutic Understanding: An Alternative to Nomological Explanation

Describing an action or ascribing behaviour is not reporting a bare fact that forces itself upon us in a simple observation. In the social sciences, explanations often consist of more than subsumption under general laws. For a relevant description of human behaviour we need to grasp the meaning, to understand the context, and sometimes even the culture. To capture this idea, the anthropologist Clifford Geertz (1973) borrowed the notion *thick description* from the philosopher Gilbert Ryle (1971). To understand the meaning of human behaviour one has to go beyond a passive camera-like registration of movements; one has to give a thick description, 'sorting out the structure of signification … and determining their social ground and import' (Geertz, 1973: 9). Whether, for example, the contraction of an eyelid is an involuntary twitch, a conspiratorial signal cheating card players use, an attempt to seduce the lady at the other end of the bar, or a parody poking fun at a boring lecturer cannot be 'read off' the physical movement, which is identical in each case. Human actions are part of a 'culture which consists of socially established structures of meaning' (ibid.: 12).

The need for understanding and interpretation is the reason why some philosophers of science contend that the social sciences need a completely different methodology from the natural sciences. As early as the second half of the nineteenth century, when sociology and psychology were still in their infancy, a *Methodenstreit* (dispute about methods) took place. German philosophers such as Dilthey, Rickert and Windelband distinguished on the one hand *Naturwissenschaften* (natural sciences) and on the other *Geisteswissenschaften* (literally the sciences of the spirit, the humanities), including history, the history of art, and philology.

Historical science was seen as very important in these sciences because it supplies one with the sensitivity to understand the wealth and variety of human life. While the natural sciences try to find universal laws of nature and generalizations – their **nomo-** | glossary
thetic (positing laws) characteristic – the human sciences and history try to under- stand or to interpret unique events – their **idiographic** (*idios* is particular, personal) | glossary
characteristic. These different and irreducible orders of phenomena, namely the natural and the mental, require radically different methods.

While in the natural sciences we are concerned with explanation (*Erklären*), with subsuming a multitude of equal and disconnected objective facts under general laws, with replicable experiments and observations, and with causal connections, in the human sciences we have to understand (*Verstehen*) actions, meanings and intentions. Understanding is about lived experience, about creating one's culture and self, about unique and unrepeatable individuals, cultures and historical epochs, not about general laws of nature. Understanding what Napoleon was doing in Moscow requires under- standing his motives, the calculations, hopes and fears of a unique individual in unique circumstances; **Verstehen** results from the inside, not from the application of general | glossary
laws and universal causes.

What many philosophers hoped for was that understanding actions and other human or mental aspects would develop into a methodology typical of and adequate for the human sciences, **hermeneutics**. Originally conceived as a method in theology, | glossary
philology and jurisprudence in order to make sense and to be able to reconstruct the meaning of classical and authoritative texts, hermeneutics was extended to all cultural products that were supposed to reflect any meaning, intention and feeling. Historical periods, texts, artefacts were all interpreted as reflecting some kind of spirit – the spirit of the Middle Ages, the meaning of *Hamlet*, the intentions of Julius Caesar.

Wilhelm Dilthey (1833–1911) and others dreamt of making hermeneutics into a strong and central methodology of the human sciences. It was their intention to protect these studies against the obtrusive natural sciences and to guarantee their autonomy. The central idea is that human creations, such as literary products, arts, buildings, laws, social institutions and behaviour, cannot be objectified as things disconnected from human subjects; instead they are laden with values and must be understood in the context of their time and cultural setting. While the mathematical-natural way of explaining requires an analysis into meaningless elements, the historical understanding necessitates the part being held up against the whole, and vice versa. The famous notion of the *hermeneutic circle* means that we can never understand a particular product with- out considering its cultural background, and for understanding the wider background you have to study the details. Interpretation goes continually back and forth, in a cyclic way, between the part and whole. For example, you have to obtain an idea of a patient's whole personality to understand his test results, but the tests help to fill in the picture.

Hermeneutics aims at reconstructing the meanings and experiences objectified in cultural products. It is hopeless to explain the French Revolution in terms of laws and causes and disconnected events; rather one has to feel its spirit, reconstruct its unique meaning. Enumerating a lot of objective observations, and trying to state a causal law about them, simply misses the meaning of it all; the meaning has to be understood, 'read off' the context, lived through, so to say.

It seems that such a methodological divide is still with us, when it is argued that subjectivity and meaning can never be explained by scientific methods. Psychology still seems to be haunted by an antithesis between scientific respectability and human interest, between scientific explanations and understanding lived experience (e.g. Bruner, 1990; Varela et al., 1991). In psychology, understanding is not generally considered a viable method, since one of the criteria for a scientific method is that it can be stated in the form of explicit instructions, in principle understandable and learnable by all. Psychotherapy, however, at least in psychoanalytic and Rogerian settings, has something in common with the hermeneutic enterprise (see Terwee, 1990): the therapist is concerned with reconstructing meaning, with exploring the way a unique individual (the patient) makes sense of the world, rather than with observing objective facts (like behavioural movements per se). She has to bring in her own feelings and prejudices to get the dialogue going. Unfortunately, as more scientifically-minded psychologists quickly remind us, therapy is a highly subjective and intractable affair, with dozens of deeply divided schools and approaches. That points to an important problem with hermeneutics considered as a scientific method: lack of objectivity.

The hermeneutic considers interpretation not as a kind of detached objective observation, but more as a dialogue where the interpreter brings his own 'horizon', his cultural baggage, his opinions, subjective norms and prejudices and confronts them with the cultural spirit of his text. Such a cultural background is indispensable, but is never completely made conscious. Interpretation is in fact only possible when it starts from such 'prejudices' (more about this in Chapter 4.2) and never completely detaches itself from them. When these prejudices are revised in confrontation with the meanings of the text, there is no external objective criterion for correct understanding, there is only different (revised and refined) understanding. The hermeneutic dialogue is a circle, from which there is no escape to objectivity (Gadamer, 1960; Bleicher, 1980).

In modern times the ideal of a *methodological* hermeneutics has been transformed, at least in the German tradition, by philosophers such as Martin Heidegger and Hans-Georg Gadamer, into a *philosophical* hermeneutics. The claim is that humans have a fundamental hermeneutic relation not only with their cultural products, but with the world in general. This relation with the world is mediated by our knowledge, formed by language and therefore saturated with the subjectivity of tradition and communication. Humans are historical and social beings and so is their most important product, knowledge. *Verstehen* is, therefore, the fundamental epistemological characteristic of human beings and turns hermeneutics into the foundation of philosophy. In our days, in the hands of Jürgen Habermas, Richard Rorty and others, hermeneutics has become a critical philosophy questioning the role of science and technology and the course philosophy itself has taken in the Western world. We will discuss some of these deeper issues in Chapter 4.2.

In this section, the classical nomological view of explanation (subsumption under causal laws), and the hermeneutic view (understanding unique and individual intentions and meanings) were discussed. We suggest that the rigid dichotomy between nomological explanation and hermeneutic understanding is mistaken. Understanding and explanation can be considered as lying on a continuum from real life to more rigidly regimented forms of inquiry. The former is closest to real-life concerns, and serves as informal inspiration for more objective investigations: for example, we have to understand first, from the inside, what the meaning of frustration is, and what counts as aggressive behavior in a culture, before we can start measuring and looking for general laws. Thus, at least in psychology, we always have a mix of explaining and understanding, or put differently, psychological explanations seem to lie on a continuum from the hermeneutical, for example psychotherapy, to the nomological, for example cognitive science or biological psychology.

To sum up, nomological explanation is, roughly, the standard in the natural sciences, and some kind of hermeneutic understanding seems crucial for social sciences. Both are present to some degree in psychology. In the next section, a third methodological approach, functional and teleological explanation, is discussed which seems adequate for biology and the biological aspects of psychology. It can be situated roughly in between the nomological (focusing on hard sciences, universal and timeless laws), and hermeneutics (focusing on meaning and intentions of unique individuals in historical context): functional explanation involves goals and functions rather than laws.

BOX 2.2 Hermeneutic understanding

- Understanding is explicating meaning of behaviour and texts.
- Describing meaningful relations in context (like a text, a web of meaning).
- Interpreting individual cases and unique events, no laws, no generalizations, no predictions.
- Reasons, motives and lived experience, not causes; actions, not movements.
- Starting from interpreter's own prejudices: circular.
- Hermeneutic circle between part and whole, between detail and context.

- *Problem*: no objectivity, not verifiable (or falsifiable, see Chapter 3.6).

2.4 Functional and Teleological Explanation

What is function?

As a first approximation, functional explanation says about a thing what it *does*, rather than what it *is*. A simple example: describing something as a mousetrap is attributing a sort of function to it (catching mice), no matter what the thing is made of (wood, plastic, poisoned cheese or perhaps a little guillotine). A more complicated kind of functional explanation is when the function of a system is analysed by showing how it works, more precisely, by showing how the organization of its components works. For example, you can analyse an assembly-line turning out cars by drawing a diagram of a series of tasks or functions, like welding the chassis, hinging the doors, fitting the engine, and so on. These subtasks are simpler, more 'stupid' than the capacity of the whole system to build cars; in that sense functional analysis explains the way an assembly-line works. The diagram describes functions at a certain level of abstraction, that is, it does not matter whether blue-collars workers, robots, or Martians execute these functions. Flow charts or schematic diagrams explain how the device as a whole exercises a capacity as an organized or programmed exercise of its component capacities. In this way, Cummins proposes that a function can be defined as what contributes to the capacity of a system (Cummins, 1983 and 2000: 125).

This kind of explanation is quite common in cognitive psychology, where a flow chart of boxes and arrows is presented to explain the workings of cognitive capacities like selective attention, memory, or reasoning. Cognition is explained as a set of functions, and analysed as a series of information-processing operations. Memory, for example, is explained as a product of boxes and arrows depicting functions like storage, retrieval, STM, LTM, WM, template match, etc., that contribute to the capacity to selectively retain and retrieve information. Cartoons in psychology textbooks often show a factory-like diagram with little men (homunculi) dragging around images, churning out percepts, and initiating motor reactions.

It is important to realize that functional analysis is different from **deductive** **nomological** subsumption under general **laws**. Showing how thinking through chess problems can be broken down in subroutines is different from finding the general laws of chess-playing behaviour. In fact, one could argue that these laws do not explain anything interesting, since they just describe trivial regularities, but the functional analysis of chess playing does show in an interesting way *how* the trick is done – 'How does it work?' is a more interesting question for psychology than 'What are the laws?' (Cummins, 2000).

glossary

BOX 2.3 Functional explanation

- The presence of a trait is explained by its function (why is it there?).
- Adaptation, not physical causation, not interpretation of meaning.
- Functional analysis shows how systems work, their design and functioning, not general laws, no predictions.
- Functional organisation and abstract design, not physical causes.
- *Problem*: cheap, circular, pseudo-explanation.

Function, teleology and evolution

Function, adaptation, design, teleology and purpose are overlapping concepts. **Teleology** is a controversial subject in the history of science. The (now discredited) Aristotelian view of the universe was that everything has a nature which determines the intrinsic goal to which that thing strives: stones have a weighty nature, which is why they tend to move downwards to their proper place on the ground, and acorns have a nature that makes them develop into oaks. This goal (α) thus explains the development and the design of organisms. This Aristotelian view is bad science. First, the explanation is circular: acorns become oaks because that is their nature, and you know their nature by seeing them grow into oaks; of course, that doesn't explain anything. Second, goals do not fit in a causal physical world. **Causes** precede their consequences, but goals apparently work backwards in time (the oak sort of motivates the development of the acorn).

glossary

glossary

Teleological explanation, invoking goals or functions, therefore has a bad reputation in science. Nevertheless, in biology, teleological terms like design, purpose, adaptive function, are quite common. Looking at organisms, it is obvious that they exhibit some kind of design: the eye for example is such a great piece of engineering, so obviously designed with the goal of making sophisticated vision possible, that for the theologian William Paley (1802, see Dawkins, 1985) it was proof of the existence of a Creator. Darwin's theory of evolution has made the notion of design respectable: natural selection provides a scientifically acceptable basis for teleology. The eye has its clever design as a result of zillions of random variations, the most successful of which has survived selection in the course of evolution. Modern biologists believe that a blind, mechanical, natural process of variation and selection has produced organisms with adaptively designed functions (Dawkins, 1985; Dennett, 1995). It is illuminating to describe or explain the presence of properties or organs as serving some goal or function; we have lungs to breathe, a heart to pump blood, etc.: these design features (the eye, the heart) exist because they helped survival (and are inheritable).

So, in evolutionary biology, ascribing a function to a trait is an indispensable part of explaining organisms. Ascribing functions in biological and psychological contexts often involves the evolutionary notions of adaptation and fitness (for example, the giraffe developed a long neck for picking the top leaves). That may be problematic: it is easy to think up functional explanations that are vacuous, or just plain silly; for example: the cork-oak's bark's *raison d'être* is to enable us to cork our wine bottles. In Voltaire's novel *Candide* (1759), Maître Pangloss keeps explaining that things are what they are because we live in the very best of all possible worlds – which is, of course, the most vacuous explanation you can imagine.

Explaining traits as adaptive or as contributing to fitness runs the risk of such 'panglossian' reasoning (Gould and Lewontin, 1979): everything is there for the best, otherwise it wouldn't be there; mammals have a heart because it should be there, that's why. The source of this tendency to churn out 'cheap', easy functional explanations is *adaptationism*, the wrong idea that natural selection is the only cause of phenotypic features of organisms, that it always produces the optimal design, and that therefore a straightforward evolutionary function can be attributed to each and every feature of an organism. In reality, many features are by-products that come with the design, or just a coincidence. It is a mistake that for every trait an adaptive function can be found. In fact, evolutionary biologists demand a well-specified selectional history before accepting functional explanations (see Brandon, 1990). We will encounter this problem again in the penultimate chapter (see Chapter 9.2) on evolutionary psychology.

Nevertheless, functional explanations are the bread and butter of many biological and some psychological explanations. We may distinguish two kinds of function: one about current function ('How does it work?'), the other about the evolutionary origin ('Why did this function originate?').

Two kinds of functions: causal role and selected functions

The famous evolutionary biologist Ernst Mayr (1988) distinguishes between two kinds of biology: functional biology and evolutionary biology. Functional biology considers the operation and interaction of structural elements, and their contribution to the system (the 'how?' question). Evolutionary biology looks at selectional history (the 'why?' or 'how come?' question). Correspondingly, philosophers of biology distinguish several notions of function that serve different explanatory interests: some explanations focus on current and future systemic function ('how?'), others on historical adaptation ('why?') (Amundson and Lauder, 1994; Enc and Adams, 1992).

The 'how come?' question is answered by the *etiological* notion of function which holds that giving a (functional) explanation of a trait is to show that it has been *selected for a specific effect* in the past. The function of pumping has caused (or contributed to) the presence of the heart in present-day mammals. The fact that it has been selected for that effect explains why mammals have a heart; it has increased fitness and provided some sort of selective advantage, and that explains why it is there (Wright, 1973). The etiological approach ties functional explanation to selective events in the past (Millikan, 1989). The function of the beaver splash (striking water with its tail) is to signal danger because it has been selected in the past for that function (non-splashing beavers presumably became extinct because they were less adept at avoiding danger).

The *causal role* concept of function considers the contribution a trait makes to some capacity of the whole system. Causal role function corresponds to Mayr's functional biology – the 'how?' question. Cummins' (1980, 1983) idea of function mentioned above is an example of this: it is called causal role function or systemic capacity function. This is basically an engineering-style of explanation, looking how a trait contributes to overall capacity of a complex hierarchical system. In contrast with Mayr's evolutionary branch of biology, this is ahistorical, ignoring evolutionary history. Whatever caused the presence of a trait (for example, a bird's feathers presumably developed for thermal isolation), its function is what it will do for its owner now and in the future (enabling flight).

In the philosophy of biology it is a hotly debated point whether evolutionary selection is a necessary part of function. Amundsen and Lauder (1994) argue that the functions a physiologist ascribes to an organism under study would not change if some evolutionary missing link were found where the same organ had a different role – that is, they don't care what the history of a trait is, as long as it contributes to the organism's capacity. Mitchell (1995) points out that different kinds of functional explanations are not necessarily competitors. They may serve distinct explanatory purposes: dispositional explanation answers the question how a trait contributes to survival in a certain environment, whereas the etiological explanation answers the question why a trait is present. Such explanations simply answer different, equally legitimate and interesting questions, and it depends on the questions asked which kind of functional explanation we are interested in.

Seeing more: the use of functional explanations

Returning to our mousetrap, illustrating that function may sometimes be more interesting than physical characteristics, there is an important reason why one would bother to look for functional explanations rather than staying within the classical nomological framework. A single function can be realized in many physical structures, and functional analysis is a way to generalize over physical diversity, to see functional unity. Functional concepts show how otherwise unconnected mechanical or neural or biochemical processes hang together in serving a purpose or being part of a design: knowing that the eye is for seeing suggests why the physical details are what they are. Functional explanation shows what physical or neural structures do, what purpose they serve; and it shows new ways of grouping phenomena, and points to new problems and phenomena to explain (Enc and Adams, 1992). Lots of biological concepts are functional in this way – for example, fitness or reproduction, but also genetic coding or genetic information (Maynard-Smith, 2000). The same function, coding for a phenotype, may be associated with entirely different biochemical processes, and only from a functional perspective the common functional factors can be seen, which would escape us if we had only the physical or biochemical description.

In psychology, interpreting a brain image involves functional concepts, describing what the brain is *doing* in terms of (for example) selectively attending to input, constructing a three-dimensional representation, retrieving memories, and so on. This is more than specifying the laws of electrochemical conduction across synapses. Thus, functional perspectives allow us to see more: goals, purposes, design and information, where there would otherwise be only mechanisms (Cummins, 1989; Dennett, 1991b). Attributing purposes should at least do some explanatory work. Functional generalizations predict that in a system with a certain goal, a form of behaviour will occur because it brings about the goal. That does help with understanding complex ('intelligent') systems, like animals, people and computers: students working for an examination presumably have the goal to get a degree, which helps understanding their diligence.

Psychology: functionalism
explains the mind as a virtual machine

Functionalism is the idea that mind can be seen as a function (e.g. Putnam, 1961; Fodor, 1968; Block, 1995), and that much of its mystery can be solved that way. Applying   `glossary` the idea of functional explanation to psychology means that we can see the mind as a kind of virtual machine; mental states like pain, hunger, beliefs and desires can be explained in terms of their functional roles, their contribution to cognitive capacities. This is in fact the subject matter of Chapter 7, but we will give a brief preview of the idea here. Functionalism holds that a mental state like hunger can be defined not by what it *is* neurologically, but what it *does* in an organism: its causal role or *function*, the way it mediates between the 'input' (perception) and 'output' (behaviour), and the way it interacts with other mental states. Functions can be *multiply realized*: the same causal role can be filled by different mechanisms. Remember the mousetrap, which can be made (realized) from all sorts of materials, and in different ways that have nothing physical in common.

A useful analogy of the relation between function and realization is that between software and hardware. Just as a computer program can be realized or implemented by different hardware configurations, so can a mental program be realized by different organisms or systems with different physiological or physical make-up, be it humans, dogs, computers, aliens from another galaxy, or the stones of Stonehenge. In this theory, you and a computer could share mental functions (like solving chess problems), without sharing underlying physical structure. Mental states (pain, hunger, desire) are defined by their causal roles, their causal relations to input, to output and to other mental states (looking for food, remembering foraging opportunities, etc.), roughly in the same way as computational states of a computer program (reading, symbol manipulation, storing, writing) are defined by what they contribute to the functionality of the machine. Although mental states do not exist without a brain in which they are realized (as computational states only exist in hardware), their neurological realization or 'implementation' is in principle not relevant for functional explanation. Functionalism thus implies a weak kind of **materialism**, *token-materialism*: a function does not exist in a 'disembodied' way; it needs some kind material realization. However, that material base can in theory be anything: a mental kind (hunger, or pain) can be realized in (correspond with) a whole array of material things (human brains, computers, octopuses' nervous systems). *Type materialism* in contrast assumes that a certain kind (or type) of mental state can be directly identified with a certain type of neural state (for example, hunger is always neuronal firing in the hypothalamus).

glossary

glossary

The **computational theory of mind** is committed to functionalism: it holds that the study of cognition can be practised as a study of an abstract machine (or 'virtual machine') (see Chapter 7).

Note that this idea of function as causal role is somewhat different from the biological notion discussed above. It is a kind of *machine functionalism*: biological function has been stripped of goal-directedness and adaptation to the environment (Sober, 1985) and is now seen as analogous to a computer program.

Teleological functionalism in contrast implies environmental constraints, which are missing, or at least not prominent, in Cummins' (1983) functional analysis (Bechtel, 1986). The problem with mechanistic causal role function (machine functionalism) is that it lacks biological plausibility: it can be argued that the role of the environment is crucial, not only in biological, but also in psychological explanation (Harman, 1988).

We could distinguish here between *narrow* and *wide* function. Wide functional analysis includes a (usually implicit) reference to the environment, and involves teleological functional considerations about the relation between the organism and its environment. Narrow functional analysis only looks at the system as such. Harman (1988: 20) thinks that 'only a wide psychological functionalism can motivate appropriate distinctions between aspects of a system, irrelevant side effects and misfunctions'. Applied to psychology, this notion of teleological functional analysis means that one should look beyond the mental apparatus as such to the way it deals with its environment.

BOX 2.4   Functionalism

- *Mental processes* are functional states of a machine or brain.
- *Functions* have a *causal role* in producing behaviour.
- *Functions* are *multiply realized*, the physical details are irrelevant, no reduction.
- Every function is *materially realized* – materialism, no dualism.

- *Example*: cognitive psychology: flow charts as abstract structures.

Explaining complex systems by analysing and decomposing functions

Functionalism as sketched above is just a global idea on the nature of complex systems and the mind in particular. For a real explanation, we need to show how the working of such systems can be explained by analysing and decomposing them in (sub)functions (Cummins, 1980, 1983; Bechtel and Richardson, 1993). The question to be answered by functional analysis is: in virtue of what can a system have such and such properties or capacities? Functional explanation according to Cummins *decomposes* functional capacities (or dispositions) into a number of simpler functions, *subfunctions*, which together instantiate the analysed function. For example, by showing that a desk calculator has modules (subfunctions) for basic operations, that it has a stack for storing numbers, and functions for adding and subtracting, and so on, you can explain why it has the capacity to calculate. A simple psychological example: when you know that memory consists of long term, short term and working memory, and what each of these do and what their limitations are, you can (start to) explain memory capacity. (e.g. if rehearsal in WM is blocked, there will be no storage in LTM).

Functions are often part of a *hierarchy*: a given function can be specified by further analysis into subfunctions that in turn consist of sub-subfunctions, and so on. This results in a hierarchy of functions within functions within functions (a sort of Chinese boxes) – what is a function on one level is a structure supporting that function at the lower level; each lower level fills the role specified by the higher level, and is simpler than the higher. For example, the circulation has the global role of delivering nutrients to tissues; this can be analysed (and thus explained) by the heart that pumps blood, the liver and kidneys that filter it, the arteries that channel it, etc. (Craver, 2001). Craver (2001) points out that functional analysis provides interesting explanations when it integrates mechanisms in a multilevel perspective. Demonstrating how mechanisms (like the heart) can be situated in a context to which it contributes (looking up for the role it plays, in this case the circulation), and analysing its constituent mechanisms (looking down for mechanisms it consists of, like contracting muscles) shows an integral hierarchy of how higher level functions are executed by lower level structures.

So, finding the components and how they are organized within a system, and to show how systemic behaviour is a consequence of the functions of the components, and of the way these interact (Bechtel and Richardson, 1993: 17), amounts to a genuine explanation.

To sum up

The concern about functional and teleological explanation in the philosophy of science in the late 1950s was whether it was not a form of crypto-vitalism, appealing to immaterial causes or backward causation. More precisely, the question was whether functional explanation could be fitted into the received view, the D-N (deductive-nomological) model, by replacing *goal-directed* explanation by an equivalent *causal* explanation. Such attempts have not been successful (see Salmon, 1990). At present the consensus seems to be that functional explanation is *sui generis* and has a legitimate place alongside causal explanation (Cummins, 1983; Rosenberg, 1985; Mayr, 1992; Cummins, 2000; Looren de Jong, 2003).

In conclusion, we can distinguish three modes of explanation: functional, nomological (causal) and hermeneutic. Functional analysis, explaining the behaviour of a system by the way it is organized, and how it interacts with its environment, is the basic pattern in biology and to some extent in biologically oriented psychology. We have seen that it involves many pitfalls, but is nevertheless an indispensable tool. In psychology, many processes are described functionally, in terms of what they do. The classical D-N model of subsuming a phenomenon under a covering law is of very little use here (Cummins, 1983, 1989, 2000), and the hermeneutic approach has little to say about the biological aspects of mind.

BOX 2.5 Types of explanation

Nomological explanation	Hermeneutic understanding	Functional explanation
Hard sciences	Humanities, social sciences	Biology, psychology
Explains events	Explains actions	Explains adaptive traits

BOX 2.5 **Types of explanation** (Continued)		
Nomological explanation	*Hermeneutic understanding*	*Functional explanation*
Causes are explanations	Motives, reasons are explanations	Functions are explanations
Discovers laws	Unveils meaning	Shows why design (a trait) is there
Objective	Intersubjective	Objective, observer relative
Generalizing	Unique cases	Individual (decomposition in subfunctions)
Psychology: laws of conditioning	Psychology: psychotherapy	Psychology: modelling in cognitive science

2.5   Reduction and Levels of Explanation

What is reduction?

Reduction has a bad reputation in some of the many mansions of psychology. It is often associated with a 'nothing-but perspective' – man is nothing but a machine, nothing but a digital computer, or a neural network. Especially in the 'soft' parts of psychology, such views are immensely resented; it seems that typically human, warm concerns are replaced by cold mechanisms. On the other hand, reduction is closely related to explanation, which is the core business of science. For instance, thunder is nothing but an electric discharge, it is not the wrath of the thunder god riding the sky. It may be useful to distinguish between *reduction*, an explanation of a macro-phenomenon through underlying micro-mechanisms, and *reductionism* as the philosophical position that all phenomena are ultimately reducible to something like basic physics.

In the philosophy of science, two aspects of reduction are of interest. The first is that reduction entails a claim about the structure of the world: that complex things and events are aggregates of simpler things. The second is that reduction is a relation between theories: *theory reduction*. Perhaps all sciences can ultimately be reduced to one basic science (some future idealized physics), and can be unified in one theoretical structure, so that laws about complex events (say, human behaviour, politics, economics) can be deduced from general theories plus knowledge about initial conditions under which these laws operate. On the other hand, it can be objected that the variety of knowledge interests, interesting questions, phenomena and styles of explanation is too diverse for a single framework. We suggest that several levels of explanation can coexist in psychology – genetic, physiological, neurophysiological, computational, personal, social, and so on. The most interesting cases are no doubt those where connections between those level relations can be established; for example, neuropsychological explanations for psychological deficits, social psychophysiology genetics of anxiety and depression, and so on. Such connections do not amount to reduction, however.

Reduction and the structure of the world

Reduction is sometimes put forward as a claim about the structure of the world. An intuitively plausible view of reduction is that it involves a chain of 'whys' and 'becauses'. To borrow Weinberg's (1992) example: Why is chalk white? – because it reflects the whole spectrum, and does not absorb a particular wavelength; this, in turn, is so because light comes in photons, and chalk does not absorb photons; and this, in turn, is because a photon has a definite energy and the atomic structure of chalk does not have an electron that could absorb a particular photon of any wavelength. Thus, reduction is following the arrow down from the macro-phenomenon of everyday objects to basic physics: chalk is white because of some deep micro-physical things like electrons and photons. The idea is that the arrows of reduction all point the same way and converge on a final theory that does not require reduction to other principles. As you may guess, the final theory does not yet exist, though physicists (e.g. Hawking, 1988; Weinberg, 1992) are confident that it may be found one day.

This view of reduction is thus in fact a claim about the way the world is made. Reality is an aggregate of elementary physical constituents. The converging arrows of reduction point towards the most basic constituents of the world. Physics deals with the fundamental laws of nature. The idea goes back at least to Newton, who thought that reality at the most basic level consists of particles in motion (forces), and the ultimate aim of Newtonian physics was to know the position and velocity of all particles. That is really all there is to know, and it would allow perfect prediction of everything in the universe. (This is *Laplace's dream*, after Pierre Simon Laplace (1749–1827), a French mathematician.) Reality is nothing but matter in motion.

We can call this the *complexity assumption*: complex things can be understood by breaking them down into their constituents. It is also the background of the classical deductive-nomological model of science.

'Nothing-buttery': reduction and elimination

In the chain of 'whys' leading down from everyday phenomena to elementary particle physics, the characteristics of the higher-level phenomena are lost (photons replace the experience of colour in the chalk example above). Intuitively, reduction seems to imply a 'nothing-buttery' perspective: the idea that most of the everyday phenomena we know can be explained away by science. For example, altruism is 'nothing but' the blind drive of the selfish gene, evolutionary psychologists tell us (see Chapter 9.2); thinking is 'nothing but' symbol manipulation; consciousness is 'nothing but' the working of a neural network (see Chapters 7, 8 and 10). Thus it is suggested that any reduction eventually leads to an elimination; in psychology this would mean the displacement of so-called 'folk'-psychological explanation by presumably neuro-physiological language, so that we turn out to be causally determined machines, rather than intentional and rational beings (see Chapters 7.3 and 10).

More precisely, the idea here is that reduction equals *elimination*, that is, entails a correction or displacement of the reduced theory (Churchland, 1981, 1989a). To use a well-worn example: 'Water is really H_2O' means that only H_2O exists, and the everyday use of the word 'water' refers to an illusion. However, it can also be argued that the possibility of reduction does not affect the legitimacy of everyday reducible concepts, and even that the discovery of a physical correlate legitimizes the use of everyday concepts. If, for example, pain has a distinct neurophysiological correlate, mental events are real, and mental idiom does refer to genuine things.

The archetype of this problem is Eddington's two tables (Schwartz, 1991); the scientific one of elementary physics, and the everyday one. The apparently solid table is an illusion, from the viewpoint of physics; the real table is, as physics tells us, a void full of electric charges. The scientific table is, according to Eddington, the only real one, and there is no obvious way to connect the two. However, as mentioned before, it is also arguable that the scientific story underwrites the common-sense story about the table. The solidity of the everyday table can be explained, to some extent perhaps corrected, by the theory of molecular bonds. In this view, we are talking about the same table. So, in some cases, reduction can retain common sense: we still talk about 'water'; in psychology, mental concepts can be preserved to some extent (and perhaps to some extent corrected) in a future psycho-neuroscience. More precise and technical aspects of this correction will loom large in the discussion of 'new wave reductionism' below.

On the other hand, note that reduction in psychology can be very interesting; knowing the mechanisms of memory, for instance, makes comprehensible why you cannot retain more than seven digits in memory. And, more generally, knowing the trick, so to speak, behind a phenomenon does not necessarily eliminate or debase it; knowing that life is a matter of duplicating RNA does not make it less interesting than it was under the old explanation in terms of a *vis vitalis* (life force) or *generatio spontanea* (spontaneous generation). Rather, it may even increase our sense of wonder. At the very least, proposals for reduction in the human sciences can serve to sharpen our sense of what exactly is left out in reduction, and in exactly what way human beings are more than science explains.

Theory reduction and the deductive-nomological model

Recall that in the D-N model the explanation of an event (more precisely, a statement describing the event) follows logically from a general law or set of laws (plus boundary conditions). As we will see in the next chapter (Chapter 3.2), in Logical Positivism, at the beginning of the twentieth century, theories were conceived as axiomatic, logical and unified logical structures. Its ideal was the *unification* of all sciences in a single theory, under a single methodology, namely the D-N model of explanation. The logical positivists' view of the reduction of a science to a more basic science is an outgrowth of their view of explanation. In this classical view (Nagel, 1961), reduction is essentially *theory reduction*: in a nutshell, it holds that reducing a higher-level theory is showing how it can be deduced from a lower-level theory plus boundary conditions. A lower-level science may thus explain the phenomena or laws of a higher, more complex level: for instance, neuroscience might explain behaviour; biochemistry explains genetics.

More precisely, the classical model of reduction conceives of reduction as a relation between theories in the sense that a more complex theory can logically be derived from a more basic one. It sees *reduction as a logical deduction of higher-level laws from lower-level laws plus boundary conditions specifying the qualifications under which the latter operate* (Hempel, 1965; Nagel, 1961; Oppenheim and Putnam, 1958/1991). As mentioned above, explaining according to the D-N model is deducing a statement (the explanandum) from general laws plus statements describing initial conditions. Note that classical reduction looks much like D-N explanation – only now it is a higher-level *theory* that is deduced, not a statement describing an explanandum. An often quoted example is the deduction of Boyle's gas laws ($PV = cT$) from statistical thermodynamics (Nagel, 1961: 338–445; see however Sklar, 1999).

Nagel (1961: 354, 433–35) gives two conditions for theory reduction: *connectability* and *deducibility*. The deducibility condition implies that theories are finished and formalized. *Bridge laws*, establishing equivalences between the two theories and connecting concepts across levels, take care of the connectability condition. In the case of Boyle's law, the bridge law is: temperature (of a gas) is average kinetic energy of molecules in an ideal gas. In this way, the (formalized) theory of thermodynamics can (ideally) be *deduced* from (i.e. reduced to) statistical mechanics. The bridge laws make sure that the reduced theory's concepts will map nicely onto those of the reducing theory. When bridge laws have established cross-theoretical identities, the equivalence of the two (sets of laws) is more or less a matter of translation. This equivalence is in itself not yet a complete reduction. In addition to bridge laws, it must be possible to derive (*deduce*) higher-level laws from lower levels.

The idea is that progress in science consists in smoothly incorporating formerly disjointed knowledge in a single theory: '... a relatively autonomous theory becoming absorbed by, or reduced to, some other more inclusive theory ...' (Nagel, 1961: 336–7). That means that the older theory is more or less retained, its **ontology**, and general view of the world is incorporated in the new more comprehensive theory – it is *reduced*, but not *eliminated*; for example, Galileo's astronomy could be fitted into Newton's mechanics. In the thermodynamics case 'temperature' does not figure in statistical mechanics, but the gas laws can be derived from the laws of kinetic energy. Another example might be the subsumption of Mendel's laws of inheritance under the biochemical laws of DNA transcription. To be incorporated seamlessly, as the classic view of reduction demands, the older theory must be basically correct; only then can its concepts be mapped by bridge laws onto concepts of the new theory, and its ontology retained within the more comprehensive successor.

glossary

This presents a problem: when the old theory is to some extent false, it cannot logically be consistent with the new, presumably correct, theory (the deducibility condition is not satisfied). When the concepts of the old theory are abandoned there can be no bridge laws (the connectability condition is not satisfied). And, of course, many if not all theories will have got it wrong somewhere.

Why the classical view of theory reduction doesn't work: bridge laws and meaning change

The classical theory reduction model has never been very successful in describing real science. In practice, the reduced theory is almost always corrected, or even entirely eliminated: bridge laws are about as frequently seen in actual science as the Loch Ness monster.

First, something seems to get lost in the process of reduction. This could be called the non-transitivity of explanation (Putnam, 1980). In Putnam's example, the fact that a square peg does not fit into a round hole is explained by the rigidity of the material, and the rigidity of the material is explained by its micro-structure; however, an interesting explanation of the rigidity of macro-objects is not an explanation of something which is explained by this rigidity. Explanation does not carry over from molecule level to the level of macro-objects. Even if the behaviour of a system can be *deduced* from its description as a system of elementary particles it does not follow that it can be *explained* from that description. The relevant features may be buried in a mass of irrelevant detail. Such higher-order patterns will be lost when we move, for instance, from macroscopic objects to elementary particles. The organization of elements determines the higher-level features (the form of the wooden peg), and the form is accidental from the point of view of physics – physics has no concepts for it. Hence, although the system has a physical basis, it cannot be explained by it. The fact that elements are organized in a particular way suggests a kind of autonomy of higher-level features, like psychology and sociology. The idea of deduction of higher from lower level is a mistake because it ignores the structure of the higher level. Putnam's (1961) thesis of the non-transitivity of explanation over levels is directed against the unity of science approach (Oppenheim and Putnam, 1958/1991) that tried to incorporate higher levels in the basic laws of physics.

Another serious problem lies in the demand of *connectability* by bridge laws. As Paul Feyerabend (1968, see next chapter) understood quite early on, when an old theory is reduced by a new theory, the meaning of its terms is usually changed in the process. A standard example is the difference in meaning associated with the concept of mass in Newtonian and in quantum physics, respectively. This makes identification impossible, and therefore cross-theoretical identities in bridge laws are almost never established. Moreover, since the old theory is usually corrected by the new, the former cannot, strictly speaking, be consistent with the latter, and hence cannot be deduced from it.

This makes the classical model implausible: corrections and changes in the meaning of theoretical terms are essential for empirical progress (Feyerabend, 1968): as Kuhn (1970) (see Chapter 3.7) famously argued, real progress, as distinguished from puzzle solving, requires revolutions where world views change and ontologies are abandoned. The classical view of reduction thus cannot give a plausible picture of scientific practice and scientific progress: the framework it proposes as the ideal type of reduction does not fit obvious cases of progress and successful reduction, and does little to clarify what constitutes reductive success.

glossary We can distinguish two responses to the failure of the classical reduction: if we cannot find bridge laws connecting, for example, psychological and neuroscientific theories, then we can opt for non-reductive **materialism**, and assume that psychological theories will remain autonomous (the road chosen by *functionalists*, explained above; see also Chapter 7). The other option is that the failure of incorporating psychology in the fabric of basic physics warrants the elimination of psychology: we drop the idea that the ontology of the reduced theory must somehow be retained, and allow extensive revision or replacement – the road chosen by *eliminativists* (see Chapter 8).

Beyond classical reduction (1): Non-reductive materialism and supervenience

glossary Behind the ideal of reduction is the metaphysical conception of **physicalism**, the claim that basically everything is physical and, ultimately, only physics can describe and explain the nature of the world. This is highly implausible: as explained above, functional generalizations can show patterns that are not visible in the laws of physics. The equivalent of bridge laws in the philosophy of mind are empirical identifications of mental and physical entities, the standard example is: pain is firing of C-fibres (the glossary **identity theory** of matter (brain) and mind is discussed in Chapter 6.2).

The phenomenon of multiple realization (see above: the octopus may have pain in a different kind of nervous system) makes that very implausible. Not many one-to-one identifications of mental concepts and neural concepts will be found. Psychology somehow should be autonomous, independent of the physical sciences. glossary However, **dualism** should be avoided; the idea of functionalism, set out above, aims to reconcile materialism with an autonomous psychology. It allows a less radical kind of materialism than the reductionism of the identity theory. Functionalism chooses a level of describing mental phenomena as functional states of physical entities: every function is materially realized, but not reducible to physical processes, since these realizations may be different each time. So, it seems we can avoid dualism without embracing reductionism and we can combine materialism with autonomy for psychology.

glossary The concept of **supervenience** (the term suggests something like 'following, accompanying') has been proposed by philosophers to underpin non-reductive materialism. It should help to understand the relationship between the different domains of the mental and the physical. The philosopher Donald Davidson is one of the first who made mention of this supervenience relation in the context of the mind-body problem:

[M]ental characteristics are in some sense dependent, or supervenient, on physical characteristics. Such supervenience might be taken to mean that there cannot be two events alike in all physical respects but differing in some mental respect, or that an object cannot alter in some mental respect without altering in some physical respect. (Davidson, 1980b: 214)

The mental is dependent on the physical, in the sense that every mental change requires a physical change (a brain process): there is no disembodied mind. In roughly the same way, the functions of a table supervene on its physical composition and on its spatial construction: whether you can use a thing to support your coffee cup depends on its form and solidity. The properties of the brain fix the properties of the mind: if we could make a completely identical physical copy of you, with exactly the same brain, it would have exactly the same mind as you. But although physical properties determine mental properties, the reverse is not true: not every mental property is associated with the same physical property: the determination or dependency relation between mind and brain is asymmetrical. And that precludes reduction: when trying to work downwards from mind to brain, we see that the arrow of reduction fragments, so to speak, in different brain processes (in the same way as the function of coffee-cup-support can be associated with many different physical objects). Supervenience goes hand in glove with functionalism. It nicely supports non-reductive materialism: mental processes are determined by, but not reducible to, material processes.

So, the initial response in the philosophy of mind to the failure of classical reduction (no connectability, no cross-theoretical identities, expressed in bridge laws, between mental and physiological processes will be found) was to turn it into a virtue: the autonomy of psychology vis-à-vis neuroscience (Fodor, 1981a, 1981b, 1997b). The domain of psychology was identified as that of multiply realized functions, and multiple realization supposedly means that no one-to-one bridge laws can be found between psychological and neural concepts, only a messy jumble of many-to-many realization relations. Supervenience helps to understand the asymmetric dependency between mind and matter and saves materialism without reductionism (Heil, 1992).

Beyond classical reduction (2):
New wave reductionism and eliminativism

The other response to the lack of cross-theoretic identities was **eliminativism** `glossary` (Churchland, 1981), of which new wave reductionism (NWR) (Bickle, 1998) is the latest and most sophisticated offshoot. In a nutshell, the idea is that neuroscience will replace or radically reconstruct, rather than reduce, psychology. NWR responds to the failure of connectability in a way different from the autonomy view. Rather than declaring the higher-level theory autonomous, and in a way immune to reduction, NWR proposes that it should be corrected to some extent. This correction can range from classical reduction where the old reduced theory is smoothly incorporated into the new reducing theory, to complete elimination (Schaffner, 1993: ch. 9; Churchland and Churchland, 1994). The corrected version of the to-be-reduced theory (e.g. psychology) can then be deduced from the new reducing theory (e.g. neuroscience). In NWR no connecting principles (bridge laws) are needed, since the reduced (corrected) theory is rewritten to fit in the reducing theory (Bickle, 1998 and 2001).

The degree of correction may range from almost perfect retention (smooth reduction) to complete rejection (bumpy reduction). The identification of temperature with mean kinetic energy is an example of a smooth reduction, where the thermodynamic concepts map almost completely on those of statistical dynamics, while the phlogiston theory of combustion, which was entirely replaced by the oxygen theory, is an example of a bumpy reduction. The 'smooth reduction' end of the continuum corresponds with classical D-N micro-reduction where the ontology of the reduced theory is retained, the other, 'bumpy', end with Kuhnian revolutions and a different world view (Bickle, 1998: 30; Churchland and Churchland, 1994). The complete abolishment of an old theory (its *elimination*) can thus be a case of successful reduction, and the demands of connectability and derivability for a successful reduction are thus simply rejected.

In the case of psychology and neuroscience, Bickle (1998: ch. 6; Bickle, 2002) points out that cognitive psychology is only an *approximation*: it gives a global, abstract, coarse-grained description of the phenomena (for example, generalizations of retaining and forgetting in memory research); the reducing theory, neuroscience, explains the real underlying dynamics causing these phenomena (in memory, biochemical processes in synapses). Bickle (2002) makes it clear that he expects the higher level (psychology) to become obsolete and redundant when the whole explanatory story is told in neuroscientific terms. The functional concepts only approximately describe the phenomena which in reality are molecular processes at neural synapses. So, when psychology cannot be reduced to neuroscience in the classical way, it can still be corrected or just *eliminated*. All the explanatory power we may want is provided by the story of molecular neuroscience, according to eliminativists. In Chapters 8 and 10.2 we will discuss Churchland's proposal to eliminate 'folk' psychology as an obsolete theory.

Coevolution versus elimination

Thus, new wave reductionism (Churchland, 1981, 1989a; Bickle, 1998) gladly accepts abandoning or thoroughly reconstructing the psychological level, and in his more radical moments Churchland considers successful reduction as equivalent to the possibility of elimination; in his less radical moments, he paints a picture of a slowly maturing marriage rather than a sudden takeover (Churchland and Churchland, 1994: 53).

Looking carefully, there is an ambiguity in this picture: the reduction–replacement continuum seems to see all *reduction* as theory *succession*. We might, however, distinguish between this *diachronic* dimension of intertheoretic relations and a synchronic dimension. The diachronic case is theory succession, where an old theory is more or less corrected and replaced by or smoothly integrated into a new theory. The *synchronic* dimension is when at the same point in time several theories coexist and influence each other. In the latter case, theories *coevolve*. Theories at several levels exert selection pressure on each other, both top-down and bottom-up. So, this is quite different from functionalism and dualism, where the upper level (psychological level) is seen as autonomous and isolated from the lower, neuroscience level. And it is also quite different from eliminativism, where the upper level is supposed to be replaced by the lower. There is in our opinion no reason why psychology would not continue to coevolve with neuroscience, and continue to exert influence on theory choice at the lower level (Schouten and Looren de Jong, 1999).

Explanatory pluralism (McCauley, 1996) or multiplicity of explanation (Clark, 1989) is in our view a much better model than elimination. We think there is overwhelming theoretical and practical evidence for believing that reality is best described at different levels, and every level – chemical, anatomical, physiological, neurophysiological, biological, mental, social – has its own theoretical concepts and theories with their own explanatory power.

Looking back on the somewhat detailed and technical discussion of reduction, we can see that it leads (at least in the present authors' opinion, which eliminativists will not share) to a view of explanation as a multilevel affair. Reduction in the classical sense where psychological theories can presumably be translated into neuroscientific theories does not work; the elimination of psychology and its replacement by neuroscience is, in our opinion, not a realistic prospect. Hence, we think that different kinds of explanations will continue to coexist in psychology, at different levels, with different and irreducible perspectives and explanatory interests.

BOX 2.6 Varieties of reduction

Classical Reduction:

- Theory reduction: deducing a higher-level theory from one or more lower-level theories, connected by bridge laws.
- Old theory smoothly incorporated, meanings of its terms unchanged.
- Requires connectability (identities between terms of both theories) and derivability (formal or mathematical theories).

- *Problem*: old theory is almost always corrected, revised, or abolished.
- *Classical reduction fails* as an account of scientific progress (e.g. no classical reduction of mind to brain).

Non-reductive Materialism:

- Responds to failure of classical reduction: higher level autonomous.
- Supervenience: no changes in upper level (mind) without changes in lower level (brain).
- Lower level determines higher levels, but no reduction.
- Multiply realized mental processes, therefore no bridge laws (no identity) between mind and brain processes.
- Mind dependent on matter, but not reducible to matter: autonomy for psychological theorizing.

BOX 2.6   **Varieties of reduction** (Continued)

New Wave Reductionism, Eliminativism:

- Responds to failure of classical reduction: higher level eliminated.
- Old reduced theory is to some degree false, obsolete, or incomplete.
- Old reduced theory is to some degree corrected or even entirely replaced by lower-level reducing theory.
- Functional, psychological theories only approximative, coarse descriptions.
- Cognitive phenomena can better be explained by neuroscience.

2.6 Reasons and Causes

As we said earlier, human behaviour, in general, can be taken as the subject matter of the social sciences. Some psychologists classify psychology among the social sciences for this reason. Many claim, however, that psychology studies determinants of behaviour, some of which are, but others are not, social. These psychologists prefer to designate psychology as a behavioural science. If we give credit to this idea of determinants we will have to confront the classic problem of 'reasons for' and 'causes of' behaviour. Are these expressions equivalent, or not? We have already referred to the glossary concept of **action** as a terse and adequate description of human behaviour. In the context of the earlier discussion we suggested that along explanations of human behaviour there is much room for understanding human actions. In this section about reasons and causes we hope to clarify the connected distinctions. By doing this we will have the opportunity to make a case for the conceptions of different epistemological strata and the multiplicity of explanation.

What do we want to hear when asking the question why John slammed the door? Probably not that John put more than average energy into his act, giving the door more speed (which resulted in a heavy collision of the door with the doorpost, a loud noise and the lamp rocking back and forth). We normally are not interested in a report of the chain of causes and effects leading up to the slamming. Neither do we expect to hear a report about micro-processes in John's body causing his movements. The why-question asks for reasons – 'He felt offended', for instance. Even when we think in a materialistic frame of mind that the state of being offended can be traced in John's brain, even then we normally will not be interested in an answer in neurological terms. So, normally, in our day-to-day why-questions about people's actions we expect to hear about their reasons.

But are reasons different from causes? Are actions nothing but movements, and if so, should science not trace the causes that set bodies in motion, by identifying, let us say, motives, attitudes, traits; or even further by showing up these psychological entities as neuro-activities? Are not reasons and actions in fact clumsy or facile expressions of ordinary language? Some radical materialists, who deny such expressions' scientific status, think that reasons are part of **folk psychology**, the common-sense glossary psychology we use every day, which consists of bad theories, a totally obsolete and inadequate account of our internal activities. 'The folk psychology of the Greeks is essentially the folk psychology we use today, and we are negligibly better at explaining human behavior in its terms than was Sophocles' (Churchland, 1989a: 8).

When doing science, according to Paul Churchland, we do better to eliminate these concepts just as we got rid of 'phlogiston', the fire principle that in the seventeenth century was thought to depart when a body burned. Scientific psychology has to be a physical, a neuroscientific, enterprise.

A less radical materialist proposition, defended once by Donald Davidson (1963), glossary is to consider reasons as causes. Actions are caused or produced by a set of **beliefs** plus desires (or 'pro-attitudes'). So, we have a causal relation between two types of material events: mental events which are inner and distinct both in time and in place from outside behavioural, that is, bodily events.

We have already in a preliminary way dealt with some materialist positions concerning the mind–body problem and we will return to this problem, but for the moment we assume that actions are not the same as movements, that reasons cannot be equated with the causes of these movements and that, therefore, everyday psychology rightly acknowledges the differences.

Consider an illustration, given before, of the fact that one and the same movement can express different actions – by raising one's hand one can greet, urge someone to stop, or simply mimic. Sometimes one acts by not even stirring a finger, when protesting by not shaking hands, for instance, or when offering resistance by not speaking up. Some actions are so comprehensive that it is unclear what movement could be responsible: for instance, the act of committing fraud.

We think that actions have another ontological status; that they exist in a different way than as the movements or non-movements by which they are expressed. Actions and movements do not belong to the same category. Actions are more like descriptions and interpretations of these events and movements. They convey meanings, have symbolic import and take their identity and meaning from the context. That is why they have to be 'understood'. The same can be said of reasons. Reasons, framed in intentions, desires, emotions and beliefs, are heavily laden with meanings and interpretations communicated between people. We ask about someone's reasons when we want to assess her conduct. Actions and reasons share the same level of explanation, and the relation between them is normative, not causal. Reasons are appreciated as arguments and are not 'like forces whose intensity can be measured in advance and whose effects can therefore be accurately predicted' (Moya, 1990: 168).

So it does not help to trace reasons in the micro-activities of the actor's brain. And it remains to be seen if throwing away ordinary psychological language will provide a better psychology. Isn't this what at least part of psychology is all about – understanding people's behaviour? (See also Chapter 10.3 on mental causation.)

Some philosophers of science maintain that because of this 'change' of cognitive interest – from 'explaining' why the actions *qua* events in space and time had to come about, to 'understanding' actions from reasons and intentions – social sciences are in essence hermeneutic sciences. To 'understand' persons as agents is not to confront them as objects in the same sense as in a non-organic nature, but to meet them 'as "subject-objects" who in relation to us preserve their status of being virtual co-subjects of interaction and communication … This virtualization of the dialogical relationship to other persons seems to me to be the very condition of the possibility of hermeneutic sciences' (Apel, 1982: 33).

But, of course, there is more to understanding people than is revealed in communication only. We cannot *act* without our brain and body – our neurophysiological and bodily make-up are among the necessary conditions for thoughts and behaviour. We should expect mixed explanations in many cases. Psychology is a science with more than one or two levels of explanation. It consists of different types of question and accordingly different types of answer (Noble, 1990).

Returning to the issue of levels of explanation, we feel that understanding and explaining (both causal/nomological and functional) can be seen as distinct, coexisting and mutually influencing levels. These are neither autonomous nor simply reducible or replaceable. In many psychological phenomena, especially the cognitive ones, such as perception, learning skills, memory and emotions, the conceptual interdependence of different levels is, we think, pretty obvious and as scientists we should, therefore, make use of different levels and models. The distinction between understanding and explanation, reasons and cause is therefore not absolute, but rather something of a continuum. Some domains of psychology are more nomological, others more functional, others more hermeneutical, but all these have (or should have) a lively border traffic with others: the genetics of depression, the measurement of therapy, the neural correlates of empathy, the biochemistry of memory, are a few examples among many of bottom-up and top-down influences between levels of explanation in psychology.

2.7 Conclusion: The Multiplicity of Explanation

In this chapter, we discussed different modes of explanation, nomological explanation, subsuming a fact under a general law, hermeneutic understanding, bringing out the unique meaning of an event, and functional explanation, explaining the working of organisms and mechanisms. We spent some time on the third type, function, that has only recently been developed, and seems specific for psychology and biology. In our opinion, the objects of science can be situated at different levels of complexity, and the physicalist drive to unify science is misguided: we need (at least in psychology) different types and styles of explanation. In psychology, both mechanical and hermeneutical approaches can be used, since behaviour results from a complicated mix of causes and reasons.

Reduction is essentially about the relation between theories and explanations at different levels: we suggest that both eliminativism (or new wave reductionism), replacing psychology by neuroscience, and autonomy, isolating psychology from neuroscience, are wrong. We suggest that theories on different levels can coevolve and influence each other, both top-down and bottom-up. Explanation is not, as physicalists dreamt, a one-science-takes-all game, but is diverse and manifold.

FURTHER READING

Newton-Smith, W.H. (ed.) (2000) *A Companion to the Philosophy of Science.* Oxford: Blackwell. An encyclopedia of the important issues in the philosophy of science.

Rosenberg, A. (2000) *Philosophy of Science: A Contemporary Introduction.* London: Routledge. A systematic introduction to the most important issues in the philosophy of science.

3. PHILOSOPHY OF SCIENCE (I)

Logical Positivism and Its Failure

PREVIEW: This chapter introduces the 'received view' in the philosophy of science, Logical Positivism, and its classic and highly influential ideas on objectivity, the nature of theory and observation, verification and progress in science. Positivists aimed at a criterion for distinguishing science from pseudo-science. This ideal proved unworkable, and with Kuhn's paradigm concept the positivist story ends in post-positivist relativism.

3.1 Introduction: Scientific Methods, Objectivity and Rationality

In the previous chapters, some characteristics and basic concepts of science were sketched. We now turn to a more principled reflection on the scientific enterprise: philosophy of science. The philosophy of science has for a long time been characterized by the quest for a so-called **demarcation** *criterion* to distinguish science from pseudo-science, [glossary] and to be used as a yardstick against which to measure progress. A demarcation criterion is an account of a universal, ahistoric and general method for rationality that can be applied in an algorithmic fashion, leaving nothing to subjective factors like individual taste or judgement, or to social and historical factors. The (logical) positivist movement in the philosophy of science was motivated by the conviction that only a universal, general and ahistoric account of the methods of science can distinguish science from pseudo-science.

Furthermore, a clear account of scientific *method* is required to account for scientific *progress*: what makes chemistry better science than alchemy, Einstein's theory better than Newton's, cognitive psychology better than behaviourism.

The political and ethical import of this idea will be appreciated when one realizes that the famous group of (logical) positivist philosophers, the *Wiener Kreis* (Vienna Circle), operated in the intellectual and moral corruption of post-First-World-War Vienna. One of its members, Moritz Schlick, was actually murdered by a Nazi. Popper's rejection of totalitarian political thought (Hegel, Marx) is of a piece with his attempt to demarcate science from pseudo-science (Freud).

Recently, the quest for a demarcation criterion has come under fire. Toulmin (1990) explains the restriction of rationality and the obsession with mathematical certainty in the seventeenth century (Descartes and Newton) as a reaction to the failure of Montaigne's open, sceptical and tolerant view in the face of religious conflicts. He interprets the Wiener Kreis as part of this modernist 'quest for certainty', which acknowledges only one type of rationality, and discards the possibility of open dialogue between different points of view within a historical context.

Feyerabend, who was the most vociferous antagonist of methodological standards, seemed motivated by a loathing of pompous, pontificating philosophers, who claim the authority to tell other people what to do, who see themselves as guardians of a supposedly universal rationality, and who stifle spontaneity and common sense.

The **foundationalist** attempt to find an Archimedean point outside history and [glossary] society in the pure and unquestionable certainties of universal standards of rational conduct, on which a secure science can be built, is now definitely out of fashion, at least among philosophers. It is nevertheless instructive to follow the undoing of the demarcation criterion – paradoxically, its demise was mainly driven by the attempt of its partisans to work it out in a thoroughgoing and coherent way. Internal criticism from within the neo-positivist community has probably contributed more to its collapse than the outside and somewhat faddish rejections of its point of view. Again, it is important to realize the significance of demarcation; in the traditional view, universal method is the only stronghold against barbarism, the hallmark of rationality, a bulwark against **metaphysics** and ideological muddles. [glossary]

In the next sections we will discuss the positivist philosophy of science, and how it came under attack in the 1960s and 1970s. This attack on this so-called standard view of science came from two sides. First, **empiricism** was challenged from within the [glossary] Anglo-American tradition itself; and second, the traditional aversions to empiricism on the other side of the English Channel intensified and broadened. The main actors were Sellars, Quine, Wittgenstein, and Hanson (section 5); Popper (section 6); Kuhn,

Lakatos and Feyerabend (sections 7 and 8). In Chapters 4 and 5 we will give an overview of some recent alternatives to positivism. One line of alternatives is relativistic and social and sociological in its orientation. In Chapter 4 we will examine some problems of relativism, as well as realism. Another line of alternatives to positivism has a penchant for a moderate, that is, pragmatically reconstructed realism that we will discuss also in the next chapter.

BOX 3.1   Demarcation

- Demarcation criterion is a *criterion separating* rational scientific knowledge from metaphysical speculation, irrationality, superstition and pseudo-science, underpinning cumulative progress of science.
- Demarcation citerion belongs to the *context of justification*, and finding such a criterion was seen as the core business of the philosophy of science.

The *logical positivists* proposed as demarcation *verifiability; Popper* proposed *falsifiability*. Neither works.

Post-positivism concludes that no hard and fast rule can guarantee scientific rationality, that scientists have a dogmatic faith in their theories, and that theory choice is socially and historically determined.

3.2 Logical Positivism and Demarcation

 Logical positivism was the dominant philosophy of science from the 1920s to the 1960s. With the ascent to power of the Nazis, many members of the Wiener Kreis (Carnap, Feigl, Neurath) emigrated from Vienna and Prague to the United States, where the Vienna Circle became a major force in American philosophy. Although probably no one would use the label logical positivist these days, the consensus among practising scientists about the nature of empirical research, data, theories, confirmation and so on still reflects the basic ideas of positivism. The previous chapter illustrates this.

Empiricism and the problem of unobservable theoretical terms

Logical positivism started more or less as a reflection on the role of *observation* in science, which had become problematic at the beginning of the twentieth century. The classical idea of physics relied on observation as the only legitimate method, and it was thought that careful experimentation would in the end lay bare the naked facts.

This view had never been a very accurate picture of history; Galileo, the celebrated founder of classical mechanics, introduced new concepts that were not directly related to empirical facts, and probably even 'cleaned up' his measurements to fit his theory better.

As an ideal, the model was called in doubt by the rise of the theory of relativity and quantum mechanics, in which theoretical considerations rather than experimental results played a leading role. These could not (initially) be verified by direct observation, nor could they be directly compared with the Newtonian theory on empirical grounds. Concepts like space, time and **causality**, which had seemed evident for all the world to see, also became problematic.

glossary

This poses a problem: if carefully collecting objective empirical facts is not the (whole) business of science, then what is? If introducing concepts without (complete) empirical support is permitted, how can one stop quacks and metaphysicians and crooks introducing kooky speculations (racial superiority, the spirit of the age, snake oil, you name it) and claiming scientific respectability? If scientists use unobservable terms, what distinguishes science from metaphysical rubbish?

Verifiability is the test of meaningfulness

The members of the Wiener Kreis were hard-nosed scientists, mathematicians and logicians. Their philosophy aspired to be as precise and exact as (natural) science. In their analysis of the legitimacy of scientific knowledge, they demanded that statements should be empirically verifiable. The meaning of a statement is the way it can be verified; and if and to the extent that a sentence does not specify how it could be proven true or false, it is just nonsense, meaningless. Pure observation statements ('The liquid in the test-tube has turned red') and operational definitions ('Intelligence is what an intelligence test measures') are models of meaningful utterances. Metaphysics, poetry, Heideggerian philosophy, and theology are meaningless ('non-sense') – one does not, strictly speaking, know what they are talking about.

However, the logical positivists understood that scientific textbooks and papers contain many '*unobservables*', theoretical terms that are not directly observable, such as 'electron', or 'personality'. It is, of course, unacceptable to abandon these as 'meaningless'. Their solution to this problem is aptly summarized in the label 'logical positivism': science consists of statements describing positive objective facts, plus logical relations between these statements. These should be knit together in a closed logical system, built from elementary axioms, in such a way that the statements of a **theory** (a collection of statements describing states of affairs) can be logically derived from the axioms. Axioms are connected with observation statements through so-called *correspondence rules*. Correspondence rules define theoretical terms in (possible) observations.

glossary

Theoretical terms without direct empirical content can, through a deductive network, be linked to empirical observations ('Intelligence is a score on an IQ test'). So, correspondence rules were introduced as an attempt to account for unobservables, recasting them (indirectly) in observation statements. Those statements that cannot in any way be logically connected with observations should be purged from the theory.

glossary **Verification** then is the cornerstone of science. As long as the conditions can be specified that would make a statement true, that statement is scientifically respectable. When you can tell what should be done to verify a sentence, it is a meaningful claim, although of course it may still be factually wrong. And unverifiable statements ('God is love') are nonsense – they cannot even be wrong.

Unified science

The positivist picture of science is that theories are linguistic structures, consisting of statements expressing a state of affairs, and logical relations between them (conjuctions, implications, negations). Ideally, theories are formalized systems, so that statements can be deduced from each other – think of Newtonian physics, where knowing force and mass allows you to deduce acceleration. Or, see Chapter 1, how explananda glossary can be logically deduced from a **law** and initial conditions. Such a system supports a deductive-nomological method. Hypotheses (predictions, explanations: see Chapter 2) can be deductively derived from the theory. A statement, for instance, that a particular piece of copper will expand when put on the stove can be derived from the general law that all copper expands when heated. Thus, explanation is subsumption of statements describing events under a general law.

Along the same lines, reduction is establishing relations between theories – Mendelian genetics, for instance, can be reduced to molecular genetics: the gene can be identified with the chromosome, and the 'rational reconstruction' (axiomatized theory) of both laws allows derivation of Mendel's laws from biochemical laws. In the positivist scheme, reduction is deducing a higher-level theory from a lower-level theory plus bridge laws connecting terms from both theories (see Chapter 2). For example, thermodynamics can be deduced from statistical mechanics using the bridge law that temperature is average kinetic energy (of gas molecules). And ideally, biochemistry can be deduced from chemistry, biology from biochemistry, neuro-science from biology, psychology from neuro-science, sociology from psychology, and so on (Oppenheim and Putnam, 1958/1991).

Thus, science is ideally a single unified system, in which the same methods can be applied across the board, and higher-level sciences (biology, psychology, sociology) are just special cases of, and reducible to, basic sciences (physics). Psychology, history, etc. were supposed to use the same physical language (Carnap, 1931, 1932), describing objective observations, and to be formalized in the same nomological framework as physics. To the extent that they do not fit, they are simply not real sciences.

Whereas the positivist view has yielded interesting and illuminating analyses of the structure of theories and explanations in physics, it has been far less successful in clarifying the nature of research in psychology and the social sciences. In psychology, behaviourism tried to implement the demand that only objectively verifiable observation statements are acceptable, by limiting itself to observable behaviour (physical stimuli and responses). Its failure indicates that unification is probably not such a good idea (see also Chapter 2.5 on multiple explanations).

Justification versus discovery

This idea of unification also indicates that science is *cumulative*: research is incorporating ever more facts into an integrated deductive network, comprehending ever more complex higher-level laws. Since all respectable sciences consist of observation statements, there can be no serious qualitative differences between them. For example, observations by a medieval astronomer are just as valid as today's, even though his theories were completely wrong. Objective facts must just add up, so progress is assured by stacking up empirical observations.

The logical positivists argued that what really matters in scientific knowledge and rationality is justification. The ideal of verifiability, observation statements, and a deductive-nomological view on theories is normative; they define how science *should* be done in the **context of justification**. How science is *actually* done, however, belongs in the **context of discovery**. Considerations, such as Einstein's, and Galileo's theoretical preferences, and other contingent circumstances at the moment of discovery, can be considered as belonging to the context of discovery, and may be left to psychologists. Whether a scientists finds a bright idea by drinking coffee, staring in the fire, or jogging, has no impact on its scientific status. This distinction between the two contexts, justification and discovery (see also Chapter 1), opened up the possibility of *rational reconstruction* of scientific practice. It is obvious that not all (good) scientists (not even physicists) spend their time juggling axioms and logical formulae. Nevertheless, philosophers hold up logic as an ideal of scientific rationality, and only demand that the final results can be reconstructed as rational arguments and written up as verifiable hypotheses and observations.

The standard view

The main, and the most hotly disputed, presuppositions of the positivist philosophy of science, the 'standard view', or the 'received view' of science as it was also called, can be summed up as follows:

- The basic elements of scientific knowledge are **sense data** and the *observation* statements reflecting them; the senses give us access to the world. The standard view is committed to empiricism (see Chapter 1). These observation statements (*Protkollsätze*) reflect elementary facts.
- Apart from observation statements, a science also contains *theoretical* terms and expressions, that are not directly observed, like gravity or energy. These are only to be admitted in theories if they can be related to controlled observations (for example, by defining them in terms of measurement operations, like temperature is what a thermometer measures).
- Theories are linguistic entities: knowledge is only knowledge if embodied in propositions, and these are ordered in a *logical* structure. It is important that a theory is a system with a sort of logical backbone: this allows deducing propositions from other statements. Science has a deductive-nomological structure (see Chapter 2.2);

the different sciences have essentially the same observational methods and the same logic. Therefore, their respective systems of statement can be *unified*. Unification in practice means the annexation of other sciences by physics.

- In the assessment of scientific products, like hypotheses and theories, it is only the *context of justification* that counts, that is, strictly logical, methodological and sound epistemological criteria. This evaluation has nothing to do with the *context of discovery*, the historical, social or psychological process and circumstances by which these products are discovered and created. The psychology of the investigator, or academics' politics, are irrelevant when evaluating a hypothesis; what is relevant are the empirical and the logical underpinnings that count in accepting an idea as 'true' and valid. The task of the philosophy of science is, in the context of justification, to explain how and why science is successful, and to discover, protect and promote the permanent criteria and standards for sound scientific method.

- Science is *cumulative*; scientific progress is made by amassing empirical data and connecting these into logically structured theories. The belief that this knowledge is reflected in technical achievements in all kinds of applications (for example, scientific management) that benefit society is called 'scientism' (cum technology: 'technocracy').

The most basic and probably (with hindsight) most vulnerable assumption is that *neutral observations* are possible, and that observation statements picture elementary facts. Positivism wants to keep scientists honest by demanding observation statements for every theoretical claim; and with verification they demand that observations are kept pure and unadulterated by theoretical prejudices. Below, we will see how the impossibility of theory-neutral observations undermined positivism.

BOX 3.2   **The standard view of science**

- The basic elements of scientific knowledge are sense data; observation statements reflect sense data; the senses give us access to the world; observation statements (*Protkollsätze*) reflect elementary facts.
- Theories are sets of statements (*propositions*) that can be either observation statements or theoretical terms.
- An ideal, formalized theory has a *logical* backbone that allows *deducing* propositions from other statements (a deductive-nomological structure).
- Unobservable theoretical terms must be translatable in terms of observations.
- All sciences should use the same methods of observation, explanation and theory building and can, therefore, be unified.
- Scientific progress is cumulative, getting ever closer to a true picture of the world by collecting more and more objective facts.
- The task of the philosophy of science is to explain how and why science is successful, and to discover, protect and promote the permanent criteria and standards for sound scientific method.

To be fair, to some extent the above is a caricature, and the positivists were more subtle than that. Positivists have been accused of **foundationalism**, trying to secure glossary once and for all the foundations of science. The two pillars were formal logic and immediately given sensory data (or neutral observation sentences). However, as Friedman (1991) points out, the positivists were in fact more interested in founding epistemology on science than the other way round, and their empiricism did not rely on undigested immediately given sense data, but recognized an indispensable role for concepts (mathematical and otherwise). Positivists were no naive empiricists. For example, Rudolf Carnap (1891–1970), a member of the Wiener Kreis, allowed much freedom in choosing one's linguistic framework and allowed pragmatic or conventional preferences for certain forms of language (logic, theories) over others (see p. 72). Some even doubt that Carnap's view is that much different from postpositivism Kuhnian-style (see below on Kuhn's idea of a paradigm) (Irzik and Grunberg, 1995).

However, even if the discussion above does not do justice to the members of the Wiener Kreis, it does summarize what was and in many respects still is (roughly) the 'received view' in philosophy of science and methodology – see Chapter 1 for many mainstream ideas on laws, observations, generalizations, hypothesis testing, and so on, that originate in Logical Positivism.

BOX 3.3   Three problems with logical positivism

1   Theory and observation are not independent: completely objective observation is impossible (*see sections 3.3, 3.4, 3.5: Wittgenstein, Sellars, Quine, theory-ladenness*).
2   No satisfactory demarcation criterion is found, no cumulative progress is guaranteed (*see sections 3.6, 3.7, 3.8: Kuhn, Lakatos, Feyerabend*).
3   Some philosophers argue that objectivity is not only impossible, but also undesirable in the humanities (including psychology): the humanities are about understanding meaningful action, objective observations are uninteresting (*for examples of anti-positivist views see Chapter 4: Hermeneutics, Social Constructionism; see also Chapter 5 for social theories of science*).

3.3 Wittgenstein's Volte-face

To see how the demise of positivism started, let us look at Ludwig Wittgenstein, whose ideas have twice had direct importance for the philosophy of mind and language, and by consequence for the philosophy of science – each time in a different direction. The first phase of Wittgenstein's philosophical work was, along logical positivist lines, about the ties between language and the world. He thought that elementary states of affairs in the world are, somehow, pictured in language. The 'logical form', or the structure of states of affairs in the world, is mirrored in the logical structure, the logico-syntactic calculus, of language. Elements of propositions, and the logical relations between them, resemble the elements and their relations of states of affairs in the world – think, for example, of the way that the structure of a musical score resembles the structure of the piece of music, or a map is isomorphic with the landscape. Wittgenstein put down this so-called picture theory of the proposition in his famous *Tractatus Logico-Philosophicus* (started in captivity after the First World War, in which he fought in the Austrian-Hungarian army, published in 1921), which had an enormous impact upon the logical positivist movement.

In his second phase, starting in the mid-1930s on, he began to criticize the positivist theory of language, including his previous views. He opens his *Philosophical Investigations* (written 1929–1949, published posthumously in 1953) with an attack on the idea that the meaning of a word is what it stands for, and that we explain the meaning of a word by ostensive definition, explaining, for instance, 'red' by pointing to red objects. The assumption of this reference theory of meaning, that Wittgenstein is now about to abandon, is that there is a timeless and context-free link between language and reality, between propositions and facts. He criticized the assumption that propositions, or statements, are to be considered on their own, reflecting elementary facts, and that their truth and meaning can be tested separately by verifying them separately. It became clear to him that propositions form an interconnected whole.

In this second phase, Wittgenstein became interested in the analogy of games. Language can be compared to games, like chess; words and statements are like the chess pieces: they can be used according to the rules of the game, and their meaning is the way they can be used in the context of a particular game. You can move chess pieces to force a checkmate, and you can use words to order a meal. Games are played in conformity with rules, which may be implicit, unconscious, or made up while we play. Briefly, words and statements have meaning only within the language game, and the rules of the game determine how they can be used.

glossary A **language game** is an activity and the meaning of an element of the game is displayed in the actions, in the way it is used:

> … the term 'Language-game' is meant to bring into prominence the fact that the *speaking* of language is part of an activity, or of a form of life. (Wittgenstein, 1953: para. 23, original emphasis)

This is the core of Wittgenstein's new theory of meaning: *meaning is use*. Words and sentences get their meaning in a context of social exchange: sentences are used as tools to assert, to command, to question, etc. Whether the shopkeeper understands the meaning of my note 'Five red apples' will be made clear by her subsequent actions.

There is a multiplicity of language games: words can be used in many contexts, there are many different sets of rules, and we have different ways with words (Wittgenstein, 1953: par. 23 lists, among others: giving orders and obeying them, describing, reporting, play acting, joking, guessing riddles, presenting the results of an experiment, asking, thanking, cursing, greeting, praying). This multiplicity of language games, as Wittgenstein notes, is clearly at odds with the bare-bones single-purpose logic of his own *Tractatus*.

To understand meaning requires mastery of the practice, a form of life. The meanings are part of forms of life which dictate how we see and handle things, and negotiate with the other players. When you ask: 'Is there any coffee left?' you are in the game of asking someone to pour you a cup, not in the game of assessing an objective fact on coffee (you would be surprised if you get the answer: 'Yes, about 123 ml'). The games themselves cannot be true or false – they rest on no foundation of facts; rather, some language games are in the business of creating facts (in Wittgenstein's list quoted above, presenting experimental results is one of many other games). Facts are convictions, the way we see things, and are embedded in language games.

Wittgenstein's radical change of mind brings an entirely different view of language and meaning. In his logical positivist phase he saw the meaning of statements as picturing objective facts, in his second phase Wittgenstein saw meaning as use in a practice (form of life). This threatens the positivist ideal of observation language as the (demarcation) criterion for legitimate science.

It is hardly surprising that some philosophers developed a relativistic viewpoint out of this. For example, the social psychologist Kenneth Gergen interprets this idea that all seeming assessments of facts are forms of social exchange (see Chapter 4.3). The consequences of this theory for the conception of knowledge and science are dramatic because it invites us to replace the quest for timeless foundations by the idea of the social character of knowledge; to see science as a social institution, as practices, which may be different in different times and places. In this view there is no such thing as neutral observation. Wittgenstein's change of mind, turning away from his earlier positivist ideas towards a contrasting account of language and meaning, was a major force in undermining positivism (but, of course, no conclusive proof against it). We will encounter Wittgenstein's inspiration again in hermeneutics and social constructivism in the next chapter.

3.4 The Impossibility of Logical Empiricism: Observation and Theory

In this section we will set out arguments that challenge positivist **empiricism**. These `glossary` arguments focus on the nature of observation and they undermine the basics of the image of science created, from 1930 till 1960, by positivist or logical-positivist (sometimes called 'neo-positivist') philosophers of science.

Sellars on the 'myth of the given'

The 'myth of the given' is perhaps the central pillar of Western **epistemology**, which `glossary` held up from the seventeenth century until the demise of logical positivism in the

1960s. The myth has been the target of devastating attacks on the foundations of psychology and traditional epistemology by Richard Rorty, Daniel Dennett, Paul Churchland and Paul Feyerabend. It is a sort of background to the positivist idea of observation and observation language.

In Wilfrid Sellars' (1963) diagnosis the myth holds that (at least some of) our mental states are 'given', that is, that we can be directly aware of them. This direct access is privileged and incorrigible: no one else can tell whether a person indeed has a specific mental state, except the owner of the mind in question. Someone can be absolutely sure that he remembers standing on the Eiffel Tower – his recollection may be wrong and he may never have been in Paris, but his feeling of remembrance, the mental state, is indisputable. Direct access implies that mental states are self-evident, self-transparent, self-disclosing and provide their own cognitive legitimation: *you just know what you know.*

With only slight exaggeration, it can be said that the 'myth of the given' – that (some) mental states are directly known, essentially private, self-presenting, self-justifying and incorrigible – was generally accepted by philosophers for centuries. Richard Rorty summarizes it as follows: 'the notion of a single inner space in which bodily and perceptual sensations …, mathematical truths, moral rules, the idea of God, moods of depression, and all the rest of what we now call "mental" were objects of quasi-observation' (Rorty, 1979: 50). These mental objects are directly present to consciousness ('given') as the states they are, since mind knows itself best. These mental objects provide absolute certainty, and thus can serve as the foundation of knowledge. As this phrasing suggests, psychological and epistemological issues are lumped together by the myth: the (psychological) feeling of evidence is turned into the foundation of scientific certainty.

In psychology, introspection, the observation of the events in one's own mental realm, was the method of investigation during most of psychology's history. Unfortunately, different schools saw different scenes in the mental theatre, and as a method of psychology introspection has long been defunct. There are serious doubts that reports by experimental subjects are reliable, let alone that they have direct and infallible access to the workings of their own mind – subjects may confabulate all sorts of reasons for their own essentially random behaviour (Nisbett and Wilson, 1977): we just don't know what moves us. This indicates that there is something wrong with the 'given'.

Sellars invents another myth

The myth held not only psychology, but also *epistemology* in its grasp. Traditional epistemology was built upon the idea of directly given sensory (or, sense) data (e.g. Russell, 1988), also known as knowledge by acquaintance. The mind knows its experiences directly, while knowledge of the external world is indirect – it must be inferred somehow from sense data (see Chapter 4.4 on Locke and indirect realism). Sellars (1963) contrasts the 'myth of the given' with a story invented by himself – the 'myth of Jones'. Let us assume that our ancestors were practising behaviourists, and that one of them, a certain Jones, hit upon the idea that all behaviour is directed by language – through verbal instructions, which may sometimes be inaudible inner speech. Jones now develops the habit of explaining the behaviour of his fellow men as a result of inter-nal statements, that is, he predicts their behaviour as guided by their 'thoughts' – where thought is inner speech. This strategy works, even if these people would not admit to finding such internal statements in their minds. Next, Jones goes a step further: he finds that the strategy can be applied to himself as well. He starts to think of his own behaviour in terms of his thoughts. The first-person use ('I think') is even more accurate in its predictions than the third person ('he thinks'): Jones is obviously an authority on his own thoughts. Jones' method becomes common usage, till this very day.

Thus, mythological Jones has invented both third-person and first-person mental language – reporting on others' and his own mind. The moral of the story about Jones, as Sellars would like us to interpret it, is that reports of the presumed 'given' are *not directly* perceived, but are basically **theory-laden**: just like an empirical claim about | glossary | the external world, descriptions of mental events are not reports of what is 'given' but are theoretical, and hence fallible and empirically falsifiable. Jones has a 'theory' about mental life, not direct access to his mental data. The story in first-person mental dis-course may be to some degree more reliable than third-person discourse, but it is not fundamentally private or infallible.

The radically new epistemological consequence then of the 'myth of Jones' is that knowledge becomes irredeemably linguistic – suspended as it were in discourse, and that it loses its moorings to an intrinsic indubitable 'given'. Attempts to ground knowledge in self-evident mental space have become impossible. Knowing something is defending it in the face of one's linguistic peers, rather than having mental data, or, as Rorty puts it: 'think of knowledge as a matter of being disposed to utter true sen-tences about something, rather than in terms of the metaphor of acquaintance' (1982b: 331). Vindication of knowledge claims must come from prediction and control, or from convincing one's fellows, not from some sort of intrinsic mental evidence.

3.5 Further Trouble for Logical Positivism: Holism, Underdetermination, and Theory-ladenness

Quine on 'Two dogmas of empiricism'

In his widely influential article 'Two dogmas of empiricism' (1961), Willard Van Orman Quine attacked two positivist assumptions. One is the belief in some funda-mental dichotomy between true statements which are *analytic*, that is, explaining the meaning of their terms (A circle is round); and truths which are *synthetic*, that is, informing about the world (This book has ten chapters). The other assumption is the belief that each meaningful statement is in itself an observation, a report of immediate experience of the world, and that each of these can be considered in isolation of other statements.

Analytic statements are merely about language, about definitions and the meaning of words. For example: 'A bachelor is an unmarried male.' Synthetic statements are about states of affairs; their truth depends on the world. Analytic statements are a priori, we know their truth before any data are in; synthetic statements are a posteriori, and can only be checked empirically. Empiricist philosophers (following Hume) think that these two kinds of statement, synthetic a-posteriori statements about matters of fact, and analytic a-priori statements about meaning and language, exhaust the domain of meaningful language. The positivist needs a clear distinction to keep observation and theory apart: for verification, the data may not be influenced by theoretical prejudices.

Now, Quine attacked the dogma of this dichotomy by showing that the distinctive criteria of analytic statements are not clear at all. What is or is not the 'meaning' of an (analytical) term is not at all absolutely clear, and all sorts of attempts to define it (via synonyms, definitions, etc.) have failed. The meaning or definition of a term is not pre-existing and pre-given, but is grounded in usage and dependent on contexts, according to Quine (cf. Witgenstein's ideas on meaning as use). Looking carefully, no sharp dichotomy can be made between the synthetic statements (grounded in fact) and analytic statements (true by definition). There are no statements totally based on sense-experience, nor are there pure analytic and a-priori statements without experiential content at all. This is bad news for positivism because pure neutral observation statements thus cannot exist.

The attack on the second dogma of empiricism follows naturally from this – the belief that it is possible to test a statement in isolation from other statements or context. The positivists thought that every meaningful empirical statement is translatable into a statement about immediate experience; that is, in sense data. A single statement maps onto a single state of affairs in the world, and can be empirically confirmed. According to Quine, however, an individual statement has no empirical content on its own. Words get their meaning from their relations to other words. We cannot compare *single* statements with the world. Rather, *whole theories* are confronted with the world. Our statements about the external world 'face the tribunal of sense experience not individually but only as a corporate body' (Quine, 1961: 41).

So, there is no neutral, or independent, foundation of given immediate experiences upon which we could build our scientific statements. We could sum up this thesis – sometimes called *epistemological* **holism** – in two points: (1) no knowledge is a priori and immune to empirical refutation, and no knowledge is completely theory-independent; (2) in cases of conflict between theory and observations we cannot summon certain statements in isolation; the whole system of beliefs, or large parts thereof, must stand to trial.

What we learn from this is that observations do not have direct access to the world but are interpreted against the background of a whole theory. There is no sharp distinction between observations and theory, because observations reveal their meaning only against the background of the theory. The totality of our knowledge 'is a man-made fabric which impinges on experience only along the edges' (Quine, 1961: 42). Quine considered this epistemological holism (not to be confused with a kind of New Age holism) a form of **pragmatism**:

glossary

glossary

Each man is given a scientific heritage plus a continuing barrage of sensory stimulation; and the considerations which guide him in warping his scientific heritage to fit his continuing sensory promptings are, where rational, pragmatic. (ibid.: 46)

It is this non-given, non-neutral and theory-laden character of observations that became a recurrent theme in the new philosophy of science.

Underdetermination: the Quine–Duhem thesis

The final nail in the positivists' coffin was the so-called Quine–Duhem thesis. A consequence of Quine's holism is that any statement can be *held* true, 'if we make drastic enough adjustments elsewhere in the system'. And even a 'recalcitrant experience', an observation clashing with the theory, can be accommodated by 'any of various re-evaluations in various alternative quarters of the total system' (Quine, 1961: 44).

Verification, or confirmation, is not a simple all-or-nothing check of a theory against the data. Rather, observations can be reconciled with a theory in many ways. A similar thesis had already been defended by the French philosopher and physicist Pierre Duhem (1861–1916) in 1906. Duhem pointed out that discrepant experimental results can be made to fit – the experimenter just makes small or larger changes in the theory. The evidence itself does not unambiguously either support a hypothesis or lead to its rejection. Theories are underdetermined by evidence, data, or observations.

Of course, the Quine–Duhem thesis is a blow for the positivist notions of verification and the theory-observation distinction. Put in the most general form, underdetermination of theory by observation means that many theories can be made to fit the pattern of the data, and theory choice cannot be decided in a straightforward fashion by empirical results. Obviously, this makes a mockery of the idea of verification – recall that for the positivists verification was the acid test of meaning, the demarcation criterion for real versus pseudo-science. If there is no strict separation between observation and theory, between analytical and synthetic statements, changing some part of the inner theoretical core can help to accommodate discordant results at the periphery. If scientists are allowed to massage the theory and the data, the door seems open to all speculative pseudo-science that positivists wanted to keep out.

If Quine is right that the whole belief system is confronted with reality, then in principle all sorts of adjustments can be made anywhere. Holism seems to lead to a kind of relativism: if any observation can be accommodated in any theory (Klee, 1997: 65), then anything goes. However, that is too rash. We can agree that verification requires some human judgement, some wriggle room, to be decided by us humans, not to be dictated by nature (Klee, 1997: 66). Theory choice is a pragmatic affair, a human choice that cannot be farmed out to Mother Nature, or mechanical procedures. But not every choice is equally good. Quine himself (1992) rejected the relativist interpretation of his 'Two dogmas' paper: he maintained that there is a continuum from almost pure theory (logic and mathematics) to reasonably theory-independent observation. The foundations of logic or the postulates of quantum mechanics are well beyond simple rejection. In practice, it is not true that anything goes. Theory choice is not entirely unconstrained, not any experimental result will fit in any theory. Underdetermination has been exaggerated, and no radical relativist conclusions follow from it (Laudan, 1996; Klee, 1997).

These considerations have taken us into a debate that only later got off the ground (see below on Kuhn, and Chapter 4.4 on relativism and realism). For the moment, the take home message is that the observation-theory distinction is highly problematic. If Quine is right that theory and observation are part of a holistic web and cannot be separated, positivism is in deep trouble.

Hanson on the theory-ladenness of observation

> Imagine Johannes Kepler on a hill watching the dawn. With him is Tycho Brahe. Kepler regarded the sun as fixed: it was the earth that moved. But Tycho followed Ptolemy and Aristotle in this much at least: the earth was fixed and all other celestial bodies moved around it. Do Kepler and Tycho see the same thing in the east at dawn? (Hanson, 1958: 5)

This is the question with which Norwood Russel Hanson begins his *Patterns of Discovery*, his study of observation, theories and what he calls 'the conceptual foundations' of science. Answering that the two astronomers see the same thing just because their eyes are similarly affected would be a fundamental mistake. To say, as the empiricist would do, that they *see* the same thing because they get the same sensations or sense data, and that after this experience they *interpret* what they see in different ways, would be a mistake as well. 'One does not first soak up an optical pattern and then clamp an interpretation on it' (ibid.: 9). On the contrary, the 'what' of the seen object is in the visual experience from the outset. There is more to seeing than meets the eye. That Tycho and Kepler see different things, though perhaps their eyes receive the same sensations, depends on their knowledge and theories. Seeing is *theory-laden*. To observe a watch is to *know* the concept of a watch. The observation

glossary

is shaped by that prior knowledge and takes with it a **background** of knowledge; it appears in a context of background information. I could answer questions about what I see and I could tell, for instance, that the little hand indicates the hours and the big hand the minutes, that the figures stand for hours, etc. The eye and knowing fit together. Without this knowledge, nothing seen would make sense. Seeing goes hand-in-glove with interpreting.

Because observation is theory laden, science is 'not just a systematic exposure to the world; it is also a way of thinking about the world, a way of forming conceptions' (ibid.: 30). With a wealth of historical illustrations from the work of physicists, such as Kepler, Galileo, Newton, Descartes, Helmholtz and Maxwell, and influenced by the Gestalt psychologists and by Wittgenstein, Hanson criticized the deductive-nomological philosophy of science. This system does not tell us how laws are decided on in the first place.

When paying attention to what scientists *do*, you have to acknowledge that they do not start from laws, nor from hypotheses: they start from data. However, data appear intelligible only within theories. Theories 'constitute a "conceptual Gestalt". A theory is not pieced together from observed phenomena; it is rather what makes it possible to observe phenomena as being of a certain sort, and as related to other phenomena. Theories put phenomena into systems' (ibid.: 90).

BOX 3.4   The problems with observation

- *Positivism* assumes theory-neutral observation statements, verification of a statement by observations. Observations (sense data) are independent of theory.
- *Positivism* assumes that the meaning of a statement is the way it can be verified (unverifiable talk is non-sense). Meaning is reference, correspondence with a state of affairs.
- *Wittgenstein* (*Philosophical Investigations,* 1953): meaning is use, part of a 'form of life', a language game. Language is an instrument of social exchange, not a picture of a state of affairs (cf. pragmatism, social constructionism in Chapter 4).
- *Sellars* ('myth of the given', 1963): there are no indubitable sense data as the basis of theory-neutral observations. All knowledge is 'theoretical' (introspection is a story (a theory) about oneself, not direct observation of inner data).
- *Quine* ('*Two dogmas* of *empiricism'*, 1961): no clear-cut separation of observation and theory, observation statements not verifiable one by one, in isolation from other statements. Theory is holist network of observation and concepts. Theory choice is underdetermined by the data (Quine–Duhem thesis), hence conclusive verification impossible.
- *Hanson* (*Patterns of Discovery*, 1958): observations are theory-laden, there are no uninterpreted data, having different theories makes observers literally *see* different worlds.

3.6 Demarcation Revived – Popper

As mentioned, the original impulse of positivism was to distinguish between science and pseudo-science. The logical positivists thought that only statements that specify how they can be verified are meaningful – it is clear how to find out whether 'Water boils at 100°C' is correct. Unverifiable statements are literally non-sense; it is not clear what the factual content of 'God is love' is, and thus it makes no sense – it cannot even be called false. Essential for the positivist project was the design of a new unambiguous language in which facts can be stated in a purely observational fashion. Ordinary language is too messy, imprecise and ambiguous to denote observations.

The positivists conceived the world as a collection of facts (states of affairs), and hence the scientific language as a collection of *Protokollsätze*, basic statements expressing a state of affairs (meter readings, colour of a chemical solution, number of lever presses a laboratory rat performs, etc.). *Verification*, then, is comparing statements derived from a theory with observation statements. Thus, verifiability was proposed by the Wiener Kreis as the demarcation criterion, distinguishing legitimate knowledge claims from nonsense, metaphysics and other claptrap.

Recall that the main tenets of positivist philosophy were: (1) the verifiability theory of meaning; (2) the notion of confirmations of theories; (3) a strict distinction between observation and theory; and (4) the view of theories as logical edifices, from which predictions can be logically deduced. In the previous section, we discussed some of the deeper reasons why the positivist view of science, language and reality behind these assumptions is untenable: in a nutshell, the observation-theory distinction does not work. Observations are theory laden, and there are no isolated observation statements to be checked off against states of affairs. Below, we will consider how later thinkers tried to prevent the disaster that seemed to follow from this failure: that it seems impossible to find a demarcation criterion for distinguishing good science from pseudo-science.

Karl Popper (1902–1994) was one of the most influential philosophers who tried to salvage the ideal of a demarcation criterion while abandoning the criteria of verifiability and confirmation.

The problem with verification (and confirmation)

As we have seen, the positivist programme soon ran into considerable trouble. The idea of comparing language with the world in itself proved incoherent, and the strict theory-observation dichotomy had to be abandoned. Furthermore, verification of general statements (laws, theories) is strictly speaking impossible. A simple hypothesis like: 'All swans are white' may have been corroborated a zillion times by observing white swans, but the logical possibility remains that the zillion-and-one swan will turn out to be turquoise: this is the notorious problem of **induction** (see Chapter 1). General laws are about an, in principle, infinite domain, and can never be conclusively verified.

Sensitive to this problem, Rudolf Carnap (1891–1970), a member of the Wiener Kreis, introduced the concept of **confirmation**. It was intended as a more practical and less rigid alternative to verification. Rather than demanding that the truth of a statement can be assessed with absolute certainty, Carnap suggested that some degree of confirmation must be possible for a statement to be meaningful. Confirmation is a matter of probability, varying from 0 ('unconfirmed') to 1 ('verified'), and depends *prima facie* on the number of observations that support a statement; usually, scientific knowledge claims will be less than perfectly verified and remain to a certain extent hypothetical. However, since general laws can be more or less confirmed, even when not completely verified, the problems surrounding verification and demarcation were supposed to be solved. Carnap formulated a logic of induction, providing the rules for generalizing from observations to general statements, in more or less the same way that in formal logic the algorithms for **deduction** are specified. Such a procedure

glossary

glossary

glossary

could provide a measure of the degree of confirmation of a theory. However, the logical apparatus never worked. Popper's work suggests some reasons why not.

Popper (1974, 1979) radically rejected the ideas of verification, confirmation and induction as foundations of the legitimacy of scientific knowledge claims. He replaced the notion of confirmation (verification) by **falsification**. While abandoning the 'rock bottom' of knowledge in observation statements, he remained within the tradition in the philosophy of science that tries to create a foolproof demarcation criterion distinguishing science from metaphysics. Keywords of his philosophy are: falsification, criticism, anti-dogmatism.

Popper on confirmation and falsification

Popper argued that, strictly speaking, only *falsification* is possible, not verification. A lot of accumulated evidence is no guarantee for the truth of a hypothesis: as soon as the first turquoise swan has been spotted, the much-confirmed statement that all swans are white is falsified and must be rejected. Confirmation cannot be measured, since one never knows how many disconfirming instances may be around. However, what is logically certain is *falsification:* if a theory predicts an effect, and it doesn't turn out, then the theory must be false. Popper shows this by making a simple logical point: while induction cannot be made certain, deduction can. Look at the logical form of the *modus tollens:* If *T,* then *P;* not *P;* therefore, not *T;* when a conclusion follows from the antecedent, and the conclusion is false, the antecedent must logically be false as well. In common language, whenever from a theory (*T*) a prediction (*P*) can be deduced that turns out to be false in experiment or observation, the theory must be rejected. This idea of falsification becomes the linchpin of Popper's system: don't try to confirm your theories, try to *refute* them. Look what observations it predicts, check these, and reject the theory when the predicted effects do not show up.

A good theory then specifies in advance not what observations would confirm it, but what would make it *untrue* (e.g. if creationism is true, there should be no fossils). A theory is only interesting to the extent that it (*ex hypothesi*) rules out certain phenomena, and it is more interesting the more it rules out – that is, the more *improbable* it is. In fact, confirmed and probable hypotheses are the least interesting. It is easy to formulate probable (often confirmed) generalizations, but such a strategy would favour uninformative truisms. The prediction that the temperature will be above zero in August in Amsterdam is highly probable, but hardly informative. Scientific progress can be made only by advancing bold, improbable conjectures, and then ruthlessly trying to falsify them. These conjectures should involve as many new predictions, pose new problems, and suggest new experiments and observations as possible; they should not just add to already known facts. The empirical content of theories is the number of possible falsifications: a theory forbids certain events, and the more general and precise it is, the more phenomena it forbids. Among competing theories, which have so far survived all tests, we should accept the one with the largest empirical content.

Of, course, since no confirmation is possible, no theory can ever be sure. Unlike the logical positivists, Popper sees no conclusively established facts. Knowledge is provisional, always revisable, 'piles driven into a swamp', and there are no absolutely secure foundations. Theories that have stood the test are only corroborated, never verified or confirmed: they may still be proven wrong any time. It seems hard to imagine that long-established theories in physics could be proven wrong – but nevertheless that was what happened, for example, with the replacement of Newtonian physics by quantum theory. At the end of the nineteenth century, physics seemed more or less complete and unshakeable, but even so it was uprooted by Einstein. This indicates that in principle no theory can be immune to refutation.

Inventing hypotheses is completely unconstrained, in Popper's view: unlike the Wiener Kreis, he thinks that theory building need not be regimented by empirical support or logic. The bolder the hypothesis, the better, provided that it is subsequently rigorously tested and mercilessly rejected if found wanting. Hence, *conjectures and refutations* (Popper, 1974) are the staple trade of science.

One could consider the process of conjectures and refutations, and provisional corroboration of theories, as something like natural selection: unfit theories perish, and the best, most adapted theories survive – for the time being. In this sense there is real progress and growth of knowledge. However, Popper abandons the positivist conception of cumulative growth founded on observation. There is no hoard of objective facts, as the logical positivists thought, but all knowledge is theory-laden, and the nature of accepted data may be entirely reinterpreted when theories are refuted. Newton's physics was experimentally corroborated many times, but had to be completely revised after Einstein.

Popper on demarcation and dogmatism

glossary

As said, the aim of logical positivism was to provide a secure foundation for science in empirical facts. Popper abandons the quest for certainty, but sticks to the ideal of demarcating science from **metaphysics**. Having rejected induction, verification and confirmation as yardstick, he defends falsifiability as the hallmark of rationality. Rather than looking for secure foundations on which to build a scientifically respectable theory, he accepts the uncertainty and provisional nature of theories – respectable science is provisional, and a critical attitude to any knowledge claim is the demarcation between science and pseudo-science. Rationality lies in a ruthlessly critical attitude towards any claim to knowledge, rather than in accumulating bits and pieces of confirmed facts.

Popper is a radical *anti-dogmatist*: discussions should be absolutely free, any claim should be criticized. Any hypothesis is in principle legitimate, as long as it is refutable. *Criticism* then is the mark of real scientific rationality. (Incidentally, Popper himself was notorious for the relentless dogmatism with which he defended anti-dogmatism: 'Always be critical' – 'yes, professor'.) Popper sees an absolute difference between critical and dogmatic thinking. Theories that are advertised as certain and immune to criticism are pseudo-science. Examples are Marx and Freud and other builders of closed dogmatic philosophical systems, which can explain anything under the sun, and its negation, for that matter. Freud and his followers are known for finding post-hoc explanations for practically any behaviour. Such systems cannot be criticized, let alone refuted; they require some dogmatic belief from their followers and are thereby the opposite of scientific rationality. Their aim is not to increase knowledge, but to prove that the believers are right. Especially pernicious is such dogmatism in political philosophy: Popper's targets are systems like Hegel's and Marx's, which he calls 'historicism' (Popper, 1961, 1966), and which pretend to know and understand the Immutable Laws of history, and therefore tend to totalitarianism. A critical, anti-dogmatic attitude is as indispensable for democracy as it is for science.

Problems with falsification

Popper thinks that repairing a falsified theory by way of adding ad hoc hypotheses is dogmatism: the principle of criticism demands that whenever facts turn up that do not fit its prediction, the whole theory must be ruthlessly rejected, and a new set of conjectures is drafted, or a competing theory is selected for further testing. Unfortunately, this is not the way researchers work: it was quickly noted that working scientists often consider their favourite hypothesis too good a story to be spoiled by the facts. When a prediction fails, they come up with ad hoc hypotheses (faulty apparatus, artefacts, etc.) to explain the deviant results, rather than rejecting the theory. Sometimes they hypothesize additional mechanisms or expand the theory to explain the refractory data. In real, successful science, falsification is rare. Another problem is that there are not always competitors for the falsified theory to choose from. Whereas the philosopher Popper considers dogmatism a sin against the Holy Ghost of science, and a critical attitude as the hallmark of rationality, in reality scientists can be stubborn and dogmatic in upholding a hypothesis against the evidence – and often with success. Sticking to one's prejudices, and looking for reasons why reality fails to behave as it should, can be a fruitful strategy that brings new discoveries. When a philosopher of science, like Popper, prescribes a method inconsistent with real, successful scientific practice, then the philosopher has a problem, not the (successful) scientists who go against his prescriptions. There must be something wrong with falsificationism then. The sophisticated falsificationist will recognize that there are no undubitable observations, and hence (Lakatos, 1970) that there are no hard and fast rules for when a theory has to be rejected. The conclusion must be that falsification in the strict sense can be no demarcation criterion.

In the 1960s the full consequences of Hanson's notion of theory-ladenness and Quine–Duhem's thesis on the interdependence of data and theory began to sink in, namely, that in a sense theories produce their own facts. This implies that theories cannot be matched against theory-independent facts, as required by a strict application of the falsification (or verification) criterion. Hence, facts cannot be used to choose between better and less adequate theories. The full relativistic implications of this view have been elaborated by Kuhn and Feyerabend (see below). Popper also recognized that observation statements are never certain, and depend on a (revisable) consensus among researchers on what count as basic facts in their field, but he nevertheless continued to believe that a theoretical framework can ultimately somehow be undermined by the data (Popper, 1994).

BOX 3.5   Verification, confirmation, falsification

- *Verification* is assessing the fit between a theory (better, the prediction generated with the theory) and empirical facts.
- Verifiability is the logical positivists' proposal for a demarcation criterion (specification on how to find empirical facts that make rejection or acceptance of the statement possible) as the criterion for a meaningful theory.
- *The induction problem* shows that it is *impossible to verify general laws,* they can only be confirmed.

- *Confirmation* is showing a statement to be supported by empirical evidence. The induction problem suggests that verification is impossible, but perhaps a degree of inductive support could be assessed, logical positivists thought. A theory can only be *corroborated*, but can never be confirmed conclusively.

- *Falsification* is showing a statement to be false. A statement or theory can be proved wrong with absolute certainty. According to Popper, a theory is to be rejected when predictions derived from it turn out to be false. A theory can never be verified, but Popper maintains it can conclusively be falsified.
- *Falsifiability* is according to Popper the demarcation criterion for distinguishing science from pseudo-science.
- *The problem with falsifiability* is that Kuhn and Lakatos show that scientists do not reject but try to rescue theories in the face of falsifying evidence, by constructing ad-hoc hypotheses.

3.7 Demarcation Abandoned – Kuhn on Paradigms and Scientific Revolutions

In criticizing empiricism and positivism, post-positivist Anglo-American philosophers effectively moved the centre of gravity from the observed object to the knowing subject. The knowing subject is not the passive observer the empiricists thought he or she was. On the contrary, the things we see and come to know are incorporated in a
`glossary` **theory**, or even more, they are part of a worldview or of a long-established life-world with roots in history and culture. And this worldview we inherit, build and share intersubjectively. The new philosophers of science, the 'second generation' (Callebaut, 1993), became more interested in the ways by which scientists reached their theories and hypotheses than in the logical structure of theories. They began to highlight context and history, the *context of discovery*, whereas the positivists favoured the *context of justification*, the assessment of the scientific products, and focused on (rationally reconstructed) theories. This introduced an element of subjectivity and interest-relativity that the logical positivists had tried to eliminate, and that seemed to open the door to relativism.

A role for history

Thomas Kuhn's *The Structure of Scientific Revolutions* (1962, second edition with a new postscript 1970) was a watershed in the philosophy of science. It caused its own revolution and created its own paradigm. The book was translated in some 20 languages, it sold a million copies and is a recognized classic in all courses in the philosophy of science. A major reason for its impact was that it introduced a role for history in the heart of scientific development. In the positivist era, scientific rationality was timeless logical theorizing, and progress was cumulative and incremental, piling objective fact upon objective fact. The scientist is an applied logician, theories are formal structures, the experiment is just a form of observation, and observation is entirely in the service of evaluating theories. The only concern of the philosophy of science is the context of justification. Historical, social and personal factors are only of interest in the context of discovery.

Against this view, Kuhn's revolutionary idea was that the criteria for rationality and justification vary with history, that theories and social practices determine what is accepted as rational method and legitimate evidence. Doing research into the history of science, Kuhn found that that in history myth is difficult to separate from rational thought. In Elizabethan England, in some sense the cradle of science, occultism was intermingled with scientific hypothesis. The obvious way to keep science pure and keep out the historical element is to identify real science with what turned out to be the right hypothesis (for example, Isaac Newton's physics), and pseudo-science (for example, the selfsame Isaac Newton's mystical theology) with what happened to be wrong. This is known as presentism, and implies that our current views are the criterion for correct science – but, of course, we could be just as wrong as previous generations. If we don't want presentism, we have to admit that rationality is tied to context, place and time. That signals the end for a timeless ahistorical criterion for (pseudo) science.

Paradigms

Kuhn famously introduced the notion of **paradigm**. It denotes the historical and social `glossary` framework of science, and has become a label for the dogmatic, self-perpetuating and collectivist aspects of science – which Popper thought characteristic for pseudo-science. A paradigm is (among a lot of other things: see Masterman, 1970) a framework that determines which data are legitimate, what methods may be used, what vocabulary is to be used in stating the results, and what kinds of interpretation are allowed. Second, a paradigm not only includes theories and even a kind of worldview, but just as importantly also methods, typical results, laboratory equipment, and mathematical techniques. Furthermore, a paradigm also comprehends the social organization of research, including the perceptual training, the socializing of apprentices in the laboratory and the scientific community at large. Students and junior researchers are trained to adopt the frame of reference, the vocabulary and the methods and techniques of the existing community.

In complete contrast with Popper's ideal of open and critical discussion, research communities can be as authoritarian and dogmatic as the Catholic Church or the Mafia. If a junior researcher cannot reproduce the canonical results of the paradigm, he will be out of a job, rather than having falsified the paradigm. Recognizing and reproducing so-called exemplars, the typical results and usually success-stories of a paradigm are part of the training. Since a paradigm is a comprehensive worldview, scientists cannot take different views at the same time: paradigms succeed each other – they cannot coexist.

In contrast with the theory-centred view of the logical positivists, Kuhn considers a theory as part of a whole structure of methods, frameworks, concepts, professional habits and obligations, and laboratory practices. This structure determines the general approach to research, it defines what counts as legitimate observations, and without it no research problems would exist. Thus, a paradigm comprises, first, a school, a community of researchers; second, all the methods, mathematical techniques, laboratory equipment, etc.; and third, the conceptual frame of reference. It includes practical skills as well as theoretical knowledge; recognizing 'exemplars', paradigm cases, requires training in special ways of looking and in the use of concepts and apparatus. (In Chapter 4.7 the role of skills and practices in research will be discussed, in contrast with the traditional purely theory-centred view.)

Furthermore, paradigms are *incommensurable*, that is, no rational comparison is possible between competing paradigms. This has the very serious consequence that there is no way to measure progress and rationality in the history of science; or better, that philosophers have been unable to find a hard and fast criterion for rationality. Another important relativist implication is that a paradigm cannot (rationally) be rejected in the way Popper advocated. Facts exist only in the context of a paradigm; therefore, selection between and rejection of theories by assessment of their empirical adequacy, according to unambiguous criteria for empirical progress, is impossible. Paradigms exemplify theory-ladenness.

BOX 3.6   Paradigms

Paradigm is a whole complex of:

  (a) theories, statements, concepts and worldview
  (b) techniques and laboratory apparatus
  (c) social processes and institutional structures (laboratories, funding)

which together determine what are legitimate problems and solutions in a field of scientific research.

Exemplars – problems, phenomena, success stories, typical results that characterize a paradigm and that a pupil is trained to recognize and reproduce – are a crucial part of a paradigm.

So, facts are theory-laden, paradigms *make* their data.

Revolutions

Kuhn starts his book with a plea for a role for *history* and he aims to provide a general sketch for the development of science. He emphasizes that the cumulative-progress idea the positivists propagated is not the way science really works. He suggests that the distinction between context of justification and context of discovery does not work, since the criteria for justified knowledge change with the paradigm; nor are fact and theory separable in the way the positivists thought. So the positivist way of keeping history out of rational science has failed. Science proceeds according to a historical cycle of normal science and revolutions. The general pattern of historical development Kuhn proposes is as follows. It starts with preparadigmatic science, followed by *normal science* after the establishment of a paradigm; then the emergence of anomalous results causes a *crisis*, that can either be solved by finding some way to incorporate the anomalies, or may trigger a *revolution* after which a new paradigm is established; after a period of normal science the next crisis starts, and so on. Preparadigmatic science is characterized by competing schools and approaches; discussions about the proper metaphysical foundations and the right methods rage, but after the first paradigm is established, the number of schools decreases, and there is only one dominant view.

Kuhn's probably most shocking and controversial claim is that paradigm shifts really have the character of political *revolutions*. Rather than through reasonable debate according to rational procedures, paradigms are abandoned as a result of some irrational kind of mob psychology. After a paradigm has run into anomalies (results that it cannot easily explain, or explain away), tensions start to accumulate, which lead, suddenly and inexplicably, into a wholesale rejection of the old paradigm, and the establishment of a new one. Note that there is no conclusive or rational reason for the point where anomalies must lead to crisis: within a paradigm one may decide that anomalies should be put aside for later generations and can be ignored for the time being. Usually, these anomalies are used by a young guard that propagates a new paradigm, which, they promise, may turn anomalies into puzzles for revolution, or: it involves a radical change in viewpoint, where existing results are reinterpreted beyond recognition. A crisis is characterized by the controversy between the supporters of the established paradigm, who have built their career on it, and by a gradual release of the grip of the old paradigm's methods, and the young guard promising new ways of thinking. During a crisis, the battle for a new paradigm is fought by persuasion and propaganda, not with evidence, since the new paradigm does not yet have results – no established methods, techniques, and exemplars.

The dogmatism of the old guard, keeping the theory and discarding anomalies, would be anathema to Popper, who demands outright rejection of a refuted theory. Kuhn, however, doubts whether falsifying instances in the strict Popperian sense exist at all. Anomalies are not even facts of science, since facts appear only within a paradigm. Therefore, the data cannot be used as a neutral base for judging the merits of the old paradigm and its competitor. Kuhn compares paradigm shifts to Gestalt switches: you cannot simultaneously see both interpretations of an ambiguous figure (like the famous duck-rabbit), but you have to choose one of them more or less voluntarily, and neither view is inherently better or more correct than the other.

Analogously, 'facts' are products of a specific paradigm, and they cannot be used as an observational basis to decide which paradigm is empirically better or more progressive: paradigms are **incommensurable**. The first effect of a crisis is usually a loosening of the rules, so that new phenomena are now recognized as legitimate observations. Paradigm shifts are a matter of persuasion and depend on essentially circular reasoning (the promise to explain the facts better, but these facts are of its own making). Embarking on a new paradigm is a kind of conversion that can, strictly speaking, only be done on *faith*. Note also that a paradigm cannot be abandoned without a new one being chosen: research would simply stop without one.

glossary

Normal science

Revolutions contrast sharply with periods of *normal science*. Here, the framework cannot be criticized. Doing research is essentially puzzle solving, filling in the gaps in a generally accepted framework by applying the generally accepted methods and interpretations. In normal science, work consists of redetermining the previously known; measuring with more precision what was already accepted, establishing more facts that were anticipated by the paradigm, and articulating the theory by finding quantitative laws, seeking new areas of application, etc. Briefly, research is working out the paradigm under the assumption that there is a well-defined solution to the remaining uncertainties which can be found by the usual methods. Puzzle solving is no small matter: the only way to move forward on detail and precision as well as on extending a paradigm to new fields is to stick to the essentials, not to question the framework. Falsificationism would be counter-productive; progress is in filling in the details, measuring parameters with increasing precision, extending the existing theories and methods to new domains and new applications. Only when the puzzles do not come out, a vague desire for new rules, for retooling the approach, may raise its head. So, both normal science and revolutions are necessary for progress: without revolutions, science would get stuck in more of the same; without normal science no in-depth elaboration and expanding of the framework would be possible.

BOX 3.7   Revolution and normal science

- *Normal science*: paradigm is used as a generally agreed framework; it is filled in with new data; it is expanded to new domains; its measurements get more precise; its methods are refined; but the framework is not criticized or falsified. Normal science is 'puzzle solving'.
- *Anomalies* are shelved during normal science.
- *Revolutions* are a change of paradigm, after a crisis, in which methodological rules are relaxed, and a new generation promises to turn (eventually) anomalies into exemplars.

BOX 3.7   Revolution and normal science (Continued)

- Paradigms are *incommensurable*: they make sense of the world in terms of completely different categories, concepts and meanings; they may not even recognize each other's research questions.
- Revolutions are *irrational*, since paradigms are incommensurable, and criteria for rationality are valid only inside a paradigm, not between paradigms. Revolutions are driven by propaganda, mob psychology, power struggle.
- *Working in a new world* after a revolution: after a Gestalt switch, a new worldview. Therefore no cumulative progress: seeing differently, not better.
- *No demarcation criterion between paradigms.*
- *Phase model of scientific development*:

  0   Preparadigmatic phase (data collection, disagreement on framework and core problems)
  1   Paradigm (normal science between revolutions: puzzle solving)
  2   Crisis (anomalies, old paradigm loses grip, new methods, promises of success)
  3   Revolution (new paradigm takes over, new institutions, methods, criteria, theories)
  4   New paradigm (normal science) ➜ 1, until next crisis

Laboratory practices

It is important to realize that a paradigm is more than a theory. It requires a set of commitments, not only to concepts and theories, but also to instruments and methods, and to metaphysical or foundational assumptions (like materialism, or corpuscularism). Thus, social and pragmatic factors are part and parcel of scientific research. Kuhn emphasizes that the shared commitments in a paradigm are more fundamental than explicit methodical rules and concepts. Learning to be a researcher involves developing the skills and know-how to handle the exemplars (the canonical examples of a paradigm) to interpret results, more than knowing explicit theories. A paradigm may be more specific than explicit methodological rules. The latter may be shared by a number of research communities, who nevertheless have different work styles, other problems and exemplars of typical results and approaches. Research is not a matter of explicit knowledge of abstract rules, and is never learned that way by the junior researcher; it is a matter of doing successful work.

Later developments in the philosophy of science also rejected this theory-centred view of science, emphasizing practice, intervention and laboratory skills (pragmatism, see Chapters 4.6 and 5.5).

Incommensurability and relativism

Kuhn compares a paradigm to a *worldview*; a change of concepts and procedures can transform objects into something else: the data themselves change. Obviously, here the notion of theory-ladenness is taken to its limits. A historical example of such a deep and radical vision is the refusal of Galileo's opponents to verify his claims by looking through his telescope: they simply did not accept it as providing legitimate data about the stars (Feyerabend, 1975: ch. 10). In their opinion, following Aristotle, the laws governing celestial bodies were essentially different from those on earth. Galileo's innovation was not the telescope (it had been used before for navigation) but the new way of looking and creating data. So there was indeed no compelling rational argument why they should accept his data.

The reason we think Galileo was obviously right is that textbooks rewrite history in Orwellian fashion, presenting the current view and distorting or ignoring justification for the historical theory. Of course, they could not do otherwise, since the 'Gestalt switch' prevents them from seeing the other image, while the historians know what really went on and smile ironically at the sanitized presentist textbook accounts. (Incidentally, Kuhn seems to assume that, unlike ordinary scientists, the historian can see the historical case as it was – he does not tell how.)

glossary   So, the driving force behind paradigm shifts and crises is not the **truth** or a better approach to reality, but the struggle between competing research communities. And such a struggle can be nasty: keeping grants and research opportunities, publication glossary   outlets and jobs away from the competition. **Relativism** (irrational social and historical factors, not truth, decide the outcome of a crisis) seems inevitable.

Kuhn himself never was comfortable with the relativist interpretation. In his postscript (1970) he tries to attenuate the irrational character of crisis and revolutions, suggesting that communication between competing groups is possible, and when both sides recognize that the other side uses concepts differently, it may be possible to find a translation rule. There is no hard and fast method for this, but neither is it completely random or irrational. Perhaps paradigms can be compared to Wittgenstein's glossary   **language games**, as forms of life (Kindi, 1995). They require implicit know-how, are essentially social, and are about use and practice, not about explicit rules. Between different forms of life there is no easy communication, but some degree of hermeneutic understanding is possible: think of the anthropologist studying a foreign tribe, who can understand the tribe's network of associations (Geertz's 'thick description', see Chapter 2.3), without giving up his own cultural framework. Language games are rooted in forms of life, and therefore are not completely arbitrary or irrational. In this way relativism can perhaps be kept at bay, and some kind of rationality can be saved (Kindi, 1995).

However, the kind of scientific rationality the positivists tried to capture, the cumulative progress of objective science, the cumulating of data phrased in objective theory-neutral observational language, has proved a chimera. Kuhn demolished this neat picture by showing that social and historical factors are part of science and the context of discovery cannot be separated from justification.

3.8 Rational Reconstruction and Methodological
Anarchism: Lakatos and Feyerabend

Lakatos on rational reconstruction

Imre Lakatos (1970) has attempted to combine Kuhn's analysis of paradigms with
the possibility of a rational reconstruction of scientific progress, effectively keeping
relativism at bay. While acknowledging the dominant role of dogmatism and puzzle
solving within scientific research, he tries to stave off relativism by allowing for
progress and rationality in terms of competition between *research programmes*.
Lakatos defined a research programme as a complex of theories which succeed each
other in time. It consists of a set of hard-core theses which are essential and not open
to criticism, and a protective belt of auxiliary hypotheses that can be modified to
explain deviant results. The hard core defines the negative heuristic: refutation is not
allowed here, as long as the programme anticipates novel facts. The test for superiority of one programme over another is whether the empirical content increases. A
programme that has to invent an ever increasing set of ad hoc hypotheses to counter
anomalies in order to protect its hard core counts as degenerating. But when such
hypotheses work, open new areas, and trigger new research it is considered progressive. For example, in the history of astronomy, a mathematical theory (a rather
cranky one, in modern eyes) led Kepler to postulate yet unknown planets, while
retaining the core of the theory. These were ad hoc hypotheses (Losee, 2001: 202–6)
but the subsequent discovery of Uranus proved them right, so that the empirical
content increased.

Scientific progress results from competition between research programmes. Each
programme tries to uphold its own hard core by protecting it in a Kuhnian dogmatic
way against anomalies through auxiliary hypotheses. However, in contrast to Kuhn,
Lakatos thinks that progressive and degenerating research programmes can be dis-
cerned. If a programme shows no empirical progress, anticipates no new facts, but
only subsists by patching up its core with ever new excuses, it is degenerative. If, however, the programme has heuristic power, its empirical content tends to increase, and
new facts are discovered, it will win the competition. In the astronomy example, if the
unknown planet is indeed discovered, the programme progresses; if, on the other
hand, the programme has to make all kinds of guesses, none of which is confirmed, it
degenerates.

Thus, although Kuhn is right that *within* a research programme dogmatism reigns,
nevertheless some form of Popperian fallibilism and falsification can be salvaged:
there is a rational choice, according to some kind of demarcation criterion, by way of
a-posteriori selection *between* programmes. Progress and rationality can be attained by
picking the programme that happened to be on the right track and proved to be more
capable of empirical growth than the competition.

So, although there is no criterion for instant rationality, a-posteriori *rational reconstruction* of scientific progress is possible; there may be good reasons to reject a research

programme, and paradigm shifts are not entirely a matter of mob psychology. The winning programme is objectively better if it has the same empirical content as its competitor, and a bit more. Unfortunately, there is no hard and fast measure of empirical content, and we do not always have a choice between two programmes.

Feyerabend on science in a free society

Paul Feyerabend (1978) has, in debate with Lakatos, radicalized Kuhn's relativism. His position has become known as *methodological anarchism*; it holds that 'anything goes' in methodology, that there is and should be no demarcation criterion. He argues that the methodological law-and-order approach, implied in the quest for demarcation, is disastrous to scientific progress, and that framing hypotheses which go against established theories is the way science proceeds. Established theories have carried the day usually by coincidence, rhetoric, superior persuasive or political powers of their defenders, and the like. As Kuhn argued, they then produce their own evidence, entrench themselves using the support, obtain grants and prestige that comes from their privileged position. Big science is successful because it controls the resources to churn out ever more results that confirm it. The competition lacks the laboratories and the manpower to produce its own evidence, and hence has no data to show. So it is only natural that new hypotheses should clash with accepted wisdom, and seem ill-supported by the evidence. However, lack of confirmation is in this view no disadvantage. Rather, being counterintuitive is highly desirable, since that is the way to unsettle the established ideologies, and realize real progress. Not surprisingly, Feyerabend became a kind of cult figure in Californian counterculture in the late 1970s.

So, 'anything goes' means that no hypothesis should be rejected as falsified or unconfirmed; on the contrary, notoriously unscientific-like ideas, such as voodoo, magic, or alternative healing, should be given a try. Moreover, they should not be rejected in the face of conflicting evidence; a maximum of empirical immunity should be granted to wild ideas. Application of a universal method that suppresses ideas with insufficient empirical and methodological backing would be disastrous for progress. Scientific progress, rather than being the epitome of rationality, needs a firm dose of irrationality.

It will come as no surprise that Feyerabend does not recognize the distinction between context of discovery and context of justification. The acceptance of new scientific ideas is as much due to social and accidental factors (discovery) as to rational methods (justification). Methodological rules hamper progress; 'counterinduction', choosing the unjustified and unconfirmed, is the road to new discoveries.

Furthermore, he argues that science is not essentially different from ideology and mythology. Only the establishment has a vested interest in selling science as superior to common sense and as the epitome of rationality, and in fostering an uncritical belief in its superiority. Feyerabend defended a separation between state and science, in the same way that church and science have been separated. Children in school should not glossary be indoctrinated with the dominant scientific **ideology**, and free citizens in a free society should not be patronized by philosophical know-alls.

It should be emphasized that the main thrust of Feyerabend's methodological anarchism is his disdain for pompous philosophers who try to lay down the law for scientists, and try to prescribe to society at large what is rational and scientifically respectable. His style has been deliberately provocative: he cultivated his image as a kind of anti-philosopher and certainly lived up to his own maxim: 'Always contradict'. By his own admission, he did not have a new philosophical doctrine of knowledge (Feyerabend, 1980: 284), but wanted to blow up the established ideology from the inside (ibid.: 285). As a philosopher of science, he probably has made no lasting contribution. Having read (and sometimes enjoyed) his diatribes, one realizes that he fails to answer the rather crucial question: why is it that established science has delivered such impressive results, and alchemy, voodoo and witchcraft have not? What distinguishes the former from the latter? To some extent, the developments in the last decades try to answer that question.

3.9 Since Kuhn: Post-positivism in a Nutshell

Three decades of post-positivism

The philosophy of science since Kuhn has flourished and diversified. Some of the sociological and relativist developments like the Strong Programme, and the 'science wars' are discussed in Chapter 5. Pragmatism as a way out of positivist and post-positivist tangles is discussed in Chapter 4.6. This section briefly discusses some attempts to salvage the positivist concern with rationality and progress (or at least with the idea of rational reconstruction), while retaining Kuhn's prominent role for social and historical factors. Several philosophers of science (Nickles, Toulmin, Laudan: see Rouse, 1998) have tried to trace the historical emergence of scientific rationality in specific domains of science. That involves case studies, looking into development of domain-specific methods and standards. No Kuhnian revolutions or incommensurable paradigm shifts, nor positivist general standards for scientific rationality are sought, rather the question is how coherent practices develop, with a kind of group rationality and internal standards that are locally valid. Philosophers increasingly turn to case studies of specific research traditions (e.g. Pickering, 1995). Another development is the increased attention for laboratory practices (Hacking, 1992; see Chapter 4.6). Mostly, this work is descriptive, not normative, it is not in the business of finding and imposing a philosophically-based methodology.

Laudan's historical meta-methodology

A good example of an attempt to develop a more or less empirically based naturalist methodology is Laudan's 'normative naturalism'. Firstly, Laudan emphasizes that there are no fixed principles of rationality – standards change in time, depending on the cognitive goals, and may change as the conceptual core as theory develops. Second, he argues that problem-solving, not truth, is the business of science. Thus, Laudan dumps much of the positivist philosophical commitments: if problem-solving, not truth, is the goal of science, then philosophical **realism**, **truth** as **correspondence**, cumulative progress as the hallmark of science, theories as linguistic edifices, and other positivist ideas that went awry can be defused. Progress is being able to solve more problems; rationality is instrumental in realizing a cognitive goal. Since cognitive goals may differ (for example, applied sciences such as meteorology or engineering may demand less rigourous mathematical proofs than pure mathematics), there is no single criterion for scientific rationality. Choosing theories involves a trade-off between maximal empirical success in problem-solving and minimal anomalies and conceptual frictions. Acceptation and rejection is relative to such cognitive goals and trade-offs. There is no abstract or absolute rationality, just pragmatically instrumental rules of the thumb (avoid inconsistency, prefer new hypotheses, etc.).

glossary

In this framework, Laudan sees a possibility for a naturalistic meta-methodology using historical methods. This tries to assess which methods (say, verification, falsification) have been more successful in history than their competitors in attaining specific cognitive goals – that is, methods are evaluated as just means towards cognitive ends. Methodology from a naturalistic viewpoint consists of just if-then rules: if you want to achieve so-and-so, then do so-and-so. And methodological norms can in principle be empirically evaluated.

In Laudan's diagnosis, positivism perversely led to relativism: when philosophers realized that demarcation criteria for general ahistoric rationality did not work out, they saw no other possible conclusion than abandoning objectivity and progress altogether. Laudan suggests that when we dispose of the 'sins of the (positivist) fathers', we can escape from relativism, and retain a notion of progress and rationality in science. For example, Quine–Duhem underdetermination does not mean that any theory is as good as any other in the face of the data: there are many cognitive goals that allow a legitimate pragmatic choice even if there is complete empirical equivalence between theories.

Methodological standards change with history and with cognitive goals – so far Kuhn was right, but the relativist conclusion does not follow. Changing standards is not necessarily a sign of irrational paradigm shifts: changing cognitive ends or changing conceptual frameworks may have provided good pragmatic reasons. Laudan's historical metamethodology thus combines a role for history that Kuhn emphasized with a normative methodology that may identify the rules that have been most effective in realizing a given cognitive goal. Methodological rules are then just as empirical, fallible and pragmatic as scientific hypotheses. The pragmatic idea is that success counts, and that the meta-methodology should find the most successful methods for a given goal. That defuses the relativist menace that 'anything goes'. To sum up, the developments in the philosophy of science after Kuhn increasingly focus on science as it is really done, in its social and historical context, and at the same time tries to escape the bane of relativism. More on this in the next chapter (4.4–4.6) – realism, relativism and pragmatism.

3.10 Conclusion: The Moral on Demarcation

So, the story of the philosophy of science in the twentieth century is to a large extent the history of the quest for a **demarcation criterion**. It can be summarized roughly as follows.   glossary

The logical positivists of the Wiener Kreis designated verifiability as the criterion for meaningfulness. Popper realized that verification in the strict sense is impossible, and proposed falsifiability. Quine undercut the dogma of the distinction between empirical and logical statements and demonstrated that scientific statements cannot be isolated from the whole web of theories. Wittgenstein maintained, against his former positivist self, that meaning is not a fixed one-to-one relation between a term and an object, but forms part of a 'language game', a 'form of life'. Hanson introduced the notion of 'theory-ladenness': there is no 'immaculate perception', observations are not independent of theoretical presuppositions, and hence cannot be used to reject or confirm the theory. Likewise, Sellars unmasked the 'myth of the given'.

Kuhn introduced the celebrated term 'paradigm', one of its implications being that scientific collectives make their own data, which are 'incommensurable' with data from other collectives or periods: paradigms determine what is seen, and no rational comparison in terms of empirical adequacy or progress is possible. Hence, no demarcation criterion can be specified, and all-out relativism seems to follow. Feyerabend exploits the notions of theory-ladenness and paradigm in the service of methodological anarchism: any attempt to impose standards is arrogant and paternalistic: so, 'anything goes'. Lakatos tries to rescue rationality in backward fashion, combining dogmatism within a 'research programme' with the possibility of progress through identification of progressive and degenerating programmes. Later developments allow a role for historical and social factors, while trying to steer clear of relativism.

One could interpret the developments from logical positivism to Kuhn and Feyerabend as the demise of a demarcation criterion for scientific rationality, the undoing of the quest for iron-clad methods and standards, and consequently as the victory of all-out relativism. However, one could also consider it as the introduction of more human and contextual elements in the philosophy of science. Science is now seen as a human activity. Already in Popper, framing hypotheses is an essentially free, creative and unconstrained human activity. Kuhn emphasizes the social nature of science, and the contextual nature of knowledge claims: only on the basis of shared practices within a community is research possible. Wittgenstein II reached a similar conclusion: knowledge starts from a pragmatic and social matrix; it depends on prejudices and prereflexive practices. So the developments in the philosophy of science seem to converge somehow with strands from continental philosophy. In the next chapter, philosophies of science which emphasize this social and pragmatic, if you will, hermeneutic matrix of inquiry will be introduced.

FURTHER READING

Losee, J. (2001) *A Historical Introduction to the Philosophy of Science*, 4th edn. Oxford: Oxford University Press.
A compact informative survey of the philosophy of science, chronologically ordered.

Kitcher, P. (1993) *The Advancement of Science*. Oxford: Oxford University Press.
A rich, ecumenical account of progress, rationality and realism in science.

Chalmers, A.F. (2003) *What Is This Thing Called Science?* Maidenhead: OUP/McGraw-Hill.
Third edition of a popular systematic and historical textbook on science and its development.

4. PHILOSOPHY OF SCIENCE (2)

Recent Proposals and Debates on Scientific Knowledge

PREVIEW: In this chapter we will introduce the reader to views on science developed out of a rejection of positivism. Thus, we will proceed with the discussion we started in the previous chapter. The fundamental issue had become how objectivity claimed by science is possible. It raises deep epistemological problems, which have to do with questions about the reliability of psychological performances such as knowledge and perception. In these performances the relationships between firstly the knower and perceiver (scientists) and the world, and secondly relationships within communities of scientists (or subjects in general), play an important role. How important these relationships are is heavily debated, as the discussion on realism and relativism will show. In trying to find a balance between extreme positions we will at the end present some pragmatic considerations.

4.1 Introduction

After positivism collapsed as a result of devastating criticism by a first generation of post-positivists and positivists themselves, philosophers of science faced a completely new task for their trade. The era of *normative* philosophy of science, with its longing after ahistoric criteria of scientific respectability and clearcut demarcation between objective knowledge and human and social interests, and its prescriptions of how to do science properly, had ended. It had to be acknowledged that this ideal image of scientific knowledge was out of reach because, as William James already remarked: 'The trail of the human serpent is thus over everything' (1907/1975: 37). Philosophers of science faced again the fundamental epistemological problem of how to know the (social) world with at least some objectivity, if objectivity is possible at all.

glossary **Objectivism** (realism) and subjectivism (relativism) were confronting each other. According to the relativist philosophers the time had come to look carefully at what scientists were really doing, in which contexts, and what were their (pre)suppositions and their (unexpressed) intentions and interests. They adopted a *descriptive* philosophy of science that found its natural domain in historical and sociological accounts of the construction of knowledge. This sociology of knowledge will be the subject matter of Chapter 5. In this fourth chapter we will discuss different proposals on the possibility of scientific knowledge and objectivity. First, elaborating the introductory remarks in Chapter 2 (2.3) on hermeneutic understanding, we will present the epistemological position of hermeneutics which grew out of German philosophy; we will also address some arguments for and against the epistemological dissimilarity between natural sciences and the humanities. In the third section attention will be paid to social constructionism, a position that has become quite popular among social scientists. Rhetoric is related to constructionism; both positions stand on the relativistic side of the spectrum. In section 4 relativism and realism are confronted; and in section 5 modern versions of realism are discussed. Versions of pragmatism try to overcome the realism–relativism dichotomy, as will be considered in the last section of this chapter.

4.2 Hermeneutics

We saw in Chapter 2 that in the continental philosophical tradition of hermeneutics was already a much respected approach to the social sciences. It was introduced in the English-language philosophy of science by, among others, Thomas Kuhn and Charles Taylor in the 1970s, Richard Rorty in the following decades. Criticism of glossary positivism and its **empiricist** epistemology, and serious doubts about the idea that the methods of natural science should be held up to the social sciences as the ideal standard merged with the view 'that there is an unavoidable "hermeneutical" component in sciences of man' (Taylor, 1971: 3). Let us rehearse some hermeneutic ideas.

An important element in hermeneutics is the sensitivity to *history*. A major thesis of the influential German philosopher, Martin Heidegger (1889–1976), was that the glossary quest for a timeless **foundation** of knowledge, for absolute truth and certainty, ignores our own radical, insurmountable historicity and finiteness. In his major work *Wahrheit* *und Methode* (*Truth and Method*) (1960) the German philosopher Hans Georg Gadamer elaborates this theme and explains the essence of understanding and interpretation, the hermeneutical epistemological concepts in the human sciences, by comparing understanding a human situation or behaviour with how we understand a work of art. We understand a work of art not by objectifying it, ourselves being detached and disinterested spectators. On the contrary, in understanding it we are involved in and participate in the work of art, starting from our own situation and prejudices. Or, consider attending the theatre: the spectators are not disinterested; they as well as the players participate in the play. This happening is never finished and never the same; the work of art is never an object in itself: it is the essence of a play and a work of art that they should be perceived by spectators who become involved in interpreting and understanding them. And every time staging and interpretation will be different because the interpreter brings his own history with him and the work of art is passed on through tradition.

In this way interpretation brings with it a sensitivity to history or, what is more, a sense of historical existence. To understand the meaning of a work of art, or a text in general, we should become conscious of our own situatedness. We should resist the naive temptation of objectivism, the belief that there is a stable pre-given object or world to be known as a secure truth on its own. Between subject and object there is a historical, hermeneutic interaction. Therefore, in understanding a text we cannot possibly remain neutral or 'objective' observers; on the contrary we should be aware of our own prejudices. To understand a text from the past, for instance, is to understand it from our own situation, though our situation is also a product of history. To understand something is to re-enact it in our own situation; to interrogate it as it were, in order to get an answer to a question of our own. In this dialectic, dialogue-like, process of questions and answers we do learn things about the world, as well as about ourselves. What a text means does not necessarily coincide with the intentions of the initial author (if any). Human knowledge and experience, in general, is a constant conversation with tradition applied to the questions of our times. As it is the means of communication, language is the most important medium of the hermeneutic experience of the world: the world presents itself in language and communication.

This portrayal of Gadamer's book has to be a very short and fragmented rendering of a typical continental philosophical, sweeping, deep, and erudite work, sometimes almost obscure to the reader who is not familiar with continental philosophy. It should give the flavour of hermeneutics, which Heidegger and Gadamer turned from a method for the human sciences and for the interpretation of texts into a universal or ontological hermeneutics concerned with the fundamental mode of human existence, our being in the world. What does concern us here is that some ideas of hermeneutics tie in with the post-positivistic philosophy of science, such as the idea that 'the given' is a myth, epistemological **holism** (the Quine–Duhem thesis), the glossary **theory-ladenness** of observations, and the importance of the historical context of the scientific products and its authors.

BOX 4.1 Hermeneutics

What was once a method for understanding difficult legal and biblical texts has been turned from the nineteenth century on by German philosophers such as Dilthey, Heidegger and Gadamer into a philosophical (a fundamental epistemological and ontological) approach of experiencing and being in the world. One needs to understand the meaning of things to be able to experience (seeing, hearing, knowing) them. But the meaning is part of a whole network of meanings, a network that refers to historical and social embeddedness.

And so understanding becomes a complicated and insecure interpretation of what there is and what happens, especially of someone's behaviour (actions), because an interpretation has no conclusive objectivity or truth; it is constantly changing and there is no impartial arbiter around.

Interpretation and meaning

What then is this hermeneutical epistemology? Let us follow Charles Taylor (1971) for a tentative answer. The objects of the sciences of man, or the humanities, such as a text, a situation, an **action**, a **reason**, a purpose, have meanings; and these meanings are to be interpreted or understood by subjects. Meaning has an essential place in the characterization of human behaviour. Something has a meaning only in a 'field', that is, in relation to the meaning of other things. There is no such thing as a single, unrelated meaningful element. A term like 'shame' refers to a certain kind of situation leading to a certain mode of response, like hiding oneself. But this 'hiding' which is not the same as hiding from an armed pursuer cannot be understood without reference to the feeling experienced. So, we are back where we started: 'We have to be within the circle' (Taylor, 1971: 13). We meet here the *hermeneutic circle*: 'the readings of partial expressions depend on those of others, and ultimately of the whole' (ibid.: 6). Just as words make sense in the context of the sentence, and the sentence in the context of the whole text, we can only make sense of a certain behaviour if we understand it as part of an entire practice. The practice of hermeneutical understanding is a movement from part to whole and from whole to part. This holist line of argument, writes Richard Rorty (1979: 319), 'we shall never be able to avoid', be it a strange culture, practice, theory, language, or whatever that we try to understand.

The readings or interpretations will never be clear-cut and the same, and will not relieve us of the uncertainty of interpretations and subjectivity. This epistemological predicament, Taylor (1971) writes, would be intolerable for the positivists, who demanded clarity, certainty and formalization as a way to avoid the circle of interpretation and subjectivity. Behaviourism failed at exactly this point; you cannot define, says Taylor, the response without the stimulus, and vice versa: interpretation gets in between, making any 'objective' definition of situation and reaction to it impossible.

glossary

A certain behaviour, say, writing a name on a piece of paper and putting it in a box, makes sense only as part of a whole, namely voting, which is a social practice. Social practices like voting, promising, negotiating, blushing, etc. carry with them certain vocabularies and rules which 'constitute' these practices, not necessarily obtaining in all societies. Here, hermeneutics meets Wittgenstein's notion of **language game** and 'form of life'. Social practices, rules and vocabularies make up the necessary context of the meanings of particular behaviours. So, understanding human behaviour requires more than knowledge and description of spatiotemporal superficialities, more than 'brute data', as Taylor (1971) calls them, 'whose validity cannot be questioned by offering another interpretation'. Understanding human behaviour requires hermeneutical epistemology by which one is aware of the intersubjective and common meanings embedded in social reality. The empiristic epistemology of the positivists is not adequate to make sense of meanings supplied by humans in various contexts.

Natural versus social (human) sciences

But is there, then, a difference between the methodology of the natural and of the social or human sciences? Is there something special about the subject matter of the latter which tells us not to adopt for it the method of the former sciences? Positivist-empiricist philosophers favoured the belief that the exact natural sciences set the methodological standard, and they adhered to a methodological monism. Already at the end of the nineteenth century the German philosopher Wilhelm Dilthey, one of the founders of the hermeneutical epistemology, proposed to distinguish between natural sciences and humanities, each with its own method; hermeneutics for the humanities. But some modern hermeneutic philosophers do not believe, for their own reasons, that we should distinguish between natural and human (social) scientific methods. Richard Rorty, who is very sympathetic to hermeneutics, takes sides with the *universal hermeneutics* of Gadamer. This is an attitude, a general intellectual position, not a universal method. After the demise of positivism and empiricism there is no place for an objective, ahistorical foundation of any knowledge. There is no ahistoric structure of rationality. 'We have not *got* a language which will serve as a permanent neutral matrix formulating all good explanatory hypotheses, and we have not the foggiest notion how to get one' (Rorty, 1979: 348–9). Rorty sees **epistemology** and hermeneutics as opposites (1979: ch. vii); epistemology being the hope of absolute objectivity and agreement based on the alleged existence of a common ground (of e.g. empirical data and the mystic correspondence between objects of reality and the intellect); hermeneutics as the negation of all this. For this reason Rorty thinks that 'there is no requirement that people should be more difficult to understand than things' (ibid.: 347); that is, there is no essential difference between human and natural sciences (ibid.: 321); both are hermeneutical, in the sense of interpretation, involving understanding. Neither are we justified in accepting the traditional distinction between **explanation** in the natural and **understanding** in the social sciences.

Taylor, however, rejects this claim of universal hermeneutics. The kind of understanding involved in the two kinds of science is different. This is so because in the natural sciences the task is 'to give an account of the world as it is independently of the meanings it might have for human subjects' (1971: 31). But this 'requirement of absoluteness', the requirement to avoid subject-related terms, is inapplicable to human sciences. Here we have to understand the world as it makes sense to the humans themselves. We have to grasp the significance of things for them, which can only be articulated in subject-related terms. In human sciences the experience of subjects plays an indispensable role. Here is one of his eloquent examples:

> When I know that a situation is humiliating, I know more than that the subject is averse to it; I know that his aversion has a different quality than to a situation which is physically painful, or one which is embarrassing, or one which awakens guilt in him, or unbearable pity, or which induces despair. There is here a set of alternative terms for feeling or reaction: 'guilt', 'shame', 'despair', 'embarrassment', 'pity', which are correlative to and are only understood in terms of the type of situation: wrongdoing, the humiliating, the hopeless, the embarrassing, the pitiable. (Taylor, 1980: 35)

For almost the same reasons Herbert Dreyfus (1980), who has become famous for his critique of artificial intelligence (see Chapter 7), rejects Rorty's (1980) conclusion that there is no important difference between the natural and the social sciences. We never can escape the hermeneutic circle, because our beliefs, communication, actions, develop against a shared cultural '**background**' of social practices, of know-how and skills, which cannot be made entirely explicit because it is presupposed (see also Chapters 9 and 10). It is the necessary context that makes communication and understanding possible in the first place. But, whereas in natural science the scientists can take this background for granted, making normal science possible, social scientists must take account of it, thereby constantly disagreeing about interpretations. It is the basic job of the social sciences to explore the background of practices and their meaning, 'the unique feature of human behaviour, the human self-interpretation in our everyday know-how' (Dreyfus, 1980: 17). Natural science 'succeeds by decontextualizing, while the human sciences have to deal with the human context' (ibid.: 20).

glossary

As mentioned, Rorty denies that we can give a natural scientific account of the world as if it were independent of the meanings it might have for human subjects. He repudiates the notion of a 'requirement of absoluteness', because he claims that the notion of 'mind-independent reality' is incoherent. Rorty sees no distinction between natural and human sciences in this respect: the universal hermeneutics, following the demise of positivism, is the recognition that inquiry proceeds without a universal canon of rationality. Rorty takes sides with the relativistic line in hermeneutics. In section 4.4 we will pursue this issue of relativism versus realism.

The philosopher of science Mary Hesse (1980) claimed that it has increasingly become apparent that the empiricist standard of scientific rationality has fallen apart; that the logic of the natural sciences cannot serve as a model for the social sciences; and that the traditional contrast between the natural and social sciences should be reconsidered. What counts as facts depends on the theory. Hence, the circularity emphasized by hermeneutics is also apparent in the natural sciences. The language of natural science is 'formalizable only at the cost of the historical dynamics of scientific development and of the imaginative constructions in terms of which nature is interpreted by science' (Hesse, 1980: 173).

Thus Hesse recognizes that human and social factors are intrinsic to all science. She charts the demise of classical positivist philosophy of science and shows much sympathy for the hermeneutic view of the role of interpretation and the hermeneutic circle between data and theory. Because almost every point made about the human sciences has been made about the natural sciences, the resemblances between this post-empiricist/positivist account of natural science and the hermeneutic approach to the human sciences appear very close (see also Bernstein, 1983).

4.3 Social Constructionism and Rhetoric

An important element of classical positivism and empiricism was its theory of **truth**, glossary
the correspondence theory, according to which a description is true if it corresponds to the object or event in the world which it describes. This notion of correspondence is the major bone of contention for social constructionists like Kenneth Gergen and John Shotter. What is that correspondence relation supposed to be? It is an illusion to think that we can establish secure and determinate relationships between words and world referents, that knowledge mirrors nature, and that scientific theory serves to reflect or map reality in any direct or decontextualized manner. 'How can theoretical categories map or reflect the world if each definition linking category and observation itself requires a definition?' (Gergen, 1985b: 4). In this kind of criticism they follow the lines of post-positivist argumentation we have already encountered. What makes them rather special is the radical and relativistic conclusions they draw from it. Because the positivist claim that science can and must strive for full objectivity, in terms of mental mirroring of the world, has proved untenable, the social constructionists infer that scientific knowledge is only the product of **social construction** and glossary
convention.

'Social constructionism,' writes Gergen, after Rorty (1979), 'views discourse about the world not as a reflection or map of the world but as an artifact of communal exchange' (Gergen, 1985a: 266).

The function of language, and thus of our theories, is not that they refer to the world at all; they have no truth-value. The basic function of language, according to Shotter, 'is *not* the representation of things in the world … It works to create, sustain and transform various patterns of social relations.' And he adds that if some words stand for things, 'they do so only from *within* a form of social life already constituted by the ways of talking in which such words are used' (1991: 70, original emphasis).

Social constructionists think that there is no such thing as objective understanding: 'reality is negotiable'; what there is depends on what society agrees about. They endorse an interpretative social science, chiefly concerned with 'conceptual transformations of social life', the theories of which are not 'mapping devices for a pre-existing reality', but 'render experience intelligible' and 'give meaning to such experience' (Gergen, 1980: 258).

From these considerations about the construction of knowledge of social activities and relationships, the social constructionists infer that there are no empirical grounds of scientific knowledge at large and that the epistemological question, what are facts and what is true or false, is constituted in the lap of communities:

> Scientific formulations would not on this account be the result of an impersonal application of rigorous and decontextualized method, but the responsibility of persons in active, communal interchange. (Gergen, 1985b: 13)

It is sometimes suggested that social constructionism pertains to concepts of social science, but the general epistemological claims are clearly directed to all knowledge.

> All knowledge is derived from looking at the world from some perspective or other, and it is in the service of some interests rather than others. (Burr, 1995: 6)

BOX 4.2   Theories of truth

- The *correspondence* theory of truth: truth consists in the correspondence (mirroring ?) between a thought or its utterance and reality. This theory is associated with realism.
  Problem: how can we assess the correspondence, how is comparing reality and thought possible?

- The *coherence* theory of truth: truth consists in the coherence between a thought or its utterance and other beliefs (sometimes: the more beliefs in a system are coherent, the truer they are). This theory is associated with idealism (and relativism).
  Problem: there is no mind-independent reality; reality is a fiction of the mind.

- The *consensus* theory of truth: truth is what is agreed upon by common consent. This theory is associated with relativism (social constructionism).
  Problem: there seems to be no mind-independent reality; reality is socially constructed; it could be that truth is dependent on group-think.

- The *pragmatic* theory: truth (better: reliability) of a belief or its utterance is shown in activity; it cannot be conceived of apart from its practical consequences, but is demonstrated in subsequent experiment, test, or action.
  Problem: caricatured as: true is what works.

Psychology in social constructionism

These arguments are being put forward in the context of a critique of the prevailing categories, concepts and views in (social) psychology by which one gains understanding of personal and social actions and interactions. Social constructionists challenge the supposedly objective and universal basis of much psychological knowledge, the subject of enquiry of tradional psychology. Traditional psychologists search for states and processes *in* the mind. For social constructionists, in contrast, 'the chief locus of understanding is not in "the psyche" but in social relationships' (Gergen, 1997: 724; for further constructionist criticism on cognitive psychology, see Chapter 9). Topics and concepts such as gender, aggression, person, self, emotion, schizophrenia, child, mother's love are *social artefacts*, products of historically situated interactions among people.

Though highly critical of traditional psychology, social constructionism does have a place for psychology, according to Gergen (1997). There are ways in which constructionism might contribute 'to a more fully enriched and broadly effective psychology'. For instance, by unmasking and deconstructing ideology, interests and rhetorical strategies in much psychological theorizing and professional practice. And by the social reconstruction of the individual and the mind; that is, by giving the social primacy over the individual and approaching individuals as 'culturally immersed', and by seeing mental processes as reflecting social processes.

For this reason constructionists are sensitive to cross-cultural psychological or ethnographic studies which reveal that psychological conceptions differ among wide-ranging cultures because they are produced by and sustain the social, moral, political and economic institutions. Forms of psychological understanding are not directly dependent on the nature of things but on the vicissitudes of social processes, such as communication, conflict, negotiation; they are forms of negotiated understanding and as such tools for praising or blaming, assigning or diminishing responsibility, rewarding or punishing, and exercising censure.

Another example of constructionist concern is that social scientists encounter the identification of actions (Gergen, 1980; see also above, Chapter 2.6). Empirical evidence does not help to understand what is going on when, for instance, 'Ross reaches out and momentarily touches Laura's hair'. We cannot identify any given action in itself; because what it means is embedded in an ever-unfolding context. To understand the meaning of the action, we have to rely 'on a network of interdependent and continuously modifiable interpretations' (ibid.: 242).

To conclude, social constructionists oppose realist metaphysics and a correspondence theory of truth and language with its view of science in which 'there is a single, knowable reality' (Gergen, 1997: 724). In this assessment they do not stand alone, as we have seen in the previous chapter. However, they radicalize the social component to the extent that science and scientific knowledge is nothing but social activity and social construction. Constructionism thus ends up in all-out relativism. Though much of their evaluation of prevailing psychological theory and practice is fair and respectable, it is the generality of this radical epistemology that is questionable. It leads to a proliferation of theoretical perspectives without the means to weigh the valuable and sound, and the non-valuable and un-sound. For to eradicate a theoretical perspective would be 'to silence a community of meaning making' and 'result in losing a mode of human intelligibility' (ibid.). This 'pluralist ethic', however, might be too radical and too liberal, indeed.

Rhetoric

According to the social constructionists science, wrought as it is in language, is not meant to map the world; it is discourse, that is, a social interchange. In this light, Michael Billig (1987) concentrates on the character of discourse. The most important element in this human activity is argumentation and it is Billig's intention to promote this argumentative aspect of thinking. Since ancient times, rhetoric has had a bad press; it is degenerated grandiloquence and stylistic conceit used merely to impress the audience. But this rhetoric of adornment is not the argumentative rhetoric which concerns Billig.

Following in the footsteps of the Greek philosopher Protagoras, Billig draws attention to the social-psychological principle of science, the fundamental two-sidedness of thinking. Because there are no fixed truths and no fixed **laws**, it is useless to try to discover the fixed essences of truth, as was Plato's vision. 'Plato may have dreamt of an end to argument, but in Protagoras's philosophy there is no escape from rhetoric' (Billig, 1987: 44). Knowledge is not absolute but is the interim product of debates between adversaries, a never-ending dialogue. In this context of argumentation, it is possible to argue both sides of a case. Contrary statements can each be reasonable and justified, and both can be open to criticism. Western philosophers have assumed that truth is one; that thinking is, or should be, reducible to logic, and that, therefore, contrary statements cannot be both true and reasonable. However, this would end argumentation, and that is, in fact, an illusion, according to Billig.

Emphasis upon the argumentative context of discourse has a number of theoretical implications for cognitive psychological issues. Billig refers, for example, to the problem of meaning (1987: 90ff.). According to social constructionism words do not refer to the world and do not possess fixed meanings; they take their meanings from communal exchange. That being so, argues Billig, one must understand words in relation to the argumentative contexts in which they are being used. One should examine them in terms of the contest between criticism and justification. 'Without knowing these counter-positions, the argumentative meaning will be lost' (ibid.: 91). One cannot properly understand an argument if one fails to grasp what it is arguing against: 'Thus, if one is puzzling over an extremely difficult piece of intellectual work, whose meaning seems too abstruse to grasp, one should ask oneself not "What is this about", but "What is this attacking?"' (ibid.: 92).

Another example, taken from cognitive psychology, to which Billig applies his rhetoric theory, is the problem of *categorization* (ibid.: 120 ff.), the placing of a particular stimulus or object within a general category. To see Billig, for example, as a representative of scientists who approach science exclusively from a social-psychological

glossary

point of view is making a categorization, sorting him into a group. Cognitive psychologists, whom Billig sees as heirs to objectivism, assume that categorization is an essential function of organisms because it is based upon the need to reduce, simplify and distort the infinite variety of information. This assumption of biological necessity, however, expresses only 'one side of the many-sidedness of human nature', according to Billig (ibid.: 123). Categorization as used by cognitive psychologists is linked with prejudiced thought because it shuts out complexity by the imposition of stereotypes, or group schemata. By categorization the particular is robbed of its particularity. By defining categorization as a biological necessity the cognitivist over-values the inflexible aspects of thought and reduces a perceiving person to a bureaucrat who processes the messiness of the world into orderly categories. Categories and schemata determine the information process – what will be coded, what retrieved from memory. The categorizing thinker appears as a rather dull person, being inherently prejudiced and programmed to bureaucratically pigeonhole. The 'cognitive miser', limited in his capacity to process information, must take cognitive 'shortcuts', and 'consequently, errors and biases stem from inherent features of the cognitive system' (Fiske and Taylor, 1984: 12). The implication that stereotyping is merely an instance of normal cognition is 'not just depressing it is also one-sided' (Billig, 1987: 126), leading to a one-sided image of the person, as a routine- and rule-follower, without tolerance, flair, wit or sagacity which 'seem to have been edged out by the demands of organization and stability' (ibid.: 129).

By his rhetorical approach Billig opposes objectivism, and challenges the scientist's quest for law and order. He argues in favour of the versatility of life, the particularity of individual cases and the contestability of points of view. He attempts to establish 'the primacy of rhetoric over logic' (Billig, 1990: 50), because logic or mathematics cannot supply a higher realm of discourse, in which truths have an absolute status. He recommends ordinary discourse rather than scientific methodology:

> Science is … an intrinsically rhetorical, or persuasive, activity, and, consequently, a rhetorical analysis of science is not so much an exposé, but an analysis which looks at the way that scientists argue and discuss their scientific cases. (Billig, 1990: 50)

To conclude: after a survey of classical empiricism, its quest for **demarcation** and glossary certainty, and its demise, we have sketched the reintroduction of human, subjective and social concerns as essential components in the practice of science. In the work of Kuhn, and in hermeneutics, prejudices are indispensable factors in research, rather than corrupting influences. However, it seems that these subjective influences detract from the realism of scientific theories: they seem more about us than about the world.

So, having rejected the idea of detached objectivity, the question becomes how to escape all-out subjectivity, the view that the truth becomes relative to the viewpoint of a particular observer as member of a social group. Would such relativism undermine science and rationality? If there is no external yardstick, no demarcation criterion to distinguish between scientific and pseudo-scientific, and between progressive and degenerating programmes, if 'anything goes' and voodoo is not, by any rational criterion, inferior to conventional medicine, why spend time and money on research?

4.4 Problems of Realism and Relativism

Kinds of relativism

If the quest for universal criteria for objective knowledge fails, a major problem faces us: How realistic is science? or: How relativistic? Is science at the mercy of subjectivity because objectivity is not attainable? Before we consider some arguments for and against both pictures of science, realism and relativism, we present some different types of relativism (Hollis and Lukes, 1982; O'Grady, 2002). We do not address here *moral relativism*, the idea that there are no universal grounds for morality; that moral rules are group inventions and that they necessarily differ from one locality or culture to another. Within the context of science at least four other forms of relativism can be distinguished.

First we have *ontological relativism*: it holds that what there is depends on our concepts, classifications, categories. Matter, persons, **consciousness**, for instance, do exist as constructions, that is, only because of the concepts we happen to have, not as parts of a world independent of us. Further, the relativist maintains that our concepts and distinctions depend on interests, paradigms, language, culture, and so on. These define the furniture of different worlds or at least different world pictures.

glossary

This takes us to *epistemological relativism*: even if it existed, we cannot know a subject-independent, mind-independent, or culture-independent world. Knowledge cannot be objective in the sense that it rests on safe, certain and common foundations, given to us all in an objective and ahistoric (non-constructed, non-social) way. Thus, facts are (social) constructions, are taken-as-facts. Observations, experiments, instruments are theory-laden. Meanings are not grasped, but originate and function internally in a social environment. This leads to the claim of incommensurability between different networks of meanings (e.g. paradigms, see Chapter 3, and below). The notion of **natural kinds** with which some realistic philosophers pronounce their belief that nature itself contains different kinds and species, and that we must classify the world in terms which represent them, is rejected by relativists stressing that every taxonomy is human-made and therefore variant.

glossary

Relativism of truth denies that truth can be found or mastered outside human interests. Because the ancient correspondence theory of **truth** (see Chapter 1.2), the idea that words, sentences, **beliefs** or whatever can 'picture', 'fit', or otherwise stand in a special relationship to 'things'or 'events' in the world, is rejected; a non-human truth is branded a myth. Truth is the expedient result of social practice, of communication, negotiation, **consensus**.

glossary

glossary

If one is a *relativist of rationality* one rejects that there is a universal standard for rationality; that there are universally valid criteria (e.g. logic) for testing inferences, beliefs and reasons; that there are grounds for reasoning common to the whole of mankind. Relativists contend that beliefs, reasoning practices are local, relative to the context of culture, time and place.

For many relativists there is an interdepence between all these forms of relativism. But there are in fact many positions with different blends of relativisms. One can even reject a relativism of truth and rationalism, but show some sympathy for a certain degree of epistemological relativism.

BOX 4.3   Relativism

- *Ontological*: the existence of objects (of what there is) depends on our own thoughts, concepts, categories and classifications.
- *Epistemological:* we cannot know a mind-independent world (even if it existed).
- *Of truth*: we cannot find truth outside human interests, the interests of communities, groups, etc.
- *Of rationality*: there is no universal standard for rationality, or rational discourse.
- *Of morality*: there is no universal standard for morality; there are no universal norms for right or wrong.

Problems for realism

Realism also comes in various flavours, some of which we will discuss later. But first we will rehearse the main worries about realism. The first problem for realism or objectivism, heavily stressed by anti-realists, is the *failure of empiricism* as a theory about perception and concept and belief-fixation, already dealt with in the previous chapter. There are no neutral data which we reproduce, as in mirrors, in our concepts and which we could use in a justification of theories. We should give up the view that the terms of our observations, scientific or not, are given in sensations and are causally dependent on natural information, and that the natural physical information (at a particular moment) is necessary and sufficient for conceptual observation and theory formation. Neither will it do to suggest that we receive neutral data from the world, after which we switch to the interpretation mode. Our judgements about what there is and what we see are theory-laden from the outset and are coloured by wide experience, beliefs and practices. The old realist picture that the world does dictate those descriptions is mistaken.

From this follows, secondly, that there are *no indubitable foundations* for knowledge. 'There is no special subset of the set of human beliefs that is justificationally foundational for all the rest', in Churchland's (1979: 41) summary of the myth exposed by Sellars (see previous chapter and below). There are no free-floating truths we have to grasp, no knowledge we have to pluck from the air. What we think and say, what we know about the world, is known by us; and this knowledge is not part of the objective world itself, but is the set of beliefs about the world. And, might the relativist add, those beliefs are wrought by us as participants in cultures, sharing languages, world-views, theories, hopes and expectations, practices and institutions, and reflecting a rich matrix of intersubjective relations.

These two problems for objectivism lead to the third one, the *fallibility* of scientific theories. History teaches us that no theory is immune to alteration and even complete rejection in the course of time. Every science has its exemplars of broken theories in the attic. Psychology's well-known example is phrenology and its gadget cranioscopy, the measurement of skulls in pursuit of the bumps of psychological qualities, much in vogue during the nineteenth century. Whatever the value of theories of knowledge, their truth and the supporting evidence cannot be absolute. Truth and objectivity, if philosophy of science can still use these terms, appear to be limited qualities. Though much science is successful, the standards of rationality by which the success was measured were also local and historical. After positivism many philosophers have brought home to us that we have to give up the illusion that there is a permanent set of ahistorical standards of rationality (Bernstein, 1983; Kitcher, 1993; Laudan, 1990).

Do we, then, have to give up realism completely? Do we have to choose the relativistic alternative that truth has indefinitely many faces? Is science nothing but a matter of rhetoric, is it nothing more than arbitrarily endorsing one set of beliefs rather than another? Many scientists, especially social scientists, and the wider intellectual community have come increasingly to suppose that science cannot claim objectivity and therefore is as reliable or unreliable as any product of human imagination.

There are, however, also many scientists who think that there are no reasons to consider ourselves 'cut loose from the anchor to reality' (Churchland, 1979: 41). The philosopher of science Larry Laudan writes:

> The displacement of the idea that facts and evidence matter by the idea that everything boils down to subjective interests and perspectives is – second only to American political campaigns – the most prominent and pernicious manifestation of anti-intellectualism in our time. (1990: x)

Problems for relativism

Before we come up with reasons and suggestions for different versions of realism (next section), let us first discuss some problems regarding relativism.

In a sense relativism is *self-defeating*. To declare that no utterance can be true because it is a product of the one who utters it is devastating for the statement itself. 'Notoriously, there is no room for the assertion of relativism itself, in a world in which relativism is true' (Gellner, 1982: 183). If no thing is true, relativism is false. Nobody would take this absolute form of relativism seriously, so we should perhaps not overstress this. Nevertheless in relativistic circles one tries to overcome this problem of 'reflexivity'; we will come back to this in Chapter 5 on social and psychological dimensions of science.

It is a relativist claim that 'we' ourselves provide the criteria for what is true or false, for what is rational or not. The question is who 'we' might be? How do we delineate the relevant subject who is responsible for a particular viewpoint? Few relativists would
glossary designate the individual as the relevant subject, because it would lead to **solipsism** ('I am the only reality'), not very popular among the '-isms'. More popular is the notion that what I think is true, is true for me, and what you think is true, is true for you. But it does not take much imagination to see that this stand kills every communication.

More serious is the relativist idea that it is language that is responsible for viewpoints, language games, forms of life; and that language is not private, but a social medium (cf. Wittgenstein). Therefore, rationality is *relative to groups, at least*. But which groups? Classes, determined by socio-economic factors, as a relativist of Marxist leanings would have it? Scientific communities as in Kuhn's paradigms? Cultures, communities, nations, tribes?

> Matters are clear if we deal with geographically separated tribes or nations. In a modern society, however, there are so many cross-currents of agreement and disagreement that specifying who 'we' might be is difficult. (Trigg, 1993: 43)

Apart from this problem of identification of the subject, however, the notion that truth depends on the group I happen to be in (the consensus theory of truth) is not a comforting one. A truth valid for me and my friends only must be parochial and uninteresting, and sometimes even dangerous.

This brings us, again, to the notorious **incommensurability** thesis, put forward by Kuhn | glossary | and Feyerabend (Chapter 3). Different theories or different systems of thought or worldviews, separated by scientific revolutions, are said to be incomparable, because the meanings of the descriptive terms used will vary from theory to theory. There can be no question of translating the claims of one into the language of another. Next to this incommensurability of meanings there is the problem that one cannot evaluate another system of thought because you cannot stay clear from your own viewpoint; you lack a neutral standard. So it seems that for relativists all theories are equal and that they cannot provide us with criteria for sifting good theories from bad ones. But can relativists keep up consistency in this? How can we claim a difference, in the first place, without forwarding an opinion about the alien theory, that is, as we saw in the previous objection, without *some* kind of translation? In line with Wittgenstein's thesis that understanding a way of life cannot be separated from adopting it, Kuhn himself held the view that it is impossible to understand a theory without subscribing to it (Trigg, 1973: 101). Though, on the one hand, one cannot pretend to take a neutral standpoint, according to the relativist principle, we cannot, on the other hand, get rid of the need to compare and to choose, so it seems. The claim would be that a relativist does not and cannot maintain the rigidity of the logical principle, that is, she has to use some notions of evaluation.

This borders the problem of *rationality* which, according to the relativist, has nothing but a local range (see above). But would comparison, or discussion about what to choose, or communication at large be possible without at least some minimal principles of universal rationality? O'Grady's (2002: 140 ff.) proposal of a core rationality model is attractive in this respect. It comprises four formal and methodological principles we have to conform to should a debate be possible at all: non-contradiction, coherence, non-avoidance of available evidence, and intellectual honesty. These principles are formal and methodological in the sense that they have no content; and 'they are broad enough to accommodate many of the insights about sensitivity to cultural, social and historical factors' (ibid.).

Another objection is that relativists tend to view science or knowledge as a mere *language* game. Relativists believe that all our knowledge is a matter of language and communication only. Knowledge, and even the world itself, they think, is only interpretation, human construction, and there is no way to step out of your interpretations; the world-in-itself disappears in interpretation. Actually, some go on, it makes no sense to talk about *the* world because we only have interpretations; and there are so many, according to time, place and culture and depending on tradition; therefore, all we can do is try to understand and give credit to each other's language games and modes of intelligibility (cf. social constructionism).

Pragmatism contra spectator theory of knowledge

So, relativists seem to assume that that there is 'nothing outside the text'; that statements and theories are not about the world and can refer only to each other. However, is language the only game in town? Of course, our theories, opinions and beliefs are wrought, expressed in language, but it remains to be seen if knowledge and science are restricted to this theoretical and linguistic sphere.

Knowledge will usually be expressed in language, but is it confined to language? Should we not maintain that knowledge and its expression refer to the world; that they represent our relation, our active relation to the world? Does not the statement that a chair is something to sit on express knowledge about a segment of the world, and convey a (possible) active relation to it? Is David's belief that Karen loves him not a reason for him to take some steps? Is coming to know that there is a difference between a bottle of nondescript claret and a bottle of fine Rioja not a condition for acting accordingly, that is, buying the one or the other? Knowledge can be expressed in language, or without language – to sit down is also a token of the knowledge that a chair is something to sit on. Our active contact with the world, our handling of things and participation in events are consequences of and contribute to our knowledge. This notion of activity is an evolutionist (we need knowledge in coping with the world) and pragmatic assumption; it is expressed forcefully already by the American pragmatist philosopher John Dewey in *The Quest for Certainty: A Study of the Relation of Knowledge and Action*:

> Knowing is ... a case of specially directed activity instead of something isolated from practice. [K]nowing is one kind of interaction which goes on within the world (1929/ 1988: 163)

Relativists, fixated on the liguistic reading of knowledge, tend to ignore the *subject–object* relatedness and seem to replace it altogether with *subject–subject* relations, that is, by convention, discussion, mutual understanding and negotiation, and persuasion. They see knowledge and science exclusively as a verbal social practice or institution. The unwarranted step in their reasoning is to conclude that there is nothing beyond socially constructed knowledge, and that science cannot refer to a mind-independent world; that everything matters, except the world. Many relativists acknowledge the importance of practice, but by turning this into an exclusive linguistic social practice they still ignore the object-relatedness, or what others would call the role or the constraints of the world in the production of knowledge. Here is an illustration of this conception of knowledge, a quotation from Steve Fuller:

> Knowledge exists only through its embodiment in linguistic and other social practices. These practices, in turn, exist only by being reproduced from context, which occurs only by the continual adaptation of knowledge to social circumstances. (1989: 4)

We already mentioned a few times that the **correspondence theory of truth**, defended by realists, is one of the relativist's main targets. How can we ever be so sure about the relation between a **belief** and reality, or between a proposition and a state of affairs in the world, if our only access to the world is via beliefs, and we are not in the position to check our beliefs independently, and cannot get out of our knowledge? Traditional realists, writes Gellner (1974: 74) scornfully, 'compare their own ideas with their own ideas and find, much to their satisfaction, that they match perfectly'.

Though realism and relativism take an opposite stand on the question of the possibility of correspondence, they nevertheless share an underlying belief. They both adhere to the notion that knowledge consists exhaustively in beliefs, theories etc., expressed in language, and that science is an exclusively intellectual and theoretical enterprise. This is what the just quoted pragmatist philosopher John Dewey marked as 'the spectator theory of knowledge' (1929/1988; see also next section); what he missed in this traditional epistemology was the important role of being active in the world. Both the realist and the anti-realist down-play this role of action.

Both also share a traditional view of knowledge (and perception) as framed in mental entities. In the case of realism these mental entities (such as sense data, ideas or representations) are the result of observations and are supposed to mediate between ourselves and the world; and in the case of the relativists knowledge is captivated in our own mental entities such as concepts. The idea underlies the 'myth of the given' we encountered already in the previous chapter when dealing with anti-foundationalist attacks, especially by Sellars. It can also be demonstrated when we confront traditional realism with a kind of 'direct' realism that tries to avoid the mental intermediary. We will say more about this fundamental problem of epistemology and perception in the next section, regarding some views on realism.

4.5 Realism and Scientific Realism

Putnam's revision of realism

Traditional realism holds that the terms of scientific theories correspond or refer to real things in the world (for instance, subatomic particles really exist). For many, the major problem with realism is that any theory about the relation between theoretical entities and the world is, well, a theory: the problem just multiplies like Chinese boxes. Put more formally, there is no theory-independent way of assessing whether a theory corresponds to reality, according to this criticism. Hilary Putnam's *internal realism* (1981, 1987) tried to overcome the dilemma of realism versus relativism. His slogan is 'The mind and the world jointly make up the mind and the world' (Putnam, 1981: xi). One of his targets is the classical realist notion of intrinsic, mind-independent properties that is assumed in the traditional realist view that such properties should fit with theoretical terms.

Putnam (1990) argues that it is not possible to describe the world in an absolute way, independent of a human perspective. That such a 'God's eye view' is inaccessible, however, does not, he thinks, necessarily lead to relativism.

> [O]ur image of the world cannot be 'justified' by anything but its success as judged by the interests and values which evolve and get modified at the same time and in interaction with our evolving image of the world itself ... On the other hand ... the world is not the product of our will – or our dispositions to talk in certain ways either. (Putnam, 1990: 29)

Putnam's internal realism then parts way with traditional objectivist realism, and allows for conceptual relativity. There is no such thing as a ready-made world; rather it depends on the knowing subject; reference, the correspondence between mind and world, is interest-relative, and cannot be objectively or intrinsically determined. The concept of truth is redefined along the lines set out by the American pragmatist philosopher C.S. Peirce: truth is a kind of limit; it is what we would accept in ideal circumstances, that is, when we knew all. This means that the correspondence idea of truth as correspondence with external pre-existing reality is rejected, and naive or metaphysical realism is replaced by a pragmatic criterion. Rationality, the seeking for truth, is a human activity, guided by values that cannot be reduced to objective states of affairs.

Putnam's account of 'natural kinds' underscores this. The taxonomies science creates (like the periodic table of the elements, or classification of the animal kingdom) are, on the one hand, discoveries of the real, ontologically necessary nature of things, on the other hand, dependent on historical and subjective conceptual frames. They can be revised without entirely rejecting or eliminating previous views. The medieval proto-scientist, who thought that the nature of gold was that it was yellow, and the modern scientist, who defines it by its atomic number, are both talking about the same reality. However, the way they talk about it is interest-relative and determined by historical context. There are no things, or causes, in themselves; what words refer to, or what counts as a cause, depends on the interests of the investigator. In this way the world is the joint product of the mind and the world.

It will come as no surprise that many other philosophers (e.g. Devitt, 1997) consider Putnam's notion of 'interest relativity' too much of a concession to relativism. Putnam (1999) himself has amended his views (as he was couragous to do more than once in his career) and now seems to opt for a form of 'direct realism', or 'natural realism' as he likes to call it. Before we take up 'direct realism' we must grasp the problem of 'indirect realism' and a version of 'scientific realism'.

Indirect realism

Next to the ontological claim that there is a world independent of mental activity, realists traditionally suppose that we experience the world by mediation of mental entities – **sense data**, images, ideas, representations, concepts, beliefs, thoughts. Seeing a tree is having an idea, or representation, or concept of a tree. In the realist version, the image or **representation** is caused by the world. In this way correspondence and objectivity is secured. This process of knowledge-acquisition by perception is 'indirect' because the realist supposes that the only way to perceive the world is by this interface of a kind of mental entity. The *locus classicus* of this indirect realism, for obvious reasons also called 'representational realism', is John Locke's statement:

> Since the mind, in all its thoughts and reasonings, hath no other immediate object but its own ideas, which it alone does or can contemplate, it is evident that our knowledge is only conversant about them. Knowledge then seems to me to be nothing but the perception of the connexion of an agreement, or disagreement and repugnancy of any of our ideas. (1690/1959: bk. iv, ch. 1, sect. 1 and 2)

Recall, however, that the philosopher Wilfrid Sellars discredited as a myth (see Chapter 3) the supposition that the directly given sensory part of perception is at the same time a representing mental thing, and therefore also a foundational piece of knowledge. It is a myth to think that when we see the colour green, the world gives us an idea or a belief that there is something out there which has the colour green, and that this belief is true because it is given to our mind by the world.

This is a bridge too far, according to Sellars, because a belief is a piece of knowledge and is therefore part of a whole web of beliefs; in this case that there is something out there, and that it is green and not blue or red, that I see it with my own eyes, etc. In short, this is knowledge that is in no way justified by the meeting between the world and my senses. The idea or belief is not the event of the stimulation of the senses, but is a knowledge claim; it is a *judgement* and therefore belongs to a 'logical space of reasons' (Sellars, 1963: 169). Whereas the visual stimulation is an *event* or a state of affairs in the world; it does not have truth conditions, it just is there or is happening, or it does not. If there is anything that can be held as a objectively given, it is definitely not the belief.

Consequently, because observational beliefs cannot be taken as given and as corresponding to the world, they cannot be seen as appropriate **foundations** of objective knowledge or scientific theories. And so Sellars's exposure of the myth undermined, as we have seen in the previous chapter, empirism and logical positivism which rested heavily on the idea that observational beliefs are given and that statements which cover these beliefs as closely as possible (as in 'protocol' statements) therefore can be trusted.

Since the correspondence relation between a mental entity and a piece of the world was depreciated as a mysterious bond, and foundationalism was discarded, many contemporary philosophers, like Rorty, who claimed to follow Sellars, and like social constructionists, concluded that what we take as the deliverance of the senses is in fact framed in concepts of our mind; that we cannot get beyond these concepts; that objective empirical knowledge is, therefore, an illusion; and reference to the world-outside is out of order.

This started an idealistic or a relativistic train of thought. Because we cannot say anything about a reference to a world outside our mind we are left with our own concepts and classifications, that is, knowledge constructed by ourselves. The best knowledge we can get cannot be other than knowledge that belongs to a coherent network of beliefs, and because those beliefs are language-driven, as these philosophers think, they are intrinsically social by nature. The conception of 'experiencing the world' should be replaced by 'understanding one another'. Therefore, 'truth', if you want to keep the word at all, means at the most something like 'social aproval'; rationality is being negotiated, is local and wrought in history; facts are social constructions; etc. Though in this anti-realistic frame of mind mental entities cannot, of course, be taken as mediating between us and the world (since reference to the world and therefore mediation is out of the question), mental entities still are the only ingredients of knowledge we have. And in this conception of the priority of mental entities, you could say, that anti-realists, again, share a notion with realists.

Scientific realism

Sellars himself, however, did not explain away the sensory part of experience; on the contrary he tried to account for the sensibility to the world. The observationally 'given' conceived as a foundational piece of knowledge may be a myth, but we nevertheless have to admit, according to Sellars, that the world impinges on our senses. There is a world out there; we take part in it; and we somehow experience the world. How to explain this, without falling into the trap of the myth? We still have to face the problem, how we should account for the process of experience. Sellars himself expressed a kind of *scientific realism*. This kind of realism creates a dichotomy between everyday perception and the 'real' underlying nature of the world. The problem is known in one form as Eddington's 'two tables': the manifest table we see and chop our vegetables on, versus the table as described by quantum physics, a void filled with subatomic particles. The objectivist line holds that only physical properties (the 'primary qualities' as the empiricist Locke called them) are real. Sellars (1963; see also Chapter 1), too, relativized the manifest image and preferred the scientific image. At first sight, objectivism seems to vindicate naive realism, the belief in the reality of everyday objects, through science; science tells us that the world really exists and that it is no figment of our imagination; it dispels the idealist, anarchist, relativist doubts about the reliability of our knowledge of the world. However, it undermines in fact the legitimacy of everyday experience (Putnam, 1987) by correcting and replacing it with scientific concepts.

A prominent defender of scientific realism is Richard Boyd (1984), who formulated four central theses of scientific realism (see Box 4.4).

BOX 4.4 Scientific realism

1 *Theoretical terms* in scientific theories (that is, non-observational terms) should be thought of as putatively referring expressions; that is, scientific theories should be interpreted 'realistically'.
2 *Scientific theories*, interpreted realistically, are confirmable and in fact are often confirmed as approximately true by ordinary scientific evidence interpreted in accordance with ordinary methodological standards.
3 The historical *progress* of mature sciences is largely a matter of successively more accurate approximations to the truth about both observable and unobservable phenomena. Later theories typically build upon the (observational and theoretical) knowledge embodied in previous theories.
4 The *reality* which scientific theories describe is largely independent of our thoughts or theoretical commitments. (Boyd, 1984: 41–2, italics added)

The problem with these tenets is that probably almost every modern realist would modify one or more of them. But many contemporary philosophers working in the field of cognition follow a kind of scientific realism, functionalist philosophers of mind and connectionists, for instance. Philosophy of mind or cognition is the subject-matter of later chapters in this book, but let us here, in the context of realism, follow the line of thought a little further. To avoid the pitfall of the given, modern cognitive philosophers maintain that the problematic judgemental sense of a mental entity, an idea, a belief or knowledge, should be seen as or replaced by a cognitive *process*. We should look for what happens in the world of our cognitive apparatus as an effect of what is the case and the cause outside; and we should not allow mental figments, such as judgements, interfere in this causal process. Some do this by introducing a cognitive network of representations in the shape of a formal cognitive code, a 'language of thought' or a syntax (Jerry Fodor and the functionalists). Others contend that this abstract language 'of thought' still harbours too much of the old myth, and they therefore stick to the mechanisms of brain processes (Churchland and neuro-cognitivists). We will clarify these points in Chapters 7 and 8.

Direct realism

So, in both cognitive theories, about a language of thought and about the goings-on in the brain, processes play the central role in the sense that they are caused by the world. Both theories can be called realistic. Nevertheless, they still are being criticized (e.g. Putnam, 1999) for the notion of an indirect process, an interface between ourself and the world; in the one case, a network of representations, in the other, neural networks. This disapproval leads to a revival of 'direct realism'. This is a view of realism quite different from traditional 'indirect realism', as understood by classical epistemologists (or philosophers of perception) like the empirist John Locke. Many modern (cognitive) psychologists endorse his representationalism, as we already suggested in the previous paragraphs; they advocate the conception of an intermediary (be it a mental entity, or a cognitive or brain mechanism) and they maintain a gap between the perceiver and the world. It creates the problem of the cognitive relationship between the representation and the object. Another worry is how to avoid the **homunculus**, the 'little man' in the system. When trying to explain along this line of representation, for instance, the perception of an object outside, you unexpectedly are confronted by a second problem, a duplication of the first, that is, the internal perceptual problem, how this representing cognitive entity is perceived, or who or what is cracking the brain code (see Chapter 6; see for discussions on theories of cognition without mental representations: Chapters 8 and 9).

glossary

Direct realism can already be found in the philosophy of the Scottish philosopher Thomas Reid (1710–1796) who criticized the British empirists, and the pragmatist philosopher-psychologist William James (1842–1910). Among contemporary philosophers who favour (versions of) direct realism we mention just a few: Dancy (1985), McDowell (1994) and the recent Putnam (1999). There is also a resemblance between this philosophical direct realism and J.J. Gibson's (1979) ecological theory of 'direct perception' (see also the conclusion of this chapter). Next to the realist assumption that there is a world of objects and properties independent of our experiences, the direct realist's thesis is that in perceiving an object and its properties we are directly aware of its existence and its properties.

This sounds rather *naive*, and therefore the *scientific* version would be preferable, making it possible that some properties we perceive will not be found in the world independent of perceiving beings, as is the case with colours, for instance (though there are philosophers who defend that colours exist in reality; see for a recent debate Byrne and Hilbert, 2003). This means that the scientific version allows some distance between us and the world. But this distance is not as wide as the gap that is created by indirect realism, where mental entities like sense data, ideas or representations are supposed to be the intermediairies, and at the same time import the problem of how they relate to objects in the world. The gap and the self-created problem are prey to be dramatized by opponents of the realist assumption and, as we have seen, open the door for dangerous moves – deny the independent world (idealism), or maintain that we cannot know what and how the world 'really' is, or downplay the subject-object relation. Mental entities turn into a linguistic affair, and in the end our knowledge appears to be completely human-made. Something like this is the relativist's position. And thus, by its indirectness, indirect realism runs the risk of breeding relativism.

BOX 4.5 Realism

- *Indirect realism*: the realist supposes that the only way to perceive the world is through mediation by mental entities. Knowledge is having a belief or a mental representation, and these supposedly correspond with objects in the real world (see Box 4.2).
- *Direct realism*: the object is perceived directly without intervening mental representations; organism and environment are directly coupled through perception–action cycles without mental mediation.

So, the scientific or sophisticated version of direct realism seems to be the best option to ward off the spectre of relativism. It has the advantage that it supports the normal worldview of many scientists themselves, as well as that it takes common sense and everyday experience seriously, that is, to a certain extent. The supposition is that there is a mind-independent world; and that the human animal has developed a perceptual system that is able to take care of what there is and what is happening. How exactly this system works may be not crystal clear, but we understand enough of the global picture to prefer this option. By supporting this sophisticated realism one is not committed at all to disregard the distance and latitude that concepts and classifications create in our explanations. Of course, there is much construction in our explanations and theories, but not as we like it. The world somehow constrains our liberty (McDowell, 1994).

Here lies an answer to a criticism by Richard Rorty. Opposing John McDowell's *Mind and World* (1994), Rorty complains that (direct) realists always 'treat perceptual judgments as a model for all judgments'. Normally, scientific statements and at least the statements in social sciences and the humanities are much more complicated than simple mundane perceptual judgements:

> To say that 'this is red' is 'directed towards the world' or 'answerable to the world' is intuitively plausible. But such phrases seem less applicable if one's paradigm of a belief is 'We ought to love one another,' or 'There are many transfinite cardinals,' or 'Proust was only an effete petit bourgeois.' (Rorty, 1998: 138)

But again, a realist need not close her eyes to the constructive leeway of explanations and theories. Though there is the mind-independent world, the distance of reference to the world might be rather large, especially in the domains of the social sciences, literary criticism or ethics.

Devitt against 'fig-leaf realism'

A warning by Michael Devitt might help here. In his *Realism and Truth* (1997) he defends the maxim that we have to 'distinguish the metaphysical (ontological) issue of realism from any semantic issue' – the first is the ontological assumption of the existence of an independent world, the latter is the epistemological issue of meaning or reference to the world, the issue of how we come to know the objects of the world. And he insists in the next maxim that we have to 'settle the realism issue before any epistemic or semantic issue'. It is his opinion that the main arguments against realism start from the wrong end, from the epistemological a priori that we cannot refer to the world at all, that our knowledge and explanations are constrained by humans and communities, and by them alone, and that therefore there *is* no mind-independent world, or one not to be worried about. Though Devitt underwrites most of the epistemological contentions of anti-realists like Kuhn (e.g. theory-ladenness), he blames them for not settling the ontological question first, and thus for renouncing his last mentioned maxim (1997: ch. 9).

glossary   Devitt takes the settling of **ontology** seriously by specifying what the world consists of – common sense and physical scientific things. He is motivated to do so, he writes, because many anti-realists admit that there is a world outside our thinking, but that this is the only statement we can make about it. We cannot go beyond human-made decribing, conceptualizing, or classifying that world, they contend. So, if there is a world outside we cannot know it at all. Here we meet the limit of realism, the 'thing-in-itself', as the philosopher Kant proclaimed. Devitt calls it a 'fig leaf' or 'weak-realism', no realism worth fighting for (Devitt, 1997); it figures mostly as the introduction to idealism and constructionism where ontology is swallowed up by epistemology.

To sum up

It may not be necessary, however, to specify in advance, metaphysically and a priori, what the furniture of the world is. Although Devitt's maxim might be the right move, there is, perhaps, no need for his ontological reductionism. We encounter, explore and explain the world on many levels (see Chapter 2.5), and perhaps this practice allows a liberal ontological stance by which it is permitted to ascribe 'independent' existence, in a certain sense, to things, properties, processes, and functions of, for example, the social segment of the world (e.g. income tax, a nuclear anti-proliferation act, the enemy), of the psychological (rage, sense of humour, imagination), or the ethical context (perfidy, loyalty).

Because history teaches us that in the past many 'things' were taken to exist, such as phlogiston and witches, which we nowadays do not accept anymore, there is no need for the radical constructionist conclusion that common sense and scientific terms do not refer to things in the world, at all. Though our theories might be wrong in certain aspects, certain objects are far from uncontested (e.g. souls), and even some modern objects might be debunked in the future (let's say, for the sake of argument, superstrings); there is an overwhelming amount of things in the world we live by succesfully, and we have enough good reasons to suppose that, by doing science, we learn more about brain, animal behaviour, space, the earth, evolution, etc.

So, being and acting in the world seems to give confidence in some notion of realism. Pragmatist philosophers took inspiration from this worldly attitude. In the last section

of this chapter we turn to pragmatism. But under the same banner of **pragmatism**, glossary
positions may be different. Richard Rorty, who impresses many modern social constructionists and stimulates discussion on hermeneutics, adheres to a rather different
notion of pragmatism than, for example, the philosopher of science Ian Hacking.

4.6 Pragmatism

Rorty's pragmatism

According to Richard Rorty a major consequence of pragmatism is that it avoids the
metaphysical dichotomy of appearance versus reality. It is the traditional view that
science addresses the eternal reality behind appearances, which is supposedly independent of human interests, that science unveils things as they are in themselves. This
theory sees the whole mental apparatus of beliefs and representations as reflections of
reality. The pragmatist alternative is that beliefs are tools for dealing with reality. They
represent nothing, so that no correspondence theory of truth and no account of the
mapping between **representation** and reality is necessary or even possible. Pragmatism glossary
is, according to Rorty, *anti-representationalism;* truth is not a correspondence between
language and reality, because there cannot be such comparison between them: **truth** glossary
is relative to a given language system, and cannot be elevated out of the linguistic
realm. Knowledge is no 'Mirror of Nature', but derives from language only: nature
emerges in discourse. Therefore conversation is 'the ultimate context in which knowledge is to be understood' (Rorty, 1979: 389). Objectivity is not a matter of beliefs
corresponding to objects, but a matter of getting together with other subjects: 'there
is nothing to objectivity except intersubjectivity' (Rorty, 1998: 71/2). Rorty's reading
of pragmatism, and he is aware that he separates out some ideas of pragmatism for his
own purposes (1998: 292), is this anti-representationalism and anti-correspondence,
and thus anti-realism: 'no image of the world projected by language is more or less
representative of the way the world really is than any other'; even natural science is
'simply one more image'; there is no '*one* image that corresponds to reality' (1998:
293/4, original emphasis). James's and Dewey's transformed empiricism and realism,
without representationalism and without correspondence, is still too much empiricism and realism for Rorty. Rorty's pragmatism is one of linguistic practice and conversation; it has nothing to do with everyday activity in the world or with scientific
practice or investigation (cf. Diggins, 1994: 416 ff.).

Other interpretations of pragmatism

Ian Hacking (1983), on the contrary, claims that *experimental work* provides the
strongest evidence for scientific realism. Experimental physicists are generally realists
about the theoretical entities they use; and why not? Using these entities, for instance

electrons, means manipulating them, building new kinds of device and exploiting the causal properties of the entities to explore nature further. Entities are tools not for thinking but for doing. Hacking distinguishes realism about entities and realism about theories. Realism about theories is perhaps less central to the concern of the active scientist; it is a belief in the aims of science, a value, and perhaps a matter of psychology. Anti-realism is popular among onlooker-philosophers, endorsing what he, following the pragmatist philosopher Dewey (1929/1988), calls the 'spectator theory of knowledge' (Hacking, 1983: 274). But the lesson is: 'think about practice, not theory' (ibid.: 274). So, Hacking's pragmatism is, indeed, practice, intervention (see Chapter 5.5).

Rouse (1987) argues, in the same vein, that truth and reality only figure within a background of scientific and everyday practices. The idea of knowledge as tool for action rather than a mirror of mind-independent reality tallies with the rejection of representations and sense data as the stuff knowledge is (entirely) made of. This relational view of knowledge, reality and truth is characteristic of the pragmatists. As Rouse puts it:

> [W]hat there is cannot be intelligibly separated from what we can encounter through the successes and failures of specific practical engagements, where scientific theorising is among these practices. (1987: 211)

4.7 Conclusion: Knowledge as Skill

In the philosophy of science attention has shifted recently from a view of knowledge as (linguistic and theoretical) representations, to knowledge as skills and practices; that is, it has shifted from representation to manipulation. Hermeneutics and social constructionism emphasize the indispensability of prejudice, tradition, and human concerns in science, and agree with post-positivists like Kuhn on the collective nature of science. Pragmatism considers scientific knowledge as a matter of actively disclosing the world rather than merely picturing it. This suggests a more pragmatic, interactive view of reality, as dependent on practical exploration, than is implied in the classical realist tenet of a monolithic mind-independent reality that can be mentally represented: 'science [is] a pragmatic exploratory coping with the world' (Rouse, 1987: 149). The pragmatic success of science is not a matter of a theory or mental representation corresponding with a mind-independent world, but is grounded in pre-reflexive practice: the real is what we manipulate (Hacking, 1983; cf. Von Wright, 1993). Hacking emphasized the original contribution of the laboratory to science – empirical success, the creation of new phenomena depends on technical innovations, not only on new theories. The laboratory is a micro-world, the only place where data are created, so in this sense research is local, not universal: data are not everyday phenomena, but are created in a specific practice, not to be found anywhere in the world outside the laboratory. That data are created in specific domains by specific skills does not mean that they are unreal fictions. We will come back to this practical view of science in the next chapter where we will discuss the social import of laboratory practices (section 5.5).

Rouse (1987) argues that Kuhn's notion of **paradigm** involves such shared skills, and glossary shared instruments – a field of practices rather than a logical edifice built out of propositions. The Kuhnian picture suggests that research is first and foremost a matter of using research tools, and of learning to extrapolate from concrete cases (exemplars). Rouse connects this with what he calls 'practical hermeneutics' (inspired by Heidegger); it holds that skills ('knowing how') precede theoretical knowledge ('knowing that'). The implications of this view are that all knowledge is local, situated, from the perspective of an embodied agent, and rooted in practical daily activities (see Chapter 9.3).

When we abandon, Rouse argues, the traditional idea of truth as a correspondence in the sense of a 'copy' relation between theory and reality, and acknowledge that reality is only grasped in dealing with the world through practical skills (the real is what we manipulate), then it becomes clear that practical hermeneutics does not make the world as it is (that is, in an idealistic or relativistic sense), but allows it to show itself the way it is. There is no such thing as uninterpreted reality, apart from human practices; the world is what shows up in our practices.

Engineering, not theorizing, is the best proof of scientific realism, is Hacking's (1983) thesis. As Rouse (1987) puts it, the world reveals itself under humanly created conditions; laboratory practices are in his view grounded in the ordinary pre-reflexive practices of the kind Heidegger and Dreyfus described in their criticism of the Cartesian theatre of the mind. Thus, in recent views on the philosophy of mind, as we will show in Chapter 9, the focus is on interaction, and on information-for-action rather than on picturing the world. The interaction of environment and exploration constitutes reality. Information is information for action, embedded in exploratory practices which are a precondition for any talk about reality or environment.

Mind-world activity

In an interesting overview, Arthur Still and James Good (1998) picture how aspects of different traditions in philosophy and psychology, especially theories of perception, come together in this action-directed view on reality. According to the pragmatist philosophers William James and John Dewey, our mind and the world are not separate moments of reality (as in empiricism and the behaviourist S-R conception); it is only in their active relationship, that is, through activities and manipulations of the perceiver (by touching, moving around, hearing etc.) that the world can be experienced as an environment of objects.

Much inspired by James, the phenomenologist Edmund Husserl concluded that we are related to the world through constant motion; it is by this fundamental (ontological) relation that our everyday, what he called, Life-World (*Lebenswelt*, Husserl, 1970: 104) can come into being.

In his 'ecological' approach to perception J.J. Gibson (1979) maintained in an analogous way that kinesthesis and locomotion, and the way the information in light is structured and changes with the perceivers, play an essential role in seeing objects under different aspects. To stress this he invented the concept 'affordance' (instead of static 'sensations' 'caused' by objects); it highlights the relational structure, the way in which both the environment and the perceiver work together to make perception possible. His theory of perception is about whole 'perceptual systems', including motor systems, not only about senses.

For obvious reasons Still and Good (1998) called this fundamental coupling (in which the social is a third component) 'mutualism'. In Chapters 8 and 9 we will hit upon more appreciations of these active mind-world relations.

Naturalism

Emerging from the failed quest for a universal criterion for scientific rationality is the 'naturalistic turn' in the philosophy of science. Philosophers have to some extent turned away from the a priori specification of universal standards, and have started looking at how the actual practice of science is done (Callebaut, 1993). Instead of trying to lay a priori foundations, on which science has to build, it is argued now that philosophy is continuous with science, and has to elucidate and systematize its results a posteriori. Especially with respect to perception, belief-fixation and knowledge, psychology is an important supplier of **naturalistic** insights. One-time philosophical **epistemology** has turned partly into cognitive psychology and philosophy of mind, as we will see from Chapter 6 on.

Finally, the bogeyman of relativism has disappeared. It is realized that the absence of a universal criterion for rationality is not the same as the absence of rational discourse.

glossary

FURTHER READING

Burr, Vivien (1995) *An Introduction to Social Constructionism*. London: Routledge.
Gergen, K. (1999) *An Invitation to Social Construction*. London: Sage.
A reader on social constructionism in psychology: relational selves, practices and emancipation.

O'Grady, Paul (2002) *Relativism*. Chesham: Acumen.
A well-reasoned introduction.

Bleicher, J. (1980) *Contemporary Hermeneutics*. London: Routledge & Kegan Paul.
An introduction to hermeneutics with selected readings.

Delanty, G. and Strydom, P. (2003) *Philosophies of Social Science: The Classic and Contemporary Readings*. Maidenhead: McGraw Hill.
A recent well-edited collection with readings from various traditions.

5. SOCIOLOGY AND
PSYCHOLOGY OF SCIENCE

PREVIEW: In this chapter the discussion in Chapter 4 will be continued. Since the quest for universal criteria for objectivity has failed, the upshot of the previous chapter was that, though forms of subjectivity play a role in the way science is done, scientists are not at the mercy of all-out relativity, since successfull coping plays an important role in the cognitive relationship between the scientist and the world. In this chapter we will widen the scope by paying attention to, first, the social background of scientific knowledge and practice. This has been the subject-matter of the *sociology* of science. Secondly, we will review some research on the *psychology* of science, much less integrated into a field of its own, but nevertheless a promising contribution to studies on scientists and their work.

5.1 Introduction

In Chapters 3 and 4 we saw that in the philosophy of science concern for the purity of science and demarcation of science from non-science yielded to the study of the (pragmatic) relation between the knower and his or her world. Can we claim disinterested objectivity for our statements or theories, or are the subjects themselves the measure of things and are they somehow dominantly present in what they assert? Is knowledge only related to the observer and the knower and the group he or she belongs to, or does it refer to the observer-independent world? Philosophers of science have developed arguments for either realism or relativism, but they have also tried to overcome the dichotomy. Most philosophers of science have come to understand that somehow time and community make a difference, although the extent of this subjective influence is under discussion.

glossary The arguments of philosophers boil down to the thesis of the underdetermination of theories by the evidence (Duhem, Quine) or, put differently, the thesis of the **theory-ladenness** of observation (Hanson, Kuhn). These theses do not immediately prove that social factors *completely* explain scientific claims; if no evidence is conclusive for the acceptance of a theory, the door is in principle open to *all* kinds of evidential support, not only social factors (Laudan, 1990: ch. 6). On the other hand, we no longer have grounds to exclude social studies of science, as happened under the regime of positivism. For the positivists carefully distinguished the *justification* from the *discovery* of theories and assumed that the context of justification was the same at all times and places. As contrasted with the positivists' ideal, however, it is held nowadays that we cannot make a sharp distinction between two contexts or domains with their own independent stories, one in which methodology of rationality and logic brings about objective scientific knowledge, and one where cultural, social, political and economic interests and events generate possibly erroneous and partial beliefs.

Philosophers of science have entrenched themselves in the domain of epistemology, working on theories about the nature of knowledge in general. The positivistic assumption was that science developed in a continuous and natural trajectory towards progress and enlightenment and that the production of objective scientific knowledge is beyond and without social explanation. In the light of this assumption history was considered of no great importance because the latest state of the art always carried more truth than before; and the history of science could be no more than a set of anecdotes of superseded theories. According to this so-called *internal* history, science is an autonomous enterprise above and beyond the petty social interests of scientists; it develops apart from the general history of society, it has its own progress and its own rules. Science *is*: and *has to be* (normatively) a pure, value-free, detached and rational search for truth. However, with the alternative idea of the constitutive character of the social and historical origins of science – meaning that the shaping and therefore understanding of scientific knowledge is conditional on the historical situation – the positivistic ahistoric image of science came to be substituted.

In this chapter we will present the ideas of *sociologists* of science, who take the relativity of scientific knowledge as their point of departure. They investigate the historical context and determinants of scientific theories or, more radically, the 'socially constructed' character of science. The ideal is to explain science and knowledge sociologically. Attention is paid to the social factors that produced them, rather than to the truth and justification of these beliefs.

The nineteenth century social philosopher-revolutionary Karl Marx can be considered as one of the inspirators of the idea. The next section of this chapter will deal with the concept of ideology, proposed by Marx, which was meant to designate the societal character of science and culture in general. For Marx 'ideology' referred to the false ideas of the opponents of the working class; he was convinced that those ideas were determined by the socio-economic position of those who held them. Karl Mannheim, however, gave the concept a general epistemological interpretation and eventually preferred the concept of 'sociology of knowledge'. The concept of ideology inspired leftist social scientists to criticism of established ideology, which the Frankfurt School developed into a 'Critical Theory'.

The three other sections deal with sociology of science 'proper'. There happen, however, to be different brands. To give some order to the mass of studies in the field we distinguish three categories: the social history of science or the macroscopic approach, broad cultural and socio-economic influences on the development of science (5.3); the sociology of knowledge, social epistemological claims about scientific knowledge itself (5.4); and the sociology of practice or the microscopic approach, recent interest in what scientists do in their laboratories in their production of facts, and in the instruments and experiments they use (5.5). In the 1980s and 1990s social studies of science and technology became very influential in academic circles. Some drew radical conclusions and developed political anti-science ideas from them. The so-called 'science wars' then ensued (5.6).

In the last section of this chapter we consider *psychological* aspects of scientific knowledge. The psychology of science is psychology's contribution to the so-called 'science of science'. This section can also be seen as a stepping stone to the next chapter about the philosophy of mind or cognition which will be presented as a naturalized epistemology, being of fundamental importance for the understanding of the mind-world relationship and the development of (scientific) knowledge.

5.2 Ideology and the Critical Theory

The German revolutionary and political economist Karl Marx (1818–1883) did not invent the term **ideology**. He took it from French philosophers of the eighteenth-century glossary
Enlightenment who criticized the residue of religion and superstition in scientific thought. Marx introduced the term in 'Die deutsche Ideologie', a critical study of the German social and political situation at the time. He held that the socio-economic structure of a society determines its legal and political organization and institutions, its art and literature, and its moral, religious and scientific ideas. Ideology, the production of ideas, reflects the material basis of a society. What a person thinks, how he judges and what motivates him to act stem from his ideology, which is a reflection of his social and economic position. And because ideology conforms to a certain social position, it is partial, it distorts the truth. Individuals and socio-economic groups are unaware of their partiality, and believe that their moral and political views are objectively and universally true and right: they have a 'false consciousness'. Only in a classless society, the ideal of the working class, will the right worldview be gained.

This notion of false consciousness allowed the Hungarian-German sociologist Karl Mannheim (1893–1947) to make the distinction between the 'particular' and the 'total conception of ideology' in his famous 'Ideology and utopia' (in Mannheim, 1936). At first, the particular conception was intended to expose certain ideas of opponents.

These were stamped as lies, distortions or half-truths, to be interpreted in the light of, and as a function of, the social position and interests of those who proclaimed them.

Within the 'total conception of ideology', however, ideas are interpreted as a function of the 'life situation' of the subject. Here we are not interested in specific ideas but in the whole worldview of the subject. This may seem only a slight difference, but Mannheim had a deeper distinction in mind: not so much the content of certain ideas, but the form, the way in which knowledge in general happens to develop as a function of the life situation. What he intended was a broadening of the original concept of ideology in the direction of a *sociology of knowledge* (*Wissenssoziologie*), a 'method of research in social and intellectual history' (Mannheim, 1936: 69) which is concerned with the mutual relationships of the two histories. The general basic assumption is that 'the thought of every group', not only of your adverseries and even of yourself, is seen as 'arising out of its life conditions' (ibid.).

Sociology of knowledge should be non-evaluative, according to Mannheim. It does not aim at exposing specific lies or distortions but conducts a search into the ways in which, in general, cultural and scientific knowledge are interwoven with life conditions, defined by social and historical circumstances. The subjective, local and changeable nature of every knowledge claim, including your own, is unavoidable. Thought is 'a particularly sensitive index of social and cultural change' (ibid.: 74). (Scientific) thought has no history and domain of its own, apart and independent from its socio-economic determinants. The sociology of knowledge aims at explaining theories from social factors.

Though Mannheim proposed, in 'The sociology of knowledge' (in Mannheim, 1936), to avoid the term 'ideology' as much as possible, the term is still in existence. It has been used, however, rather ambiguously; sometimes it refers to Marx's critique of society and to 'the false ideas' of the class-interested establishment; sometimes it is used merely as a descriptive term to denote some complex of social and political ideas as a whole, such as the Marxist, the liberal, socialist, or Christian-democratic ideology; and sometimes it is even used to refer to a philosophy or a vision about anything whatsoever. In all these shades of meaning the notion of unmasking ideas as subjective or as biased has been more or less preserved.

BOX 5.1   Ideology

The *particular* conception (Marx): the false ideas of a political class (especially the class of capitalists) reflecting its dominant socio-economic position; it supports the political status quo, by picturing this as natural or given. This is a psychological/moral/political interpretation of ideology.	The *total* conception (Mannheim): ideas as a function of the socio-economic position, or 'life'-situation of everyone or every group (workers, bourgeois, capitalists, scientists, whatever).This is a general epistemological interpretation of ideology, resulting in a 'sociology of knowledge'.

The Frankfurt School and Critical Theory

In the wake of Marx and Mannheim neo-Marxist students took exception to the ahistoric, positivistic 'neat' image of science. They claimed that science is a social enterprise and, as such, is part of general history, reflecting interests, and social and cultural change. This was part of the philosophy of the so-called Frankfurt School, the Institute of Social Research in Germany, which came into existence in the mid-1920s. In this Institute the philosophy of Hegel, Marx and other idealist and materialist philosophers and their importance for social theory was much discussed. The staff of this avowedly Marxist organization, among whom Max Horkheimer, Theodor Adorno, Herbert Marcuse and Erich Fromm were the senior and the most famous members, was almost exclusively of Jewish descent and had to emigrate, mainly to the US, when Hitler came to power in 1933; but despite dispersion the Institute managed to remain more or less intact (Jay, 1973). *Critical Theory*, as their social philosophy was called, adopted Marx's critique of Hegel's idealist philosophy, that there is no abstract spirit as such, apart from material circumstances, but that the thoughts of people were rooted in their socio-economic conditions. Their target was the closed systems of thought they saw emerging around them, such as Nazism and Stalinism. Concern for the 'open society' also guided Popper's study of science; his conclusion was rather that science could and should withdraw from the political scene. In the view of the critical social scientists, it was possible to be socialist without being totalitarian, and sociology can and should contribute to social change.

Many of the themes of Critical Theory, popular among the generation of the 1960s, were reiterated and elaborated by Jürgen Habermas, a post-war student of the Frankfurt School, in his famous essay 'Technik und Wissenschaft als "Ideologie"' (Technology and science as 'ideology': published in 1968, see Habermas, 1971) and in other influential work. In his view, the expansion of the state and bureaucracy in capitalist society and the increasing predominance of economic and technological thinking have killed independent thought and rational discussion of values and goals. Critical reason is reduced to *instrumental* reason, the search for the best (technical) means for the attainment of a given end (e.g. economic growth); this end itself, however, is no longer rationally criticized or reflected upon. Values are considered as merely subjective, a matter of taste, and beyond rational debate. Social problems are defined as technical problems, the solution to which is best left to experts (technocracy). By mainly offering technical solutions, science and technology constitute instrumental rationality preeminently. They have become the leading forces in the economic progress of society and the only accepted forms of legitimation. In this way, instrumental reason has reached social life and has become the 'background ideology' of the depoliticized mass of the population, according to Habermas' analysis.

A central theme, especially in Habermas' later work, is the interaction of people. Interaction is symbolically mediated, that is, by language. In this Habermas was influenced by American pragmatists, especially George Herbert Mead (1863–1931) who defended the thesis that the individual mind emerges only in relation to other minds and that this interaction involves shared meanings and communication. Mead's ideas were first of all adopted by Herbert Blumer (1969) in the sociological theory of 'symbolic interactionism'. Things in the world are mediated through their symbolic content, their meaning. They are not inherently meaningful; they become meaningful by the way people act towards them. In their communicative interactions people share meanings or symbols. And so reality and the social order of norms and rules become the creations of actors, and every language user internalizes them. To under-stand the life of a group you have to identify its world of objects, that is, its symbols.

glossary Kindred ideas can be traced in **hermeneutics** and **social constructionism**.

Habermas is especially interested in the problem of rationality, the way we assess knowledge, our arguments and behaviour. For him the kernel of sound rationality is *communicative action* (Habermas, 1984), a way of life in which undisturbed commu-nication, unforced agreement and mutual understanding are possible. The goal of knowledge and science is not to search for correspondence with reality. On the con-trary, there is no independent reality to catch in value-free theories. Habermas advo-cates a **consensus theory of truth** and his view of knowledge and science is that they guide communication about the world. One should arrive at consensus and shared opinion, which is made possible in a communicative community in which individuality and intersubjectivity, knowledge and morality, tradition and critical reflection are combined. This contrasts sharply with the rationality he criticized in his earlier work, as mentioned above, instrumental reason; for this 'partial' rationality places discus-sions about values and interests, wrongly, outside rational discourse.

5.3 Social History of Science

The social origins of science and knowledge, already studied by philosophers and sociologists of more or less Marxist leanings, became a central issue after Kuhn's seminal *Structure of Scientific Revolutions* of 1962. Though the concept of paradigm did not at first carry a socio-economic meaning, in the ensuing debate on changes in scientific knowledge the social aspects of the production of knowledge and the con-cept of ideology or sociology of knowledge became central notions. Anglo-American critics of the **positivistic** picture of science, German philosophers and sociologists, and Marxists joined hands. They all agreed that scientific knowledge cannot be simply 'read off' from the world, but is a socially conditioned phenomenon.

The sheer mass of studies presented as sociology of science or social studies of science is so overwhelming – in the words, not without irony, of critic Mario Bunge (1991–92), 'it has become a growth industry' – that we cannot hope, within the scope of this book, to do justice to all the differences in approach, emphasis or selection of problems. For the sake of some ordering we will briefly set out three broad categories. The first class consists of historical studies of social or cultural influences on the devel-opment of scientific institutions, ways of thinking, concepts, methods, etc., in short, the *macroscopic* approach (this section). The second category is concerned with the production of scientific knowledge itself and the four claims of the so-called 'Strong Programme', prescribing how sociological research of science should be done (5.4).

Third, we discuss the more recent studies on laboratory practice of producing scientific facts – the *microscopic* approach (5.5, see also Box 5.3).

The external or contextual history of science is the oldest tradition in the sociology of science. This consists of studies of science in relation to wider social changes and refers to external factors as the explanation for scientific development. In the 1930s Robert Merton discussed in his famous doctoral dissertation, 'Science, technology and society in seventeenth-century England' (1970), the modes of interplay between society, culture and science. It is, he stated in the original preface, 'an empirical examination of the genesis and development of some of the cultural values which underlie the large-scale pursuit of science' (1970: xxxi). In the 1970 preface he paraphrased the main sociological idea of the book, maintaining that 'the socially patterned interests, motivations and behaviour established in one institutional sphere – say, that of religion or economy – are interdependent with the socially patterned interests, motivations and behaviour obtaining in other institutional spheres – say, that of science' (ibid.: ix). And because the social structure is such that the same individuals have multiple social statuses and roles, scientific and religious, economic and political, it makes for the interplay of seemingly autonomous institutional spheres. Merton's study grapples, for instance, with the much debated question of the interplay of science and religion (Puritanism) in the seventeenth century, the thesis that the new Protestant religious ethos sanctioned natural science with its rationalism and empiricism, assuming that the study of nature enables a fuller appreciation of God's works. Merton stresses that the different institutional spheres, in this case religion and science, are indeed interdependent, and warns against the doctrine that there are universally dominant 'factors' in social development which result in claims to 'the economic determination of historical change', or its technological or political determination (ibid.: x). So he seeks answers to such questions as: 'How does a cultural emphasis upon social utility as a prime, let alone an exclusive, criterion for scientific work variously affect the rate and direction of advance in science?' And, once science has evolved forms of internal organization: 'How do patterns and rates of social interaction among scientists affect the development of scientific ideas?' (ibid.: ix).

Merton was the founder of the sociology of science in the English-speaking world, and numerous studies of the social or cultural history of science followed his example, especially after Kuhn's (1962) work. For instance, studies about the importance of hermeticism and alchemy for the development of science in the late sixteenth century (Yates, 1964, 1972); the social and cultural background of the development of mesmerism (Darnton, 1968); eugenics (Allen, 1976); phrenology (Shapin, 1975; Cantor, 1975); the use of social science in American industry (Baritz, 1960) and its application to other social problems (Napoli, 1981); the influence of *fin-de-siècle* Viennese culture on philosophy and psychoanalysis (Janik and Toulmin, 1973), to name only a few that have become classics.

Other subcategories within this historical branch of the sociology of science tradition are the historical studies of scientific institutions, such as Hahn's study of the French Academie des Sciences (1971); and histories of the scientific professions, such as Geuter's history of the professionalization of psychology in Nazi Germany (1992).

5.4 The Social Character of Scientific Knowledge and the Strong Programme

While studies of the social circumstances and influences on the development of scientific theories, institutions and professions continued to appear abundantly, some sociologists of science began to focus their attention on the construction of scientific knowledge itself, and this can be seen as a shift in the sociology of science. In his analysis of the development of sociology of science, Steve Woolgar (1988) has contended that the old sociology of science – the work of Merton and others – placed emphasis on science as a social institution and on the social relationships between knowledge producers, their social roles and the norms they followed. By doing this such studies adopted a view which was essentially a 'sociology of *scientists*' and neglected the very relationship between *scientific knowledge* and what was still seen, wrongly according to Woolgar, as 'the objective, natural world'. In Woolgar's eyes the old sociologists of science were not radical enough. More recent work, he continued, 'emphasizes the relativity of scientific truth, calls for a sociological analysis of technical content' (1988: 41). What has to be studied is the way scientific knowledge is constructed and how what is considered true or untrue is the outcome not of a neutral and rational endeavour but of a *social* process: the very content of scientific theories, not only the organization of research, is studied as a function of social circumstances.

So, whereas Merton and others concentrated on the institutions or group processes, a new sociology of science endeavoured to explain the very content of scientific theories as products of social factors. This is rather an epistemological concern, a reflection on knowledge itself.

Though Mannheim's and Kuhn's work can be regarded as steps in the direction of the sociology of science as knowledge, rather than the sociology of science in the sense of a community and its institutions, the breakthrough in this social epistemological research was brought about by the so-called 'Strong Programme' in the sociology of scientific knowledge launched by Barry Barnes, David Bloor and Steve Shapin (at the University of Edinburgh).

In his *Knowledge and Social Imagery* (1976) Bloor stated that the sociologist of scientific knowledge employs a definition of knowledge that is rather different from that of the philosopher:

> Instead of defining it as true belief knowledge for the sociologist is whatever men take to be knowledge. It consists of those beliefs which men confidently hold to and live by. In particular the sociologist will be concerned with beliefs which are taken for granted or institutionalised, or invested with authority by groups of men. (1976: 3)

glossary Not the questions of what **truth** is, or how we can arrive at true knowledge – these are the *philosopher's* questions, he writes, but questions such as: 'How is knowledge transmitted; how stable is it; what processes go into its creation and maintenance; how is it organised and categorised into different disciplines or spheres?', are the *sociologist's* questions.

Bloor formulated four tenets (Box 5.2) which define what he baptized 'the Strong Programme in the sociology of knowledge' (Bloor, 1976: 4–5).

BOX 5.2   The Strong Programme in the sociology of knowledge

1   The sociology of scientific knowledge should be causal, that is, concerned with the conditions (social, economic, political, cultural, psychological) which bring about knowledge (claims).
2   It should be impartial with respect to truth and falsity, rationality or irrationality, success or failure.
3   Therefore, it should be symmetrical, that is, the sociologist should invoke the same causes for success and for error in science; he or she should not credit rationality and logic for success stories and blame social factors for failures, as the standard image of science would have it. In a joint article Barnes and Bloor (1982: 22–3) define this requirement as an equivalence postulate, meaning 'that all beliefs are on a par with one another with respect to the causes of their credibility'. So, the sociologist must search for the causes of a scientific belief regardless of whether she or he evaluates the belief as true or rational, or as false and irrational.
4   The sociology of scientific knowledge should be reflexive; the patterns of explanation should be applicable to sociology itself; sociology is not immune to sociological analysis.

In other words, the sociologist of science must not only investigate the beliefs of other scientists, but must also attend to his or her own beliefs. So, the problem for the sociologist of science is how to avoid the danger of self-refutation. It seems that Barnes and Bloor think to escape this danger by their neutral standpoint on matters of truth and rationality, required by the third tenet. According to this they need neither to claim nor to negate the rationality of their own sociological theory; hence they get the chance to circumvent the danger of self-refutation (Derksen, 1985: 122).

The importance of the Strong Programme lies in the renewed attempt to ground relativism and the social construction of all (scientific) knowledge. The concept of truth is essential here. The process of judging a **theory** is an 'internal' one, according [glossary] to Bloor – not a correspondence of the theory *with reality* but of the theory *with itself.* We never have independent access to reality: 'all that we have, and all that we need, are our theories and our experiences of the world'. And by 'experiences' he means 'our experimental results and our sensori-motor interactions with manipulatable objects' (Bloor, 1976: 34).

This seems to bring him near to a refined, pragmatic realism, as becomes clearer when he contends that we cannot altogether abandon the concept of truth. This concept does a number of jobs (ibid.: 35–6). First there is what he calls the discriminatory function – we cannot but order our beliefs. Second, there is the rhetorical function – the labels 'true' and 'false' play a role in argument, criticism and persuasion. The third job of the concept of truth is its 'materialist function', the 'obligatory character of truth' (as one of the fathers of sociology, Durkheim, called it): 'all our thinking instinctively assumes that we exist within a common external environment that has a determinate structure'. And Bloor adds: 'in practice the existence of an external world-order is never doubted' (ibid.: 36).

These ideas are remarkable for their slight undertone of realism, so it seems, as in the following passage where Bloor opposes the anti-relativist 'assumption' that if something is a convention then it is 'arbitrary'. He replies that conventions are not arbitrary at all. The acceptance of a theory by a social group doesn't make it true, because the relation of a belief 'to the basic materialist picture of an independent world precludes this' (ibid.: 38). This seems to ring a realistic bell, indeed. Is there still a distinction between subject and object, between the scientist (knower) and things and events in the world? But then, does not the social construction of scientific knowledge preclude such a distinction? Apparently, even Bloor cannot avoid acknowledging the object side of scientific knowledge. And what about the object of the sociology of science itself? One critic, Roger Trigg (1993: 155), writes that the sociology of scientific knowledge takes as its focus 'the work and assumptions of scientists' and therefore is 'as dependent as any other form of intellectual activity on the idea of truth, and on the separation of subject … and object'.

Relativism in the Strong Programme

On the other hand, the Strong Programme is presented as a radically subjectivist one. Already in the first of Bloor's four requirements, causality, he claims that there is no question of mere social influences, but that social factors *cause* scientific beliefs; that all knowledge, even mathematics – Bloor's case study – is shaped by society. A basic argument is that because 'what we count as scientific is largely "theoretical"' and because theories are not 'given in our experience', but 'give meaning to experience by offering a story about what underlies, connects and accounts for it, … this theoretical component of knowledge is a social component' (Bloor, 1976: 12–13). It is, however, far from clear that the underdetermination of theories by data, as the premise suggests, leads to the conclusion that what is added should be social by nature. Behind this claim is the ubiquitous argument that because science is a social activity, which nobody would deny, science can only be understood in sociological terms. But, as Laudan writes, 'science is a multi-faceted process':

> To argue that because science is a social activity we should view sociology as the primary tool for its investigation is like arguing that because syphilis is a social disease it is only or primarily the sociologist who can have scientific knowledge of syphilis. (Laudan, 1981: 194–5)

The Strong Programme rests on 'a form of relativism', writes Bloor in the conclusion to his book (Bloor, 1976: 142). We saw in the previous chapter that one of the criticisms of relativism is that a relativist cannot discriminate among different theories or knowledge claims. The recipe is – in the words of Gellner (1974: 48) – 'when in Rome, do (and above all, think) as the Romans do'. And Gellner adds that the recipe is empty: 'It is like the injunction "meet me at the town entrance" when the town has countless entrances, or none' (ibid.: 49–50).

According to Bloor, however, his relativism does not mean that 'anything goes'. His 'methodological relativism', summarized in the symmetry and reflexivity requirements, is the opposite of absolutism; no knowledge, not even sociology which designates the determining social factors, is absolute and final. The sociologists of science, Knorr-Cetina and Mulkay (1983: 5), call this 'epistemic relativism', which asserts that knowledge does not just mimic nature but is rooted in a particular time and culture. It should be distinguished, they say, from 'judgemental relativism' which claims that all forms of knowledge are equally valid and that we cannot discriminate among them, a position the authors reject.

Nevertheless, there is reason to be concerned about the consistency of Bloor's Strong Programme. It is strange, to say the least, to claim that the sociology of knowledge is a contribution to scientific knowledge, and at the same time to define that knowledge as 'whatever men take to be knowledge' (Bloor, 1976: 2). Should we not think that knowledge, however fallible, is in principle a claim to universality (not in an absolute sense, though) and deserves to be called knowledge if it is 'properly' grounded? Should not science require that those grounds should be open to public scrutiny and rational debate?

Here we come across the appeal to rationality. This is an appeal to a common sense of rationality; to universal grounds for acceptance or rejection of knowledge and beliefs, their reasons and arguments; to the very conditions that make thinking, believing, arguing, communication, and also science possible in the first place. But what if one relativizes rationality (see Chapter 4.4), arguing that notions of rationality are also local and relative to social contexts and cultures, and denying that there are universal conditions of rationality. This relativity of rationality, which mostly ties in with relativity about truth, about a mind-independent world, and about knowledge, is what Barnes and Bloor (1982) and many others (e.g. Rorty, 1979) maintain. It is the antifoundationalist treatment of knowledge and science, meaning that there is no common ground that holds the conditions for adjudicating knowledge claims. In Chapter 4.4 we already suggested that it might be helpful to distinguish between, on the one hand, the content of a knowledge claim or the substantive view of rationality, for example in a statement like 'All animals and plants have souls', and the methodological view of rationality. In this methodological stance one could try to find some general principles of rationality making possible a rational discussion in the first place. We referred to O'Grady's proposal for a 'core rationality model' (O'Grady, 2002: 140; see also p. 103).

5.5 The Sociology of Scientific Practice

If one is convinced that the content of scientific knowledge is a product of social creation, the step towards direct examination of scientists at work follows naturally.

A precursor of this kind of sociological analysis can be found in a book by the Polish bacteriologist Ludwik Fleck (1896–1961), *Genesis and Development of a Scientific Fact* (1935). This book is in the first place a study of the origin of the concept of syphilis. But that case study also grounds epistemological claims about the origin and nature of *facts,* and about the working of 'collective thinking' (*Denkkollektiv*) and 'style of thought' (*Denkstil*). Fleck argues that the scientist shares in an exchange of ideas and that his or her thoughts are socially constrained by the existing preconceptions and the stock of knowledge of the research group in which he or she participates. Whereas in positivism facts are elements of what is seen as absolute reality and should be cleared of human colouration, in Fleck's conception facts do not exist a priori and are not extracted from or found in the world but are the social and historical products of collective understanding; they cannot get cleared of the human colouration. Kuhn, in *The Structure of Scientific Revolutions* (1962), acknowledged his debt to Fleck's book.

Since the end of the 1970s more studies in the sociology of knowledge show a preference for the *empirical* study of scientific *practice* itself. What is investigated are the judgements, interpretations and activities of the scientists, the practice of the scientific enterprise. Besides preference for the 'microscopic' study of the production of science, these studies tend to give 'priority to the question HOW rather than to the question WHY' scientists act as they do; and they adopt a *constructivist* perspective (Knorr-Cetina and Mulkay, 1983: 7), that is, they take social processes as 'constitutive of the production and acceptance of knowledge claims' (ibid.: 9):

> Whereas we now have fairly detailed knowledge of the myths and circumcision rituals of exotic tribes, we remain relatively ignorant of the details of equivalent activity among tribes of scientists, whose work is commonly heralded as having startling or, at least, extremely significant effects on our civilisation. (Latour and Woolgar, 1979: 17)

This ethnographic analogy is chosen deliberately. What these studies do, especially *Laboratory Life* by Latour and Woolgar (1979), is share the daily life of scientists in the laboratory, in this case the Salk Institute for Biological Studies, a private laboratory in California. The focus of *Laboratory Life* was the 'routinely occurring minutiae' of the work carried out there, for instance the daily encounters, the working discussions, the production of papers and the culture of publication. They called the project an *anthropology of science* for a number of reasons (ibid.: 27 ff.).

First, they provided, just as an anthropologist would do, a body of observations presented as a preliminary research report about the 'belief system and material production' of one specific group of scientists. Second, in order to retrieve the 'craft character of scientific activity', they collected and described the observations in a particular setting because understanding of science had been dogged by the problem that the reports of the scientists themselves are silent about the ways and the circumstances in which science is done and 'conceal the nature of the activity which typically gives rise to their research reports'. The prolonged immersion of an outside observer in the daily activities of scientists was regarded as one of the better ways to answer such questions as, 'How is it that the realities of scientific practice become transformed into statements about how science has been done?' Third, in order to reduce the mystery which surrounds scientific activity they adopted, paradoxically, the anthropological notion of strangeness, that is, they bracketed their familiarity with the object of study and did not take too much for granted. Because 'there are no a priori reasons for supposing that scientists' practice is any more rational than that of outsiders', they made the activities of the laboratory seem as strange as possible, by approaching it in as unprejudiced a way as possible. By framing their methods in this way Latour and Woolgar intended to comply with the requirement of *reflexivity*: to subject their own sociological methodology to the same rigour as they did the objects of their scrutiny.

The constructivist perspective

The constructivist perspective of the book is clear. In order to demonstrate the 'idiosyncratic, local, heterogeneous, contextual, and multifaceted character of scientific practices' (Latour and Woolgar, 1979: 152) the authors want to show the microprocesses at work in the constitution of phenomena such as 'having ideas', the way **beliefs** are created and adopted in a 'group's thinking process'. They point to the use `glossary` of logical arguments and proofs, suggesting that the logical character of reasoning is only part of a complex of interpretation which comprises 'local, tacit negotiations, constantly changing evaluations, and unconscious or institutionalized gestures' (ibid.). One of the conclusions of the work is that 'facts' are socially constructed:

> The construction and dismantling of the same statement can be monitored by direct observation, so that what was a 'thing out there' can be seen to fold back into a statement which is referred to as a 'mere string of words', a 'fiction', or an 'artefact'. (ibid.: 180)

Because of the epistemological assumptions this genetic and microscopic approach within the sociology of knowledge is called 'the programme of *constructivism*' by Karin Knorr-Cetina (1981; Knorr-Cetina and Mulkay, 1983). In opposition to the notion that scientific investigation is descriptive, and that it concerns the factual relations between its products and an external reality, the constructivist interpretation considers the products of science 'as first and foremost the result of a process of (reflexive) fabrication' (Knorr-Cetina, 1983: 119). Accordingly it involves an investigation of 'how scientific objects are produced in the laboratory rather than a study of how facts are preserved in scientific statements about nature' (Knorr-Cetina, 1983: 119). Elsewhere Knorr-Cetina says that 'the world as it is, is a consequence rather than a cause of what goes on in science' (in Callebaut, 1993: 180). Nowhere in the laboratory, she writes, do we find 'nature' or 'reality'; on the contrary, scientists operate upon and within a 'highly preconstructed artifactual reality' and their 'instrumentally accomplished observations intercept natural courses of events' (Knorr-Cetina, 1983: 119); scientific reality is an artefact. The network of decisions and selections of methods, measurements, formulations and interpretations contribute to this artificiality and invest scientific products with a 'decision-impregnated character'. In short, scientific consensus is not fully based on evidential considerations and not fully accounted for in terms of technical rationales.

BOX 5.3   Sociology of science

Historical studies of broad social influences on scientific ideas and institutions; also called the *macroscopic* approach.	The *sociology of knowledge* proper; *epistemological* studies on the social production of scientific knowledge. In this category the so-called 'Strong Programme'.	*Social-psychological* studies on the *day-to-day practice and conventions* of scientific research in laboratories and scientific institutions; also called *microscopic* or *anthropological* approach.

Discourse analysis

Because language is of the utmost importance in the sociological constructivist and in the social constructionist approach (see Chapter 4), discourse analysts came to highlight the importance and even the priority (Mulkay et al., 1983) of their methods for the micro-genetic study of scientific investigation. *Discourse analysis* is a method of analysis of all kinds of discourse, of the government, the police, the classroom, the media. Analysis of scientific discourse shares with the sociology of science, of course, the epistemological conviction that scientists' data, methods and products are a result of social construction. It contends that not only are the conversations and discussions about professional organization, publicity, fund raising, etc. social by nature, but the discussions in learned journals and during congresses, constitutive of scientific knowledge itself, are also social and contingent. Behind the formal scientific literature lie personal and social contingencies. Therefore, a systematic investigation of the social production of scientific discourse is 'an essential preliminary step in developing a satisfactory sociological analysis of action and belief in science' (Mulkay et al., 1983: 194).

In *Science: The Very Idea* (1988) Woolgar reiterated in a radical way his critique on the assumptions of traditions in the history, philosophy, and even (old) sociology of science: namely, the view that science is 'something special and distinct from other forms of cultural and social activity', whereas in Woolgar's view, scientific beliefs and products are 'rhetorical accomplishments'. The traditional idea was 'that the objects of the natural world are real, objective and enjoy an independent pre-existence', whereas Woolgar thinks that the contents of scientific knowledge are social by origin. And he criticizes what he calls 'the persistent notion of knowledge as an individualistic and mentalistic activity', 'the enduring respect for the work and achievements of "great men"', and the complete failure 'to take up the relativist themes' (1988: 26).

Underlying these assumptions, according to Woolgar, there is a basic *fallacy* – the supposed distinction between 'representation' and 'object', such as the distinction between knowledge and facts, between voltmeter reading and voltage, between documentary evidence and the historical situation, between image and reality, between questionnaire response and respondent's attitude (ibid.: 31, his examples). The problem that follows from this fallacy is 'the adequacy of connection' between the two. What he means, of course, is the epistemological idea of truth as correspondence: first, there is the object which, then, is represented; and this representation is understood as corresponding to the object. But, says Woolgar, there is an 'intimate interdependence' of representation and represented object, such that 'the sense of the former is elaborated by drawing on "knowledge of" the latter, and knowledge of the latter is elaborated by what is known about the former' (ibid.: 33). This ideology of representation is the kernel of **objectivism** `glossary` and even sociologists of knowledge, who should know better, sometimes commit this fallacy. Therefore, Woolgar thinks, the fallacy should be deconstructed; we should invert the order: the representation precedes the represented object; and we should resist 'the persistent construal of science as a distinct topic for study, an object "out there", beyond us *qua* observers/inquirers, and essentially separate and distinct from our own writing practices' (ibid.).

Scientific practice

Various authors have expanded in the 1980s and 1990s on the topic of practice and experimentation (Ackermann, 1985; Gooding et al.,1989; Pickering, 1989 and 1992; and many others). In his famous and controversial book about the social construction of quarks, Pickering (1984) contends that modern physics could have developed in another direction; the theory of quarks was not inevitable. Quarks are the result of laboratory work, an intricate meddling and fitting of theories, experiments, apparatus, and data. And this was not determined by the world. It was not determined by the scientists either, in the sense that they did not decide to go in the direction of quarks. The taken direction was, however, a result of social steps. What has been fleshed out in these studies is the relationship, the mutual relationship, between data and theory. Recall that Duhem (and Quine, see Chapter 3) maintained that observations are never judged in isolation, meaning that if data appear to be inconsistent with the theory, one usually revises the theory or the hypotheses. For the sociologists of science (or of experimentation), recommending a practice-oriented approach, the next step is to acknowledge that the practical scientist tunes her or his theory to data; to the instruments with which the data are gathered, to the interpretations; and that all the elements of the scientist's work happen to be interrelated and often interdependent. Hence, data are as instrument-laden as they are theory-laden.

In his book *Representing and Intervening* (1983), Ian Hacking urged a shift in the focus of the philosophy of science from knowing to practice, or in terms of his title, from representing to intervening. In Chapter 4 we introduced him as a pragmatic realist; his realism is, as he says, not about theories but about practice, the practical realism which is the concern of the active scientist. In later work Hacking (1992) elaborated his conception of scientific practice in accordance with this recent trend in the sociology of science, and proposed a 'new vison of what practice is' (Pickering, 1992). Data, he thinks, are not so much *theory* laden but material artifacts, that is, graphs recording variations in time, photographs, tables, displays, productions of instruments used in the laboratory, in short:

> The format for writing up a laboratory report is inculcated in school and preserved, modified, or reinforced – in ways that vary from discipline to discipline – in preprints and journals. The modest uniformity is largely an artifact of how our scientific culture wants to conceive itself and has much to do with our construction of what we call objectivity. (Hacking, 1992: 43)

He offers a taxonomy of three categories of items used in the laboratory – 'ideas', such as questions, background knowledge, theory, hypotheses, and modelling of the apparatus; 'things', such as targets, tools and data generators (e.g. micrographs, scanners, or simply people who count); and 'marks', such as data, assessment, analysis and interpretation. Whereas in traditional conceptions of science knowledge is prior to experimentation, Hacking's picture of science as experimentation is that all these elements can be mutually adjusted. Theories and laboratory equipment 'evolve in such a way that they match each other and are mutually self-vindicating' (Hacking, 1992: 56).

The taxonomy of elements is 'internal' to an experiment; what Hacking has left out (mainly for practical reasons, as he writes) is the broad, rather metaphysical 'worldview', 'style of thought' or 'horizon' which possibly operates in the background and guides thought and practice in general (cf. Merton's work); as well as the social-psychological, political and infrastructural way of experimenters' scientific life; the influence of communications, negotiations (cf. Latour's concerns), and allocation of funds and flow of money (in studies on science policy).

5.6 The 'Science Wars'

Though mindful of the intricate theory and practice relationship, Hacking remains critical of the doctrine of social constructivism. His bundle of articles (1999) offers a forceful argument to fend off the by then proliferous constructivism in social studies of science and technology. One has to distinguish between science as an assemblage of hypotheses and science as an activity; that the activity is social is almost trivial, he writes. Perhaps it is 'the idea of quarks' which is the social construction; the quarks, the objects themselves (*pace* Pickering), 'are not constructs, are not social, and are not historical' (Hacking, 1999: 30, see also 65 ff.). He counters the contructionist's belief that classifications are convenient ways in which to represent what we think the world is with 'a strong sense that the world has an inherent structure that we discover' (1999: 32).

In the 1980s and 1990s the sociologists of scientific knowledge (SSK) and Latour's actor-network theory (ANT) became highly influential in academic circles; numerous science and technology studies (STS) appeared. Bruno Latour, the founder of the French school of sociology of science, and his followers gathered many ideas of the

STS and the SSK in the actor-network theory. Latour's methodological textbook was *Science in Action: How to Follow Scientists and Engineers through Society* (1987). ANT focuses upon the work of scientists and engineers in their endeavour to defend and extend their beliefs, classifications, definitions etc., and to turn them into 'objective knowledge'. Networks are social concentrations of human actors as well as (non-human) machines, instruments, journal articles, grants etc. For this reason 'actants' were substituted for 'actors' in the subsequent jargon. The work of these actants is building the network and extending it, to enroll and to shape allies, to control the definitions, to make predictions indisputable (see 1987: 180–4); in short, to define and claim rationality. Hence, among the heralded principles we find:

> [U]nderstanding what facts and machines are is the same task as understanding who the people are. [I]rrationality is always an accusation made by someone building a network over someone else who stands in the way. (Latour, 1987: 259)

There is much drama in this. From an empirical point of view much science may be done in this social and strategic ways, but to extrapolate this to what science and scientific knowledge is all about may be a bit over the top. The object of ANT and many science and technology studies became (Western) science. Radical cultural and women's studies ('the inherent masculinity of science'), and French postmodernism and decon-structionism joined in. Their message was that science and scientific knowledge was a social enterprise and a matter of convention. All theories were epistemologically on a par and their truths equal to all truth claims: inherently social (see Chapter 4.3). What scientists did was work to expand their network and develop strategies in order to win in the game of scientific rhetoric, discourse, and rationality. Therefore, science was nothing but a social construct; nothing but texts the social interests of which needed to be deconstructed. Radicals developed an anti-(natural) science attitude and jumped to political conclusions – since scientific beliefs cover nothing but social and political interests, the whole game was about power and money. It was, writes one analyst of these decades, Segerstråle (2000: 6), 'as if, the sociologists were the self-appointed psychoanalysists of scientists, knowing their "true" motives, unbeknownst to the scientists themselves'.

In 1994 the marine biologist Paul Gross and the mathematician Norman Levitt took up for the scientists themselves with a book under the telling title *Higher Superstition: The Academic Left and its Quarrels with Science*. This was their first ominous sentence:

> Muddleheadedness has always been the sovereign force in human affairs – a force far more potent than malevolence or nobility.

Their subject was to clean up much of the muddleheadedness in a 'large and influen-tial segment of the American academic community which, for convenience but with great misgiving', they called 'the academic left' (Gross and Levitt, 1994: 3–4). With this label they went after the cultural studies and critiques of postmodernists, radical feminists, traditional Marxists, deconstructionists. They put it bluntly: 'The academic left dislikes science.' The book was followed by a conference of (social) scientists and philosophers of science and the proceedings were edited by the same authors (Gross et al., 1996). The response came in counter-attacks (Ross, 1996), and a polarized climate with pretty much ad-hominem arguments was the result – the 'science wars' had broken out. The war was fueled by a postmodern science criticism, written by the physicist Alan Sokal and submitted to the cultural studies journal *Social Text* (Sokal, 1996a). Although the journal had published it as a serious scholarly article, it was revealed as a parody ('the Sokal Hoax'; see also Sokal, 1996b). Next to flirtations with 'morphogenetic fields', Rupert Sheldrake's 'bizarre' New Age idea, and mysterious suggestions about the connection between quantum field theory and Lacan's psycho-analytic theory, Sokal quoted 'controversial' philosophical pronouncements of Heisenberg and Bohr and asserted that quantum physics was profoundly consonant with postmodern epistemology. Because it contained citations (ironically and in the way of pastiches, of course) of French philosophers and social scientists such as Latour, the feminist Irigaray, Lacan, Derrida, Hippolythe, the French reacted furiously, some accusing the Americans of an anti-France campaign. The fight took place in con-ferences, readers, and more books, and reached the wider public through articles by friends of both sides in newspapers and journals such as the *New York Review of Books*, *Le Monde* and the *Times Literary Supplement* (see Further Reading at the end of this chapter).

5.7 Conclusion: The World and the Social Nature of Knowledge

All the interrelations of elements of theory and practice, all the internal and external influencing factors make up a very complicated picture of science, indeed; much more complicated than philosophers' simple subject-object, as well as abstract realism-relativism considerations, we have to admit. Accepting that knowledge is never absolute, that the prejudices of knowing subjects are involved in the determination of what there is, does not preclude, however, independent counter-pressure from the world, constraining the interpretations, measurements, methods and local decisions scientists may uphold. Just because we do not meet the world in ideas and theories only, and since we do not live in the world only as theorizing and talking creatures, we sooner or later have to act upon our beliefs so that in this sense we cannot arbi-trarily and with impunity believe what we want. It is no naive realism to suppose that knowledge is to be seen as a subject–object relation and that this epistemology need not be replaced by one in which a subject–subject understanding is all there is. Knowledge is fallible, but beliefs and theories, informed and adjusted by our inter-ventions, help us to get a useful picture and a more or less reliable grip on the world, and enable us to live in it. Concepts and conceptual systems are held by humans, but they have referents, are about something outside the knowing subject, the existence and nature of which can be a source of disagreement. We need knowledge about the world that is properly grounded and can be trusted; we have to discriminate between true and false, between the trustworthy and the dubious, in order to be able to act. The very *raison d'être* of science is information about the world – 'securing answers to our questions about how things stand in nature in terms of description, classification and explanation' (Rescher, 1987: 36) – as a preliminary to actions and communication.

Humans have a firm hand in how the 'external' world looks, and pure nature, untouched by humans, is nearly extinct, but we do live in a world which is not altogether a human or scientific creation and of which we too are in part the products. Despite the artificiality of much scientific investigation, we do not live in a world that is altogether artificial. And even when nature and culture are merged, even when nature is almost 'acculturated', humans find themselves in that world and need knowledge about it. Scientists allow themselves to construct virtual realities for a while, but sooner or later their products as well as the scientists themselves have to face the reality of which they, like everybody else, are inhabitants. That science, as a social venture, has been used for political reasons and that scientists 'are strategists, choosing the most opportune moment, engaging in potentially fruitful collaborations, evaluating and grasping opportunities, and rushing to credited information' (Latour and Woolgar, 1979: 213) are probably correct historical and empirical descriptions of the scientific enterprise, but this acknowledgement is no reason, we think, for drawing radical epistemological conclusions, like saying that knowledge is 'whatever people take to be knowledge' (Bloor, 1976: 2).

The overall purpose of knowledge and science, and therefore of scientists as well as of non-scientists, is to know what there is and how it works, however they might be distracted by local interests, however they might be part of the social mechanisms of communication and interaction, and however they might be unreliable in their beliefs or be biased by their instruments. Some sociologists of knowledge pretend to replace epistemology, but, by their own admission, they cannot do this in the name of truth, since they consider truth to be local – so, one could say, why should we worry about those theories? It remains to be seen, *pace* the 'Strong Programme', if staying neutral in matters of truth is enough to ward off this danger of self-refutation. Sociological analysis of science and knowledge has to be taken seriously, no doubt about that, but extreme ontological conclusions from epistemological premises have to be avoided; Devitt's (1997) maxim of the order is important here (see Chapter 4.4).

So, social studies of science are highly relevant to the understanding of the processes and development of science and the 'manufacture of knowledge' (Knorr-Cetina, 1981), but we take them as contributions in the same way as studies in the psychology of science (next section) investigate certain aspects of the production of scientific knowledge.

The realism and rationality, we think, that we have to preserve are stripped; what we have left is not a realism and rationality of content, that is, not an a priori statement of what there is and universal rules on how we have to think, but regulative principles or methodological guidelines, making thinking, acting, explaining, understanding and communicating, in short, life, possible in the first place. They contain a primordial grasp of the world and ourselves, and of principles making reliable conceptions attainable. The world outside our minds constrains our minds in a hardly describable way, but it at least stems our freedom – we cannot say of the world as we please. In a realist and pragmatist frame of mind Putnam writes:

> The notion that our words and life are constrained by a reality not of our own invention plays a deep role in our lives and is to be respected. (1999: 9)

5.8 What about a *Psychology* of Science?

Though the investigation of psychological aspects of science and scientists seems to be in a less advanced state than the sociological approach to science and knowledge, the concern for the social genesis of scientific knowledge is in part a psychological, a social-psychological, concern. There are, however, many more psychological aspects and objects of overall science that can be studied in the context of *science studies* (or the 'science of science', or 'metascience'). In fact there is already a considerable psychological literature pertaining to science studies, but the field is not well structured and the many studies of psychological aspects of science are scattered (see for many titles the bibliography in Fisch, 1977; for a more recent reader and many references, Gholson et al., 1989). The psychology of science can be seen as the fourth 'core discipline' of science studies, next to the philosophy, history, and sociology of science (Houts, 1989). Adopting the definition of the psychology of science given by Gholson et al. (1989: 9), 'the scientific study of scientific behaviour and mental processes', we suggest for the sake of some ordering and to give an impression of the field the broad categories as shown in Box 5.4.

BOX 5.4 **Psychology of science**

1. *Social-psychological studies of the scientific enterprise*, the scientific community, and the receiving public. In this category you could find (historical) studies on the religious background of scientists; culture of publication; political influences; institutional mechanisms; career patterns; the peer review system; reception of scientific beliefs and concepts; the making of psychological society, etc. In fact, many studies in this category have been started and developed within the sociology of science.

2. *Social-psychological studies of the acquisition of scientific knowledge*, that is, social influences on cognitive processes, such as mechanisms of socialization into a scientific belief system; psychological accounts of theory change; the social basis of scientific discoveries (Brannigan, 1981); scientific networks; and many of the so-called ethnographic laboratory studies (the behaviour of scientific communities) we became acquainted with in the previous section.

BOX 5.4   Psychology of science (Continued)

3. *(Cognitive) psychological studies of scientific knowledge*, that is, concerning the structure and processes of the generation and fixation of scientific beliefs; studies about scientific thinking (Tweney et al., 1981; Nersessian, 1992) and reasoning (Faust, 1984; Magnani et al., 1999), creativity (Gruber, 1974; Amabile, 1983; Sternberg, 1999), the genius (Simonton, 1988), scientific discovery (Kantorovich, 1993; Shrager and Langley, 1989), conceptual change (Thagard, 1992).

Carruthers, Stich and Siegal (2002) is a recent volume with contributions by a number of cognitive psychologists who take science as subject. One of the questions they try to answer is: 'What is it about human cognition which either enables us, or fits us, to do science?' These cognitive psychological studies (thus, of the third category, in Box 5.4) can have a general approach, or can be person-oriented (by means of case studies).

It will be clear that the psychology of science will in fact overlap with studies of science from the other disciplines, the philosophy, history and sociology of science; take for instance the psychohistorical case studies of scientists, such as *A Portrait of Isaac Newton* by Frank Manuel (1968); or the cognitive historical case studies, such as Ryan Tweney's work on Faraday's thought (1985, 1989). Sometimes a new programme is launched to stress the interface between two disciplines as, for instance, *cognitive history*; it 'draws on historical and biographical studies of creativity to shed light on the cognitive nature of the creative process' (Dasgupta, 2003).

Perhaps one will feel a tension between the second and the third categories (Box 5.4). The social constructionist approach denies the importance of individual cognitive processes, because beliefs, reasoning and facts are supposed to be social by nature. On the other hand, traditionally, the other disciplines of metascience, especially philosophy, had a distaste for psychological inquiry, as we saw in Chapter 3. As one of the tenets of positivist philosophy of science was to divorce epistemological questions from psychological questions, many authors 'ridiculed or explicitly dismissed the psychology of science as an undesirable flirtation with subjectivism, irrationality, and relativism – those legendary foes of the Western philosophical tradition' (Houts, 1989: 50).

However, appeals to extrahistorical foundations of scientific rationality, to the independence and autonomy of logical laws and criteria, considered as the general laws of science, and to the notion of the 'proper' study of science (the philosopher's ideal science) are undermined, as we saw in previous sections; and many think that at least some subjectivity in the scientific enterprise has to be considered. One of the early authors on the psychology of science, Mahoney (1976), contends that we cannot separate (scientific) knowledge from the knower, nor epistemology from psychology. The social psychologist Kruglanski (1991) asserts that because of the non-unique character of science, as well as because of its unique aspects, science is highly amenable to study from the social science perspective. The relevance of psychological inquiry derives from the assumption that scientists as humans abide by the regularities of social behaviour and cognition. In this sense, science shares its modes of knowledge acquisition with everyday practice. And in so far as 'Western science is a unique societal institution that is committed to a unique set of values, subscribes to a unique set of assumptions, interacts in unique ways with other societal agencies, and regulates its own internal affairs (allocations of funds, publication and communication) in its own unique ways' (Kruglanski, 1991: 226), the sociological and the psychological perspective are highly relevant.

Cognition

The third group of psychological studies of science, mentioned in Box 5.4, borders on the study of cognition, which is in part the business of psychology: for example research on observation, thinking and reasoning, problem-solving, experimentation, motivation etc. In the last decades it has become clear that cognition is a multidisciplinary phenomenon. It began as a chapter of philosophy, namely, the study of knowledge or epistemology. Understood as the groundwork for science it became the most significant part of the orthodox philosophy of science. However, in post-positivistic philosophy it has been acknowledged that **epistemology** is not the concern of philosophy alone, but that it has to be continuous with science. This is sometimes called the *naturalistic turn:* epistemology should be **naturalized** (Quine, 1969a; Kornblith, 1994; see also Chapters 4.5 and 10).

glossary

glossary

Kantorovich (1993), for example, 'naturalizes' the epistemological concept of discovery by applying the evolutionary model to it. One of the most important kinds of creative discovery in science, he writes, are 'serendipitous discoveries'. These discoveries are made when scientists unintentionally solve a problem while intending to solve a different one. In his book he demonstrates that a serendipitous discovery, like a biological mutation, 'can be explained as an "error" which infiltrated a routine procedure – a research program' (Kantorovich, 1993: 7). In this way he borrows the element of chance from the natural selection model and applies it to the concept of discovery, a facet of scientific creation which he labels 'tinkering', adopting the notion that the French biologist François Jacob (1977) uses for characterizing, in a Darwinian way, the evolutionary process. The generation of novelty in science is not a matter of sheer chance, however; serendipitous discoveries contribute to the adaptability of science, making science a major tool by the use of which the human species 'does not wait passively for environmental changes to occur but creates the changes by its own activity' (Kantorovich, 1993: 208).

Experimental research

Problem-solving and the reasoning process are among the favourite subjects in empirically based and experimental cognitive psychology, and it stands to reason that an interest in scientific discovery and the scientific reasoning process should appear on the agenda. Klahr and Dunbar (1988) developed a model of the scientific reasoning process. They propose that scientific reasoning requires search in two problem spaces: a hypothesis space and an experimental space. They placed subjects in a simulated scientific discovery context by first teaching them how to use an electronic device and then asking them to discover how a hitherto unencountered function worked. The subjects had to formulate hypotheses based on their prior knowledge, conduct experiments, and evaluate the results of their experiments. The general model of Scientific Discovery as Dual Search (SDDS) shows how search in two problem spaces shapes hypothesis generation, experimental design, and the evaluation of hypotheses. Computer programs play a major role in this kind of research (Shrager and Langley, 1989) because the idea is that thinking is a computational process, and artificial intelligence research is concerned with designing models of information processing. Kulkarni and Simon (1988) developed a program, KEKADA, which models the heuristics Hans Krebs used in his discovery of the urea cycle in 1932, an important event in biochemistry.

Paul Thagard (1992) deals with conceptual change. Since Kuhn (1962) we have been acquainted with the concept of scientific revolutions. But how exactly do conceptual revolutions occur? What *are* the conceptual systems whose transformation is so fundamental to scientific development? Conceptual change is of general psychological interest (see also Nersessian, 1992), since people other than scientists also experience it, writes Thagard (1992: 4). 'Children's acquisition of knowledge is not simply a matter of accretion of new facts. Rather it involves an important restructuring of their conceptual systems' (ibid.). His approach to the thinking process in the history of science and in developmental psychology is, as with the other experimental cognitivists we mentioned before, computational. But, whereas **artificial intelligence** (AI) researchers [glossary] have concentrated on cases of learning by accretion of knowledge, Thagard wants to extend AI and machine learning research to phenomena of revolutionary replacement of complexes of concepts. He offers a theory that explains cases of conceptual change in the history of science, and tries to answer questions such as: Why did the oxygen theory of combustion supersede the phlogiston theory? Why is Darwin's theory of evolution by natural selection superior to creationism? For this reason he examines, among other reasoning processes, how we in general infer to explanatory hypotheses, and how we determine the explanatory coherence of a hypothesis, that is, how we assess the credibility of hypotheses, their fit with the evidence and other hypotheses; in short, how we infer to the best explanation (see Chapter 1).

These are only a few examples of research that is carried out in the field of the psychology of science. There is more (see for a recent volume Carruthers, Stich and Siegal, 2002), but the work is scattered; the field is still in need of a framework.

Philosophy of mind, the subject of the following chapters, is the philosophical contribution to the multidisciplinary science of cognition and it raises important theoretical issues in its own right. However, philosophy of mind can also be understood as a contribution of philosophical psychology to the study of knowledge and the 'science of science', insofar as it helps us to understand how people – or scientists, for that matter – make sense of the world, by observation, interpretation and intervention. As such it has a hand in the programme of *naturalizing epistemology* that we already referred to. Thus, this concern can be seen as part of the 'science of science', more specifically the psychology of science we outlined in this section. An author, for example, who frequently makes cross-overs from philosophy of cognition to philosophy of science is Paul Churchland (1989a, 1995).

FURTHER READING

Parsons, Keith (ed.) (2003) *The Science Wars. Debating Scientific Knowledge and Technology.* Amherst, NY: Prometheus Books.
A well-balanced reader on constructivism, for and against.

Carruthers, P., Stich, S. and Siegal, M. (eds) (2002) *The Cognitive Basis of Science.* Cambridge: Cambridge University Press.
A reader on psychological studies on science.

6. INTRODUCING PHILOSOPHY OF

MIND, BRAIN AND COGNITION

PREVIEW: This chapter is a brief introduction to the main themes of the philosophy of mind. It provides definitions of mental processes (intelligence, intentionality, consciousness), and the rough outlines of traditional theoretical frameworks for understanding the relation between mind and brain (behaviourism, dualism, materialism). In the last paragraph we sketch three perspectives (or levels of analysis) for describing and explaining complex, mindful organisms.

6.1 Introduction: The Nature of Mind

Philosophy of mind: a cluster of issues

In this chapter we discuss some basic issues and problems in the philosophy of mind. At the most abstract level, philosophy of mind is concerned with the most fundamental notion of psychology: what is mind? In more or less the same way the philosophy of physics is concerned with the nature of time and space, and philosophy of biology is concerned with the nature of life or the concept of natural selection. The big question is: What is the nature of human thought, rationality consciousness?

Broadly speaking, problems in the philosophy of mind can be clustered into five categories.

1   What *are* mental states? What are they made of? How can we get a grip on the spooky stuff of thoughts, images, desires? One proposal is that they are computation, that is, they are (roughly) something like a computer program. Another view is that they are neural activation. Note that on the former, but not on the latter proposal, computers can be said to have thoughts, or even consciousness.

2   What is the relation between mental and physical (more realistically, neurophysiological) processes (the famous mind–brain problem)? Can thoughts, images, dreams be understood as in terms of material processes, or is the mind something over and above and separable from the body?

3   What is the relation between mind and world: how is it possible that our thoughts (and words, for that matter) refer to real things, and how can a mental representation correspond with the world? In philosophy such questions are phrased in abstract and technical vocabulary, like mental content, representation, intentionality and meaning (semantics).

4   What is the status of 'folk psychology'? Can common-sense knowledge of one's fellow beings as persons with knowledge, goals, and intentions, acting rationally, be reconciled with the scientific view of humans as neural and computational machines?

5   How special is consciousness? Even if we agree (as probably a majority of philosophers of mind do) that in the end thoughts, representations, and rationality will be explained in naturalistic and scientific terms, not everyone is convinced that consciousness will yield to the same treatment. The argument is, very briefly, that you can imagine a system (a 'zombie') that does all the clever mental things, and can be said to have internal representations like pain or hunger, but nevertheless lacks the conscious feeling. Thus, maybe consciousness (feeling 'what it is like') resists incorporation in an objective account of mind (more about this in Chapter 10.5).

Three features of the mind: intelligence, consciousness, intentionality

We want to take stock of possible answers to the first main question: what is, at core, the nature of mind? What are the job specifications of mind, what does it do, and what would count as successfully explaining mental states and processes? Let us start with a useful distinction between three aspects of mind, between intelligence, **intentionality**, and **consciousness**.

glossary

Intelligence   A first aspect that comes to mind is intelligence, difficult to define, but very roughly the capacity to execute complex tasks. Traditionally intelligence is considered as more or less the same as reasoning: to think methodically and cogently, arriving at the right conclusions. In philosophy, the traditional definition of man was *Animal rationale*, the rational animal; thus, intelligence was identified with the human mind and was seen as a distinguishing property of humans, setting them apart from the poor brutes of (the rest of) the animal kingdom. In the philosophy of mind and cognitive psychology of the 1960s and 1970s, the rational conception of intelligence spilled over to the idea of **artificial intelligence (AI)**. Following the idea of the glossary seventeenth-century English philosopher Thomas Hobbes that 'reason … is nothing but reckoning, that is, adding and substracting' (1651/1968: 111), modern philosophers of mind claimed that intelligence was nothing but computation and that it could be built in machines and robots (see the following chapters). Early enthusiasts in AI thought that the human mind could in principle be completely understood in that way.

But others suppose that mind must be more than intelligence, and also a lot messier than just cool reason. Having false ideas, thinking confusedly, but nevertheless thinking, must be a feature of mind too. A person overwhelmed by emotions and taking the wrong steps does not forfeit his intelligence, let alone his mind. Therefore, the conception of human intelligence has become much broader than rationality alone. It has come to include emotions (and 'emotional intelligence') and other functions, like intentions, motivation and **actions**. Another reason for abandoning the idea that logical reasoning is glossary the essence of mind is the evolutionary perspective that having a mind cannot be an all-or-nothing affair: all complex systems develop gradually from more simple ones, so intelligence must be something of a continuum: other animals than humans may have their own little bit of rationality as well (see for these extensions of mind and intelligence Chapters 9 and 10).

Consciousness   Is there another mental property that might distinguish humans from animals? Descartes saw consciousness as the essence of the human mind, and many authors feel that any serious philosophical account of mind has to explain consciousness. However, modern psychology has until recently found consciousness subjective and intractable, and no methods to study it seemed available, so that a more scientific, physical, and objective treatment of psychology was opted for and consciousness was simply dropped from the agenda.

Recently, however, it has become the subject of lively debate. Some philosophers demand that the essential subjectivity and the first-person nature of consciousness be taken seriously; these experiential properties are called **qualia**, because they have a glossary qualitative character, a '*how it is like*' (Nagel, 1980) for you to have a feeling. Others, however, try to reduce consciousness to physical, informational or neural states and processes, thus making it amenable to science. In this debate the very existence of qualia is at stake: some (like Dennett, 1991a) maintain that they are illusions.

One way of explaining consciousness (or explaining it away) is to show how it can be derived from intentionality (see below), and/or from information processing capacities of the mind/brain (e.g. Dretske, 1993; Lycan, 1987; Dennett, 1991a; Flanagan, 1991); that is, notions like representation and information are seen as primary, and consciousness as secondary, as derived from information processing. Searle (1992) has tried to reverse the tables, and argues that conscious experience logically precedes cognition: cognitive processes are either conscious or can be brought to consciousness. The brain processes that cannot be conscious are not cognitive (for more about qualia and consciousness see Chapter 10.5).

Intentionality   Another concept that is traditionally considered as the characteristic of mind in contradistinction to matter is the particular property of mind that goes by the somewhat technical term of intentionality.

The Austrian philosopher Franz Brentano (1838–1917) is usually credited with the definition of intentionality as the 'mark of the mental'. The *locus classicus* is Brentano's *Psychologie vom empirischen Standpunkt* (1924). According to Brentano, the defining characteristic of mental states, distinguishing them from physics, is their property of being *directed* towards an object, or having some content:

> Jedes psychisches Phänomen ist durch das charakterisiert was wir ... die Beziehung auf einen Inhalt, die Richtung auf ein Objekt (worunter hier nicht eine Realität zu verstehen ist), oder die immanente Gegenständlichkeit nennen würden. [Every psychological phenomenon is characterized by something we would call a directedness towards a content, an object (here not a thing in reality), or something immanent.] (Brentano, 1924: 124–5)

Thus a mental state, unlike a physical state, includes an object or content within itself: the intentional object. This implies that *aboutness* is a criterion for the distinction between mind and matter. Intentionality, defined as the ability of the mind to refer to something outside itself, to be about something, distinguishes the mental from the physical. Your thoughts represent things, a cup of coffee or the mountain Fujiyama, but things (a cup of coffee or a mountain) are not *about* anything. It will be clear that notions like representation, meaning and mental content are closely related to intentionality. They all refer to the ability of mental or cognitive states to indicate something beyond themselves. And therefore they play a central role in the modern philosophy of mind and cognition, as we will see in later chapters (especially Chapters 7, 8 and 10)

One might argue that some non-mental things or states have meaning or content; for example, that this book is about or represents theoretical issues in psychology or that traffic signs mean to bring about certain kinds of behaviour. However, such signs or texts have only *derived intentionality* – they depend on some original intentional system (a human mind) that can interpret them (Searle, 1992).

Brentano himself presented his concept of intentionality in the context of the demarcation between mental (*psychische*) and physical (*physische*) phenomena (Brentano, 1924: 111–24). In this view, the entire world can be divided into the two mutually exclusive categories of mental and physical phenomena (ibid.: 109). And for many philosophers of mind a definite 'mark of the mental' is important because it provides a last line of defence against the attempts to reduce the mind to physical or physiological processes (see e.g. Bechtel, 1988b; Flanagan, 1992).

A major issue in modern philosophy of mind is whether intentionality is indeed an exclusive property of mind – or whether it might be possible in physical systems (brains or computers) as well. The latter implies the project of **naturalizing** intentionality. Since most contemporary philosophers of mind are **materialists**, who believe that physical processes are all there is, they feel compelled to give an account of the phenomena of intentionality in natural, mechanistic or physical terms. Descartes' and Brentano's position, that mind is an irreducible entity apart from nature, is seen as unscientific, invoking mysterious unexplainable entities. The naturalists' ideal is to understand intentionality as a property of natural systems, something that at least biological organisms can have, and perhaps machines and computers too; and to explain it in mechanistic, computational or biological terms.

BOX 6.1   Intentionality, beliefs, representations, folk psychology: some connections

- *Intentionality* is 'aboutness', the property of mental states to represent states of affairs.
- *Intentionality* is a typical property of mind, not of matter (material things like books may have derived intentionality).
- *Beliefs and desires* are typically intentional states (believing, desiring something).
- *Intentional states* have semantics: they represent, or mean, or refer to something – they have mental content.
- *Cognition* is an intentional state – it involves internal representations.
- *Folk psychology* explains behaviour as a result of beliefs and desires, as a product of intentional states.
- *Naturalizing intentionality* is showing how physical systems like brains and computers can represent, think, desire, etc.
- *Naturalizing intentionality* is sometimes seen as a necessary condition for scientific explanation of representatition, cognition and folk psychology.

6.2 Traditional Views on the Nature of Mind: Dualism, Materialism, Behaviourism

In the following, we will see the five questions mentioned above surface in several ideas and theories in the philosophy of mind.

Although contemporary views are strongly influenced by the ascent of computer models and more recently neuroscience, some important questions date back to the pre-computer era. Before, say, 1960, roughly three options were available for conceptualizing the nature of mind and its relation to the brain: dualism, materialistic reductionism (the mind–brain identity theory), and linguistic behaviourism. We start with a brief historical overview to put the traditional concepts and positions in place. This section is mostly about pure philosophy, analysing concepts and building arguments from the armchair. In Chapter 7 we turn to the classical computational theory of mind, which is more of a reflection on empirical work, including artificial intelligence. This view has been contested in the last three decades by connectionism. This will be dealt with in Chapter 8 and the recent views on mind as interacting with its environment (dynamicism and the extended mind) will be the subject of Chapter 9.

The philosophy of mind can be said to combine two different tacks: traditional analytical philosophy, and the naturalistic view on the role of philosophy as continuous with empirical science. The former is at work in philosophical analysis of concepts like reduction, **supervenience**, the mind–brain problem, etc. as an exercise in conceptual
glossary

analysis and **metaphysics**. One of the masters of such work is Jaegwon Kim (1996, 1998). The latter approach is exemplified by the naturalism of P.M. Churchland and P.S. Churchland (inspired by Quine), who look at the way science is really done, and how cognitive and neuroscience bear upon philosophical issues; for example, how the nervous system realizes intentionality and mental representations. In Patricia Churchland's (2002a) and John Bickle's (2003) recent books on the philosophy of mind and brain, many traditional philosophical subjects have yielded to discussions of neuroscience. In Chapter 10 we will return to the more traditional philosophical issues, like consciousness, intentionality, mind–brain supervenience, and so on.

But first we will briefly go into some answers that were given before the cognitive revolution of the 1960s.

Dualism

The traditional view was **dualism**: the doctrine that mind and body are different substances and should be studied by different methods. The historical culprit was René Descartes (1596–1650). He distinguished a material substance (*res extensa*) and a thought substance (*res cogitans*) which are independent. He then, of course, ran into the problem of how these might interact: how one's thoughts lead to movements of one's limbs; and how a blow on the head leads to a feeling of pain; how to account for the obvious interactions of bodily and mental processes, as in fatigue, alcohol effects or psychosomatic diseases. Descartes suggested that the pituitary gland was the locus where the thought substance and the nervous system interact, which leaves the philosophical problem as mysterious as it was. This position is known as *interactionism*: it holds that there must be a point of contact where the mind and the body interact.

In our own time, Popper and Eccles (1977) state that through cortical modules the immaterial Self monitors and directs its brain. Of course, this only transforms the problem – how can the immaterial mind influence bodily processes? – into the question: how can the Self, the immaterial mind, act upon cortical structures? Popper and Eccles contribute little in answer to that conundrum.

Another position within the dualist mainstream is *epiphenomenalism*: it holds that mental processes are by-products of bodily processes, without any causal influences on the body, more or less like the whistle on a steam engine, which reflects the physical process, but doesn't change it.

A position not strictly dualist is the *double-aspect theory*, also known as *property dualism*: mind and matter are not separate substances, but aspects of a single underlying substance. An organism can be described either in mental or in physiological terms, and these descriptions are mutually irreducible.

Cartesian dualism is routinely ridiculed in philosophy textbooks. However, until quite recently it seemed incomprehensible that material systems could possess consciousness and intelligence. Therefore the view held by most psychologists was something much like property dualism: it was conceded that there is no independent mental substance, that mental processes are properties or products of the brain, but it was deemed practically impossible to study them by neurophysiological methods (fortunately, because therefore psychologists were free to go about their business without paying attention to physiology). Obligatory references to the brain notwithstanding, psychologists have, at least until recently, been dualist for *methodological* reasons (unlike Descartes' ontological dualism).

Materialism and reduction

Another view on the relation of mind and brain can be found in a number of materialist or reductionist theories. The most explicit in the 1960s and early 1970s was the so-called *mind–brain* **identity theory** (Feigl, 1967; Borst, 1970). Its first formulation `glossary` was in a brief paper by the British psychologist U.T. Place (1956/1970) that suggested the possibility of empirical identification of consciousness and brain processes. It held that mental states like pain or seeing a yellow after-image are *not a priori* logically identical with a neural event, that is, that we have distinct perceptions and different concepts for mental and physiological states. Nevertheless, it might turn out that conscious states can in empirical research be identified with neural events like the firing of certain nerve fibres. The standard example is that pain might found to be identical with the firing of C-fibres. (Incidentally, the philosophers who recycled the example at the time apparently failed to notice that it is neurophysiological nonsense, since C-fibres are characterized by myelin sheaths and conduction velocity, and some C-fibres do subserve pain, while others have different functions.)

Much ink has been spilled over logical questions associated with such identifications. For example, can mental properties like pain which have no physical location be considered identical with events that take place in specific locations in the brain? At least, there seems to be a difference in location, so logically they cannot be considered identical, it was argued.

The death blow for the identity theory was the doctrine of **functionalism** (see also `glossary` Chapters 2.4 and 2.5), first put forward in a paper by Hilary Putnam (1961). Putnam suggested that functionally identical mental processes can be realized in different ways in different physical or physiological systems, where these realizations have little or no physical properties in common. We might say, for instance, that a computer 'thinks' about a chess move in about the same way as we do, although it has a physical make-up completely different from ours. This so-called **multiple realizability** effectively pre- `glossary` cludes identification of mental and physical events. Or, most people have a speech centre (or centra) in the left hemisphere, but in a small percentage of the population it is found in the right hemisphere. Here speech is in a sense multiply realized. The idea can be illustrated by considering a computer program, which can be run on different types of computers. The program will be functionally identical, will work in the same way, independently of differences in the computer chips.

Analogously, mental processes like speaking, or being angry or thinking about chess can be functionally identical in beings with completely different nerve systems or processors. (We will come back to this in Chapter 7.2.)

Linguistic behaviourism

Linguistic behaviourism was the third view on the nature of mind; it was initiated by the later Wittgenstein, and by Ryle and Malcolm.

The linguistic focus comes from Wittgenstein's conceptual analysis, which explores the rules of common-sense discourse. The role of philosophy is to clear up the conceptual confusions that are the source of metaphysical problems, such as the mind–body problem or the problem of free will. Philosophical psychology is about exploring the 'logical geography' of our mental concepts, not about discovering empirical facts about the mind.

Gilbert Ryle (1949) launched a devastating attack on the Cartesian myth of the 'ghost in the machine', the idea that the mind is an inner realm of ghostly events (sensations, thoughts, pains, intelligence), which reside in a 'second theater' alongside the real life theatre of physical events and public behavioural acts. His thesis is that this myth rests upon conceptual confusion, more precisely, on a *category mistake*.

Suppose you show a visitor around Oxford. You point out the buildings of the colleges, and when you eventually sit down exhausted in the Bear over a pint of Hall's Bitter, she asks which of the buildings you have shown her is Oxford University. She makes the category mistake of assuming that the university is a building among the others, rather than the collective of the colleges. Likewise, assuming that *the* mind is a thing like the body; that mental events are events like physical ones, only in a non-physical realm, are category mistakes, according to Ryle.

Ryle goes on to expose the confusion that results from juxtaposing mind and body, as in: 'We have a body *and* a mind', and mental to physical events; and treating mental events as if they were immaterial causes and effects in a 'mental theatre'. If you think that you can explain seeing something as the having of an internal mental ghostly event (mental recognition), then you have to explain a whole internal chain of ghostly causes and effects. If you think that acting consists in having a mental event (an intention) that causes your limbs to move, then you are stuck with the 'wire and pulley question': how an immaterial event can interface with and cause a physical movement.

Ryle's way out of the confusion caused by 'inner realm' explanations of external behaviour has been called *linguistic behaviourism*. It holds that mental concepts refer to *behaviour* and behavioural *dispositions*. A disposition is a tendency to behave in a certain way in certain circumstances; for instance, glass being brittle is a disposition, it means that it will shatter when hit. Referring to someone as intelligent means that she will behave in certain ways under certain conditions; for instance, that she will score high marks in mathematics, that she will win a game of chess, etc. The concept of intelligence as we use it in daily life does not refer to an inner mechanism of immaterial cogs and wheels, but it serves to describe and predict behaviour. No reference to the inner life of a ghostly Cartesian mind-substance is needed. For example, looking at someone, you can sometimes see from the outside that he is engaged in deep thoughts (he looks just like Rodin's sculpture *The Thinker*), and that leads to several predictions about his behaviour (when someone with such a mien is addressed, he may cry 'Eureka', or ask you not to disturb him).

The linguistic behaviourist story about the nature of mental talk is not to everybody's taste. It seems intuitively plausible that there is something behind the behaviour; that there is some inner life going on that causes and explains behaviour. Another reason that linguistic behaviourism is out of fashion these days is that it cannot go beyond what is implicit in common-sense knowledge. It aims at describing the 'logical geography' of our concepts; as a philosophical approach, it tries to dissolve conceptual confusions by exposing traditional metaphysical problems as conceptual fallacies, and thus to solve (or dissolve) metaphysical problems. Ryle's (1949) classic is a philosophical delight to read, but having done so, one knows little more about mind than before. Linguistic analysis is a great way to undermine 'bad habits of thought', but does little to increase our knowledge. Reflecting on the use of daily language and its rules, straightening its fabric, showing where it goes off the track is hardly likely to produce new knowledge and compete with new discoveries in the age of neuroscience. New interesting facts about the mind will come from empirical research in psychology, and linguistic behaviourism has very little to contribute on that subject.

Ryle (1949: 21–4) has, however, a strong argument against the mentalist (Cartesian) approach, the myth of the 'ghost in the machine': it tries, in vain, to explain outer behaviour from inner mental mechanisms (like physicists have found the underlying mechanisms that produce material events and objects). But by defining inner mechanisms as private, accessible to the owner of the mind, the myth at the same time makes explanation impossible. Mind is a spectral machine, driving its bodily movements, but we have no way of getting access to the immaterial mechanisms. By trying to find the springs of overt behaviour in the mind, we block any useful explanation, since the immaterial Cartesian mind is unknowable anyhow.

The myth starts from the intuition that mind is special and that it is the quintessential difference between humans and beasts (Descartes thought that animals were automata, and the human body is likewise a kind of robot). If that were true, we would never be able to find that very difference, since mind is unobservable according to the selfsame myth. Of course, in real life we know mindless from rational creatures by observing their behaviour, Ryle argues, and assuming an unknowable ghost in the machine is no help at all.

The very point, whether we can get a hold on unobservable cognitive processes, will be the subject of the cognitive revolution in the following chapters.

BOX 6.2   Dualism, materialism, behaviourism

Dualism: *mind and matter (or body, or brain) are somehow different*

- *Interactionism*: brain and mind influence each other.
- *Epiphenomenalism*: mind is a by-product of brain processes, does not influence the brain.
- *Property dualism*: mind and brain are different aspects of one underlying reality.

BOX 6.2 Dualism, materialism, behaviourism (Continued)

- *Methodological dualism* is not committed to any view on the nature of mind or brain; it just holds that some processes can be studied by neuroscientific methods, other processes require psychological methods.

Materialism: *mental processes are really brain processes*

- *Indentity theory*: mental states can be empirically identified with brain states.

Linguistic behaviourism:

- Words for mental processes really refer to behaviour (or behavioural dispositions). Dualism is the result of conceptual confusion.

6.3 Three Perspectives on Mind and Brain

The different perspectives of materialism, methodological dualism, and (in a more indirect way) also linguistic behaviourism can be detected in Daniel Dennett's proposal that intelligent complex systems like minds, brains and computers can be described and predicted from three different 'stances'. We will briefly discuss Dennett's ideas to set the stage for a multiple explanatory perspective on the mind/brain, which is consistent with our penchant for multiple (levels of) explanation in psychology (Chapter 2.5). We will encounter Dennett's three-level scheme again in the section on intentionality (Chapter 10.1).

Three approaches to intelligent systems

Daniel Dennett has an interesting proposal for combining intentional explanation with neuroscience – the kind of combination that Brentano and his followers thought impossible. Although Dennett is committed to **objectivism** and materialism, which leaves no room for intrinsic and irreducible subjectivity, immaterial consciousness and so on, he acknowledges the value of the intentional way of talking about behavior in terms of thoughts, plans, and knowledge.

He distinguishes (1978) three stances:

1   The *intentional stance* is the kind of explanation that considers prediction and description of behaviour in terms of beliefs and desires, or in slightly more

scientific terms, of goals and information. It cannot only be used for humans, but also for artificial agents, or any intelligent purposive system in general. For instance, a chess program is credited with the knowledge of openings, a repertoire of moves, and the goal of winning through checkmate. The computer does not really have thoughts or desires (the real causes of its behaviour are ultimately just electrical currents), but it can very usefully be described as such. When we know that it tends to play aggressively, or has a limited knowledge of endgames, we can predict its moves, and perhaps win the game. The computer, of course, has not literally a strategy, or style, or knowledge, only program statements and electronic pulses.

2   The *design stance*, another way of looking at intelligent systems, is concerned with precisely these underlying mechanisms: the design stance specifies the algorithms or the design that produces this intentional behaviour. The design of a chess computer, the specific chess rules and inferences, the subroutines and intermediate goals the programmer has put in, explain why it seems to have 'knowledge' and plans and an apparent 'desire' to win. In the same way, knowledge of neuropsychology will tell us (eventually, ideally) what sort of neuropsychological functions underlie human purposive, rational behaviour. The design stance is an instance of functional explanation, discussed in Chapter 2.4 and Chapter 7.2. It gives the 'program', the functions that the system can perform (think of perception, memory storage and retrieval, selective attention, and so on), and it describes these (more or less) independently as 'hardware'.

3   The *physical stance*, finally, considers the hardware, and is relevant for explaining the system's behaviour when something goes wrong with the electronics or the power supply.

The intentional stance employs notions that are traditionally considered bad explanations: it seems to invoke rational and intentional thinking, information and goals, to explain rational and intentional behaviour. It presupposes what it explains, a notorious error known as circular reasoning , or the **homunculus** fallacy: it invokes a `glossary` little man (homunculus) or 'capacity' inside that does the thinking. Why does someone play superior chess? Because he has a superior capacity for chess playing. That doesn't help, of course, because we now want to know what exactly causes this capacity, and what it is that makes the homunculus so clever. (Recall Ryle's devastating criticism of the Cartesian myth, which assumes inner intelligent causes of observable intelligent behaviour.) Dennett, however, points out that we can legitimately use this homuncular intentional language if we consider it a 'loan on intelligence', a kind of explanatory debt, that has to be paid by providing explanations at design stance level.

Moving from the intentional to the design stance means that the single intelligent 'homunculus', the chess playing capacity, is replaced by an 'army of idiots', by agents with simpler job descriptions (speedy computation, clever heuristics, a repertoire of inference rules). These simpler subroutines can in turn be decomposed into even simpler mechanisms until the level of physics is reached. Instead of goals and knowledge, program subroutines and properties of electronic circuits are invoked as explanations. The strategies and knowledge of a chess computer (as seen from the intentional stance) are explained in terms of the rules, data structures and subroutines of its program (from the design stance).

Even without unpacking into design descriptions, the intentional stance can give useful explanations and predictions. For example, when constructing a lightning rod, you may assume that the lightning will 'want' to take the shortest route to earth, and 'try' to take the easy way down (Dennett, 1987). A thermostat can fruitfully be described as striving to maintain a comfortable temperature, or a chess computer as considered as pondering on its next move. There is no real thought or intention in lightning of course, but the intentional stance is a useful device for description and prediction nevertheless. In principle, there is no limit for the applicability of intentional explanation; it is legitimate whenever it works.

Instrumentalism

Thus Dennett (1987) manages to exorcize the homunculus without throwing it out with the bathwater. *Intentionality* depends on the stance, on the concepts and perspective; briefly, it is in the eye of the beholder. Attributing intentionality, goals and information is a manner of speaking, an instrument for describing and predicting behaviour, not a reference to underlying mental mechanisms.

However, it is no illusion, no fiction, and it is not an entirely arbitrary decision whether to describe something as intelligent. The intentional stance reveals real patterns of intentional behaviour (Dennett, 1991b) that would not have been visible without it. If an alien from Mars could completely predict our behaviour from a physical stance (let us assume that Martians have a superior knowledge of physics), and could tell all our body movements with perfect accuracy, he would still be missing something, namely the intentional pattern in them. Compare the statement that a boxer is practising a left uppercut because he wants to win a match, with a list of his muscle contractions: you could not tell the former from the latter.

In Dennett's view all there is for a system (human, animal or computer) to being a 'true believer' is that it must be predictable by the intentional stance, in terms of beliefs, desires, goals and knowledge. No real intentionality, no inner facts of mind, are necessary for such prediction and explanation of intentional behaviour. The intentional stance is just an *instrument*, a conceptual tool, a convenient fiction. Instrumentalism glossary contrasts with (intentional) **realism** which holds that beliefs refer to something real in the world.

glossary In Dennett's **instrumentalism** we can see his Wittgensteinian and Rylean heritage. Wittgenstein and Ryle argued that the meaning of mental terminology depends on glossary **language games** (see Chapter 3), rather than on a reference to inner events. Likewise, Dennett thinks that intentionality and consciousness depend on their concepts. What the weight of a stone is, is intrinsic, but whether something is a bathtub or a boat depends on the way it is used. Even more significantly, what counts as love, or whether an act is aggressive or heroic, gallant or macho, may vary with the concepts of the community.

This marks his bitter disagreement with realists like, for example, Searle (see below, Chapter 10.1), who considers the real first-person experience and consciousness, that is, intrinsic intentionality, a fact of life, whereas Dennett (1990b) thinks original intentionality is a myth. Dennett thinks that his intentional stance, nevertheless, yields a robust criterion for the relative reality of intentional folk-psychological categories, such as beliefs, goals and intentions. A rich semantic system with lots of intricate representational states must correspond to a certain specific environment; this puts enough constraints on interpretations. Whether a thermostat 'knows' the 'right' temperature is a matter of interpretation, but it is not arbitrary. Whether it is useful to interpret some internal feature of a system as a representation depends on the complexity of its design and how that fits into the environment; rich inner states that fit well in a complex environment can usefully be described as 'true believers', knowing subjects. The aboutness that Brentano considered the mark of the mental resides in the system's connection to, embedding in, its environment.

A criticism that might be levelled against Dennett is that he seems to take the design or neurophysiological stance quite literally. It is not clear why the design stance should thus be privileged above the intentional stance, unless one already has a scientistic bias that takes folk-psychological discourse less seriously than scientific idiom (cf. Baker, 1995).

Soft materialism, multiple explanations

Dennett's framework of three stances can also accommodate functional explanation and folk psychology, and perhaps even to some extent hermeneutics (see Chapter 2). Dennett (1990c) draws a parallel between four seemingly quite different styles of explanation as: (1) the classical hermeneutical enterprise of interpreting the meaning of a text (what can Shakespeare's Hamlet tell us); (2) the interpretation of people's beliefs and desires; (3) the interpretation of artefacts (as archeologists do when digging up unfamiliar objects from extinct cultures); and (4) the interpretation of organismic design in evolutionary biology (recall the types of explanation discussed in Chapter 2). Adaptationism in biology (all properties are functions aiding survival), the intentional stance in psychology (all behaviour is a product of information and goals and rational thought), and hermeneutics (all texts have (hidden) meanings) are methodological principles from the same cloth: all answer 'why' questions (What is it for? What does it mean?) in roughly the same way, by assuming good reasons. In all cases, they are warranted by their success in explaining.

The attractiveness of this framework is that it accommodates the soft, humanistic reason-oriented style of explanation, as well as the functional, biological goal-oriented, and also the hard, scientific cause-oriented styles of explanation (see Chapter 3) in a single framework. We could call it (methodological) dualism, or better pluralism, since it recognizes that for complex systems we need other ways of looking ('stances') than physics can provide. Dennett (1995) is an impeccable materialist: the natural, blind, causal mechanisms of evolutionary selection are the source of all meaning, design, intelligence (see elaborations of this naturalist view on consciousness in Chapter 10.5, and on free will in Chapter 10.4). However, there are real meaningful, intentional patterns of behaviour that can only be seen from the intentional stance, not from the physical stance. In the same way, looking at organisms from a functional perspective in biology reveals what a certain trait is for, what purpose it serves; it shows patterns in nature that would be missed if we only considered the physical properties of an organism.

BOX 6.3 Intentional explanation, design stance and physical stance

- *Intentional explanation* using beliefs and desires, information and goals as explanation of behaviour is a way of viewing, describing and predicting complex intelligent systems. It is in the eye of the beholder.
- *Intentional explanation* describes real patterns of intelligent goal-directed behaviour. It is therefore also objective.
- A *'real' intelligent goal-directed system* (a 'true believer') is just a system for which the intentional stance works.
- *Intentional explanation* is a loan on intelligence that must be redeemed by specifying the *design* (computer program, electronic circuits, etc.) that produces intentional behaviour.
- The *design stance* predicts a system's behaviour by breaking it up into functional parts and showing how these subsystems or subroutines perform their (sub)tasks.
- The *physical stance* predicts the system from its physical states, and is usually invoked to explain malfunction (e.g. 'Oops, the battery is low').

6.4 Conclusion: Levels and Perspectives in the Study of Mind and Brain

This framework is consistent with what we said about causal, functional, and higher-level explanations in Chapter 2. The important point in our view is that the physical perspective is incomplete, that an eye for mechanisms only will overlook real phenomena. In that sense dualism was approximately right. However, materialists were right in emphasizing that the mind is not separate from the brain, but is the way matter is organized. (As we will see below, so-called non-reductive materialists are happy with the idea that although mind is matter, it cannot be understood in terms of the laws of physics.)

The linguistic behaviourist view that mental concepts are a way of talking about behaviour is quite consistent with Dennett's intentional stance: describing and predicting patterns of behaviour in terms of mental concepts like beliefs and desires can remain neutral as to the real existence of such mental processes. In a way, linguistic behaviourists agree with Dennett and others who are close to the **pragmatist** tradition (e.g. Rorty, 1979, 1982b, 1993) that mind is not a thing (a substance) but a relation, that it depends on the way you look at it (is only visible when one takes the intentional stance), and on how the observer describes it. So, in very rough outline, we can see how different styles and levels of explanation, combining insights from the different approaches sketched above, are required for understanding the mind/brain.

FURTHER READING

Bechtel, W.B. and Graham, G. (eds) (1998) *A Companion to Cognitive Science*. Oxford: Blackwell.
An encyclopedia of the important issues in cognitive science.

Guttenplan, S. (ed.) (1994) *A Companion to the Philosophy of Mind*. Oxford: Blackwell.
An encyclopedia of the important issues in the philosophy of mind.

7. MODERN APPROACHES TO MIND (1): THE LANGUAGE-BASED VIEW

Functionalism and the Computational Theory of Mind

PREVIEW: In this chapter we discuss the classical view of mind as the software of the brain: the computational theory of mind. It holds that mental states (thoughts, representations) are really symbol strings, and that mental processes (thinking, reasoning) are computations over these symbols. The computational theory of mind provides an integrated view on the nature of mental representations, meaning and intentionality. Functionalism is a philosophical pillar of the computational view. Artificial intelligence is the proof of the viability of the computational view, and the current state of (strong) AI suggests that computationalism is in deep trouble.

7.1 Introduction: The Origins of Computationalism

glossary

The **computational theory of mind** has, broadly speaking, three sources. First, there was the cognitive revolution in psychology, starting around 1960. It made the notion of internal mental processes as causes of overt behaviour respectable again. Before that, behaviourism had more or less banned talk about internal processes from scientific psychology, as unverifiable and mysterious (Gardner, 1987). Only overt behaviour was considered admissible; mentalist terminology was considered speculative and unscientific, and could only be legitimized if it was directly linked to, or translatable into, observed behaviour. The cognitive revolution made a case for independent internal processes that are only indirectly linked to behaviour. These underlying mental mechanisms consist in storing, processing, and retrieving information. Part of the philosophy of the cognitive revolution was functionalism, the idea that mental processes are functions that can be studied in terms of what they do (their causal role), ignoring how they are realized in brains or silicon chips (see Chapter 2.4). An important difference with behaviourism was that now overt behaviour was no longer the only legitimate subject matter of psychology: talk about internal mental processes became acceptable.

Second, on close scrutiny, many problems in the philosophy of mind resemble traditional issues in the philosophy of language that had dominated Anglo-Saxon philosophy since the days of Gottlob Frege, Bertrand Russell, and Ludwig Wittgenstein, in the early twentieth century (see Devitt and Sterelny, 1987; Harnish, 1994). These philosophers were interested in questions concerning reference, meaning, **intentionality**, `glossary` propositional mental content – that is, questions like: How can sentences or thoughts be about things in the world? How is it possible that thoughts somehow reflect reality? Similar problems now pop up under the label of *mental representation* (e.g. Fodor, 1981b; Silvers, 1989; Sterelny, 1990). Internal **representations** in the form of a kind `glossary` of sentences in the head might explain the peculiar properties of mental processes. Linguistic propositions are as it were transplanted to mental content: meaning and intentionality is a matter of having sentences in mind. Thus, the new philosophy of mind modelled some of its ideas about mind on the philosophy of language. Jerry Fodor's (1975) (in)famous **language of thought** hypothesis holds that thinking is `glossary` manipulating sentences in a kind of mental (logical) language. It is interesting to note that such ideas hardly play a central role in cognitive psychology textbooks, and if they do, it is usually with quite a different emphasis (cf. Palmer, 1978 and Fodor, 1981b). Recently, doubts have arisen whether the concerns of cognitive science dovetail as nicely with philosophical ones as, for instance, Fodor (1981b) thinks (Stich, 1992; Rorty, 1993).

Third, the rise of the computer and the promise of **artificial intelligence** boosted `glossary` the idea that thinking is symbol manipulation, and that the computer can be used as a tool for studying thought. Within AI, two approaches can be distinguished: weak and strong AI. *Weak AI* just tries to write programs that can do tasks that require intelligence, such as making a medical diagnosis, playing chess, translating and summarizing texts (e.g. a news bulletin). *Strong AI* claims to write programs that exactly simulate human thinking, and as a consequence it claims that programmed computers can literally think – and that thinking is literally computation. Obviously, only the strong variety is relevant for the computational theory of mind.

Below, we will first discuss the pillars of the computational theory of mind (CTM), functionalism, computation, and the idea of a mental language (7.2); and in section 7.3, the theory itself, as articulated by Jerry Fodor. Then we turn to the somewhat disappointing story of strong AI (7.4), before concluding this chapter.

7.2 Functionalism, Computation, and Formal Languages

Functionalism and the cognitive revolution

As discussed in Chapter 2.4, functional explanation says about a thing what is *does*, rather than what it *is*. **Functionalism** in the philosophy of mind holds that mental states and processes are functions that can be identified by their causal role, that is, by the way they cause behaviour, react to input and interact with other mental states (Sterelny, 1990). For example, hunger is a mental state that can be identified by what it does: it causes foraging, makes the organism more alert, it may lead to aggression, and so on. If mental states are functional states (of a machine, or a brain), and if it is their functional role that counts, then what they *are*, what the physical make-up of the machine (the *implementation*) is, can easily be dismissed as irrelevant to the function it realizes (a suggestion that is now contested, see below, and Chapter 8).

The cognitive revolution of the 1960s (Gardner, 1987) required some idea of mental processes that would be independent of neurophysiology. First, at that time neurophysiologists had hardly anything to say about cognitive processes like thinking (although neural mechanisms of attention and perception were studied). And second, from a political point of view, autonomy from the neurosciences would help psychology and cognitive science to claim its share of research grants: at lot of US Defence money was available, and therefore it was better to have an own identity and subject matter. That required some kind of (methodological) dualism (see Chapter 6.2), but, of course, within an objective scientific framework (no Cartesian disembodied thoughts, please!).

Functionalism provided the appropriate philosophy for cognitive psychology. Putnam (1961) and Fodor (1981b) emphasized the disadvantages of the existing competitors, the identity theory and linguistic behaviourism (see Chapter 6.2). The problem with *linguistic behaviourism* is that it is not a real theory about mental processes, and has nothing to say about inner mental processes that cause behaviour. It does not explain anything about the underlying mechanisms; it only analyses the (common-sense) descriptions. At best it clarifies what we already know. We need a theory that takes mental processes seriously as causes of behaviour, that provides explanations and laws of behaviour, not just linguistic descriptions. The problem with the *identity theory* (of mind and brain) (IT), on the other hand, is that it identifies mental states with neural states. Although this means that, in contrast to behaviourism, mental states are seen as real and causally effective, it also means that cognition as a field of study is in danger of being absorbed by neurophysiology. That does not deliver the desired autonomy for (cognitive) psychology.

Functionalism should be an improvement over both the identity theory and linguistic behaviourism. Unlike behaviourism, it holds that mental processes can be considered in their own right, apart from overt behaviour. Furthermore, in contrast to behaviourism, mental states are not just labels for dispositions to behave in certain ways, but they really exist, independently of behaviour (you can have a mental life when completely unable to move – Searle, 1992). Mental causation (see below in Chapter 10.3) is (on this view) also perfectly real and understandable: what we think determines what we do. By generalizing over mental states, psychological generalizations and causal **laws** can be found, for example: hunger will cause organisms to forage. So, by identifying mental processes with functions, the functionalists think they can at last study mind in a objective scientific way.

Against the **identity theory**, the one-to-one correspondence of mental and physical processes is abandoned. Functionalists agree that mental processes are ultimately realized in some kind of material substance (brains, or computers or whatever kind of matter), but they point out that the same function can be realized in many ways in different materials. As in the example of the mousetrap that can be made of almost anything, the same mental state (a thought, an idea) can be realized in brains or computers. Therefore, the identification of mental and neural states the identity theory required is impossible.

On the other hand, functionalism also avoids dualism. It distinguishes two kinds of identity. *Type identity* refers to the identity of kinds or categories (types), as they figure in laws and generalizations ('temperature' would be an example of a type, and it can in general and lawfully be identified with average kinetic energy). The identity theory was about such type identity of mental and physical processes: a whole class (type) of mental events should be (systematically) identified with a class of neural events (for example, all instances of pain are identical with the firing of C-fibres in the nervous system).

Token identity is a much weaker claim: it holds that every instance (token) of a mental event is a token of a physical event, but the connection may be different in different species or on different occasions or in different individuals. Hunger may be a different process in human and octopuses' nervous systems and hence hunger cannot be type-identified with a neural process. In both cases, however, it is a materially realized process, not a disembodied mental state. So, although there is no such thing as non-physical thought (mental and physical processes are token-identical), there are no laws connecting classes of mental and neural events (no type-identity). So, as mentioned in Chapter 6, functions can be *multiply realized* in physical systems.

Functionalism thus has the better of two worlds; it avoids both dualism and reduction: on the one hand mental processes are instantiated in material processes – there is no such thing as non-physical thought, no metaphysical dualism of mind and matter; on the other hand, mental processes are irreducible to neurophysiology (Fodor, 1981b, 1997a/b). This is an interesting achievement for a philosophical idea, because it legitimizes the autonomy of psychology, while being impeccably scientific, materialistic and anti-dualist. Artificial intelligence is based on similar ideas. You can know about the way a computer program like Word works, without knowing anything about the machine(s) it works on. Since the hardware is essentially irrelevant, cognition can be studied in computer simulations (artificial intelligence) just as well as in human subjects (see Chapter 7.3).

BOX 7.1 Functionalism, multiple realization and reduction, non-reductive materialism

Functionalism

- Functionalism: mental states are functional roles: they have causal relations with input, with other mental states, and with behaviour.
- Multiple realizability: the same mental process (functional state) can be realized in different physical systems (brains, or computer hardware, or whatever).
- Narrow (or machine) functionalism: considers a function solely in terms of the internal economy of the system.
- Wide functionalism: is more like the biological notion of function: it includes the role a function has in the system's environment.

Multiple realization and reduction

- Function as abstract causal role: implementation is irrelevant.
- Many possible realizations of mind in physical systems.
- There is no mind without physical realization, that is, no disembodied mind: materialism, not dualism (in ontology).
- No identification of mental and physical, hence no classical reduction.
- Autonomy of cognitive science relative to neuroscience (in methodology).

Non-reductive materialism

- All mental processes are materially realized, but they cannot be identified with a single physical (brain) process.

Multiple realization as barrier to reduction

 So, functionalism nicely combines **physicalism** (everything, including mind, has a physical basis) with the rejection of reductionism (psychology cannot usefully be reduced to physics or physiology). The **multiple realizibility** of mental states blocks reduction of a single mental state to a single neural process. An animal with a different nervous system from ours can be considered to have the same mental states; a computer which has nothing physical in common with us can be assumed to think in the same way we do. So, as in the example of the language centres mentioned in Chapter 6.2 (speech is usually in the left hemisphere, rarely but not impossibly in the right), the language faculty is functionally identical in the sense that it produces the same speech, and linguists interested in the laws of speech can go about their business ignoring neurophysiological differences. Therefore, multiple realizability is (or was, see below) generally seen as a guarantee that functional explanations are irreducible, and that autonomous psychological explanations, cut loose from neuroscience, are perfectly legitimate.

An autonomous domain has thus been carved out for cognition with its own phenomena at macro level (Fodor, 1997b), and cognitive psychologists can safely leave aside the micro details as merely a matter of implementation. Of course, whether functionalism works, whether there are any interesting (multiply realized) explanatory generalizations at the macro level, is an empirical question.

Fodor (1997b) argues that the evidence is that indeed functional macro-level generalizations are discernible in nature. When you do the science, you can find such laws; he thinks it is a brute fact that a messy intractable lot of micro processes give rise to reliable macro patterns and can be described in macro-generalizations (recall Dennett's intentional patterns mentioned in Chapter 6.3). There are an awful lot of molecules involved in the movements of, for example, an avalanche, and all sorts of different molecules (snow, mud, sand, whatever) may produce avalanches, but the fact is that these all obey the same macro-physical pattern.

Special sciences is Fodor's (1981b, 1997b) term for those sciences whose laws do not nicely map onto the basic laws of physics, i.e. cannot be reduced by deducing them from physics. (Recall that in the classical **D-N model**, see Chapters 2.2 and 3.2, all `glossary` higher-level laws should be deduced from basic laws plus boundary conditions.) No law-like generalization is to be expected between basic physics and special science. But the higher-level laws are perfectly respectable as explanations in their own right. Economics is a good example: there are perfectly respectable laws about money, but these do not map onto physical laws: sometimes money is little gold pieces, sometimes it is pigs, sometimes a series of electronic pulses through the bank's computer network. No physical pattern is to be found, no interesting generalizations are to be expected by translating economic transactions in physical laws, by finding type identities between economics and physics.

The same situation is found in psychology. Of course, in all these cases there is a *token identity* between money and some sort of material thing – it's just a different thing every time: *no type identity*. The interesting conclusion is that the special sciences have their own laws and generalizations, and have nothing to gain from misguided attempts to identify these with basic-level physics. So much for the orthodox position on autonomy and multiple realization.

Let us note that recently the ground under the multiple realization argument for functionalism has started to shift (Block, 1997; Kim, 1992; Looren de Jong, 2003). Whereas Fodor bravely sticks to autonomy for psychology, Bechtel and Mundale (1999) showed that multiple realization is no barrier to successful identification of cognitive functions with brain structures. A working assumption in neuropsychology is that mental functions can be located in circumscribed areas of the brain. Furthermore, the brains of different species (humans, rats, monkeys) are roughly similar in that respect. Bechtel and Mundale point out that, contrary to the original multiple realization argument, in neuroscience functional processing systems are identified using evidence from brain anatomy. So, in these cases the neural level is not as irrelevant as the orthodox multiple realization argument seemed to show, and the details of the implementation are not completely arbitrary (see also Block, 1997). In the simple example used above, hunger in octopuses and humans may well have something in common at the level of their neural realizers. And when researchers find that the respective brains are different, that might point to interesting functional differences in their hunger-driven behaviour – octopean hunger may be functionally different from humans (more fishy perhaps).

In sum, the multiple realization phenomenon is not the strong argument for autonomy of psychology vis-à-vis neuroscience that functionalists have tried to sell it for. In real cognitive neuroscience the realization of cognition in the brain is the subject of research, and in that context, the claim that cognition is autonomous is hardly helpful.

Thus, functionalism holds that mental states can figure in psychological laws and explanations; that the mind can be studied in principle independently of lower-level sciences; that mind is a respectable subject for scientific study; and that we can find laws (causal generalizations) that show how thoughts cause behaviour (Fodor, 1990a). There is a causal role to play for the mental in the physical world, or put more grandiosely, what we think can change the world. Functionalism elegantly reconciles materialism and anti-reductionism, and manages to take mental processes seriously as part of the physical world (if only we could ignore the problem with multiple realization sketched in the previous paragraph; see also the section on mental causation in Chapter 10.3 for more, mostly disappointing, developments).

Functionalism supports a comprehensive philosophy of mind: the computational theory of mind. Functionalism as such does not specify what exactly constitutes the mind's functions. Here computationalism steps in: it says that the functions are computations, that they consist of symbol manipulation (Fodor, 1980; Pylyshyn, 1984; Sterelny, 1990). Computation is presumably the business of the mind/brain. Intelligent behaviour can be produced by mechanical procedures (programs); then, it seems, the 'homunculus', one of the major problems of orthodox cognitivism and its conception of representations, is exorcized.

BOX 7.2   Functionalism and computationalism

- *Functionalism*: mental states are functional states of some physical system (for example a computing machine or a brain).
- *Computationalism*: kind of functionalism that gives a specific definition of a functional state: mental processes essentially consist of computation, i.e. symbol manipulation.

BOX 7.2 **Functionalism and computationalism** (Continued)

- *Fodor's Computational Theory of Mind*:
  - mental states are symbol states, strings in a formal language (such as computer language, or a calculus in logic) in the head (a 'language of thought'); mental processes are transformations of these symbol strings;
  - thinking is explained as following an algorithm, a series of formal operations (as in a Turing machine, see Box 7.7);
  - syntactical (purely formal) processes mirror semantics, meaning, representation, intentionality.

The notion of computation

The idea that the mind is the software of the brain (Block, 1995) was highly influential in finding answers to the old problems on the nature of mind and knowledge. Some inspiration came from Chomsky's ('Cartesian') linguistics (Chomsky, 1990). Abstract formal mental structures, an inborn grammar, can generate correct linguistic utterances, so it seemed plausible that other kinds of intelligent behaviour could also be explained as being generated by a formal-language-like structure in the head.

For the origin of classical (symbolical) **computational** models we have to go back to glossary developments in mathematical logic. Formal languages were the triumph of analytical philosophy and logic in the early twentieth century. Proof theory gave powerful instruments for coming to grips with mathematical reasoning. In mathematics the notion of logical proof had started to look problematic: how are we to know whether a proof is complete and certain – foolproof so to speak? It was thought that this 'decision problem' (*Entscheidungsproblem*) could be solved by specifying a set of elementary rules to be applied in a mechanical way. Thus, in principle, thought, rationality, and reasoning can be formalized and performed in a mechanical way. This requires not mysterious intuition or intelligence but consists in following a series of mechanical steps known as an *algorithm*.

The mathematician Alan Turing (1912–1954), among others, started to look for a decision procedure. The discussions on that problem among mathematicians in the first half of the twentieth century were complicated, but in Turing's view the notion of machine is part of the solution. Thought can be mechanized by means of 'intelligent machinery'. Interestingly, that opens the way for something like machine learning and machine thinking (Turing did some work on the 'mechanization' of chess). When formal systems can be implemented on computers, thinking can be done by machines – not nineteenth-century steel and brass machines, but logical devices.

In this context, Alan Turing gave his proof of a universal machine that can implement any algorithmically calculable function (not to be confused with the more controversial

Turing test – see Chapter 7.3). The theoretical foundations of the claim that thinking is computation, more precisely symbol manipulation, lie in the notions of a **Turing machine** and effective procedure.

A Turing machine is a general-purpose symbol manipulator: it reads a symbol, performs an elementary operation on it, and writes it back; the computer is in the business of symbol manipulation, transforming input symbols into output symbols. A universal Turing machine is a Turing machine that can simulate the input–output function of any other Turing machine. Anything that can be specified by an algorithm is computational and can be calculated.

This leads naturally to the hypothesis that the brain is a (tremendously complex) machine that calculates outputs, given some kind of input. The classical view of computational theory of mind, CTM, mostly associated with Jerry Fodor is, in a nutshell, that thinking consists in logical and **syntactical** operations on discrete symbols in a formalized language; it will be the subject of the next section. (The alternative view that the kind of computations that underwrite mental operations is numerical, that is, continuous computation in connectionist networks, will be discussed in the next chapter.)

BOX 7.3 Computation

Computation is manipulating symbols. The idea of a general-purpose computer was traditionally that it executes symbol manipulation according to formal mechanic procedures. One should distinguish between this classical symbolic view, as described, and the recent connectionist view on computation, as the spreading of numerical activation through a (neural) network.

Computational theory of mind (CTM) holds that mental processes essentially consist of computation, i.e. manipulation of a mental symbols network.

- CTM in its *classical* version, associated with Jerry Fodor, assumes that mental states are symbol states, strings in a formal language (imagine a computer language, or predicate calculus in logic) in the head, and mental processes are transformations of these symbol strings.
- The *connectionist* alternative (see next chapter) holds that mental processes are activation patterns in a multidimensional vector space; this could also be called a computational view of mind, although a completely different kind of computation (numerical versus logical).

The notion of a mental language

The idea of symbols and formal languages was an inspiration for CTM. Symbols can be combined according to strictly formal rules: the progress in mathematical logic in the late nineteenth and early twentieth centuries has proved it possible to formalize deductive reasoning (see Chapter 1.3 on deduction; 'If he calls Fido, the dog comes immediately' can be formalized into: p > q (p implies q); hence the formalized reasoning: p > q; p; thus q). Frege talked about *'eine der mathematischen nachgebildete Formelsprache des reinen Denkens'* (a formal language of pure thought, modelled on mathematic language). So we can compute deductive reasoning in a mechanical way by manipulating symbols, in more or less the same way as we do in arithmetic.

Effective procedures are mechanical procedures that can be executed without any insight. This means that any activity that can be specified in a series of mechanical operations, an *algorithm*, can be executed by a universal Turing machine.

Newell and Simon launched the hypothesis that such a universal symbol manipulator (Newell, 1980, called it a *'physical symbol system'*) can exhibit intelligence, in the sense that it can be said to possess goals, plans and knowledge. Symbol manipulation is instantiated in a physical system, a computer, and the existence of a mechanism that embodies logical operations, namely, symbol manipulation, made the notions of information and symbol manipulation palatable to materialists. Logic is put to work, and AI shows 'how ... rationality [is] mechanically possible' (Fodor, 1987b: 20); or in Newell's words: 'mind enters into the physical universe' (1980: 136).

So, we can see now how the revolution in computer science in the early 1960s brought, in combination with the heritage of analytic philosophy, an upswing in the philosophy of mind. Issues like intentionality, meaning, representation, already the staple trade of analytical philosophy, were now approached in terms of formal languages. CTM applies these ideas to psychology.

An idea that lies at the root of the orthodox symbolic approach is that formal languages (proposition logic, predicate logic, programming languages) give us a handle on the mind. The possibility of an abstract characterization of a system was considered especially useful after the collapse of the mind–brain identity theory (Chapter 6), since this provides psychologists with a level of description that generalizes across minds, brains and computers.

Furthermore, formalization is scientifically respectable since the languages that are used in writing computer programs are both formal and causally powerful. The idea was that some kind of formal languages is the canonical form for mental processes, that is, provides a notation for the program of the mind in which to express mental states and the mechanisms of mental transformations.

A formal language consists of a set of admissible symbols and operations on them. The idea of the computational theory of mind is that the mind is a formal system and can be specified by the same concepts as used in specifying computer programs. These basic concepts refer to inputs and outputs, machine operations and program states, all of them conceived as symbols and operations on symbols (Fodor, 1981a: 13). Mental processes are considered as operations on some sort of symbol. They are purely syntactic: only the form of the symbol string counts in determining what can be done with them – just like formulae in mathematics.

Syntax mirrors semantics

Formalism means that form is sufficient and that content doesn't matter; somewhat more precisely, that syntax determines the workings of a formal system, that the semantics do not add anything to the causal structure of a process. A formula or symbol structure or program does not change when it refers to different things. Considering the mind/brain as a computational device means that it is both a syntactical machine, or a syntax-driven machine (the program drives it through a series of states), but also, if Brentano and others (see Chapters 6.1 and 10.1 on intentionality) got it anywhere right, it must be a semantic machine that has properties like meaning and truth. Its syntactical symbols mean something; they refer to things beyond themselves, and if given a true input, will produce a true output (as is the case in logic).

A helpful analogy (Block, 1995) is the difference between numerals and numbers: numerals are manipulated according to syntactic rules, but numbers have meaning and follow the laws of arithmetic. In other words, numbers are truth preserving: true premises lead to true conclusions. In mathematics and logic, syntax presumably tracks glossary **semantics**. The numerals on your bank receipt represent the number of pounds or euros in your bank account; the bank computer or your desk calculator do their job by shifting numerals without regard for their meaning, but the result mirrors your wealth (or lack thereof). Somehow, the world is arranged in such a way that it follows the laws of logic and mathematics: the symbols 'stand for' real things, and manipulating them according to syntactic rules leads to new symbol structures that stand for true conclusions about the world.

The same kind of isomorphism between the semantic and the syntactical is characteristic for the classic computational theory. The mind/brain operates at two levels: the syntactic and the semantic.

As Fodor puts it, the computational theory of mind is a combination of two theses: that thought is mechanical computation, and that thought is representational, and that the former drives the latter (Fodor, 1994). The syntactic machine mirrors the semantic machine: reasoning, rationality, logical validity are reflected and realized in syntactic operations. Meaning correlates with the form, the symbols in the brain and the formal operations on them are in accordance with the meaning relations between symbols.

This is not unproblematic because the question remains: what guarantees the harmony between these two levels? Why are purely formal operations truth-preserving, rational, and so on? Fodor (1994) and Block (1995) vaguely point to evolution, which has presumably produced brains that perform the right syntactic operations to remain in step with reality.

More precisely, Block (1995) argues that the meaning of a symbol follows from its connections with other symbols, from its role in a network economy of the mind (the symbol for 'red' is partly defined by its connection with 'danger', 'communism', granny's Ford Mustang, Enron's accounting practices, and vice versa). This network fixation of meaning is supplemented by input systems, called transducers, which connect the inputs from the external world to input symbols. Together internal and external connections define the role for a symbol, and that defines its meaning. Intentional representational states derive their meaning from these symbol roles. So here is a complete theory of meaning, intentionality and the laws of thought for you – at least in outline. CTM is the elaboration of these ideas into a theory of what mind really is.

As a final note of caution, it deserves to be mentioned that although these ideas are still mainstream, some think that they are a misinterpretation of the notion of computation (Shagrir, 1997). Interpreting effective procedures as similar to mental causality (abstract or mental events driving behaviour) may be misguided; interpreting syntactic structures in a Turing machine as a bearer of meaning is the result of a confusion; and some think that the Turing machine analogy may be useless in understanding human cognition (Kearns, 1997). Although the computational view of mind has a long history, and is widely seen as plausible, it may be more problematic than initially thought.

7.3 The Computational Theory of Mind: Representations, Symbols, Meaning and Intentionality

Philosophical roots: computation and mind

Fodor (1981b, 1997b, 2001) has laid the foundations of a theory of cognition and meaning based upon the idea of computation, known as the computational theory of mind (CTM). CTM looks by his own admission (Fodor, 1980) a lot like Descartes' theory of mind: a mix of mentalism and nativism. It is the latest version of what could be called the representational theory of mind (Fodor, 1981b; Sterelny, 1990), which fits into a long tradition in philosophy that sees the mind as a repository of ideas (see also Chapter 4.4). But now, for the first time, so think CTM's admirers, a scientifically respectable story can be told about what exactly these ideas are.

CTM can be situated within the functionalist tradition; it qualifies mental functions as representations and operations on representations. Representations are symbol structures (roughly something like formulae in logic or mathematics), and mental operations are computations that transform symbol structures (roughly like deriving proofs in logic). The idea that representations are symbol strings seems natural since, as explained above, a symbol has a representational function, it stands in for something.

In addition, the computational theory provides a story on explanation, inspired by the computer metaphor outlined above: mental symbol structures have their causal and explanatory role in virtue of their formal syntactical role. These representational states and transitions between them are both semantic and causal; they both have **intentionality**, content and meaning, and they support the mechanics of thought and rationality. This idea brings together cognitive science, looking for the laws of thought (the causal concern), and philosophy, looking for the nature of meaning of mental

glossary

representations (the semantic concern) (Fodor, 1987b). It has a message for psychologists on the nature and laws of thinking and reasoning, and for philosophers on the nature of meaning and mind.

The big picture is to combine intentionality and causal mechanistic explanation. Computation is cause of behaviour: like the symbolic program drives the machine through a series of physical states, mental computations are mental causations (see Chapter 10.3) – the eternal riddle of how our thoughts and desires can cause changes in our brains, and pull our muscles. It is conceived in terms of the way representations cause other representations (the mechanism of the train of thought), and finally cause behaviour. Mental processes are transitions between representations, and syntactic operations constitute the laws of thought and the mechanisms of mind.

The grand scheme of the CTM is: naturalizing intentionality, showing how rationality is mechanically possible (Fodor, 1987b: 20). Basically, the argument is that intentionality requires symbols, because symbols are the only bearers of meaning we know. Symbol manipulation can be arranged so that the semantics follows the syntax (Fodor, 1994); the syntactic engine mimics the semantic engine (Haugeland, 1981). Roughly, the idea is that a formal program behaves in an intelligent way, as if it tracks referents, things in the world. A key concept here is 'truth preserving': the formal program is so arranged that true input symbols lead, after a lot of symbol crunching, to true output symbols. If that sounds like magic, recall that this is what happens in mathematics too; even the lowly desk calculator is designed so that it infallibly comes up with the true answer to an arithmetical problem.

Likewise, formal logic provides a formal mechanical recipe in reasoning: how to get to true conclusions from true premises (note that formal logic has nothing to say about what premises are true).

Important for philosophers and psychologists is the idea that a mechanical, formal structure can exhibit logical, semantic and truthful behaviour. This suggests that mechanical rationality is possible in computational, symbol-manipulating systems.

Thus, Fodor's proposal is an example of naturalism: natural science explains the mysteries of mind, the phenomena of thinking and rationality as products of natural, causal, mechanical processes (albeit a type of naturalism different from Churchland and Churchland, who would argue for a more biological perspective of cognition as a adaptation, made for survival, not for truth and semantics – see Chapter 8).

Empirical claims: language of thought

The claim that the mind is a symbol manipulator, that representations are symbol strings, implies that we need some kind of formal language that defines the symbols and the rules to combine them (like a dictionary and a grammar in natural languages, or the numbers and the rules for division, adding, subtracting and multiplying in arithmetic).

Here Fodor applies another computational idea to psychology: the language of thought (LOT); this is not a real language as spoken, but a group of formulae as in formal logic or computer languages. According to this picture, we have a head full of logical formulae, and symbol crunching is the essence of cogitation. When you think something (like: 'Chocolate is bad for your teeth') you have a token of a sentence in your mind (what some philosophers call a proposition), that is made up of basic symbols (maybe like words in a natural language), which are put together according to formal rules. Mental representations are symbol strings; transforming them according to formal rules into new symbol strings is thinking.

Below we will discuss arguments pro and con such a counterintuitive hypothesis. In a nutshell, defenders of the view that we have 'sentences in our head' argue that thinking must be very much like language, since it can be expressed in words and must have a logical structure to make reasoning possible. What is, at least according to Fodor, a non-negotiable fact about thinking is that it is compositional: elementary concepts (chocolate, bad, teeth) are combined to make strings of concepts. Logicians think that 'combinatorial semantics' is a property of logical languages: the meaning of a complex expression is the product of its constituent expressions and the connectives that combine them. The properties of thought require in Fodor's view a structure that can combine (and recombine) constituents into almost infinitely long, complex and logically structured expressions – that is, it must have a language-like structure.

The language of thought must also be innate. Learning something requires, according to Fodor (1975), that the apparatus of reasoning and hypothesis testing must already be in place. What is learned is just the filling of the LOT architecture. Note that Chomsky's generative grammar is also innate, and learning a language is essentially 'parameter setting', filling the slots in an inborn language capacity.

In that light, the notion of an internal language (half-jokingly referred to as 'mentalese') that accounts for the structure of our thinking, and that cannot come from the outside world, is less absurd than it seems, or as Fodor likes to argue, it is less absurd than alternative hypotheses. See Bloom and Keil (2001) and Pinker (1994) for many (complicated and sometimes contradicting) ideas and findings about innate mental languages (computational or otherwise), and on the possible relation between mentalese to spoken, natural languages, and how both types of language in turn might be related to thinking and using concepts.

BOX 7.4 **Syntax and semantics**

Syntax: is about the *form* of statements, that is, the logical or formal linguistic relations between sentences or parts thereof. Formal logic and mathematics deal in syntactical operations.

Semantics: is about the *meaning* of linguistic representations (utterances) and by extension of mental representations (thoughts). It is a deep philosophical question how words or thoughts can mean a thing in the external world; even more, how they can mean things that do not exist (e.g. how one can think of a unicorn). *Truth* is a typical semantic notion.

BOX 7.4   Syntax and semantics (Continued)

Sometimes the *syntax* can *mirror* the *semantics*: the formal operations on numerals in mathematics (adding, subtracting, etc.) mirror quantities of objects in the real world (e.g. a desk calculator may track the amount of money in your pocket).
Logic is *truth preserving*: if you enter true premises in valid argumentations, you get true conclusions.

BOX 7.5   The language of thought (LOT)

Mental activity has a structure like a formal, or logical, language. Mental representations are strings of symbols that are characterized by their syntactical structure. Thinking is manipulating these symbols in more or less the same way as constructing logical proofs is.

LOT's syntax is supposed to mirror the world it represents – it is truth preserving. Its formal operations track the changes in the environment – as a mental apparatus serving survival should do.

The LOT hypothesis explains the *systematicity* and *productivity* of thinking: you can think infinitely many thoughts by combining a finite number of mental elements, and these thoughts cohere with each other.

Empirical evidence

As Copeland (1993) rightly emphasizes, it is an empirical hypothesis that there is a algorithmically calculable function computed in the brain/mind, and that hypothesis has still to be confirmed. There is no compelling logical reason to assume that symbol manipulation adds up to intelligence. The computational hypothesis is defended by Fodor as a case

glossary of **inference to the best explanation** (see Chapter 1.3): it gives the least implausible account of a system that is capable of the generative capacities we know mind has. It is the only game in town, all other accounts can be seen to be non-starters. Although the theory transcends the facts, it is the story that is the most compatible with the facts. Usually, his arguments take the following form: given the properties of human thought and language, nothing less than a LOT would explain them: how could it be otherwise? We will see how this argument goes in Fodor's attack on connectionism, in Chapter 8.3.

It is not very clear how a hypothesis on the structure of the mental algorithm can be verified. Direct empirical evidence, showing that cognitive systems are symbol crunchers, is surprisingly scarce. Pylyshyn (1989) proposed some criteria to decide whether a computational simulation exhibits what he calls 'strong equivalence' to a real thinker; and these criteria seem to allow considerable leeway. Attempts in (strong) AI to build a cognitive system within the framework of a LOT, that is, as symbol manipulator, are said by some critics (Dreyfus, 1979) to be all but defunct by now. Fodor (1984, 2000a) is fully aware of this, and is downright pessimistic about the success of building a mind in the foreseeable future, but he maintains that the CTM is the only theory that is not dead in the water from the start.

Other attempts, like connectionism (see Chapter 8.2), are sure to fail, he thinks. More precisely, he thinks that cognitive science is as yet impossible because we do not know how to handle the 'holistic' properties of cognition (Fodor, 1984, 1987a): what we consider relevant and reliable knowledge, and what kinds of evidence bear upon a given belief, depend on the whole system of our beliefs. But we have as yet no way of analysing this whole in specific inferential relations between discrete propositions – we just don't know the rules and symbols of the LOT, and how it computes these inferences. Incidentally, this situation is very similar to the induction problem in the philosophy of science, where all attempts to formalize induction and **abduction** have failed | glossary | (see Chapter 3.6); it is no coincidence that Fodor (1984) refers to Quine's holism (see Chapter 3.5).

To sum up, as an account of the mind, the computational paradigm is in trouble.

Folk psychology

In the next chapter and in Chapter 10.2 we will discuss different views of **folk psychology**. For the moment, we can define folk psychology as the kind of | glossary | psychology that explains everyday behaviour by an appeal to beliefs and desires – seemingly simple **explanations** like: he is working late because he believes that is the | glossary | way to pass tomorrow's exam, which he very much wants to do.

The philosophically interesting point is that these explanations are intentional and refer to mental states with representations and goals. Furthermore, they assume rationality in the agent: her behaviour will be understandable as the most rational way to achieve her goals given her perception of the current state of affairs. Rationality is a normative principle, and at first sight it is typical for humans and perhaps some animals: we don't attribute rationality to stones falling along the optimal trajectory, or to the planets for staying in their orbit.

Folk psychology also seems to give causal explanations: our desires and beliefs produce physical behaviour, they make us labour and toil by the sweat of our brow. And these physical happenings are somehow coherent with meaningful, rational and normative criteria for behaviour. Or put differently, the causes of behaviour are not only brute physics, as when falling from a roof, but they are at the same time rational and meaningful in the light of reason and truth. The challenge is to explain how semantics and meaning can be a physical cause.

glossary Recall how the traditional view in continental philosophy of science thought reasons incompatible with causes (see Chapter 2.6), and you will see that **naturalism** would have been anathema to Brentano and the hermeneuticists (see Chapters 4 and 10). They thought that mental states have content and meaning, and this sets them apart from the physical world.

glossary Fodor's project is a species of naturalism (though surely not the only species). Cain (2002) summarizes it as the conjunction of folk psychology and **physicalism**. In contrast with linguistic behaviourists, Fodor believes that mental representation and processes are real things with causal powers, and not just convenient labels for describing behaviour. He also believes that this claim of 'intentional realism', that is, the real existence and causal efficacy of intentional states like beliefs and desires, is supported by the CTM. The CTM vindicates folk psychology, the use of beliefs and desires as explanations, and abandoning intentional idiom would be a cultural catastrophe since all our daily predictions and explanations of our fellow beings' behaviour implies it. We simply have no other way of explaining and predicting what our fellow beings do, other than in terms of what they believe and what they think.

glossary The beauty of CTM is in Fodor's view that it vindicates folk psychology. CTM explains beliefs and desires as **propositional attitudes**, symbol structures in a language of thought, that the subject has an attitude to, that is, that have a location in the computational system (belief box and desire box, respectively). So we can understand why folk psychology works in terms of computational psychology, and how intentionality and rationality are mechanically possible.

It should be realized, however, that in this picture both the computer metaphor and folk psychology have been extensively reconstructed to make a rapprochement between them possible. The man in the street who attributes mental states (knowledge and goals) to himself and others does not usually assume propositions in his head, nor mental causation. Fodor has constructed a package deal of computationalism and intentional psychology that not everybody wants to buy.

Interestingly, as we will see in Chapters 8.2 and 10.3, Paul Churchland does accept the package, and then manages both to abandon the LOT model and to eliminate folk psychology in one fell swoop, replacing both by neural network models.

BOX 7.6   Folk psychology

Common-sense psychology is the kind of explanation of everyday behaviour in terms of the goals, desires, beliefs, opinions and plans that supposedly drive one's fellow beings' behaviour.

Philosophers emphasize that folk psychology involves intentionality – beliefs and desires, representations and mental content are intentional terms.

BOX 7.6 Folk psychology (Continued)

Beliefs and desires are (according to some philosophers) literally causes and lawful explanations of behaviour; in this view, folk psychology is committed to *mental causation* (Chapter 10.3).

The possibility of *naturalization* of folk psychology, its reduction to cognitive or neuroscience, is a hotly debated issue.

CTM thinks that folk psychology can and should be preserved in a computational theory of mind.

According to *CTM*, beliefs and desires are *propositional attitudes*, consisting of an attitude towards a *proposition* (believing that *p*). The proposition is a symbol string (in LOT), and the attitude is the place where it is stored (the 'belief box', or the 'desire box').

CTM: intentionality and rationality

Drawing together some lines, we have seen how Fodor sharpens the functionalist intuition by connecting it with the idea of a language of thought, introducing the apparatus of the philosophy of language into the philosophy of mind. More precisely, Fodor (1987b) combines the cognitive-psychological problem of the nature of mental processes with the philosophical problem about the semantics of propositions. The LOT carries in its wake a lot of problems of semantics. However, Fodor (1981a) is also clear that he is in fact taking on two problems in one theory: intentionality and mechanical rationality.

The former refers to Brentano's problem: how is it possible that some (mental) states are *about* something? How are meaning and representation possible? The second refers to **artifical intelligence** and the problem of giving a naturalistic theory of `glossary` intelligent behaviour. It is quite conceivable that the former does not contribute anything to the latter, and vice versa.

Fodor (1994) tries to reconcile the two distinct claims – that the laws of psychology are intentional, that is, that they explain behaviour by citing mental content, the goals and desires an organism has; and that these are implemented in computational mechanisms.

The 'selling point' of Fodor's theory is that CTM has a story for both the philosophical problem of intentionality and semantics, and for the problem of the mechanisms of intelligence and rationality. To appreciate the strength of this claim, recall the alternative view proposed by Dennett (see Chapter 6 and again in Chapter 10.1): meaning and intentionality are not a part of the machinery of the mind, but are in the eye of the beholder. It is just an external perspective from which we describe and predict the behaviour of complex systems (Dennett, 1978a, 1987b).

Fodor in contrast is an intentional realist: he thinks that intentionality is ontologically real, a fact of nature, underwritten by computational mechanisms, not just an observer-dependent way of describing the behaviour of complex systems. At the very least, this is a strong and implausible claim. One might think that Fodor is overplaying his hand here, by trying to capture philosophical and psychological issues in one computational framework.

Another crucial and at second thought problematic aspect of CTM is the relation between syntax and semantics – the formal machinery and what it represents in the outside world. How is it possible that syntactic mechanisms run in harmony with the semantics? In the example of the desk calculator the designer has made sure that the electronics will do the arithmetic correctly, but how can a formal syntactic mind have truth preserving representations of the world?

Fodor (1994) has no very convincing answer. There is some connection, he thinks, because the computational mechanisms have a causal history of interactions with the world that generally connect the current outcome of the syntactic mechanisms with the right behaviour in the environment, that is, preserve the meaning or content of a **belief** or desire over a series of formal computations. Very roughly, evolution has guaranteed that the inner formal syntactic processes are in harmony with events and processes in the world outside. However, as he admits elsewhere, evolutionary accounts of cognition are problematic (Fodor, 2000b).

So the grand vision of CTM, to explain intelligence and intentionality (and for that matter, also to solve the mind-brain problem along functionalist lines), still has several serious defects, as Fodor will acknowledge – he just thinks that CTM is basically on the right track, and the connectionist competition (see the next chapter) is basically wrong.

7.4 Artificial Intelligence and the Idea of a Physical Symbol System

As mentioned above, in 1950 Alan Turing published his famous paper, 'Computing machinery and intelligence' (Copeland, 1993), where the possibility of intelligence in a computer was defended. The idea of a thinking machine was older than Turing's paper: in the eighteenth century a chess machine appeared in royal courts in Europe (it was a hoax, with a dwarf inside); and in the nineteenth century (1838) Charles Babbage tried to build an 'analytical engine', a calculator of brass cogs and wheels. Turing himself did not contribute much to the realization of real artificial intelligence: the first computer was built according to designs by John von Neumann (and a few others).

BOX 7.7 Turing machine

The prototype of a symbol manipulator, a Turing machine can read a symbol from tape, perform an elementary operation on it, and write the result back. The British mathematician Alan Turing proved that every task that can be written as a set of elementary operations (an algorithm) can be executed on a *universal* Turing machine. This is the basis for the claim of strong AI: when you can specify an algorithm, a set of operations, you have explained how a system performs that task, and you can run it on a computer.

The first working program played checkers (draughts) in the early 1950s. Newell, Shaw and Simon presented a program (the 'Logic Theorist') that could prove theorems from Whitehead and Russell's *Principia Mathematica* (a foundational work in mathematical logic) in 1956. Herbert Simon claimed in 1957 that 'there are now in the world machines that think, that learn and that create', and that in ten years a computer would be world chess champion, that by then a computer would have discovered a new mathematical theorem, and that most theories in psychology would have the form of a computer program (Dreyfus, 1979: 81–2).

Unfortunately, as you may have guessed, that did not happen. The consensus is that simulation of real human intelligence (strong AI) is nowhere in sight (not even in chess; the newest programs that beat top chess players partly rely on brute force). Whether that reflects negatively on the computational theory is a moot point. Nevertheless, it is interesting to look closer at the theoretical foundations of classical symbolic AI, if only to appreciate the alternative (connectionism, discussed in the next chapter) and the critics (Hubert Dreyfus, see below). Of course, we will encounter many ideas from the CTM discussed above.

Strong AI claims that in the digital computer we already have an instance of a thinking machine. The basic idea of AI is the notion of *physical symbol systems* (PSS) (Newell, 1980; see also Copeland, 1993: ch. 4; Pylyshyn, 1984). A PSS has a set of symbolic structures and performs operations on symbol strings, generating new symbol strings. All this is implemented in a physical machine with a binary code realized in electronic physical components (plus memory, input and output devices that translate physical inputs into symbols, and symbols into physical outputs – Pylyshyn (1984) calls them 'transducers'). The PSS hypothesis is that such a system can display general intelligence (and perhaps *only* such a symbol manipulator can display intelligence – Copeland (1993: 82) calls the latter view the 'strong' PSS hypothesis).

As we have seen, a symbolic language can be the vehicle of representations of the world, and therefore it seems reasonable to consider the collection of symbol structures as the PSS's knowledge. Together with appropriate input and output transducers and mechanisms for operating on symbol strings to produce new symbol strings it will exhibit intelligence – thinking, insight, learning, intuition, creativity, and common sense (Copeland, 1993; Newell, 1980).

The PSS hypothesis thus holds that intelligence can be captured in an algorithm: a procedure that is mechanical in the sense that it requires no insight – it consists of a finite number of precisely specified steps that lead necessarily to a specific result, more or less like a cooking recipe or instructions for taking apart and reassembling an engine. Turing's point was that computation is algorithmic, and any algorithmically calculable procedure (known as an effective procedure) can be executed by a universal machine (a symbol manipulating device). The PSS hypothesis says that we can simulate general intelligence by specifying the algorithm, the steps taken to solve a problem; that is, what we call intelligent behaviour can arise from a finite sequence of mechanical computations. As Copeland (1993) puts it, this is an article of the deepest faith among AI researchers, too obvious to mention.

The background of this belief is Church's thesis that if something can be characterized as a sequence of algorithmically specified operations it can be simulated on a Turing machine. So if intelligence is tractable at all, it can be executed in a series of mechanical steps; and then it will run as a computer program.

The 'if' in the previous sentence is an empirical if: from Turing to Newell and Simon (1981) it has been admitted that intelligence conceived as effective procedure is a fallible hypothesis (frankly, the possibility of failure was not unduly emphasized). The claim is that a (perhaps unknown) algorithm exists by which behaviour can be calculated; but whereas it is not implausible that the brain is a information-processing device, whether its workings are computable is another matter.

Recently, Roger Penrose (1989), an eminent physicist, has argued that mathematical thinking is *not* algorithmic, and that strong AI therefore is on the wrong track as an account of thinking (mathematical and otherwise). Penrose (1994) later proposed a non-algorithmic alternative based on quantum physics (quantum effects in the brain somehow produce consciousness – Hameroff and Penrose, 1996). Penrose's arguments are a bit too abstract and esoteric to be discussed here (see Grush and Churchland, 1995 for a rebuttal). It may be significant, however, that a respected mathematician thinks algorithmicity is problematic. See also Shagrir (1997) for doubts about the dogmas of computationalism.

Below, two other arguments against strong AI will be briefly discussed, the first empirical, the second conceptual.

The failure of classical ('strong') AI

The PSS hypothesis aimed at explaining general intelligence, the kind of all-purpose rationality that could be applied in any domain of knowledge. The claim that 'we now possess machines that think' (quoted in Dreyfus, 1979: 81) was put forward by Newell and Simon in 1958, and they predicted tremendous progress in the next two decades. This has failed to materialize. AI programs only seem to work in small and narrowly circumscribed domains – so called 'toy worlds', like a world consisting of blocks that the program has to stack. Attempts to upgrade to real or at least somewhat richer worlds have not succeeded. General intelligence seems to depend on a lot of domain-specific knowledge that has so far resisted formalizing (Copeland, 1993). In this sense the PSS hypothesis is increasingly implausible. Newell's SOAR architecture (1992) and Anderson's ACT-R (1983) are attempts to provide a general architecture of cognition. It is perhaps not unfair to say that decades after their introduction, these are still no more than a torso.

Whereas the approach in AI initially was to get things right from the outset and create a foundational system of general intelligence, the present approach seems to be more like starting from particular problems like building search engines and hoping that in the end methods and techniques will converge bottom-up to a grand scheme of general intelligence. Dreyfus and Dreyfus (1990) make some sarcastic remarks about the quest for a fundamental epistemology in early AI: precisely that has been tried in philosophy since Plato and has consistently failed – from Descartes to Husserl. The failure of founding epistemology on formal rationality Dreyfus now sees repeated in classical symbolical AI.

One of the very few remaining projects that attempt to model common sense in the classical symbolic approach is the CYC project (Copeland, 1993) (the name comes from 'encyclopaedia'). This tries to build the basic categories of our common sense into a large encyclopaedia-like system. Statements that describe the way we categorize the world (events, properties, etc.) are entered into a database, and the system can reason about this knowledge using formal logical inference techniques. The least one can say is that the project has come a long way (the database is now gigantic), but still has a long way to go – if it is going anywhere.

The *frame problem* (Dennett, 1987; Haselager, 1995) illustrates the impasse methods of specifying algorithms for common sense have got into. Very briefly, the frame problem is that humans have an uncanny sense for what is relevant in changing situations, and how to keep track of the consequences of one's actions. It seems impossible to simulate this capacity in explicit logical inferences. Philosophers have noted that essentially the same problem emerges in the philosophy of science as the induction problem. Whatever it is, it has something to do with relevance, and the holism of our belief system (see Fodor, 1984; Pylyshyn, 1987). Dreyfus and Dreyfus (1990) argue that atomism and rationalism, the idea that all knowledge can be captured in explicit rules and strings of elementary symbols, are at odds with the holistic nature of human practices and skills.

The upshot is that the AI project of capturing human intelligence in explicit rules has run into trouble. It seems that human values, engagement, commitment and risk, a sense of relevance and physical presence are essential in human knowledge, and that all this is intractable in terms of abstract knowledge and explicit rules. Hubert Dreyfus (2001), who predicted this outcome back in 1979, thinks that knowledge is essentially embodied and embedded in an environment, and that being in the world (a phrase deriving from continental phenomenological philosophers) is characterized not by explicit knowledge and rules, but by prereflexive engagement. It is not primarily theoretical knowing-*that*, the knowledge of statements and theories, but practical, embodied knowing-*how*, skills that allow us to cope with the things we encounter (see also Chapters 9.3, 9.4, 9.5). Dreyfus' diagnosis is that the 'data assumption' and 'theoretical' construals of knowledge (knowledge is a sum of discrete and explicit beliefs expressing elementary facts) are misguided (see also Dreyfus (2001) on a similar criticism of the dubious blessings of the Internet).

The Chinese Room

In his famous (1950) paper, Alan Turing proposed a simple test to solve the question of whether a machine can think. It has the form of an imitation game: somewhat simplified, the 'Turing test' works as follows: an observer tries to find out whether he communicates with a computer or with a human by typing questions and reading the answers on the screen. If he cannot identify by the answers whether his interlocutor is a human or a computer, and the computer's answers are indistinguishable from a human, it has passed the test and then, according to Turing's proposal, it can be said to think. (Since 1991, there is an annual contest (the Loebner Prize; http://www.loebner.net/Prizef/loebner-prize.html) for AI programs impersonating some (usually very small) aspect of human intelligence, for example, discussing baseball. It is usually very easy to find out which is the computer by asking catch questions, so the Loebner contest has very strict rules about the subject and the form of the questions.)

John Searle (1990b) became famous for his attack on the central thesis of the strong AI. He proposed a thought experiment known as the 'Chinese Room'. Imagine that a speaker of English is put in a room with an input and output tray, and is given a batch of Chinese characters, plus a set of instructions in English. When he finds a set of Chinese characters in his input, he has to produce a set of Chinese characters by way of output; the instruction tells him how to manipulate (read, compare, combine, order) Chinese symbols so as to come up with the correct stack of output symbols. Outside the room, speakers of Chinese know that the input characters are questions in Chinese, and they can read his outputs as answers in Chinese, insofar as the instructions guarantee symbol sequences that are comprehensible for Chinese readers. To them the Englishman seems a Chinese-story-comprehending system. In reality, however, all he does is manipulate uninterpreted symbols according to some set of formal **syntactic** rules (the 'program'); that is, the Englishman plus his instructions are imitating a computer program.

glossary

The inspiration for this story came from Schank's computer program that could answer questions about simple stories, thus presumably instantiating understanding. The English speaker/understander without knowledge of Chinese takes the place of such a program: he/it answers questions intelligently, by going through a routine of symbol manipulation. So, the crux is: 'What would it be like if my mind actually worked on the principles that the theory says all minds work on?' And the conclusion is: 'The computer is me ... the computer has nothing more than I have in the case where I understand nothing.' The Englishman plays the role of a computer program; obviously, he does not understand Chinese, and the conclusion Searle draws is that insofar as he does what an computer program does (manipulating symbols according to syntactic rules) a computer program cannot be said to understand anything.

This means that the famous Turing test for intelligence (does the system give the right answers to difficult questions, such that it is indistinguishable from human answers?) is irrelevant; the system can give the right answers in exactly the same way as a human – but without really understanding anything. It follows that symbol manipulation is not sufficient for understanding, and strong AI is wrong.

It has often been argued that Searle's thought experiment is unrealistic and misleading. One objection is that the complexity of a working expert system is not comparable with the sheet of instructions and the stack of symbols that Searle provides the Englishman with – and from that complexity might emerge genuine understanding.

Probably the most powerful objection is the 'systems reply', which holds that the Englishman is only a component of the system (see Searle, 1980). It holds that Searle's misleading trick is to picture the English symbol manipulator as human. No one would have asked whether understanding resides in a particular neuron anywhere in the brain, since it is obvious that the *whole system* (brain plus much of the rest of the body) understands Chinese or English. The Englishman in his particular role of symbol manipulator is just a *part* of the whole system. So, the systems reply is that understanding should be attributed to the whole system (input, output, program, symbol stack, and processor). The Englishman is only the analogue of the central processor, so that his lack of comprehension of Chinese does not prove that comprehension is beyond any computational system. The latter conclusion is about as silly as concluding that you do not understand this text because part of you (for example, some neuron in the back of your head) taken in itself does not understand it.

The Chinese Room is still the subject of ongoing debate (Preston and Bishop, 2002). We do not want to force an interpretation on the reader, but we feel that thought experiments are inconclusive evidence. What computational systems can do is ultimately an empirical question. Churchland and Churchland (1990) point out that Searle does not know what the future may bring, and perhaps new more brain-like computers (neural networks – see Chapter 8.2) might do the trick.

7.5 Conclusion: Classical Computationalism in Trouble

The classical view of mind as the software of the brain seems to have a bright future behind it. It is an intellectually rigorous, plausible and once promising idea. Some decades ago it seemed that the Turing machine had the potential to explain mind and cognition – computation (symbol manipulation) seemed a powerful model to capture intelligence, intentionality and representation by reconstructing mental representations as symbol strings in a language of thought. It provides a non-reductive yet materialistic solution to the mind–body problem and guarantees the autonomy of cognitive science. However, the purely formal syntactical account of mind runs into philosophical problems, and strong AI is in trouble. Although CTM still has its believers, its problems are manifold. The next chapter will present a competing model of mind with more or less the same promise: connectionism, the theory of neural networks.

FURTHER READING

Block, N. (1995) 'The mind as the software of the brain', in E. Smith and D.N. Osherson (eds), *Thinking: An Invitation to Cognitive Science*. Cambridge, MA: MIT Press. pp. 377–425. A lucid exposition of the computational theory of mind.

8. MODERN APPROACHES TO MIND (2): THE BRAIN-BASED VIEW

Neurophilosophy, Connectionism and Dynamicism

PREVIEW: In this chapter we turn to the alternatives for the classical computational view: connectionism and dynamicism. Connectionism implies that pattern recognition, embodied in activation spreading through the neural network, is the stuff the mind is made of. Dynamicism rejects the notion of internal representation, be it symbolic structures or patterns of activity, and instead offers the model of an organism dynamically coupled to its environment as the basic metaphor of mental activity. In section 8.4 we sketch how the brain-based view could contribute to such general issues in philosophy as the nature of knowledge, meaning, and the sense of self and personhood.

8.1   Introduction: An Alternative View on Mind

In this chapter, we present an alternative to the classical story of mind – more precisely, an alternative view on what cognition is, of how mind relates to brain, and what the status of folk psychology is. Prominent representatives are Paul and Patricia Churchland, and the framework they propagate is 'neurophilosophy': for answers to philosophical and psychological questions we have to turn to the neurosciences (P.S. Churchland, 1986, 2002a).

As mentioned, the main source of inspiration for the symbolic view was logic and formal language. For psychology that suggests that logic and some kind of internal language are the basis of cognition. For philosophy it entails that logical analysis is an important task, leading to insights into the true nature of things.

The Churchlands believe that the language/logic-based approach is dead on both counts. As Quine (1961) showed (see Chapter 3.4), there are no purely analytic sentences (nor purely synthetic sentences), and nothing is immune to empirical discoveries. Philosophy will have to be naturalistic, an extension of science, rather than an a priori enterprise. As to psychology, essential for Paul Churchland's attack on the (Fodorian) orthodoxy is the rejection of propositions as the basic material of cognition. Rather, since the function of cognition is representing the world in the service of survival of the organism, it starts deep down on the evolutionary ladder with sensorimotor capacities in simple organisms. Propositional language-like knowledge is secondary to and builds upon sensorimotor skills. Churchland advocated these ideas before the advent of connectionism. He presented (1979, 1981) an integrated naturalist philosophy of mind, of science, and psychology in one. An essential assumption of Churchland is that *all observation is* **theory-laden** (see Chapters 3.4 and 3.5). There is no such thing as pure observation: our mental make-up (our 'theories') determines what we see, and when our theories change (that is, when we learn) our experiences and observations change with them.

(glossary)

In the same vein, he rejects the classical view of a scientific theory (elaborated by the positivists, see Chapter 3.2) as an edifice of propositions, statements, and the logical derivations between them. In his view, a theory is a cognitive capacity to recognize and discriminate rather than a body of statements (see Chapters 4.5 and 5.5 for a similar pragmatist view of science).

In the mid-1980s, the new connectionist simulations that had come to supplement the orthodox symbolic techniques in AI, discussed in Chapter 7.4, proved a useful vehicle for undermining the orthodox symbolic view of mind. The properties of these neural networks supported the competing view of mind as a property of distributed activation in neural networks. Towards the end of this chapter we will discuss more recent developments, in some respects a radicalization of connectionism: dynamicism. Thus, we have three contenders for the true account of mind (Eliasmith, 1996, 1997): first, the classical symbolic view, based upon the symbol-manipulating **Turing machine**; second, the neural-network view, based upon connectionist techniques; and finally, the dynamic view, based on **dynamical systems theory**, but more or less continuous with **connectionism**. The first was the subject of the previous chapter. In this chapter we will sketch the latter two, and try to compare all three. Since there is a huge amount of research on building networks, we will be brief about the technical aspects (see Bechtel and Abrahamsen, 2002; Port and Van Gelder, 1995; Van Gelder, 1998).

(glossary)
(glossary)
(glossary)

Let us first turn to the controversy between the symbolic and the connectionist view. We start with a very brief discussion of connectionism, to show how the alternative for the computational theory of mind is based upon non-sentential systems (that is, systems not consisting in mental sentences or propositions).

8.2 Symbols versus Networks

Neural networks

A connectionist network consists of a set of nodes and connections between them; activation spreads through the network, and the connections have weights that determine to which extent nodes pass on activation, that is, the degree to which nodes influence each other. This is vaguely analogous to signal transmission between the neurons in the nervous system, hence the adjective 'neural'. The similarity should not be exaggerated however: real neural systems are far more complicated (Crick, 1989; Shepherd, 1990). Churchland and Sejnowski (1992) suggest that these models may capture functional properties of neural structures at a higher level of abstraction than real neurons.

A typical network will have three layers: input, output and a layer of hidden nodes in between. The advantage of networks over symbolic rule-governed systems is that they can learn and generalize. Unlike a symbolic program, where a small change can make the program ineffective, networks are robust, they can resist damages and their performance will degrade or improve gradually with deletion or adding nodes (graceful degradation). Furthermore, networks satisfy soft constraints: unlike symbolic programs where rules are fixed and formal, networks can find some compromise solution, by more or less satisfying a set of conditions simultaneously.

Learning in a network occurs through adjustment of weights according to some learning rule. To perform adequate discriminations, a three-layer network (a layer of input nodes, a layer of output nodes, and a layer of hidden nodes in between) is required. Usually the weights are set in a training period in which feedback about the right response is provided.

In a sense, the network does this training by itself, so it 'learns' to produce the correct 'solution' (activation pattern over the output nodes) for a given 'problem' (activation pattern over the input nodes). The specification of learning rules is the crux of connectionist modelling. One simple example is the Hebb rule, which increases the weight of a connection between two nodes proportionally with the product of their activations – informally, if two nodes often fire together, they stick together. This relatively simple trick is highly powerful in finding patterns and regularities. A network can learn to recognize and discriminate between different kinds of input; for example, a network in a submarine can learn to distinguish between the sonar signals belonging to rocks and mines (Figure 8.1; Churchland, 1995, ch. 4).

If we try to interpret a network as a model of the human mind, its 'knowledge' can be said to be coded in the connection weights, which determine the response to the input (that is, the flow of activation through the network). In a certain sense, the network has created this knowledge on its own account; it has organized itself to tune in to its environment. The knowledge of the network is usually *distributed* over many connections; unlike the so-called classical approach with its discrete symbols and data structures, the content of the system's beliefs cannot be localized in discrete symbol

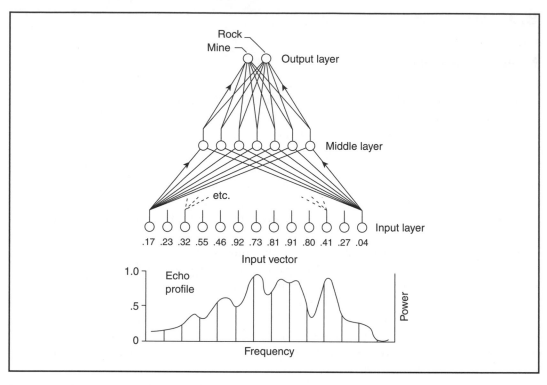

FIGURE 8.1 *An example of a network that can learn to distinguish rock echoes from mine echoes in a sonar signal. The input is the frequency spectrum of the sound signal. The weights of the connections between input and middle layer nodes, and between middle layer and output nodes, together with the activation pattern on the input, determine whether the 'Rock' or the 'Mine' output node will be activated.*

Source: *Churchland (1995: 82)*

structures or program statements. Pattern recognition by a network is the activation of a recognition vector (a vector is a set of numbers that plots (in this case) the activation of neurons in a multidimensional space; see Figure 1): the network 'sees' a solution when activation is spread in the right way over units. That could be interpreted as a 'representation': for example, the network may be said to have a representation of a mine when it produces a specific activation pattern over its hidden nodes and on the output nodes in response to the corresponding sonar input. The learning process can be visualized as a trajectory (Figure 8.2) through a kind of space of all possible weights, so that error, the distance between desired and actual response, is minimized.

There is a huge variety of network architectures and in particular of learning rules governing the learning process (see Bechtel and Abrahamsen, 2002). In practice, real networks, as they exist today, need a lot of help to do anything interesting. The researcher has to provide a highly structured situation, and all sorts of constraints

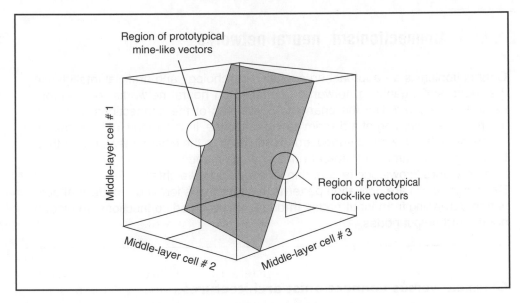

Figure 8.2 *The activation vector space for three middle layer nodes of the rock–mine network. The three dimensions picture the degree of activation of the respective nodes. The two hot spots represent activation patterns, i.e. recognition, for typical mines and typical rocks, respectively. The partition corresponds to the distinction between rocks and mines.*

Source: *Churchland (1995: 83)*

are put upon the task, the size of the network, the nature of the problems to be presented, etc. The explosively growing research in network design tries to find learning rules and network designs for a variety of cognitive tasks.

A special class is recurrent networks that feed back information from output nodes to input nodes or hidden nodes (or sometimes from hidden nodes to separate context nodes) – thus, these networks can make past activation available for current processing (Churchland, 1995), since previous activation is added to a later stage. The recurrent pathways enable a kind of short-term memory: unlike standard (feedforward) networks, they can represent not only events, but temporal sequences, like movement patterns. A recurrent network is not just wholly dependent on current input, but can generate sequences of activation patterns. (Churchland (1995) even suggests that consciousness can be realized in recurrent networks.) An interesting application is 'finding structure in time', detecting grammatical sequences of words in sentences. Elman (1992) managed to let a recurrent network discover grammatical structure (tricky word sequences, like 'boy chases boy who chases boy', were recognized). This is an important achievement because the hierarchical structure of language, until recently the monopoly of symbolically structured systems, now seems within reach of connectionist networks (perhaps) (see also p. 196).

BOX 8.1 Connectionism, neural networks

- Connectionism is an approach in cognitive psychology and artificial intelligence that uses self-organizing networks (modelled on neural networks) of interconnected nodes, in which the changing of weights of the connections underlies the network's learning of a discriminating response. In this model of information-processing the network is supposed to tune itself to the environment, rather than following a programme of pre-set rules and commands
- The network's knowledge is coded in its connection weights.
- Representations are activation patterns: recognizing is forming a pattern of activation spreading from input nodes through, via weighted connections, to hidden nodes and output nodes.

Classical versus connectionist architectures

The contrast between the *classical* (Fodor, see Chapter 7) and the *connectionist* approach will now be clear. Fodor's Language of Thought uses discrete symbols, connectionist models go by diffuse activation patterns; or, in mathematical terms, the former uses logical means, the latter uses numerical means. The classical approach holds that logical reasoning and language-like structures and processes (sentences in the head) are the essence of mind; connectionism thinks it is holistic neuron-like activation patterns. The classical approach has to assume an inborn cognitive structure, analogous to a database and a set of rules for reasoning and induction set up by a programmer. For this reason classical cognitivism has been compared to Cartesian **rationalism**, for Descartes presupposed inborn ideas: the most important ingredients for knowledge were wired in from the start. It is no coincidence that Fodor (1975) is a self-confessed nativist, and Chomsky practises 'Cartesian linguistics'. Contrary to the *pre-programmed* classical approach, the connectionist challenger claims to have a means of *self-organization*.

The connectionist approach also claims to be more biologically plausible, more in tune with the neural nature of the mind. The latter claim is pushed vigorously by Churchland to substantiate his ideas on elimination of psychological (i.e. 'folk'-psychological) categories, and their replacement by neuroscientific discourse. Its critics argue that neural networks are no improvement over seventeenth- and eighteenth-century **empiricism** and *associationism*. All networks can do is to chain elementary experiences (inputs) into composite ideas (distributed patterns of activation), using statistical patterns of contiguity and similarity.

Fodor and Pylyshyn contra networks: no combinatorial structure

Fodor is (predictably) one of the most devastating of the critics. He doubts the feasibility of the connectionist enterprise and the capacities of neural networks. Although

glossary (rationalism)

glossary (empiricism)

the Churchlands hardly entered this debate, we will nevertheless discuss it here, since it bears upon the issue mentioned above: are networks powerful enough to produce systematic thought? Fodor thinks that non-propositional representations are insufficient as 'architecture' of human cognition, and that, whatever the successes of connectionism, a language of thought is still needed (Fodor, 1990b, 1997a; Fodor and Pylyshyn, 1988; Fodor and McLaughlin, 1990). The properties of systematicity and productivity are Fodor's benchmark. *Productivity* means that in principle an infinite number of complex propositions (sentences, thoughts) can be generated from a limited number of simple constituents. This is a typical feature of languages: with a limited number of words in a dictionary, an unlimited number of sentences can be made (note how the Chomskian idea of generative grammar inspired the classical symbolic view). *Systematicity* means that you cannot have a thought without the ability to have or understand another thought that is semantically close to the first one. If you know what 'John loves the florist' means, then you will also inevitably understand a sentence like 'The florist loves John.' Fodor argues that the only way to get productivity and systematicity in a cognitive system is a language-like medium with a 'constituent structure', with, that is, discrete elements (words, symbols) which can be concatenated using standard connectives, such as 'and', 'therefore', 'or' and 'if … then'. Systematicity follows from the fact that we have discrete symbols for (in the example) 'John', 'love', and 'florist', that can be cut and pasted in new sentence combinations.

Note that Fodor (e.g. Fodor and Pylyshyn, 1988) does not hold that it is impossible for networks to exhibit logically structured behaviour. The point is that a language-of-thought-like medium has productivity and systematicity intrinsically; it comes along with the classical architecture of cognition, and the same is true of human language and thinking. That structure is not intrinsic to networks and has to be hand-crafted to let a network show logically structured behaviour.

Fodor and Pylyshyn think that networks are similar to associationist psychology, where everything can be connected to everything else (think of Pavlov's dogs). Thus, they interpret the connectionist movement as a return to association psychology of the British empiricists and the behaviourists. Fodor's battle resembles the controversy between Skinner and Chomsky on language acquisition. Chomsky showed that children cannot learn how to construct grammatical sentences just by listening to the way their parents put one word after another, as Skinner proposed. Sentence structure often requires long-distance connections – for example, embedded clauses, such as 'The woman who the janitor we just hired hit on is very pretty' (Pinker, 1994: 207), cannot be understood without grammatical structure. They need an inborn *language instinct* to unpack such structures, and learning to associate words won't help.

Fodor and Pylyshyn (1988) and Fodor and McLaughlin (1990) conclude that connectionism might be a useful theory of the way cognitive structures are *implemented* in the nervous systems, but not of the architecture of cognition itself. Networks are parallel, and the brain probably is a parallel processor, but cognition is a serial, Turing-type processor. Connectionist networks may in their view be interesting as an account of implementation: they can be compared with the hardware of a computer, or with the wetware of the brain. But just as the logic of a chess program cannot be found in the electrical pulses in the hardware, the neural network realization is of little use for understanding the serial rule-governed symbolic cognitive processes. The brain may be a parallel network, but networks are not a viable proposal for the architecture of cognition. In fact, as a proposal for the architecture of cognition, it is hardly an improvement on the associationism of Hume and Skinner. No cognition is possible without systematicity and productivity, and no systematicity is possible without constituent structure. The only viable solution to date is the language of thought.

Connectionist responses

glossary

Connectionists have countered in different ways. First, the objection that networks can do no more than pattern recognition can also be turned against the classical approach. Some argue that perhaps cognition *is* essentially pattern recognition, not rule-governed reasoning (Margolis, 1987). One could think here of Kuhn's **paradigms** and exemplars in science, which are ways of seeing patterns rather than applying formal rules. Margolis (1987) gives some examples suggesting that in reasoning a stepwise series of patterns matches occurs. Bechtel and Abrahamsen (2002: 106–118) describe a network that recognizes patterns of syllogisms: surely a symbolic task (although the network needs an extremely large number of trials compared to humans). Perhaps, then, logic is a skill, consisting in seeing valid patterns of reasoning, not the mechanical execution of program rules. Dreyfus and Dreyfus (1990) think that expertise is a holistic skill of recognizing exemplars, of recognizing problems and solutions, not a capacity of formal reasoning: for example, master chess players are not necessarily better at computing, but they *see* positions better than the novice – in fact, the novice is the one who relies on formal rules. So, one argument against connectionism might be turned into an argument against the classical approach: maybe the mind does not work with formal rules, not even in what seems the most formal logical tasks.

Connectionists have also countered by building networks that do have some sort of compositionality. The background consensus seems to be that cognitive systems must be able to represent complex structured items (Van Gelder, 1990: 356); language, and especially grammatical structure, is a paradigm case (Pinker, 1999). Bechtel and Abrahamsen (2002, Chapter 6) discuss three such strategies for realizing some kind of compositionality in networks.

The first is to construct networks that explicitly implement rules. For example, a production system that executes a rule when a condition is fulfilled (one of the techniques of classical AI) can be built in a network. Bechtel and Abrahamsen's (2002: 166–8) system for encoding logical relations (e.g. the relations between owning, giving, selling, owner, giver and object) does a fair amount of logical reasoning and makes coherent inferences. It seems successful in handling the systematicity examples ('John loves the florist'). However, since the strategy is to build systems that can execute rules known and specified in advance, this approach comes dangerously close to admitting that networks are no more than implementations of a classical architecture – which was exactly Fodor and Pylyshyn's argument for discarding connectionism as a model of cognition.

The second strategy is to realize *functional compositionality*. Van Gelder (1990) argues that a system can be compositional without being classical, when there are general rules for putting together a complex expression, and for decomposing it again into its constituents. That expression itself does not have to have a constituent structure. The classical view (Fodor) demanded that the structure of the representations must be the same as the structure of the represented items. Fodor's model is formal logic: it works by concatenating symbols into formulae, such that the symbols themselves are preserved in the concatenated expressions, just as words are still recognizable in a sentence – *concatenative compositionality*. Van Gelder suggests that a system may have *functional compositionality* without classical symbolic structure; perhaps cognition can be explained by neural networks which are only functionally compositional.

Smolensky's work is an example of this approach. His network can provide structured representations and structure-sensitive processes as a kind of by-product of pattern activation (Smolensky, 1988, 1990). The behaviour is (more or less) structured, but the real medium of cognition is what he calls the 'intuitive processor'. Mental representations are vectors, and mental processes are differential equations governing the development of the system. Thus, in reality, the causal mechanisms governing cognition are activation patterns and vector transformations, and compositionality is a macro-feature, if you will an epiphenomenon of this intuitive processing. Not unlike in physical reality, the macro-objects we see, like chairs and tables, are really epiphenomena of underlying clusters of (microphysical) atoms and molecules.

Smolensky (1988) tries to prove that networks can exhibit constituent structure in the form of ordered vector transformations. His example is that the representation 'a cup of coffee' can be thought of as consisting of a vector with a number of elements (hot, brown, liquid, contained in white porcelain, etc.), and proper transformations can preserve a plausible degree of constituent structure. Such a system has weak *compositionality* where the meaning of the elements depends on the context in a holistic fashion, unlike *strong compositionality* in Fodorian fashion where the constituents are independent of each other, as 'meaning atoms'. Note that this is a middle course between the distributed and holistic nature of representation in networks, on the one hand, and functionally discrete, fully compositional, classical architecture, on the other. Smolensky has the best of both worlds: the network is said to be structure-sensitive (like classical architecture), and at the same time context-sensitive and holistic (the forte of connectionism). However, the real, causally effective work is done by the connectionist activation patterns; the (classical) structure-sensitive properties are epiphenomena and only approximately correct. Whereas in the CTM discrete symbol structures are the rock bottom of the system's working, Smolensky thinks that cognition really works through vector activation. The *subsymbolic* level is where the real action is. Fodor and McLaughlin (1990) are not convinced; their major criticism is that structure sensitivity is not a necessary part of the system, as it is with classical architectures.

Another example of the second strategy, non-classical compositionality is the connectionist architecture RAAM (Recursive Auto-Associative Memory), which manages to implement a tree structure in a network (Bechtel and Abrahamsen, 2002: 171–8; Pollack, 1990). Structured representations like 'Pat knew that John loved Mary' (Bechtel and Abrahamsen, 2002: 171) are coded in compressed form in a set of hidden nodes and later can be reconstructed by the decoding part of the network. This seems to get close to (functional) compositionality. However, it remains doubtful how well RAAM will perform in more full-scale cognitive problems.

The third strategy Bechtel and Abrahamsen (2002) discuss is exploiting external symbols. Most of us prefer to do multiplication by writing numbers on a piece of paper rather than in our heads. Human cognition feeds upon textbooks, manuals, and instruction; it needs a cultural and linguistic embedding, and as Vygotsky realized long ago (see Chapter 9.5), internalizing external symbol systems is a necessary stage in developing higher cognitive capacities. External symbol systems are an important part of our cultural environment (see Donald, 1991 for an interesting account of how large parts of our cognitive skills are located outside us – think of the Internet). Dennett (1995) and Clark (1997) explain that the mind relies on a 'scaffold' of external symbols (see pp. 210–9) to build higher cognitive processes. Smolensky (1988) thinks that his intuitive interpreter needs explicit external symbols. Recurrent networks may be a first step in this direction: they have a kind of memory for previous states that helps to understand, for example, sequential structure in language, and a sense of context.

A cautious conclusion from these three lines of response to the classical orthodoxy is, first, that everybody (so far, but see below) agrees that cognition requires complex representational structures. Not everyone agrees with Fodor's strong claim that compositionality needs a classical symbolical architecture. Connectionist networks have been built that instantiate a fair amount of functional compositionality. Whether *distributed* representations can do the job that the classical view requires is too early to say. Some connectionists admit the need for explicit rules, and try to build hybrid systems including *both* classical rules and connectionist activation patterns. As a very brief illustration, think of language, which has words that have to be learned, and grammatical rules to combine words into sentences (Pinker, 1999). Pinker makes an interesting distinction between the cognitive mechanisms for regular and irregular verbs. Classical symbolic architecture works well for regular verbs, where rules can be applied in a formal and generalized way to produce the tables in grammar books ('walk, walked, has walked'). Connectionist architectures seem to work for patterns of conjugations that must be learned and then recognized, as in the case of irregular verbs ('ride, rode, has ridden', but: 'hide, hid, has hidden'). Language then may be a real-life example of such a hybrid system (see Pinker, 1999).

The last decade has introduced yet another change of direction. The above might be called 'classical' connectionism. The new trend is dynamicism (Port and Van Gelder, 1995; Bechtel and Abrahamsen, 2002). The anti-orthodox position seems now to have been overtaken by an even more radical development in computational modelling, which abandons computation and internal representations in the traditional sense entirely.

8.3 The Third Contender: Dynamicism: Representations Abandoned?

The main difference between these connectionists and the classical view is how the inner representational structure is built. A far more radical challenge to the classical agenda is the criticism of internal representations *tout court*. A first attack came from work on mobile robots ('mobots'), which are claimed to exhibit *intelligence without representation* (Brooks, 1995). Hence, it is argued, the reliance of classical cognitive science on the notion of representation is misguided. The theory of dynamic systems proposes that cognition is best seen as a dynamic coupling betweeen organism and environment, and the best way to describe cognitive processes is to model them as a trajectory through a state space of possible cognitive states. In this way mind is 'relocated' from an inner representational realm to an activity in the environment. On-line interaction with the environment is more important than symbol crunching, and the evolution in time is more characteristic of cognition than constructing static representations. This view is underpinned by dynamical systems theory, which is a set of mathematical tools for describing the trajectory of a system through a series of possible states (Van Gelder, 1995, 1998; Eliasmith, 1996, 2001). Dynamicists conclude that cognitive systems do not need internal, symbolic representational structures; rather, an agent is coupled to its environment, and both co-evolve in real time.

Below, we will first briefly discuss robots, and then the captivating metaphor of the Watt governor. Finally, some sceptical views about the elimination of representation will be discussed.

Robots

Brooks (1995) has a somewhat peculiar definition of intelligence. The main point of his argument is that the roots of intelligence, and the most important component of it, is the ability to move around in a dynamic environment. After all, it took evolution billions of years to get that right, and only a few hundred years to create human expert knowledge. Brooks' work is building mobile robots that can locomote in the real world (well … in his Cambridge (Mass.) laboratory for the time being), doing smart things like picking up cola cans in the office and dropping them in the recycle basket. His goal is to make robots that are able to maintain multiple goals, change these, depending on circumstances, that is, adapt to the environment and capitalize on luck; they should be robust, not collapse with minor changes in the environment. That is quite different from the classical approach to robotics, inspired by classical cognitive science. The latter is based on the 'boxology' (boxes in the head) common in classical information-processing accounts, where a system is specified in subsystems with distinct functions (boxes for feature analysers, feature integrators, long-term memory, short-term memory, motor control, motor execution, etc., arranged in succession from sensory input to central processor to motor output). The robot processes its input, tries to construct an internal representation of the environment, and issues motor commands to guide its movements, all in separate processes. Brooks in contrast rejects the distinction between the peripheral (motor and sensory) systems and central representations. His methodology is to build layers of independent behaviour-producing systems, each of which may have its own goal and provides a complete perception-activity connection. Successive new layers are then added, pursuing different goals in parallel, data-driven by the environment: for example avoiding, wandering, and exploring, which can inhibit each other (for instance, the robot wanders, when not busy avoiding things). This is called subsumption architecture. Brooks argues that no internal, in fact pre-programmed, representations mirroring the world are necessary, since the world is used as its own representation. There is no symbolic interface coding and decoding input and outputs to and from an internal medium, but each layer is under local environmental control. The layers (behaviours) inhibit and suppress each other, but there is no central controller or goal representation. The device has to seek its own way in its environment, and not to follow internal models, put in by the programmer and representing the way the programmer sees the world (see also Keijzer and Bem, 1996; Bem and Keijzer, 1996). In Chapter 9 we will explore the idea of the 'extended mind' (Clark and Chalmers, 1998), that cognition is inseparable from the world.

The 'Watt governor': a non-representational paradigm

Another school of anti-representationalism takes its cue from dynamical systems theory (DST) (Port and Van Gelder, 1995; Eliasmith, 1996). The basic idea is that cognition is a continuous and dynamic interaction with the environment, not internal symbol manipulating. DST provides tools for understanding the development of systems and their interaction across time. Van Gelder (1995) argues that connectionism is still too much focused on finding a new answer to the old question of how a system mirrors the world. The dynamicist alternative is to analyse cognition as a trajectory through state space. His quite instructive metaphor is the 'Watt governor'. This is a device that controls the throttle valve of a steam engine so as to keep power output (rotation of the flywheel) constant. If the computational approach had to solve this control problem, it would have divided it into a number of subtasks, specified by algorithms and executed by subroutines or subagents. The main tools would be symbolic representations (for instance, numbers standing for engine speed and valve position), and a kind of bureaucracy of interacting agents, busy measuring, computing, and issuing commands. The governor uses these representations to 'stand in' (Haugeland, 1991) for the real processes in the steam engine.

In contrast, the system James Watt invented simply uses the angle of a set of rotating weights attached to the flywheel to control engine speed (when speed rises, the weights rise and close the throttle a bit so that speed decreases – and the other way round, of course – see Figure 3). This does not require computation or representation, no processing steps, algorithms or sequences of discrete operations or subtasks. It is just smooth continuous coupling of the governor and the engine mutually influencing each other. The Watt governor can be mathematically described as a dynamic system, in terms of equations that describe the changing of its state. Van Gelder's claim is that cognition is better described as the realization of a dynamical system, proceeding through state space, than as a system computing internal symbolic representation to stand in for the world. Therefore, Van Gelder concludes, intelligence does not need representations. Dynamicism constitutes in his view a new Kuhnian paradigm for cognition, replacing the old representationalist one. It considers cognition as

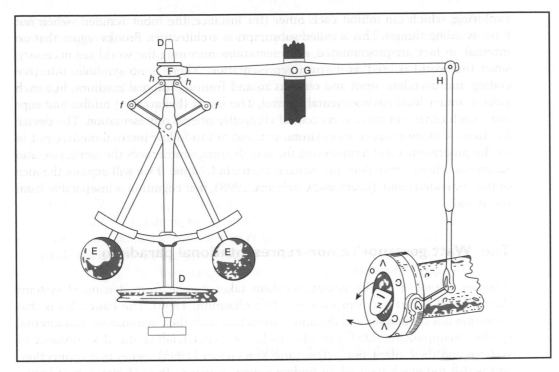

FIGURE 8.3   *The Watt governor. The vertical spindle marked D is connected to the main flywheel of the steam engine; when it starts to turn faster, the centrifugal force will lift the arms with the weights E and close the throttle valve marked Z; steam pressure will fall and the engine slows down. Decreased speed lets the weights drop and open the valve. In this way, engine speed is kept constant. This illustrates the idea of coupled systems in real time, with circular causality (the weights control the valve, and the valve controls (though engine speed) the weights).*

Source: *Van Gelder (1995: 349)*

on-line real-time interaction with the environment, as multiple simultaneous, mutual co-evolution over time; cognition is intrinsically embodied in a real body and embedded in a real environment: body, brain, world and mind are inseparable (Clark, 1997; see also Chapter 9.3); and skills and knowledge unfold and **emerge** in real time.

glossary

Dynamicism contra connectionism

Although connectionist networks are also instances of dynamic systems, the traditional networks are set up to transform static input representations into static output representations (Van Gelder, 1995) – see for example, Churchland and Sejnowski (1990) who analyse the knowledge and representations a neural network possesses in terms of the frozen image of weights and activation pattern after training, trying to find where the network stores its knowledge – so it will be clear that Van Gelder has a point in describing traditional connectionism as a 'half-way house' between classical representational and genuinely new, dynamic models.

Van Gelder (1995) draws some philosophical conclusions from this new, non-representational framework. Cognition is basically skilful coping with the world, which can be done without explicitly representing it. As such, it contrasts with the Cartesian framework which considers mind in itself. Furthermore, it is intrinsically temporal, because of its on-line, real-time interaction with the world. Hence, these new views on cognition are more naturalistic than the classical view and the conservative connectionist view. Emphasis is on continuity between lower forms of life and human cognition ('Today the earwig, tomorrow man,' as Kirsh, 1991, put it somewhat ironically), and the connection with the environment is emphasized. What is slightly disturbing, however, is the rather lowly definition of intelligence put forward by dynamical systems theory aficionados: the Watt governor is certainly not everyone's idea of a cognitive system in the full sense of the word, and Brooks' claim that locomotion is almost all of intelligence is somewhat exaggerated.

BOX 8.2 Dynamical systems theory

- Dynamical systems theory is *a general formalism for describing complex systems*, using the notions of an abstract space of possible states of the system (*state space*), and of a *trajectory* through it, governed by laws that can be described mathematically.
- *For psychological purposes*, behaviour (like approach–avoidance, or walking) can be described, in a more or less geometrical way, as evolution (or 'flow') through state space.
- Important assets are its conceptualization of the *agent-environment coupling* and the evolution over *time*.

Dynamical systems: coupled and continuous

If natural cognizers are dynamical systems, then they can be understood by applying the mathematical tools of dynamic modelling. Dynamical systems theory provides a toolbox and a vocabulary to describe the intuitive notions of coupled co-evolving systems (we will gloss over some subtle distinctions here, see Van Gelder, 1998). DST's tools are differential equations that describe the system's trajectories in state space: development can be described as a series of points (possible states of the system) through a space with dimensions that characterize the possible states. For example, a classical example from physics, an oscillator (the swinging of a weight suspended on a spring) can be pictured as a curve in a state space characterized by position and acceleration – that trajectory will converge to a point (an attractor) where the weight swings rhythmically. An attractor is a kind of equilibrium point, towards which the system will move; interesting systems have multiple attractors, as in a landscape with several basins. According to dynamicists, when used to describe cognition, these attractors may stand for different cognitive states or stored knowledge or concepts (Eliasmith, 2001).

Plausible examples of psychological theories in line with this metaphor are still scarce. Port and Van Gelder (1995) collected a number of applications of these techniques. Showcases are motor action (Turvey and Carello, 1995) and motor development in children (Smith and Thelen, 2003; Thelen, 1995). Beer (1995a, 1995b, 2000) applied dynamic modelling to autonomous agents' (robots) legged locomotion. An obvious objection is that leg use in robots (though very interesting from a robotics engineering point of view) is not very cognitive. An often quoted example of DST in psychology is Townsend and Busemeyer's model of decision behaviour as push and pull by desires and opportunities (say, hunger and the availability of food) in a quasi-gravitational way; approach and avoidance can be seen as a continuous trajectory through state space (Van Gelder, 1995). However, the model does not seem to generalize well, and looks too simple as an account of motivation or decision-making (Eliasmith, 1996).

Some problems with dynamical models

An important difference with connectionist networks is that dynamical models are supposed to be low-dimensional: unlike the many dimensions spanned by activation vectors, dynamicists hope to find few or even a single parameter governing the behaviour of the system. The ideal is to explain collective behaviour with a minimal set of variables – think of a traffic jam, where many individual cars are involved, but which may be described as some sort of flow. Dynamicists count finding such collective variables as the unique selling point of their approach – it would be a major success if motivation or decision-making could be described in just a few parameters. However, as Eliasmith (2001) points out, this could also be the weakness of the method, since these are probably too simple to capture language and concepts. He doubts therefore whether DST does qualify as a cognitive theory: there is little cognitive attraction in attractors. Where Van Gelder makes much of the temporally continuous smooth flow of the Watt governor as an advantage over digital/computational discrete architecture, upon closer inspection cognitive mechanisms may not be continuous at all.

Dynamicists think that cognitive explanations can now dispense with internal representations. For example, Beer (1995a) argues that in decomposing the internal structure of his legged robots the representational model is of little use: its states do not allow decomposition in computational modules, and the way the legs are used by the mobot is not interpretable as representations. However, looking closely at the Watt governor, it is not so obvious that it has no representation of the engine speed. It could be argued that if we define a representation as something that stands in for a feature of the environment, then the angle of the centrifugal arm of the governor is a representation of the engine speed and is 'used' as such by the system (Bechtel, 1998; Chemero, 2000). The dynamicists' anti-representationalist rhetoric may be exaggerated – in fact, in Van Gelder's (1995) seminal paper it is admitted that states of the Watt governor can be interpreted as representations, and that moving towards an attractor can

glossary be seen as recognition or as action, and the development of motor skill as **emergence** of attractors (Port and Van Gelder, 1995: 12, 17).

Some argue that connectionist networks are really dynamic systems, and that the distinction is artificial – for example, in the simple example above the network's learning to tell rocks from mines can also be described as a trajectory through state space towards the attractor, minimizing error. Elman (in Bates and Elman, 1993) argues that such dynamics (somewhat more precisely, the trajectory of a cognitive system through a multidimensional space of possible states) are more appropriate way to approach cognition than symbolic or activation patterns. The interesting thing about Elman's empirical work is that he implements the temporal aspect of cognition by copying back activation from hidden nodes to the input nodes; thus he manages to get a handle on context and achieves interesting results on the prediction of word sequences in natural language. Hence, the network is able to track sentences without internal representations of grammar and syntax. Elman emphasizes that instead of static representations it is the trajectory of the system through states (activation patterns) that is the proper level of analysis for this particular aspect of cognition. How the new dynamics will develop is too early to judge. Some suspect that representations are preprogrammed in Elman's systems as a kind of innate structure, rather than a developing trajectory; further, it is doubted that Elman's networks have the same power to generalize over grammatical phenomena as humans do (Marcus, 1998).

Two issues raised by dynamicism and connectionism warrant some more discussion, more or less independent of the value of DST methodology. The first is the role of representations. The second is the idea of organism and environment as coupled systems, continuously intertwined; this will come back in Chapter 9.3 as one of the pillars of the 'extended mind', putting together brain, body and world (Clark, 1997).

BOX 8.3   Mental representations

- *Mental representation* is a crucial but problematic concept in cognitive psychology.
- *Mental states* supposedly mean, refer to or stand for something else: they have mental content. The concept of mental representation is thus burdened with many of the problems of meaning and intentionality.
- *Classical symbolic paradigm* (Fodor, Chapter 7) assumes that mental representations have a symbolic format, as sentences in the language of thought.
- *Connectionists* consider representations as activation patterns in neural networks.

BOX 8.3   **Mental representations** (Continued)

- *Classical symbolic and connectionist theories* are both *representational theories of mind:* thinking is essentially having and manipulating representations. Both offer a naturalistic explanation for representation, meaning and intentionality.
- *Dynamicism* questions the usefulness of representation as an explanatory construct in cognitive psychology.

The value of representations

Brooks and the dynamicists think that representations are unnecessary because certain kinds of complex intelligent behaviour can occur without explicit internal representations that intervene between input and output. However, even in robots some kind of internal state stands in for aspects of the world, and in that sense can be called a map or a code or a representation (Bechtel, 1998; Wheeler, 2001). Interestingly, the notion of representation has started to shift from its original meaning as a static symbol structure: it is now related to action in the environment (Clark, 1997), as embedded context-dependent coding for action (Wheeler, 2001). It is increasingly clear that external factors determine behaviour, and therefore, the internal state cannot be said to code for the action: part of the work is farmed out to the world, so to speak. Think of a simple example: the route an ant takes is mostly determined by the troughs and peaks in the terrain; more technically, motor actions are not completely coded in the nervous system, but depend on the physical properties of the limbs. Ergonomics shows that lots of information guiding behaviour is in displays, levels and buttons, not just in the head. Long ago, Gibson (1979; see also Chapter 4.4 on direct realism; and Chapter 4.7 on pragmatism) argued that information is in the world, not in the head, and that perception is picking up invariants from the world, not constructing images in the mind. So, if dynamicists are right that body, mind and world cannot be separated, the explanatory role of internal representations is severely limited (see Wheeler, 2001).

However, it may be no coincidence that the DST seems limited to low-level sensorimotor tasks. Perhaps in more complex situations intelligent behaviour requires more than continuous coupling of agent and environment. Clark and Toribio (1994) call these 'representation-hungry' contexts: situations where the agent needs to refer to absent objects, or counterfactual situations, or situations involving distal, non-existent or highly abstract properties; or where the agent has to be sensitive to 'parameters whose ambient physical manifestation are complex and unruly' (Clark and Toribio, 1994: 419). There, coupling between agent and environment obviously breaks down, and some kind of internal representation standing in for absent objects seems indispensable. Smooth continuous coupling with the environment won't help when you have to figure out how to combine your holiday with a conference visit next year, and what to do in case the dollar falls and you don't win the lottery; or in trying to figure out in the Kiev railroad station where the train labelled MOCKBA is going, or when you plan to prove Fermat's theorem, and so on. Typically, the notion of representation is invoked as an explanation when organisms react to objects or situations that are not present in the environment (when, for instance, Claire is hoping that Count Dracula will pay her a visit tonight and she thinks that opening her window will make it easier for him to come in). We may define representations as stand-in for features of the environment that are not present, and that guide behaviour in their stead (Haugeland, 1991). But these are not necessarily explicit, symbolic and computational, and do not require Fodorian apparatus of symbolic, syntactically structured representations.

It can be concluded that Brooks' mobots and Van Gelder's governor fail to prove the general radical anti-representational case because these are just not 'representation-hungry' enough. Representations as internal information-bearing states emerge as products of filtering, recoding and transforming inputs, and this is not the case in the latter examples. And, as noted above, when some system, dynamical or otherwise, manages to bridge the 'gap between the dimensions of the relevant state space and bare, easily available input parameters' (Clark and Toribio, 1994: 424) it can be considered as representational.

To sum up: although the strict Fodorian construal of representations and even the connectionist view of representations as activation patterns might have to be rejected, the notion of representation is still indispensable for those situations where the behavioural repertoire involves higher cognitive processes. Our preliminary conclusion is that the anti-representationalists are too rash, and have based their case on too simple and selective cases – situations where a tight coupling of organism and environment exists. Intuitively, higher cognition involves some distance from the environment, and that is where some kind of internal representation of abstract or absent properties is indispensable. The 'cash value' of intentionality is to swing free from the environment (Rorty, 1993).

Probably the most promising approach to reconciling representations with a naturalistic view of mind will employ the notion of *internalizing*: higher organisms acquire the capacity to do some of their cognitive activities somehow in their head, rather than in the real world, and to use tools in a more or less decontextualized way, that is, not directly coupled to the current ambient environment. The connectionist strategy of employing external symbols suggests how this might work (see p. 190).

8.4 Neurophilosophy and Naturalism

glossary Neurophilosophy and **naturalism** entails that the mind, the self, free will, the most basic structures of knowledge and rationality, emotions and feelings are all neural happenings. Therefore, answering the eternal question on human nature, personhood, and ethics requires not abstract a priori philosophy, but a turn towards neuroscience; not the analysis of linguistic concepts, but the facts about the brain can answer philosophical questions about mind, representation, meaning and intentionality.

glossary Naturalism is closely related to **pragmatism**: it entails that there is no knowledge beyond science. Our brains are made by evolution to understand our environment,

and science is the extension of that; they are not designed to achieve **metaphysical** [glossary]
truths. The remaining task for philosophy is to critically review, interpret, intergrate
and synthesize empirical results. Recall how naturalists like Quine see philosophy as
continuous with science and concerned with the more abstract aspects of its theories.

Neurophilosophers, not just as a matter of abstract principle but in practice, try to
deploy the tools the neurosciences have provided to tackle the big theoretical questions on the nature of mind and science. For example, our sense of self and experience
of the environment are related to neural structures: when cerebral hemispheres are
disconnected, we seem to have two personalities. Even the philosophical questions
of epistemology can be approached from a neuroscience perspective (Churchland
and Churchland, 2002). For example, the centuries-old problem of appearance and
reality can thus be solved. Philosophers used to distinguish between 'objective' primary
qualities, such as mass or motion, where our experiences mirror reality, and 'subjective' secondary qualities, such as smell or our sense of heat and cold, that are just 'in
the mind'.

But let us assume that the task of the brain is to represent, in a map-like abstract
fashion, the world, and the body, both its sensorimotor situation and its internal homeostatic milieu. Evolution then must have made sure that these maps are adequate for
the animal's survival. That dissolves much of the philosophical conundrum of the
mind-world fit: representations support motion in the very real world of predators
and scarce food, so they had better be good guides and predictors. Where lower static organisms have reflex-like responses, locomoting animals can pick up higher-order
regularities in the world using movement and develop sensorimotor coordination.
Representation of permanent objects in an 'allocentric' framework, that is, positioned
in the objective world independent of the position of the animal, is probably a late
addition in evolution (Goodale, 2000).

Scientists inventing theories and abstract mathematical models is just one of many
further steps on the same evolutionary ladder (Quine, 1961). Theories are activation
points in the brains vector space (see below) that are isomorphic with categories and
causal relationships in the world. The appearance-reality problem dissolves in the
neurophilosophical approach: **theories** are aspects of negotiating the real world, and [glossary]
accurate prediction is the test for **truth** and reality, in science as well as in motor [glossary]
action. In the words of Quine (1961), science is to predict future experiences in the
light of past experiences (see Chapter 4.5).

Reduction changes the explananda

In the process of upgrading our 'animal habits' into a simple sensory model of the
world, and subsequently refining these into abstract scientific theoretical models
(Quine, 1969b), some old problems and theories will fall away as misguided. For
example, the 'problems' of alchemy and witchcraft have disappeared. In general, it is
typical of progress in science that reductive explanations emerge. Initially, some points
of contact between levels of explanation (say, single-cell recordings and systems

neuroscience; or psychology of memory and cell biology) are established. Next, the phenomena of the higher level can to some extent be explained by the lower level. So, the picture is: initial co-evolution of higher- and lower-level theories, followed by closer connection between them when both theories get more developed (Churchland and Churchland, 1994; Churchland, 2002a).

Revisionary modifications are characteristic for developing sciences: in some cases, the **ontology** of the old higher-level theory is retained (temperature is average kinetic energy), in other cases the old worldview is eliminated (oxogen replaces phlogiston in chemistry). That means that the explananda (what science started out to explain) may change in the process; hand in glove with new theories some phenomena (like phlogiston, or witchcraft) just disappear and others (like oxygen, or mental disturbance) become visible.

In the neurophilosophical framework, reduction does not mean saving the phenomena, or saving our current intuitions about mind, consciousness or personhood. Whenever an 'equipotent image', a good or better explanation can be generated by a more basic theory, the original explananda, higher-level concepts (mental processes, meaning) can be forgotten. Within the neurophilosophical scheme the mind is the brain; functional cognitive theories just specify what phenomena are to be explained, but the real explanation will have to come from neuroscience.

In the process, the psychology may change, for example, a theory of memory may have to be revised when the biochemical details of memory storage in the brain are known (Bickle, 1998; Churchland and Churchland, 1994). Recall that classical **functionalism** defended autonomy of the mental, as the software of the brain (Block, 1995). Churchland's (2002a) reply is that the hardware-software distinction is found nowhere in the nervous system.

We may expect stepwise and levelwise reduction and revision of psychological theories (although many levels of desciption will still be needed to explain the mind/ brain). Even problems in the philosophy of mind can then be seen in a new light. Below we will mention three: meaning and representations in neural systems, the neuroscientific view of selfhood, and the fate of folk psychology (see Chapter 7.3 and Chapter 10.2). Churchland (1981, 1995) thinks that folk psychology is sloppy theory that is slated for elimination, to be replaced by neuroscience.

Neurosemantics: meaning and representations

An essential part of the naturalist story is that philosophy, including philosophy of mind, is not an a priori enterprise. The influence of Quine and Sellars (see Chapter 2) is easily detected in Churchland's work. Philosophers have to give up their one-time dream of laying down a priori methods, epistemological criteria, ontological statements about the furniture of the world, according to which empirical research can proceed. On the contrary, philosophy is continuous with science and extrapolates and clarifies empirical results.

In this way, Churchland and Sejnowski (1990) set out to explain mental representation from a connectionist (neurophilosophical) perspective. Their point is that if you want to know what representations are, you should not primarily consult philosophers and linguists like Frege, Brentano and Chomsky, you should look at what the nervous system does in keeping track of the world, or at least at what a neural network does.

Patricia Churchland and Paul Churchland (1990) restate the old Brentano question, 'How is aboutness possible?' into 'How can the brain be a world representer?' And how are these representations used such that intelligent and purposeful behaviour ensues? The functionalist and **rationalist** strategy, followed by Fodor and others, [glossary] is to consider representations as symbol strings, and thinking as transformation of symbol strings. The first major problem here is to explain how such symbol strings hook on to the world. Second, the functionalist Fodorian style expressly ignores the brain (see Chapter 7).

The naturalist approach treats representation as a function developed in evolution; cognitive processes lie on an evolutionary continuum, ranging from pattern detection in lower animals to complex forms of thought and language. Thus, it looks for the basis of human cognition not in language and logic, but in elementary perception and action in animals. We are epistemic engines for the extraction, production and control of information in the service of survival.

The problem of **intentionality** and meaning then boils down to: 'How does *the brain* [glossary] represent?' The naturalist assumes (unlike Fodor) that it does not do so by way of sentences in the head, and (unlike empiricists) that it represents actively and selectively. For a model of cognition we should look at pattern recognition, for example at the way a rattlesnake recognizes a mouse (its dinner). Churchland (1989) buttressed this model using the results of the modelling of connectionist networks, which can be said to tune in to their environment, and adapt their internal structure to respond adequately to input. Network models are capable of learning, they are sensitive to the world and they mature through an active engagement with their environment. In contrast, rationalist, classical symbolist models are pre-formed and pre-programmed, bringing with them from the start everything that is psychologically important, such as rules for cognition and a language of thought.

Paul Churchland (1998) and Patricia Churchland (2002a) build upon these ideas with a more directly neuroscientific approach. Representations are activation patterns in brains and neural networks. More precisely, permanent knowledge of a network or brain is embodied in the weights of a network, and recognition of an input pattern is an temporary pattern of activation that can be pictured as a point in an abstract many-dimensional vector space (see Figure 8.2, p. 185 for a bit of explanation on how this works).

The problems of meaning, truth, and reference that concerned the orthodox symbolic approach and its philosophical ancestors (see Chapter 7) can be re-interpreted within this framework (Churchland and Churchland, 2002). Meaning can be seen as a mapping of the world by the brain. Brentano-style 'aboutness' is the mapping of the geometry of the brain's vector space with the world – the brain has in a more or less literal sense abstract maps, and having a representation is just having an activation of an input pattern. These maps reflect what is relevant to a organism (a mouse has relatively huge parts of its brain devoted to its whiskers, its most important tool to sniff out its environment), so we are equally justified to call the world a subjective construction – guiding behaviour, made to fit the organism's evolutionary interests, constructed on a 'need-to-know' basis, so to speak. (These ideas seem quite consistent with 'situated cognition' and action-oriented representations (Clark, 1997; see Chapter 9.3.)

Some (e.g. Wheeler and Clark, 1999; Keijzer, 2001) have wondered whether we still need concepts like representation, or map, or code to explain behaviour: do these concepts still cut ice, or is all the explanatory work done by detailing the neural mechanisms? In the neurophilosophical framework, this does not matter very much: whenever a better explanation can be generated by a more basic theory, in this case neural networks, the traditional notion of representation may change beyond recognition. The usefulness of representational explanations was discussed in the previous section.

Body maps, neural models and the sense of self

Another example of neurophilosophy is the explanation of selfhood in neural terms. Few things seem more intimate to us than our selves and the feeling of our own body. The question of 'Why am I, I?' could not be farther beyond the reach of neuroscientific explanations, or so one might think. However, P.S. Churchland (2002a, 2002b) argues that the root of our sense of self lies in the sensorimotor and homeostatic body images in the brain. To survive, organisms need sophisticated images of the state of the body (hunger) and the world (danger). Such body maps have been located in the brain stem, with many relays to spatial and motor areas in the hippocampus and the cortex. In addition, predicting what motor actions are required, and fine-tuning motor behaviour, is a crucial task of the brain. Damasio (1999, 2003) showed how action, planning and emotion are closely linked – patients with lesions in frontal cortex lose much of their emotions and their behaviour becomes less effective. His explanation is the 'somatic marker' hypothesis: the higher cognitive prcesses of thinking and deciding are connected with 'gut feelings', basic emotions that reflect body states. Body maps thus are an essential part of cognition, and have a role in basic survival. Unlike Descartes who thought that body and mind were separate, and that passions impede cool reason, cognition is part and parcel of the monitoring of the body, and the *feeling* of the body in the world (more on this in Chapter 9 on situated and embodied cognition; see also Chapter 10.5).

In a similar way, sophisticated representations of the world are based upon sensorimotor activity. For accurate and speedy motor actions in a hostile environment the nervous system has a set of prediction and execution mechanisms. Some of these mechanisms are simulators: the nervous system creates an internal simulation of how a motor action should be executed. The brain also keeps track of its own motor commands. The so-called efference copy (an image of the motor command to be executed) allows extrapolation used for planning elementary motor actions, and for correcting perception (for example, the brain manages to distinguish perceptual changes caused by movements of the head and by movement in the world, respectively). Body images can be manipulated and the brain can do something of a dry run of a movement.

So, even in pretty basic sensorimotor mechanisms the brain can do off-line planning and run 'as-if' simulations – it routinely does the sort of things that are attributed to intentional minds. This is the basic form of representation, intentionality, and self-reflection. Inner regulation gives rise to a sense of distinction between oneself versus non-self, between own movement and movement in the world. Lesions in centers in the brain (parietal cortex among others) that serve spatial orientation also impair the body image – for example, patients may not recognize their own limbs. So, our experience of ourselves can be fairly directly related to neural processes, and these seem to serve purposes of survival in animals. That suggests that the sense of self and non-self **emerges** from neural representation mechanisms. The feeling: 'This is my [glossary] hand', or 'Am I doing this?' is a property of the brain (see also Gallagher, 2000; Jeannerod, 2003).

To sum up, the philosophy of self and personhood, and for that matter also issues of ethics (P.M. Churchland, 2001), can be answered from neuroscience. Neuro-philosophers believe that knowing how the brain works helps to solve (or dissolve or replace) traditional problems of mind, and as the brief illustrations above show, have started to practise their belief. Personal, intentional, mental phenomena like meaning, consciousness, experience of one's own body and its place in space can be directly related to neural patterns. If these explanations work, neurophilosophy has scored a victory. Another of its battlefields is the debate on folk psychology.

The elimination of folk psychology

Recall that Fodor's computational theory of mind counted the vindication of common-sense **belief-desire psychology** as one of its selling points. Churchland [glossary] (1981) agrees with Fodor that folk psychology is a genuine theory (see Chapter 10.2 for the alternative, the so-called simulation view). But then it should be judged like any other theory: Is it progressive, producing new knowledge and new research directions? Does it converge with the rest of science? Does it explain a wide range of phenomena? and so on. Some may think that we know minds directly and infallibly, and no scientific evidence can correct our feeling that we have **consciousness**, beliefs, [glossary] intentions, free will, and so on. Many people just *know* that they act upon their beliefs, and that their fellow beings must be just as rational and intentional. When your dentist tries to convince you that you cannot feel pain now, you will tell him that you know better. But according to the naturalist introspective intuitions, the feeling of consciousness, the feeling that we have beliefs and desires – none is immune for empirical scientific evidence. They are not directly evident or 'given', but depend on theoretical presuppositions, and changing our outlook might thus dissolve or radically reconstruct deep-rooted convictions in our self-image. Churchland (1981) like Sellars (the 'myth of the given' see Chapter 3.4) believes that our concepts of mind are 'plastic', malleable, and that even our introspective judgements are theory-laden.

Traditionally, since at least Brentano, intentionality was seen as a real property of the world, distinguishing mind from matter. Churchland (1981) argues that intentionality is more a fact about *our language* in which *we* frame our views of the world than a distinction in the world itself; that language is fallible and revisable. Hence, folk psychology with its assumptions of irreducible beliefs, desires, intentionality, etc. may be replaced by new scientific theories.

BOX 8.4   Folk psychology and eliminativism

- Folk psychology (1) is normally a *common-sense psychology*, the kind of explanation of everyday behaviour in terms of the goals, desires, beliefs, opinions and plans that supposedly drive one's fellow beings' behaviour.
- Folk psychology (2) is a *philosophical construction*, called a *belief-desire psychology*, that uses intentional language to construct a language of mind, and requires representations as explanatory concepts. Beliefs and desires are literally causes and lawful explanations, and can and should be preserved in a computational theory of mind (Chapter 7).
- *Eliminativism* is the claim that folk psychological categories like beliefs and desires eventually can, and should, be eliminated and replaced by neuroscientific terms: we will talk about the firing of our neurons rather than about pain when hitting our thumb. It denies that both folk psychology (1) and (2) are useful in (scientific) psychology.
- In contrast, *reductionism* allows us to keep our common-sense concepts (like 'water') even when they are identified with scientific concepts (water is 'really' H_2O).

Churchland also gives some reasons to suppose that folk psychology is not only a fallible, but actually a *false* theory. These are, first, that it has nothing to say about important mental phenomena like mental development, mental illness, individual differences, learning, and so on. Second, it has not seen any progress for the last few thousand years, and in that sense is what we could call in Lakatos' terminology a stagnant research programme (see Chapter 3.8). Third, folk psychology does not fit into the scientific image of the world; it is isolated from the physical sciences, where real progress is being made. So, folk psychology suffers from massive explanatory failure, and should be replaced. It is time to reconfigure our conceptual schemes and start talking about ourselves and our fellow beings in neuro-speak (Churchland, 1981; Churchland, 1992).

Those who cannot imagine that neuroscience could explain mental phenomena should consider the possibility that that is a problem with their imagination, not a limitation of science. An analogy might be helpful. Prior to Maxwell, it was equally inconceivable that light could be electromagnetic radiation – magnets and microwaves do not give off light, surely. Nowadays, we understand that light is of course an electromagnetic wave. In the same way, we may come to understand how neurons can have consciousness (Churchland, 1995). In his 1981 paper Churchland could only offer some science-fiction-like speculation on the ways the theoretical framework of folk psychology could be eliminated and replaced by new ways of understanding. However, in the mid-1980s connectionism came up, and provided Churchland with a vehicle for the overthrow both of sentential models of cognition (the CTM), and of its common-sense counterpart, 'belief-desire' psychology.

A non-sentential view of theories (a theory is a capacity to recognize patterns, not a set of sentences) helps to see how folk psychology is a (failing) theory (Churchland, 1992). A network recognizes and represents input patterns as activation vectors, it recognizes similarity in terms of proximity in activation space; explanatory understanding is pattern recognition. Folk psychology is in that interpretation recognizing purposeful behaviour patterns in others. And better understanding and prediction is to be expected from neuroscience.

It will come as no surprise that the defence of folk psychology by functionalists like Fodor is rejected by Churchland (1981). Functionalism is in Churchland's view a conservative and a cheap explanation; anything can be a functional state, and declaring the analogues of beliefs and desires functional states tends to preserve obsolete theories; seventeenth-century chemists might have saved their completely false and obsolete theories by calling phlogiston a functional state. Beliefs and desires should be replaced by better (neuroscientific) concepts.

However, Churchland's eliminativism may be a bit rash. If we apply Dennett's framework (see Chapter 6.3) we could see how the belief-desire perspective can be combined with neuroscience. Humans (and for that matter, networks) can be described in intentional terms as knowing, recognizing, etc. That can yield useful predictions of their behaviour, which do not, however, necessarily correspond to inner representations in a given format (Clark, 1996a). The inner vehicles of representation (neurons, networks) may look quite different from the belief-desire description of the system. But that is in itself no reason for elimination: folk psychology serves other purposes than neuroscience and can be more 'coarse-grained' – as long as it evokes the right responses and inner activation pattern. It is not a game of 'folk psychology loses, neuroscience wins' (Clark, 1997): rather these are different (language) games, serving different explanatory purposes, and may coexist alongside each other. This picture of peaceful coexistence of different perspectives fits well with the explanatory pluralism we sketched in Chapter 2.7 (for more on the uses of folk psychology, its role in empathy, and development see Chapter 10.2).

8.5 Conclusion: Three Views of Mind: Symbols, Networks or Dynamic Systems?

First, let us repeat that both classical computationalists (Chapter 7, Fodor) and connectionists (Churchland) consider mental processes as computation; only they have different views on the stuff the mind is made of. The former's paradigm of mind is language and formal logic, 'sentences in the head'. Churchland looks for alternatives for language-based models of cognition, and has found them in pattern recognition skills, exemplified in connectionist networks. He thinks it highly implausible that the brain has anything like a program and hardware, let alone a language of thought.

Second, that implies that whereas classical computationalists think that cognition (symbol manipulation) is an autonomous level of description relative to its implementation in silicon chips or neurons, connectionists think that cognitive theories will be replaced by neuroscience.

Third, the classicists and the connectionists have opposing views of the relation between mental representation and reality. The symbolic view has as a logical consequence the Cartesian picture of the mind as its own place. Symbols moved around in isolation from the real world – just like the computer does not know what its symbols refer to, the LOT has no semantics. Briefly, CTM is (methodologically) **solipsistic** (Fodor, 1980). Connectionist networks tune into an environment (to be fair, a highly restricted and artificial environment) where their knowledge can be interpreted as adaptive. Connectionism is committed to naturalism, the biological, adaptive view of the genesis of representations factors in the environment as inseparable from the mind (more, and even more radical, ideas on the 'extended mind' in the next chapter).

Finally, the disagreement over the autonomy of functional classical architectures of cognition is interpreted by both Fodor and Churchland as having consequences for the status of folk psychology: can intentionality, mental content, etc. be salvaged in cognitive science, or will they be eliminated?

Whether connectionism has the resources to model structured representations and thereby presumably higher cognition is not yet decided. Dynamicism has a very radical solution: it rejects internal mental representations and emphasizes that cognition is a mutual influencing of organism and environment, developing in real time, and that is can be analysed as a trajectory through state space. Cognition is not in the head – it is a mind-body-world system. Although it is early days, the mood seems to be sceptical about dynamicism. It has few big successes; development may be amongst them (see Van Geert, 1995; Smith and Thelen, 2003), and motor action (see Beer, 1995a; Turvey and Carello, 1995), but for higher cognition the low-dimensional models seem too inflexible (Eliasmith, 2001).

The ideas discussed in this chapter take seriously the neural basis of cognition: the brain is the paradigm for theories of cognition. Connectionist networks are loosely similar to the neural networks in the brain; neurophilosophy looks even more directly at the brain for answers about the mind. Dynamic systems theory is not explicitly brain-based, but emphasizes the adaptive nature of cognitive processes, and thus has a certain biological flavour.

One could perhaps summarize the development of the three views of mind and brain sketched in the previous chapter and this one as a move away from language-based to brain-based models, from abstract logical processing ('Cartesianism', if you

glossary

will) to biological adaptation ('naturalism'). Cognition is increasingly seen as an interacting adaptation to an environment. The next chapter will, therefore, focus on the 'extended mind'.

BOX 8.5 **Three approaches to mind**		
Classical computationalism	*Connectionism*	*Dynamicism*
Formal, syntactical rules, symbols	Weights and activation patterns	Coupled co-evolving systems, developing over time
Preprogrammed, no real development	Self-organization, learning through adapting weights	Evolving through state space, circular causality, continuous adaptation
Brittle program rules	Graceful degradation under damage	Smooth mutual adaptation
Structured, language-like architecture, concatenating discrete symbols	'Associationism', structure dependent on environmental regularities	Development in time
Productivity and systematicity through compositional architecture	Functional compositionality	Trajectory through state space
Functionalism, autonomy for psychology	Reductionist (more or less) brain-like cognition	Emergent properties of organism-environment system, and development
Folk psychology vindicated	Folk psychology eliminated	
Representations are symbolic structures	Representations are activation patterns	No representations needed – no satisfactory account of inner representational states
Solipsism, self-contained mind	Representations are products of interaction with environment	Body, mind and world part of a single system

FURTHER READING

Churchland, P. S. (2002) *Brain-Wise: Studies in Neurophilosophy*. Cambridge, MA: MIT Press.
Looks at how neuroscience transforms the traditional philosophical questions.

Clark, A. (2001) *Mindware: An Introduction to the Philosophy of Cognitive Science*. Oxford: Oxford University Press.
An introduction to philosophical issues in cognitive science, especially dynamical systems.

Gazzaniga, M.S. (2002) Brain-Wise: Studies in Neurophilosophy. Cambridge, MA: MIT Press.
Looks at how neuroscience transforms the traditional philosophical questions.

9. THE EXTENDED MIND

PREVIEW: In this chapter, biologically, phenomenologically and culturally inspired models and metaphors for mind or cognition will be discussed, which all in some way or other go against the narrow mechanical interpretation of mind as symbol manipulation or network activation, that is, some form of computation.

9.1   Introduction

As you may have noted, in the models discussed in the previous chapters, mechanical metaphors for the mind were dominant: digital computers, neural networks, logical machines etc. In the last section of Chapter 8 dynamical systems were introduced, and it was suggested that the latest developments may be inching away from mechanics – sometimes even towards phenomenology (Van Gelder, 1995: 380–1).

This discusion on anti-mechanistic approaches will be continued in this chapter. First there is the idea that mind should be taken as a biological phenomenon. Second, a constantly recurrent theme is the notion of the 'extended mind' (Clark and Chalmers, 1998). Though the body is used as a metaphor to maintain that mind is not working as an isolated system inside the skull, it is demonstrated that external features outside the skin play an indispensible role in shaping cognitive processes as well. A third theme is that mind has to be seen in relation to its resulting activity, the cognition-action cycle. Often action is taken as normal day-to-day activities; mind as embedded in the everyday world. Finally, a fourth topic is that culture at large is a vital cognitive resource, in language and other tools. Environment is not confined to the natural, biological milieu: the social setting is just as important. The focus of study is shifted beyond the individual.

In this chapter we will move from 'hard' to 'soft' science: from evolutionary biology which is in itself not incompatible with a computational approach (section 2), to a cultural view of mind that implies a radically different perspective on mind, meaning and representation (section 5). In sections 3 and 4 all the themes just mentioned, such as the extended mind and the role of the body as a starting place of mind, will be discussed.

9.2 Evolutionary Psychology: Adaptations as Explanations

Adaptation and the mind

glossary   If we take **naturalism** seriously, we should consider the human mind as a product of evolution, that is, an adaptation. In a weak sense this was illustrated by the neurophilosophers discussed in Chapter 8.4. Intentionality, mind, cognition are explained as neural

glossary   mechanisms designed for adaptation and survival. In **dynamic systems theory**, organism and environment are analysed as continuously coupled and co-evolving systems – a vaguely adaptationist idea. In the next sections of this chapter, the view of mind as extending into the biological and cultural environment fleshes out many adaptationist intuitions. However, an emergent discipline called evolutionary psychology goes a step further and proposes to apply rigorous evolutionary biology to psychology. It aims to explain cognition, feelings, bonding and mating, jealousy and moral sentiments, language and art, feelings of revenge and cognitive illusions on the basis of the idea of the evolutionary selection that has shaped the human mind to fit into the hunter-gatherer conditions of the Pleistocene. Briefly, in the Pleistocene the men did the hunting, bringing home the bacon, and women cared for the children and gathered food.

Prominent evolutionary psychologists Cosmides and Tooby (1994) argue that the Pleistocene environment selected a mental architecture that is still present in modern man ('the stone age mind in our skull') (Cosmides and Tooby, 1994). Evolution is slow, and the change of life habits from nomadic hunting and gathering to sedentary agriculture to metropolitan life is relatively very recent (say, 1 per cent of the time of *H. sapiens* on earth), so our mind has not changed with the times. Furthermore, mental architecture is just as universal and fixed as the body's anatomy. Like all people have their ears in more or less the same place, they have roughly the same cognitive and emotional processes – the standard social science model that considers mind as a blank slate written by cultural learning is radically wrong. Each mental capacity is an adaptation for a Pleistocene problem (stereo vision for throwing spears, marital fidelity for dividing the care for offspring, and so on). Cosmides and Tooby argue that since the problems are

glossary   unrelated, the solutions must be independent as well: mind must be **modular**, consisting of a set of separate tools like a Swiss army knife.

So, according to Cosmides and Tooby mental architecture is *universal, modular and selected for a hunter-gatherer society*. These ideas are controversial (see Looren de Jong and Van der Steen, 1998), especially 'modularity' (the idea that the cognitive system is devided into rather autonomous modules, each with their own input and output devices, and their own evolutionary history, compare Chapter 7) is dubious (see Buller and Hardcastle, 2000; Fodor, 2000a, 2000b; Samuels, 1998).

There is now a booming literature on all aspects of social and cognitive behaviour (see e.g. Laland and Brown (2002) for a broad review of evolutionary approaches to behaviour, and Pinker (1997) for a survey of evolutionary psychology). The next section will discuss a brief example of evolutionary explanation of moral behaviour and emotions. In the final sections we will discuss theoretical pitfalls of the approach.

An illustration of evolutionary explanation: moral sentiments

Moral sentiments are those emotions that are associated with moral issues: feelings of altruism, love, hatred, revenge, loyalty, friendship, justice, sacrifice, and so on. Evolutionary psychology will try to explain these not as cultural institutions but as adaptations to serve transmission of genes.

To explain altruism, we have to understand the idea of a selfish gene and the notion of inclusive fitness. Fitness is defined in population genetics as the proportion of one's own genes in the future gene pool – roughly, the number of one's offspring. Inclusive fitness takes into account that one's relatives have partly the same genes, so a brother with many (surviving) children helps one's inclusive fitness. The background to this somewhat counterintuitive idea is the notion of a 'selfish gene' (Dawkins, 1989). Evolution is about the spread of genes, not about survival of the individual. The units of selection are genes, organisms are just their vehicles. Genes code for phenotypic traits that may help survival (say, long legs, or big brains), with the aim of propagating themselves: we could say that the body is under remote control, and on a mission to deliver its genetic cargo safely into the next generation.

When we start to think in terms of the gene's rather than the organism's survival, altruistic behaviour towards relatives (nephews, cousins, brothers) starts to look understandable: by laying down one's life for one's brother, one helps his and thereby (partly) one's own genes survive. This kind of altruism (genic selfishness) is known as 'kin selection'. Family values thus are a behavioural programme (more or less an instinct) that genes build into their vehicles (i.e., us) to promote their own survival.

Another, complementary, evolutionary explanation of altruism is that cooperation may be more profitable than competition. Game theory shows that in the so-called Prisoner's Dilemma consistent cooperation is, in the long run, more profitable than defection (the take-the-money-and-run strategy) if the other player does the same. Reciprocal altruism, returning favours, is common in simple animals like vampires (bats that live on blood sucked from animals): they share their harvest with other vampires, but only with those who reciprocate these favours – freeloaders are shunned (Ridley, 1996; Wright, 1994). So, in general, in the struggle for survival cooperation helps; and cooperation requires a reliable partner. This is the origin of virtue

(Ridley, 1996): emotions of justice, rejection of cheaters, sympathy for reliable partners are programmes built into our brains by our genes and help our genes survive. According to Cosmides (1989), we have a built-in cheater detection module that spot those who take benefits they are not entitled to – for example, most people get mad when someone jumps a queue, even when it hardly hurts them. This was selected as an adaptive solution in our ancestors' hunters-gatherer environment. To uphold the long-term commitments required for the division of labour, it is vital to detect those who don't play by the rules of social exchange (concerning, for example, the distribution of food and opportunities for procreation). One of the first showcases of evolutionary explanation was Cosmides' (1989) experiment in which she showed that difficult logical problems become instantly comprehensible when framed in terms of spotting those who take benefits that they are not entitled to. It should be mentioned, however, that the experimental evidence for the existence of the cheater detection module is open to other interpretations (Fodor, 2000b) (the effect may be an artefact of the way the material is presented, and may reflect the subject's inferential patterns rather than a dedicated module for social exchange), and that the Cosmides interpretation seems more and more doubtful.

Anyway, some mental tool or instinct required for reciprocation is supposedly present in vampires and hunter-gatherers, and presumably in modern man as well. Instincts that drive us to be reliable partners were selected for their evolutionary usefulness. In this light, the Victorian virtues of honesty, hard work, and modesty are quite useful, since a good reputation is an asset: it shows you as a trustworthy business partner to play the game of cooperation and reciprocation with (Wright, 1994). Virtuous people get the business, shady characters are shunned and stay poor.

The premium on being a reliable partner also helps to explain a class of moral sentiments that at first sight looks baffling: passions, seemingly irrational and self-destructive behaviour. Some people will sacrifice anything in romantic love, others will spend a fortune in time and energy to retrieve a stolen bicycle and catch the thief, where buying a new one would have been much cheaper, and the thirst for revenge can destroy a person. Passions are obviously against one's self-interest, and therefore seem unexplainable in terms of a survival strategy. However, there is an explanation: the Doomsday principle (Frank, 1990; Pinker, 1997: 407–16). The Doomsday machine in Stanley Kubrick's film *Dr Strangelove* will automatically fire missiles in retaliation for an attack, not to be stopped by anyone. It is a perfect deterrent, since a potential attacker knows that revenge is assured, even when it goes against the self-interest of the retaliator (who may be destroyed himself). A person in the grip of passion is like a Doomsday machine: he cannot back down, even when wanted; he is completely reliable because he has lost control. So the irrationality of the passions makes evolutionary sense. The fact that the outward signs of passions can be read from one's face (irrepressible muscle twitches, blushing, shaking) and cannot be dissimulated fits into this picture: the Doomsday principle only works if the potential attacker knows about it – uncontrollable anger, romantic love, and so on must show on the face to be effective. (Incidentally, in the film the Doomsday machine misfires (so to speak) badly, because the Russians kept it secret).

To sum up

Evolutionary psychology considers mental processes as behavioural programmes, a kind of instinct promoting the survival of the selfish genes whose vehicles we are: emotions are a self-serving message from our genes (Wright, 1994). Feelings of disgust are good for keeping us away from germs, love is a clever trick of Nature to spur us to procreation and gene-spreading, and patriotism and family values are a matter of kin selection. Moral behaviour is a kind of instinct, selected to facilitate exchange in hunter-gatherer societies. Cheater detection is a cognitive mechanism designed to facilitate reciprocal altruism.

One of the selling points of evolutionary psychology is that it can explain maladaptive behaviour as a result of the stone-age mind in our skull, now operating in a modern technical society. Note that Mother Nature's idea of what is good is entirely backward-looking: we are programmed to survive in the environment of *past selection*. When circumstances change, adaptive solutions may turn out to be maladaptive: an instinct like gorging on as much fat and salty food as possible may have been good when food was scarce, but quite unhealthy in today's shopping centres. Likewise, evolutionary psychologists will explain unhappiness from a misfit between our mental architecture selected in hunter-gatherer societies and modern society (Buss, 2000).

The above example of evolutionary reasoning is brief and simplistic, and only intended to give something of the flavour of the approach, and of the startling perspectives evolutionary thinking (or speculation) affords.

Spurious generalization

To understand mind as an adaptation we need biology is the message of prominent evolutionary psychologists Cosmides and Tooby (1994, 1995; Tooby and Cosmides, 1995). They think psychology should be integrated with biology – and the social science paradigm with its emphasis on learning as social shaping of behaviour (the idea of the 'blank slate' – see Pinker, 2002) should be replaced by the biological view of mind as an evolved organ. They emphasize that biology is a hard science with real laws and a genuine scientific method. That method is functional-adaptive thinking, considering a phenotypic trait as a solution to an adaptive problem in the ancestral environment in which it was selected.

Much ink has been spilled over the soundness of adaptive explanations in biology. Cosmides and Tooby (1994) claim that functional-adaptive thinking is the method of evolutionary biology, and that 'evolutionarily rigorous theories of adaptive function are the logical foundations upon which to build cognitive theories' (1994: 41). They also claim that:

> ... the modern technical theory of evolution ... consists of a logically derivable set of causal principles that necessarily govern the dynamics of reproducing systems. ... This set of principles has been tested, validated and enriched through its integration with functional

and comparative anatomy, …, genetics, … and a number of other disciplines … Modern evolutionary biology constitutes, in effect, a foundational organism design theory, whose principles can be used to fit together research findings into coherent models of specific cognitive and neural mechanisms. (Tooby and Cosmides, 1995: 1186)

Somewhat ironically, working biologists and philosophers are sceptical if not downright dismissive of these ideas. Cosmides and Tooby seem to have missed a debate in the philosophy of biology, to the effect that biology, especially evolutionary biology, is itself not integrated, and is in many respects hardly comparable with a real hard science like physics (Brandon, 1990; Schaffner, 1993). For example, Brandon (1990: 134) writes: '… I do not think evolutionary theory is a theory at all. Rather, it is a family of theories (and goals, methods, and metaphysics) related in complex and ever-changing ways.' The consensus in the philosophy of biology seems to be that biology has no, or very few real laws, that biological kinds are historical and contingent, and that natural history, not general laws or universal **foundational** principles, is the material of biological **explanation**.

glossary

So, Cosmides and Tooby are deeply wrong about the nature of explanations in biology (Lloyd, 1999; Looren de Jong and Van der Steen, 1998). Biology is about as diverse and messy as psychology. Cosmides and Tooby tend to *spurious generalization*: the misguided idea that there are general laws in biology that cover every aspect of evolution, and that psychology can be brought under these laws (see Van der Steen, 2000). A presumably general law like the principle of natural selection (PNS) (Brandon, 1990) has no real empirical content. The concept of functional explanation, as it figures in adaptive-functional explanation, has multiple meanings and multiple uses (Mitchell, 1995).

So, even within the sciences of biology, some kind of explanatory pluralism exists (see Chapter 2.5). Reduction does not work in the human sciences, where different perspectives (causal, functional, hermeneutical) will remain in use, and even within biological functional explanation the different levels and applications cannot be brought under one general scheme. Explanatory pluralism rather than reductive integration is the best way to look at psychology and its relation to biology. There are no general biological laws, hence psychological ones cannot be derived from them. Thus the spectre of biological reductionism and genetic determinism (Are we just animals? Are we just machines running according to our genetic blueprint? and so on) can be kept at bay.

The problem of 'how-possible stories': history is indispensable

Apart from the misguided overgeneralization of biological explanations, there is another problem with adaptive explanation, well known among biologists, but less so among psychologists: the danger of 'how-possible stories'. Gould and Lewontin (1979) famously attacked the uncritical application of adaptive explanations to each and every trait with their now classic metaphor of a 'spandrel' (see Chapter 2.4). A spandrel is a wall surface between two arches and a dome, as in the San Marco cathedral in Venice (strictly speaking, art historians would call it a squinch or pendentive). Adaptationists would, in the caricature Gould and Lewontin paint, routinely devise some function for the spandrel – for example, that it is designed for (has the function of) bearing mosaics. But in fact the spandrel is not designed, it is just a by-product since you cannot build a dome on arches without a piece of wall in between. There is nothing to explain, and Gould and Lewontin want to show that adaptationists are guilty of inventing pseudo-explanations. Adaptationism dabbles in just-so stories, like: the tiger has stripes because that helps fitness, otherwise the stripes would not be there. That things are just so as they are is clearly a non-explanation. Evolutionary psychologists like Buss et al. (1998) admit that there is a problem here, but maintain that when applied carefully, functional-adaptationist explanation generates useful hypotheses. Philosophers of biology tend to be more restrictive. They demand empirical facts, showing that some trait is associated with more survival in a certain environment, and what the underlying mechanisms were (Brandon (1990) shows how this works for a seemingly simple case with plants). The adaptationist has in fact no more than a 'how-possible story', showing what function a certain trait might possibly serve. What is required in addition is a 'how-actually' story, showing that the trait was actually selected. For example, language may have developed because it has conferred more efficient communication for the group, or better opportunities for procreation for the verbally gifted (Pinker and Bloom, 1990), but to support that claim evolutionary biologists need data on primitives with and without language, showing who became extinct, when, and how and why. Historical facts are indispensable for good evolutionary explanations. Unfortunately, that condition is almost impossible to fulfil, since behaviour does not fossilize: evidence of extinct speakers is more difficult to find than fossils of extinct species. Lewontin (1998) believes that therefore evolutionary psychology is impossible, while Pinker and Bloom (1990) are more optimistic.

To sum up

The consensus among evolutionary biologists is that explanation requires much more than inventing how-possible stories. And that makes the enterprise much more complicated than the simplistic-examples discussed above suggest (see also Buss et al. (1998); Laland and Brown (2002)). So evolutionary psychology opens interesting new perspectives, and the basic idea of a naturalist explanation of the mind seems sound enough (to the present writers), but its explanations should be viewed with caution. A final remark: socially-minded opponents of biological approaches to mind suspect all kinds of dehumanizing tendencies; they believe that it may lead to social Darwinism, inequality, biological determinism, even racism. In our opinion there is no reason to suspect anything like that (see Pinker, 2002).

9.3 Mind in Action: Uniting Brain, Body and World

The embodied and world-embedded mind in action

Champions of AI supported by orthodox cognitivism promised in the 1960s that in the then near future, say at the end of the century, science and technology would present artificial minds. At the beginning of his (1997) book Andy Clark asked cynically: 'Why are even the best of our "intelligent" artifacts still so unspeakably, terminally dumb?' (1997: 1). The reason was that up till the 1980s cognitivists imagined mind as a logical reasoning machine connected to a continually growing database. What was ignored was that mind is a biological asset and that it has developed to control and guide the biological body in a natural environment; that cognition and action go together. Of course this biological idea was maintained by scholars already much earlier, at least from times that the theory of evolution inspired ideas on organism and environment interactions. The **pragmatist** philosophers James and Dewey, for instance, referred continuously to the survival value of mind and the intimacy of thinking and acting (see Chapters 4.6 and 4.7). But the early cognitivist were so fierce in their anti-behaviourism that for them behaviour or action was, from a cognitive point of view, not a respectable issue. Although they rejected Cartesian dualism, they again cherished the philosopher's picture of mind as a thinking device. The Darwinian style of thinking about mental processes (see for example Tomasello, 1999) was cast away, and a static and atemporal, an **individualistic** and intellectualistic view was adopted during the first decades of cognitive science and AI.

glossary (margin)

glossary (margin)

BOX 9.1   Recent views of 'mind'

Mechanical and computational approaches:

- The *linguistic view*: mind is an inborn symbol structure of logically and syntactically linked mental propositions. This linguistic symbol structure is not essentially connected to, and therefore can be studied in abstraction from, the physical system in which it happens to be realized, as well as isolated from the outside world and its behavioural performances.
- The *connectionist* view: mind is a system of neural networks consisting of nodes and connections between them in which weights of the connections determine the activation of input and output nodes.
- The *dynamic view*: mind is a complex mathematically structured and self-organizing system of brain states which operates in space and time in a non-linear but adaptive way because of a constant coupling with its environmental objects and systems.
- The view of *evolutionary psychology*: mind is a set of modules, programmes promoting the survival of the human animal whose behaviour can be explained by the evolutionary adaptive history of its ancestors. The emphasis on function and adaptation sets the evolutionary approach slightly apart from mainstream computational models.

BOX 9.1   **Recent views of 'mind'** (Continued)

Non- (or anti-) mechanical approaches:

Other approaches differ from the mechanical mainstream in emphasizing the embodied nature of cognition, or its social and cultural roots, which are in their view neglected in the mainstream. These approaches stress the respective role of evolution, body, action, organism–environment interaction, language, education, metaphors, and culture in the development of human behaviour. Some can be said to 'relocate' the mind from the inner world of the Cartesian theatre to a mind extending into its physical and cultural environment.

We have seen in the previous chapter that **connectionist** or neural network styles of **computational** mind-modelling, the growing field of cognitive neuroscience, dynamicism and 'real-world' robotics have changed cognitive science so completely that it has been customary since then (roughly the 1980s) to refer to it as the 'second cognitive revolution'. As with the proposal of evolutionary psychology, also an effect of the general biological turn in cognitive science (see previous section), the adaptive response to an environment is supposed to be one of the basic features of mind and intelligence. In view of the general coupling between the organism and the world, between the brain-body and world, more and more cognitive functions such as perception, memory, intention, emotion, motivation etc. are being studied in terms of their contribution to adaptive action in the daily environment. The classical cognitive function of reasoning has changed from a disembodied world-aloof symbol manipulation into *situated* reasoning.

   Clark (1997), presenting an overview of research results and discussing methodological issues, suggests that development and perception psychologists, such as Piaget, Vygotsky (see next section), Bruner and J.J. Gibson (see Chapter 4), were probably among the first to notice the link between internal and external factors in cognitive development and perception. They anticipated many ideas later pursued by roboticists, such as Brooks (see Chapter 8.3). Clark mentions a number of 'landmarks' in theory and research on 'situated cognition' (Clark, 1997: ch. 2). These landmarks are closely related properties of creatures with action-oriented cognitive capacities, some of which we will present here, just to give an idea.

On-line strategies

First there is the idea of 'action loops' which can be demonstrated in the case of jigsaw puzzling. Instead of mentally representing and determining in advance whether a piece fits into a location, we actually exploit a mixed strategy of physically manipulating and rotating a piece, mentally assessing a potential fit, and then again physically giving it a shot. Completing a jigsaw puzzle thus involves 'an intricate and iterated dance' (op. cit.: 36) of perception, thought and action. Seen from a historical perspective it was in fact John Dewey who, in his critique on the reflex arc concept (the notion of disconnected and passive stimulus and response chains) (1896), already referred to a so-called 'circuit of experience', the cyclic performance of perception, thought and action. He used the example of a child who encounters a candle, making ready to reach for the flame, and learns in the activity that the thing is hot and causes pain. Instead of a passive stimulus–response connection there is a reciprocal action-perception cycle. In their dynamical system approach to the development of cognition and action, developmental psychologists Esther Thelen and Linda Smith reported in their wonderful book (1994; see also Smith and Thelen, 2003) a testing of this idea in their research on infants' leg movements, for instance crawling or walking on 'visual cliffs' (a drop covered with transparent plexiglass). They demonstrated that cognitive development is dependent on bodily factors, and that infant behaviour is constituted by continuous perception-action coupling.

Another finding is that the development of a child's cognitive capacities is not orchestrated by a single factor, such as a genetically inborn 'blueprint', and does not progress in a linear way by going through in advance determined successive and irreversible stages. It appears that such nativist and centralized thinking has to make way for a much more complicated vision in which multiple factors perform an interactive play. When learning to walk newborn infants show no neat behaviour transitions to sequential maturation stages; on the contrary, they appear to adapt strategies (e.g. stepping motions) in response to environmental circumstances, and to learn by interaction. The message is that functional locomotion is a 'confluence of organismic and environmental factors' (Thelen and Smith, 1994: 18); and also: stop searching for single factors and centralized causes when explaining complex phenomena because complex phenomena exhibit a great deal of self-organization (Clark, 1997: 40; see also Chapter 8). For instance, the flocking pattern of birds is not orchestrated by a leader bird or a pre-ordained plan, but each bird follows the behaviour of its nearest neighbours. The resulting behaviour emerges not from a single and central factor, but from the interaction of multiple local factors.

A third aspect, mentioned by Clark, is what he calls 'soft assembly' (Clark, 1997: 42). Unlike the 'hard assembly' of the precisely controlled movements by a classical pre-programmed robot-arm, on-line action, like human walking, shows different patterns of locomotion according to the circumstances – on a carpeted surface, or an icy sidewalk, with high-heeled shoes on, or tormented by blisters. This ability to readjust the pattern in response to 'intentional, organic, or environment constraints' (Thelen and Smith, 1994: 84) arises from the ability of subsystems to softly, that is, biodynamically assemble. Due to the decentralized route in the whole cognition-action dynamical system, the resulting behaviour is flexible and also robust, because when one subsystem crashes others can take over.

Finally we mention another closely related aspect of the way humans and other animals incorporate the environment in their adaptive and action-oriented cognitive tasks: 'external scaffolding'(Clark, 1997: passim), making use of features of the world in solving problems. A non-cognitive example is the feeding strategy of a sponge. To get its food by filtering water, but also to reduce costly pumping, the creature exploits ambient currents. Likewise, we often exploit aspects of the world to help thinking, planning and on-board memory, as in playing scrabble (continuously ordering physically your letter tiles) or in doing mathematics (making use of graphical devices on paper or blackboard). The overall message is that instead of following inborn programmes animals, organisms in general, display 'on-line' strategies in their adaptive behaviour.

BOX 9.2   Key ideas in non-mechanical approaches to mind

- *Embodied*: emphasizing the role of the body in (mindful) behaviour, in contrast with mind-body dualism.
- *World-embedded*: to mark the organism–world coupling in adaptive behaviour.
- *Thought and action unity*: the idea that activity is an important ingredient in explaining mind, in contrast to the 'onlooker' or 'spectator' interpretation of mind, or mind as an exclusive 'thinking' device (intellectualism) (see Chapter 4.5).
- *Externalism*: the view that we have to explain mind by looking beyond the boundary of the skin (in contrast with internalism, or individualism).
- *Perception-action cycle*: to mark the cyclic performance of thought, perception and action, and to stress the kinesthetic and mobile features in these performances.
- *Situated cognition*: indicates that cognition has to be studied in its day-to-day activities in a real world.
- *On-line strategies*: the procedures which are used by an organism in its adaptive world-embedded behaviour, in contrast to inborn programmes.
- *Emergent properties*: is said of properties arising out of the coordinated activities of many elements in a system, properties which cannot be traced back to the elements.

Artificial life

In 1987 Chris Langton gathered at a workshop in Los Alamos 160 researchers from all over the world. They did diverse research (from computer science to anthropology and ethology), many of them even idiosyncratic work, but in fact asking the same question: 'What is life?' During the conference artificial life (A-Life or AL) was born; Langton wrote the manifesto defining its agenda. It is extremely difficult, he wrote, to distinguish essential properties of life, shared by *any* possible living system, if you have in fact only one example on Earth due to 'a combination of local historical accident and common genetic descent', that is, carbon-based life. The alternative, therefore, is 'to try to sythesize alternative life forms ourselves – Artificial Life: life made by man rather than nature' (Langton, 1996: 39). Thus:

A-life is the study of man-made systems that exhibit behaviors characteristic of natural living systems. It complements the traditional biological sciences concerned with the analysis of living organisms by attempting to synthesize life-like behaviors within computers and other artificial media. (Langton, 1989: 1)

Some key principles of life are evolution, self-reproduction, self-organization, and emergent behaviour. Life is a form of behaviour, not a kind of stuff (Langton, 1996: 53); it is the result of the (self)organization of matter rather than something inherent in the matter itself. Carbon-chain molecules are not alive, but when they are put together and are allowed to interact dynamically they exhibit behaviour which we call life. Life shows the properties of non-linear systems for which (contrary to linear systems) the behaviour of the whole is more than the sum of its parts. It is the interactions between the parts, rather than the properties of the parts themselves, which are of primary importance.

glossary   Life is the behaviour that **emerges** out of the local interactions of a great number of non-living molecules; there is no centralized controller with access to a set of pre-defined data-structures. A living organism is viewed as a large population of simple parts, so you probably do best to start your study with these constituent elements and to work upwards synthetically, than with going down from the top of complex behaviour. Therefore, it is this 'bottom-up, distributed, local determination of behaviour' that AL employs as its primary methodological approach and modelling technique (Langton, 1989: 3; Bedeau, 2003).

The ideal tool for this synthetic approach to the study of life is the computer. But whereas classical AI used the technology of computation itself as a model of intelligence, AL uses computers as a tool to explore the dynamics of interacting information structures; it does not attempt to explain life as a kind of computer program. Computers themselves will not be alive; they should be thought of as a laboratory tool and experimental equipment devoted to the incubation, manipulation, and exploration of information structures of behaviour, 'substituting for the array of incubaters, culture dishes, microscopes, electrophoretic gels, pippettes, centrifuges, and other assorted wet-lab paraphernalia'. Used in this way, computers demonstrate important heuristic value (Langton, 1996: 50 ff.).

Of course, one recognizes in the (sometimes rather heterogeneous) ideas of the A-life community the notion of mind-body-world couplings that we have encountered in the discussions of biological, world-embedded, dynamic, on-line strategies and adaptive behaviour elsewhere in this and previous chapters.

A one-and-only approach or a multiple exploitation of methods?

Let us conclude this section by referring to two debated issues: do we still need glossary **representations** in explanations of cognitive functions; and which is the best method in cognitive science?

As we have seen in the previous chapter, there is much disagreement whether internal representations and conceptualizations can be missed in full-grown cognition. 'Moboticist' Rodney Brooks thinks that 97 per cent of human behaviour is non-representational (Brooks, 1995). David Kirsh (1991) disagrees. He thinks that human activities fall along a continuum: at the one end situationally determined activities such as walking and tying shoelaces; at the other end highly cerebral activities such as playing bridge and doing research. Recall that Clark referred to 'representation-hungry' situations, such as off-line imagination and reflection (Clark, 1997: 147; see Chapter 8.3). If representations cannot be missed, the notion is undergoing fundamental changes: from explicit one-to-one corresponding, chunky and symbolic representations, to representations which are highly distributed over populations of neurons and vector coded. Though it might be true that humans do process internal representations, it might be less acceptable that symbol manipulation makes up the architecture of cognition.

Closely connected is the second controversial issue, the question about method. Or to put it differently: is the dynamical systems approach, which seems to be successful in understanding what is life and the adaptive strategies of embodied and worldly embedded creatures, also the best explanatory method for understanding cognitive and neurocognitive phenomena? The brain seems to be a system with many specialized parts which can operate in modularized ways, that is, with respect to individual roles. By the dynamic approach one tries to explain adaptive behaviour of the organism-environment interactions as an emergent property not detectable in the individual components of the organism. However, by this perspective one runs the risk of overlooking the details of the parts of the brain, for instance, when they are damaged and disrupted, and how because of this they would precisely affect overall behaviour. To account for these phenomena of neurological impairment and its behavioural effects, an important task of cognitive neuroscience (see for instance the work of Damasio, 1999), one needs a modular explanation, an approach that tries to understand the inner organization of the brain system and the spread of functions among its parts. This kind of approach resembles to a certain extent the classical method which details the individual roles of the parts of a cognitive system, but without notions of a centralized homuncular controller and storage system. Nevertheless the modular explanation is relative, we like to add, because without a view of the effects in the wordly behaviour, one easily overlooks the inner specifics. Both types of explanation constrain and complement one another.

In sum, this means for cognitive science that explanations in terms of the emergence of adaptive organism-environment couplings are important, but do not completely displace classical representational-computational explanations. It is therefore likely that the cognitive scientist would be willing to exploit multiple kinds of explanatary tools (Clark, 1996b, 1997 and 2001).

9.4 The Body in the Mind

In the previous section the body played a crucial role in the action-oriented approach of dynamicists and A-Life researchers. In their vision of cognitivism, materialism, computationalism, and mechanism were still main orientations. However, embodiment has been an argument in anti-mechanist cognitive theory as well. Shanon's (1993: 109) distinction between two senses of the body may be helpful here: on the one hand, the identification with the neurophysiological system or the body in terms of motor activity; and, on the other, the body in its phenomenological sense, that is, as experienced.

It is especially this second sense that plays a crucial role in cognitive activity, according to many cognitive philosophers (e.g. Dreyfus, 1979; Johnson, 1987), who take an anti-mechanist position. Their critique, it must be said, was launched against the classical cognitivism of the early period. As later developments in cognitive theory, described earlier, made embodiment a crucial element in adaptive behaviour, there appeared a rapprochement to a certain extent.

Critique on early cognitivism was, of course, the focus on 'higher' mental functions, rational thought and the production of language, resulting in disregarding the body. Even behaviour was not a relevant topic, because it was seen by the classical cognitivist as an unproblematic consequence of information-processing. They did not see a real cognitive difference between, say, problem-solving and playing the piano. Both activities involve knowledge, and all knowledge, it was thought, can be specified and represented in symbolic mental representations. Being able to perform the activity is possessing the required knowledge.

The phenomenology of the body

What is meant by the anti-mechanist philosophers is that intentionality, our cognitive relation with the world (see Chapter 10), is mediated by our body. To perceive is to move our eyes, to grasp things, to walk around. For our daily habitation in the world we need a zillion skills, and these cannot be made explicit, spelled out in knowledge, that is, in *knowing-that*; what we use is *know-how*. Many philosophers have pointed out this distinction (e.g. Ryle, 1949). To know the rules is not the same as being able to play the piano; to think about them can even hamper the performance.

The body has a fundamental epistemological function in our *background knowledge*: this is pre-reflexive know-how, absolutely necessary knowledge we do not learn explicitly and just do not think about. To use one of John Searle's (1992; see also 1983) examples: we learn how to use a knife and fork, we hardly have to learn not to stick the food in our ears. Exploiting this concept of **background** (see below, Chapter 10), Dreyfus (1979) demonstrated 'what computers can't do'. Learning, he wrote, does not consist merely in mechanically acquiring more and more information about specific routine situations; rather it takes place against a 'background of shared practices'. This background is also implicit know-how, and not formalizable in facts and beliefs; it is 'bodily skills for coping with the world' (ibid.: 47). AI researchers had difficulty in coping with the problem of representing everyday context, since they tried in vain to make the background of practices explicit as a set of beliefs (ibid.: 56).

Many of the inspiring thoughts about the phenomenological import of the body in our daily experience and conduct, especially perception, can already be found in Merleau-Ponty's *Phénoménologie de la perception* (1945). His work has motivated

glossary

studies about the cognitive role of the body, how the body shapes the categories of our world-understanding and world-activity. Mark Johnson's *The Body in the Mind* (1987) speaks of 'embodied schemata', cognitive structures 'that are constantly operating in our perception, bodily movement through space, and physical manipulation of objects' (1987: 23). He takes as an example of embodied schemata those for *in-out* orientation in our experience, and in our use and understanding of language, as in: John went out of the room; let out your anger; hand out the information. He claims that our sense of *out* orientation in these daily examples is most intimately tied to the experience of our own body in its spatial orientation, since the body can take up the role of the 'thing contained' or the 'container'. We easily project this in-out orientation not only, to, for example, a tube of toothpaste, but also quite naturally extend a schema from the physical to the non-physical, as in: tell me your story again, but leave out the minor details; here the story is metaphorically seen as a container that can 'hold' events (1987: 32 ff.).

Metaphors in thinking and speaking

As can be seen in the above example, metaphors play an operational role in these schematic structures. They elaborate meanings and underlie understanding, combine images and memories, furnish structure to our thoughts and experiences, Johnson claims (1987: 65 ff). This creative and constitutive role in cognition was ignored in, what he calls, the objectivist view of meaning and truth. In this view there is one universal set of concepts that map directly onto the objective features of the world, independent of subjective and imaginative structures of thinking and speaking (cf. above discussions about realism and relativism in Chapter 4). In this received view metaphors are treated mainly as nothing but rhetorical or artistic figures of speech, and therefore of secondary importance in explaining the relation between mind and world. Johnson maintains, on the contrary, that metaphors pervasively constrain our thinking and reasoning.

The meaning of 'balance', he shows in another example of metaphorical power, emerges in bodily and perceptual experiences in which we physically orient within our environment (op. cit: 74 ff). Metaphorical extensions of this meaning, connected to the experience of bodily balance, are working in the notion of a system. A system is an organization of interconnected elements or members that work together to form a functional unity. An ecological system, for instance, exhibits a balance not only of physical but also of social forces, such as the migrations of animals, a balanced social interaction among the members. And so metaphorical extensions are present in our understanding of other systems, such as the nervous system; of balanced personalities, balanced views, the balance of power, the balance of justice, and so on. These metaphorical projections are understood by virtue of the balance schemata of our bodily experience, Johnson maintains.

Metaphors, in sum, act in extending cognitive structures from the physical to the non-physical. And such is the influence of embodied schemata and the role of the body in the mind.

Philosophy in the flesh

Mind is inherently embodied. Thought is mostly unconscious. Abstract concepts are largely metaphorical. These three theses Lakoff and Johnson (1999) consider as the major findings of cognitive science. These discoveries not appreciated in Western philosophy lead to a radical change in our understanding of human reason, ourselves and the world; 'philosophy can never be the same again' (op. cit.: 3).

Mind or reason is not autonomous, independent of bodily capacities, such as perception, motion, emotion, in conscious control of its intellectual functions. It uses and grows out of bodily functions, and builds upon evolutionary earlier animal nature. But what is more, the very structure of mind is shaped by body and brain. Categories and concepts are formed through our embodiment, our sensorimotor experience; and as claimed in the earlier book by Johnson (1987), metaphors and imagination play a constitutive role. It will be clear that the authors feel more at home in the second generation of cognitive science which is in many aspects a cognitive science of the 'embodied mind' (Varela et al., 1991).

Building upon their earlier work (see also Lakoff and Johnson, 1980; and Lakoff, 1987), the authors challenge in this inspiring book no less than the complete Western philosophy; they are more sweeping, unbridled, but perhaps also more superficial.

9.5 Beyond the Individual Mind: Cultural and Linguistic Origins

Vygotsky on the social origins of mind

The Russian psychologist Lev Vygotsky (1896–1934) can be considered one of the fathers of the idea that the social other plays a crucial role in the cognitive development of the individual. Two themes in his theoretical framework are of importance for his understanding of mind: the developmental approach, and the claim that (higher) mental processes in the individual have their origin in social processes (Wertsch, 1985). In the context of his research on the dynamics and prediction of children's intellectual development, for instance, he asserted that only in joint activity with others do children achieve what he calls 'zones of proximal development'. These are levels of performance beyond their individual competence, higher cognitive skills than they could attain by acting on their own. It was shown that only under the guidance of or in cooperation with an adult could three- to five-year-old children perform some tasks, which five- to seven-year-old children were able to perform independently (Rogoff and Wertsch, 1984; see also Van der Veer and Valsiner, 1991: ch. 13). In the light of the social origins of cognitive development, Vygotsky proposed a more complex method for assessing and predicting children's intelligence than the 'Western' individualistic IQ test: he focused on the relation between teaching (socializing) and cognitive development, rather than on what the child can do herself.

Vygotsky saw the mental as an 'internalization' of the social, a process in which social phenomena are transformed into psychological ones. Language is an important medium of internalization, it is a psychological tool for socializing children into the public domain, the means to communication and social contact, as well as the medium that shapes individuals' higher mental functions, such as thinking and memory. Language is by nature social, not organic or individual (Vygotsky, 1962; see also Wertsch, 1985: ch. 4).

Contrary to Chomsky's theory that language is not taught but is an inborn mechanism, a 'language instinct' (Pinker, 1994), the social tradition considers language as a social product. This is branded by Pinker as the key factor in what he disapprovingly calls the 'standard social science model', according to which the human psyche is moulded by the surrounding culture (Pinker, 1994: 23). The focus of most social psychologists is on language as social action, its pragmatic use rather than as a formal and abstract mental system, 'wired in' in a human being. Both sides of the controversy make a number of interesting observations (for an overview of the social side of this discussion and many related issues see Shanon, 1993: ch. 9; Bickhard and Terveen, 1995: ch. 11).

Sociocultural and 'situated cognition', Vygotskian style

Many commentators have pointed out the similarity of some of Vygotsky's ideas to the thoughts of the American social philosopher George Herbert Mead (1863–1931) (Looren de Jong, 1991). Mead (1934) also claimed that mind is social by origin. His idea that the self is a product of **social interactions** (see also Chapter 5.2 about symbolic interactionism) is pursued in social constructionists' studies on self and identity (Shotter and Gergen, 1989; Chapter 4.3) and by those social psychologists who postulate that, because language is inherently social, thought is collective; that individuals take part in 'social representations' created in the course of communication and interaction; and that reality is a matter of conventions (Farr and Moscovici, 1984).

glossary

Like behaviourism, (early) cognitivism understood knowledge and learning as resulting from experience 'within a stable, objective world' and acquired intrapsychically, piecemeal and incrementally by isolated individuals. Culture and society could, therefore, hardly enter into this picture, and 'only insofar as they are decomposable into discrete elements' (Kirshner and Whitson, 1997: vii). Rallying round this fundamental critique on the cognitivists and their unpromising treatment of culture and community, social, developmental and educational psychologists launched 'situated cognition' theory. Learning and knowledge are explored as processes that occur in a 'local, subjective, and socially constructed world' (ibid.; compare this constructionist notion of 'situated cognition' with the notion mentioned in Chapter 5.3).

'One source of inspiration' for the situated cognitivist is 'the robust expertise' that common people display in daily situations, such as street mathematics and grocery shopping. 'Situated cognition' holds that knowledge is not just accumulated information but entails 'lived practices' (op. cit.: 4). It takes as its central problem how cultures reproduce themselves across generational boundaries, a Vygotskian theme.

The focus of analysis, thus, may be shifted from the individual toward the activities in the sociocultural setting, in which a 'dialectical relation' has to be preferred, that is, a relation in which its individual components 'are brought into being, only in conjunction with one another' (Lave, 1988). This means that relationships between individuals develop in their shared activities and are not only the result of simple mutual effects.

In the following paragraph we will introduce you to a recent remarkably robust elaboration of some Vygotskian principles.

Hutchins: cognition in the wild is distributed cognition

An exciting account of the thesis that for real everyday cognition we have to look beyond the individual mind is given by the anthropologist Edwin Hutchins (1995). He describes what a group of people is doing when they perform together a complicated task. His case is the activity of ship navigation as practised on the bridge of a navy ship, say an entry into a harbour, or avoiding a sudden danger. The team on the bridge is taken as the unit of cognitive analysis. Hutchins describes extensively the processes and operations of a number of cognitive systems that can be identified in the conduct of navigation tasks: processes internal to a single individual, of an individual in coordination with a set of tools, of a group of individuals in interaction with one another and with a set of tools. It is shown that the important cognitive operations in relation to the navigation tasks are taking place in systems larger than the individual. He therefore shows how the cognitive properties of these systems are produced by interactions among their parts, and accordingly pushes the boundary of the unit of cognitive analysis out beyond the skin of the individual.

Hutchins describes how cognitive properties of technical and collective systems may be culturally constructed. The properties of the Mercator-projection chart used by sailors, for example, are mathematical in nature; the chart is an analogue computer. But the actual computations were performed by the cartographers and need not be a direct concern of the users of the chart. The navigator doesn't need to know, either, about the properties of the Mercator projection by which special computational meaning is given to straight lines. The computations and properties exhibited by the chart have been 'distributed over time as well as over social space'; they are culturally distributed. The computational abilities of the navigator 'penetrate only the shallows of the computational problems of navigation' (Hutchins, 1995: 173–4). One easily ascribes to individuals what has to be seen as the outcome of cultural and contextual factors. Compare this to what Clark called 'scaffolding' (see 9.3).

To analyse the organizational effects of communication Hutchins used computer simulations of communities of connectionist networks. They showed that patterns of communication within groups and over time may produce different cognitive properties. These group properties are the outcome of interaction between structures internal and external to individuals, and the generation of different interpretations by the group may be better. The performance of the cognitive tasks that exceed individual abilities, he concludes, 'is always shaped by a social organization of distributed cognition ... Even the simplest culture contains more information than could be learned by any individual in a lifetime' (op. cit.: 262).

Elaborating Vygotsky's conception of internalization (see previous paragraph), Hutchins has many interesting things to say about learning that he defines as 'adaptive reorganization in a complex system' (op. cit.: 289), inside and outside the individual.

With his analysis of everyday cognition, 'cognition in the wild' (the title of the book), Hutchins criticizes the 'Western view' of the individual bounded by the skin, in general, and the early cognitivists' notion of the cognitive symbol system 'lying protected from the world somewhere far below the skin' (op. cit.: 289). He calls his description 'cognitive ethnography' which reminds one of the characterization of the laboratory studies by science sociologists such as Latour, whose book (1986) Hutchins indeed typifies as one of the few 'truly ethnographic studies of cognition in the wild' (Hutchins, 1995: 371; see also Chapter 5.5). He is convinced that the question about the functional specifications of a cognitive system, 'What is mind for?', can only be answered by explicating the social and cultural factors.

Wittgenstein on the nature of language and mind

In our opinion, the most articulate alternative to the dominant mechanist theories of mind is a broadly Wittgensteinian position. The mechanist position is that thinking is literally symbol manipulation or network activation; in any case, some form of computation. Wittgenstein denies the possibility of identifying mental content or meaning with a physical state, and by extension, with a computational state. More precisely, although he may agree with the thesis that the brain is a **syntactic** machine, it cannot be *ipso facto* a **semantic** machine. Recall that Wittgenstein (1953) contends that the meaning of an utterance is shown in the way it is used, 'meaning is use', and cannot be isolated from its context, the language game it is part of (see Chapter 3). Therefore, meaning cannot be something in the head, constituted by syntactic patterns of neural activation, but is embedded in human customs and institutions, in a cultural context (McDonough, 1989).

Wittgensteinians strongly object to Fodor's thesis that the syntactic engine mimics semantics, that is, that semantic elements correspond with syntactic patterns, and that the thesis is incoherent; **methodological solipsism** (see pp. 206–7, 233–9) cannot be true. Wittgenstein himself later rejected his earlier picture theory, where a similar **correspondence** between language and the world is assumed. McDonough (1989) identifies some kind of picture theory of meaning as a precondition for a mechanist model of mind: meaning elements must correspond with elements of a syntactic structure. In the later Wittgenstein, however, meaning is holistic, part of a wider cultural context. Therefore, mechanistic models of mind, which assume that meaning elements can be isolated and subsequently correlated with language tokens, are rejected by the Wittgensteinian tradition. Mechanism ends where meaning begins (McDonough, 1989: 12; see also Williams, 1999).

The brain does not think

Wittgenstein's pupil Norman Malcolm (1971) emphasized that the possession of a concept (representation, knowledge) is not the same as possessing a mental image or idea in the mental theatre – rather, it is being able to *do* certain things. '[I]nner exhibition can contribute nothing to the understanding of a concept' (Malcolm, 1971: 56–7). According to Malcolm, the mind cannot be understood in isolation from the body and the community of human beings. The brain as such does not think; only a living person does (ibid.: 77).

The likeness to Ryle (see Chapter 6.2) will be clear: concepts are parts of a whole form of life, and it is the task of philosophy to explore and clarify concepts, not to explain them by inner mental causes. Philosophical conceptual analysis merges into theoretical sociology, which is elucidation of existing social conceptual practices (Winch, 1958). Linguistic analysis in a social context also touches **hermeneutics**. In contrast with the facts of natural science, concepts have a contextual structure, which is known by the members of a linguistic community, as it were from the inside, from the way they participate pre-reflexively in its transactions. This makes the hermeneutic conception of mental content clearly distinct from the naturalistic science of the mind, which is in the business of discovering empirical facts about mental processes.

glossary

Fodor rejects such a conceptual (social) construal of mental discourse. He wants real explanations, and therefore causal mechanisms of mind. McDonough (1989) argues that Fodor needs to assume that meaning is a function of elementary meaning particles (cf. the elementary observation statements of logical positivism), and that language and the language of thought is thus analogous to a logical calculus. Contrary to the Fodorian school, Wittgenstein holds that there is no underlying mechanism that explains meaning. The explanation of behaviour is not to be found in a semantic engine inside the skull, but the criteria for a semantic description of neuronal events can be traced to the semantical system outside them (McDonough, 1989: 19): a person's intentionality is to be understood, not from inside his or her brain but from the outside, the cultural context. McDonough calls this a Copernican revolution: conceptual clarification goes in the opposite direction from what Fodor thinks.

For this reason Wittgenstein had great doubts about whether psychology and (neuro)physiology did match:

> No supposition seems to me more natural than that there is no process in the brain correlated with associating or with thinking; so that it would be impossible to read off thought-processes from brain-processes. … It is thus perfectly possible that certain psychological phenomena cannot be investigated physiologically, because physiologically nothing corresponds to them. (Wittgenstein, 1981: 106)

From this non-mechanist model of mind and language, later critics of cognitivism infer that there cannot be a universal mental syntactic or 'deep' structure, conceived of in Chomsky's theory of language and in Fodor's language of thought, which delivers meanings in a mechanical way. Our ability to understand sentences is not an ability to make 'lightning-quick calculations in which we derive the meaning of a sentence from the meanings of its constituents and their mode of combination,' write Baker and Hacker (1984: 354). They see this as a false idea, a remnant of the 'ancient myth of the "given" and of what the mind, contributing structure from its own resources, makes of it'; and they add that this myth 'is not rendered respectable by being dressed up in late twentieth century garb' (ibid.: 355).

In a recent book Bennett and Hacker (2003) sum up their arguments against the cognitive neuroscience version of mechanist thinking. Their main objection contains a repetition of Malcolm's above mentioned maxim that the brain as such does not think, but that only a living person does. They call the cognitive neuroscientist's delusion the 'mereological fallacy'. Mereology is the logic of parts/whole relations. The mistake is 'ascribing to the constituent *parts* of an animal attributes that logically apply only to the *whole* animal' (Bennett and Hacker, 2003: 74, original emphasis). Referring to the work of many neuroscientists, Bennett and Hacker argue that these scientists explain cognitive capacities of the whole human being or animal by reference to the capacities of only the brain. And because this is a logical mistake it is nonsense. Again, only to complete human beings can one apply psychological attributes, can one say that they see, hear, believe, make decisions, and interpret data. The primary grounds or evidence for the ascription of these psychological predicates are behavioural; and behaviour belongs to the public, intersubjective and linguistic domain in which elements of brain or body do not take part.

To sum up, Wittgenstein and his followers can be seen as a kind of counterpoint to the dominant cognitivist paradigm, of which Fodor is an early exponent. The latter tries to explain mind by its computational mechanisms, the former consider cultural context, irreducible to physical mechanisms, as the essence of mind.

BOX 9.3 Notions inspired by Wittgenstein

- *Language games*: language is part of collective 'forms of life', and the role of words is governed by social rules as in a game of chess. Breaking these rules leads to confusion and philosophical puzzles. There is no such thing as a private language. And there is no such thing as the meaning of words in isolation; concepts belong to interdefined networks of meaning.
- *'Meaning is use'*: words are tools. The meaning of a concept can be understood in its context of activity, how it is used, and only by members of the language community taking part in these activities.
- *'Brains do not think'*: mind cannot be understood in isolation from the activities displayed in the community of human beings, in contrast with the notion of a 'semantic engine' inside the skull (or a universal mental grammar, a syntactic deep structure).
- *Mereological fallacy*: the cognitive neuroscientist's delusion of ascribing attributes to the constituent *parts* of an animal that logically apply only to the *whole* animal (like attributing thinking to a brain).

9.6 Conclusion

In this chapter, we presented a somewhat loose collection of approaches to mind that in one way or another revolt against the computer-inspired approaches outlined in the previous chapter. Biologically, phenomenologically and culturally oriented approaches all emphasize that mind should be considered in its relations to the environment. Evolutionary psychology explains cognitive capacities as adaptations to problems in the (ancestral) environment. The idea of an extended mind holds that mind is part of a rich and complex web of interactions between body, brain and world, and cannot be considered on its own. Finally, cultural psychologists argue that mental capacities rely on cultural cognitive resources, such as language and other collective mental tools.

FURTHER READING

9.2 **Evolutionary psychology: adaptations as explanations**

Buss, D.M. (1995) 'Evolutionary psychology: a new paradigm for social science', *Psychological Inquiry*, 6, 1–30.

9.3 **Mind in action: uniting brain, body and world**

Clark, A. (1997) *Being There: Putting Brain, Body and World Together Again.* Cambridge, MA: Bradford/MIT Press.

9.4 **The body in the mind**

Lakoff, G. and Johnson, M. (1999) *Philosophy in the Flesh: The Embodied Mind and its Challenge to Western Thought.* New York: Basic Books.

10. SOME ISSUES AT THE INTERFACE OF PHILOSOPHY AND PSYCHOLOGY REVISITED

PREVIEW: In this chapter we will discuss some problems that were traditionally the province of philosophy (or philosophical psychology). Issues like the nature of mental acts, the mind's place in a physical universe, freedom of will versus determinism, and the nature of consciousness are venerable philosophical problems, which have been the subject of metaphysical speculation and theoretical analysis for some 25 centuries. They are also related to central questions in the much younger science of psychology. Moreover, empirical psychologists have recently moved into domains like consciousness, folk psychology and free will. In this chapter we will present thumbnail sketches of some of the main developments at the interface of psychology and philosophy, most of which we have come across already in earlier chapters.

10.1 Intentionality

To pinpoint the difference between physical states and mental states Franz Brentano (1838–1917) re-invented the concept of **intentionality** (see Chapter 6). It indicates glossary the supposedly typical faculty of psychological phenomena or activities *to be about* things and events. Intentionality is the *aboutness* of mental states, such as beliefs and desires. We hear, see, hope, wish, always something: a bird singing, a tree blossoming, a friend coming. In our cognitive activities we are *directed towards* objects and events.

Having a mental state is being *engaged in* something. But since you can boast that you will be the next Prime Minister, though it is not very likely that you will ever become a politician, the objects or events you boast about, or wish, or predict need not be actually present or possible. You can be mistaken about something: you can think that you see a rat, though it is a squirrel. Peter can know that the liquid in the bottle is water, though he may not know what to do when smarty Fred asks him to pass the bottle of H₂O. You even can imagine or yearn after things that do not exist at all. These are all intentional mental states, though the things they are about may be imagined, absent, or non-existent.

BOX 10.1   Intentionality

Intentionality is the faculty of psychological phenomena to be about things and events; it is the aboutness of mental states, such as believing, desiring, hoping, hearing, seeing, mourning. Mental states have content, are directed to factual or counterfactual (existing or non-existing) things and events.

In its technical sense, intentionality is not restricted to having an intention or a purpose, as in the common phrase of doing something intentionally. A lot of seeing and hearing is done without intention or for no special reason. Intentionality is as well working when you happen to hear music in the park, as when you intend to go to the concert. Intending in the daily sense of planning is but one of many intentional activities in the technical sense.

Physical things do not have properties which are 'about' other things, existing or not: a rock does not have those kind of relationships with the slope on which it lies, or with the sun above; that is, whatever the relations between the rock and the slope or the sun, they are definitely not psychological, and thus not intentional. *We* can enjoy lying on a slope and basking in the sun.

At first sight, objects like traffic lights, billboards, books seem to have aboutness or significance: they are about danger, discount prices, or the life of George W. However, that is only true because someone put the meaning there, and only as long as there is someone who can read the sign or book, and understand the symbols. This aboutness derives from the original intentionality of a human mind. Searle (1992) makes much of this difference: in his view only human (and some animal) minds and brains have *original* intentionality. Computers for example will never have true understanding – at best they have *derived* intentionality (see below). Following Brentano, the phenomenological movement in philosophy (Edmund Husserl (1859–1938), Maurice Merleau-Ponty (1908–1961)) made intentionality one of the main themes of their philosophy; they identified intentionality with meaning and meaningful content of mental states. Seeing and enjoying a clown, and saying that you see one, is implicitly having, knowing, and expressing the meaning of what you see and are enjoying. In the

Brentano-conception intentionality is a property of mental states. So-called existential phenomenologists (foremost Martin Heidegger (1889–1974)), however, stressed man's embodied being-in-the-world; intentionality is the way a whole person lives in the world, rather than a property of a detached mind. We'll come back to this in due course.

It is one thing to describe the phenomenon, it is quite another to understand what is really happening or how it works. Behind Brentano's idea that mind alone displays intentionality lay his firm belief that mind differs essentially from matter, and that therefore mind cannot be reduced to matter. Modern cognitivists are mostly materialists and try persistently to take away the mystery of intentionality. In stark contrast to Brentano they aim to *naturalize* the property by somehow fitting it in the natural world, in an information processing mechanism, for instance; or by seeing it as a biological phenomenon; or by explaining it away, defending that it is a folk-psychological (bad) habit. In the following we present different interpretations.

Intentionality as a feature of the language of thought

In his linguistic view of cognition Fodor pictured mental states as attitudes to mental propositions (see Chapter 7). Adopting Brentano's notion, Fodor emphasizes that the feature of 'aboutness' belongs to mental (propositional) states. Thus, he has turned intentionality into a property of propositions of being about things: believing, hoping, wishing *that* … (for example, that your friend will come tonight). Mental propositional states can also be about non-existing situations, things of imagination, or counterfactuals. Whether or not there is such an object in the world, it can be the content of a mental state. Intentionality, therefore, adheres to the mental state proper. It has to be interpreted as a **syntactical**, internalistic, solipsistic property of a mental state, [glossary] that is a mental proposition – a kind of sentence in the head.

This is what is psychologically relevant, according to Fodor: to explain Patrick's behaviour, the psychologist has to take seriously Patrick's belief that the whole neighbourhood is after him, even if it is a delusion. It is the syntax of his **propositional attitude** which is causally effective. Patrick's beliefs cause his fear, his paranoia, his [glossary] subsequent actions. The **semantics**, whether his beliefs refer to something real in the [glossary] world, does not matter. So the semantics has no causal efficacy and is, therefore, secondary, or less important from a psychological point of view. The primary psychological fact is Patrick's (probably) paranoid belief, for it causes his other mental states and actions. The intentionality of mental states does its causal cognitive work, regardless of reference to the world. This is what Fodor's methodological **solipsism** (p. 206) is [glossary] about. Intentionality, according to this theory of mental sentence-like representations, is a feature of the language of thought, the beliefs and desires which are essentially abstract language-like *functions*, that happen to be realized in computational, physical or brain-like structures (see Chapter 7).

The question is, however, whether the semantics is secondary. It is in this solipsistic interpretation of intentionality with its world-aloofness, a consequence of the Cartesian mental linguistics, as if what you see, believe, fear or desire are mental representations inside your brain, rather than things in the world (cf. indirect realism, see Chapter 4.5). But true or not, existing or not, Patrick thinks, suspects, fears that enemies are all around him, next door and at the other side of the street, and that they spy on him; to keep them at a distance he has ferocious dogs, keeps calling his mother and the police. So, he fears what, to his mind, is *in* the world, and accordingly acts *in* the world. Fodor's internalism and solipsism are suspect indeed.

This kind of criticism might come from theorists with a biological point of view, that intentionality is a feature of a living organism adapting to its environment. They join in, so to say, with philosophers who mark man's world directedness. But first we glossary will discuss two other **naturalist** projects.

Dennett's solution: intentionality as a stance

For Dennett (1978, 1987) intentionality is a concept that belongs to the intentional stance (see Chapter 6.3), the way we normally approach systems such as human beings, animals and even (occasionally) machines, such as a chess computer or the 'speaking' navigation system in your car. We normally attribute thoughts, desires, glossary intentions, fears, **reasons** to 'intentional systems', to ourselves and our fellow human beings. This intentional idiom and psychological strategy works well; it produces accounts, explanations, understandings and predictions of their and our own behaviour. But we should not be tempted to take it literally, to assume that mental states like beliefs and desires exist somewhere at, say, the physiological level of brain states. When we attribute mental states, it is just a way of speaking in terms of states in someone's head, as in 'She has a plan' predicts her behaviour, not because we actually scanned her brain. We should not think that, when we describe someone as expecting that it will not rain this afternoon, we give a description of his brain processes.

So, adopting the intentional stance, according to Dennett, is a useful glossary **folk-psychological** approach. The intentional vocabulary is a practical instrument to describe and predict the behaviour of intentional, belief-desire, systems. In Dennett's glossary **instrumentalism** intentionality is not an ontological term referring to a specific property of human beings. By speaking about intentional systems Dennett does not say that they '*really* have beliefs and desires, but that one can explain and predict their behaviour by ascribing beliefs and desires to them' (Dennett, 1978: 7). Intentional language is a way of speaking, and a very expedient one; without it we, in our everyday interactions, would be in the dark about what people are up to, and we could not explain what our own intentions are. 'Life would be unbearably unpredictable' (Lyons, 1995: 23).

Dennett (1991b) himself is not happy with the label instrumentalism: he maintains that the intentional stance describes *real patterns* of (clever, purposeful) behaviour that are perfectly objective. When 'She has a plan' her behaviour is objectively purposeful and the intentional description taps into something real. A useful analogy is the 'game of life', a computer game that consists of simple cells, that can be either on or off, depending on how many neighbouring cells there are. When the environment is too crowded, or too lonely, a cell switches off ('dies'). The result of this very simple rule is that patterns emerge, configurations of cells that glide, or swim, or metamorphose, or eat each other; patterns of organism-like shapes can be seen to move quasi-orderly across the screen. These macro patterns are for real, not just in the eye of the beholder, although at the micro level the game is driven by nothing more than by simple rules switching single cells on and off. In the same way, intentional, intelligent, purposeful patterns of behaviour are objectively real. In that sense the intentional stance is not just an arbitrary tool, and Dennett is more than just an instrumentalist. On the other hand, without an intentional viewpoint these patterns are just not visible: if you look only at the movement of the molecules in his body, you don't see that somebody is trying to buy a bottle of wine because a colleague is coming to diner (Dennett, 1987). The intentional stance is an indispensable and sophisticated instrument for seeing and predicting behaviour of complex systems.

In certain subdomains of psychology, however, where we just want to know *how* we think, will and plan, we are interested in the physiological and neural conditions of mentality. We then approach the system from the physical and design stance and hope to learn how things *really* work backstage – what the cognitive system does in mechanical or informational terms when fed with information. Whether the processes at design level are best specified as computations in a formal language, as Fodor would have it, or as neurophysiological facts is an open question in Dennett's view.

In other psychological domains, such as clinical and social psychology, we may use the intentional way of speaking because it is convenient to do so, or because we don't have enough knowledge on the level of neural networks and its design. But Dennett thinks that from the point of view of scientific **explanation** we should replace the `glossary` intentional stance by the design stance and trade in the intentional idiom as soon as expanding computational or neurological knowledge permits us to do so. The intentional language is like a loan, a temporary permission to use mysterious and unexplained terms like intelligence and purpose, and that loan has to be paid back in hard currency: in the end, we have to find out how the mechanisms of the internal design work that cause intelligent behaviour (Dennett, 1978; see also Chapter 8).

Dennett, in conclusion, solves the problem of intentionality (and consciousness, as we will see in the last section of this chapter) not by reducing such mental concepts to basic material processes, or to a property of mental language, but by relegating them to the realm of stories about ourselves, that is, stories we live by. But, as one critic writes (Lyons, 1995: 27ff), do we have to accept that our everyday fruitful intentional strategy and successful predictions are based 'on a false or "make-belief" picture of the relevant facts', that they are 'without any firm basis'? Wouldn't it be 'quite magical and mysterious ... how humans ever did generate their intentional explanations and predictions' (op. cit.: 28)?

Shouldn't there be relevant connections between the age-old intentional language and facts about human behaviour from the outside point of view, just as newly won neurophysiological language is connected to facts from the inside point of view? Wouldn't it be surprising, on the other hand, if an intentional interpretation did resemble the interpretation of the 'lower' level. We have chosen to interpret Dennett's three stances as consistent with the idea of multiplicity of explanations (see Chapter 2), meaning that interpretations on different but highly related levels, as in this case, do have their own explanatory force and predictive power, and do not compete. Both interpretations might tell their own success story, without the one being truer or more realistic than the other, notwithstanding the material neccesity and relevance of the more basic level for the higher one.

In reaction to similar comments and criticisms Dennett tried to explain that he is advocating a 'milder sort' of realism on beliefs and desires (Dennett, 1987: 28). The intentional stance, he writes, 'provides a vantage point for discerning similarly useful patterns. These patterns are objective – they are *there* to be detected – but … they are not *out there* entirely independent of us'; they are 'composed partly of our own "subjective" reactions to what is out there' (Dennett, 1987: 39, original emphasis). Dennett's approach to folk psychology is not as radical as Churchland's **eliminativism** (see Chapter 2.5); in Dennett's view we cannot reasonably abandon the intentional stance.

glossary

Intentionality as a feature of information

A clear example of a naturalistic account of intentionality, showing how physical systems could have representational content, has been proposed by Fred I. Dretske (1981, 1988, 1995). Intentionality is a 'pervasive feature of all reality – mental and physical' rather than a 'mark of the mental' (1991: 356). Intentionality has its source in the structure of information. The concept of information is borrowed from communication theory. Think about the working of a thermometer. The amount of information transmitted from one point to another point is a 'function of the degree of lawful dependence' between the events occurring in these two locations. The thermometer carries information about its environment 'to the extent to which its state (e.g. the height of the mercury column) depends, lawfully, on the ambient temperature' (1991: 357); or put more informally, it is sensitive to the value of the temperature it is designed to measure. Any physical system which can carry information in this way is an intentional system, according to Dretske. We can also say that these systems are representational systems; they represent or indicate something else. The thermometer represents the temperature of its environment.

But can we say that the thermometer *knows* things; do instruments like a thermometer have genuine cognitive states? Dretske's answer is – no! A galvanometer cannot but carry the complete information that it is designed for. It cannot carry the information that there is a current flow between two points without carrying the information that there is a voltage difference between them. In contrast, it is possible, that you know that the galvanometer indicates a current flow between the two points, but that you don't know that this means that there is a voltage difference, or a magnetic field. The thermometer indicates the temperature – this is what it is designed for, nothing more and nothing less. But seeing the height of the temperature you can conclude that your friend is ill and that a doctor has to see her. The intentionality or the representational power of your **belief** is much more complicated than that of devices like thermometers. A prominent aspect of the intentionality of beliefs, but not the only one, is that they have the power to misrepresent. It is possible that you know

glossary

that Ronald Reagan was President of the US, but that you don't know who was the fortieth President; though it was Reagan who was the fortieth President. This is what real knowledge is – it involves meanings, concepts, beliefs, context, (mis)interpretations. Instruments cannot have this kind of knowledge.

By explaining intentionality in terms of the natural phenomenon of information Dretske has not solved the mystery, you might say, he has only displaced it to knowledge and cognitive states. How is aboutness of knowledge and cognitive states possible? Or to put it differently, how come that *original* intentionality is different from *derived* intentionality, the intentionality that is assigned to devices by human design? Dretske, however, thinks that by explaining intentionality as a feature of information he has transformed the problem of kind into a problem of degree (1991). Thermometers and the like do not have enough intentionality to be described as really knowing; it will take a lot of upgrading to implement real knowledge, but it is at least a start, Dretske thinks. At least the veil of mystery has been taken away and we can go on trying to solve the many remaining problems in a natural way, by considering, among others, biological and evolutionary aspects:

> By conceiving of mental facts ... as part of the natural order, as manifestations of overall biological and developmental design, one can see where intentionality comes from and why it is there. (Dretske, 1995: 28)

Intentionality as a biological feature

Unlike Dretske, philosophers have traditionally tried to understand the puzzling phenomenon of intentionality as it appears in its full-blown human form; to approach it from the *top down*. Following Descartes and Brentano, philosophers until recently believed in a unbridgeable gap between body and mind, animal and human nature. However, authors oriented to biology and evolution, as many are nowadays (see also Chapter 9), assume that there is continuity in nature, and they hope that we can start to understand intentionality by focusing first on its less complicated form, in simpler biological and physiological systems. And therefore some think that a *bottom-up* approach is the best way to naturalize intentionality and other psychological notions, like meaning, **representation**, **consciousness**. In the words of Dennett: glossary

> Intentionality doesn't come from on high; it percolates up from below, from the initially mindless and pointless algorithmic processes that gradually acquire meaning and intelligence as they develop. (1995: 205)

A much discussed notion in this biological context is *function* (see Chapter 2.4). Here it is defined in its **teleological** sense, not in terms of a causal role within the system as   glossary an orthodox functionalist would describe it. Considering the teleological function of something (intentionality, representations) means that one has an eye for what it is *designed* to do, for its *purpose*, or in evolutionary terms, for what it is *naturally selected* to do (see Chapter 2.4, and Chapter 9.2 on evolutionary psychology). In the teleological account, to put it more formally, the biological function of A is to do B, if A is now present, because in the past it was naturally selected to do B (Wright, 1973; Papineau, 1993). Seeing it in this way one takes into consideration the organism-environment relation, the 'adaptive hook up' as Clark calls it, that is, the system with its inner states 'to coordinate its behaviours with specific environmental contigencies' (Clark, 1997: 147). So, the biological view understands intentionality and representation as a kind of biological adaptation, as being *about* the environment (Churchland and Churchland, 1990; Dennett, 1995). (see also Chapter 9 on the extended mind, and Chapter 8 on the brain-based and dynamic view of mind.)

BOX 10.2   Views on intentionality

Dualistic conception:

Intentionality is an exclusive property of the human mind, the mark of the mental. Matter, physical things, or animals do not have intentionality.

Naturalistic conceptions:

Intentionality is a feature of *some physical systems* in general (and not only a mark of mentality); it has its source in the way those physical systems can carry *information* about their environment.

Naturalistic conceptions (1) symbolic, language-based:

- Intentionality is a property of the *syntax of the mental language* (LOT), of internal symbols that constitute mental sentences with some kind of meaning or content (aboutness). Intentionality is an essential characteristic of the folk-psychological way of speaking without which people could not make sense of each other's behaviour.

Naturalistic conceptions (2) biological, brain-based:

- In the *biological* approach intentionality is seen as a feature of the adaptive behaviour of an organism, as it develops from the mindless organism-environment relation into complex knowledge–world and other meaning-bearing relations.

Naturalistic conceptions (3) instrumentalist:

- The *intentional stance* (folk psychology) is an indispensable and sophisticated instrument for seeing and predicting behaviour of complex systems.

Non-materialistic and non-dualistic:

Intentionality is the property of a complete being, cognitive, bodily, and active in the world; it characterizes human existence, human living and acting in the world – its 'Dasein', 'être au monde', or 'being-in-the-world'.

Searle's biological view

John Searle defends a different variety of the biological view. Intentionality is a pheno-menon 'that humans and certain other animals have as part of their biological nature' (Searle, 1992: 79). Therefore, artefacts of human design, such as a thermometer, are not intentional at all. We ascribe intentionality to them figuratively or metaphorically; the ascription is merely *as-if*, and not intrinsic. When we say that the lawn is thirsty because it has not been watered for a week we speak metaphorically. These attributions are harmless in our daily conversation, but they are psychologically irrelevant. *As-if* inten-tionality is not a kind of intentionality. Here Searle obviously disagrees with Dennett, who feels that all intentionality is in the eye of the beholder (see Dennett, 1990).

We often endow non-mental phenomena such as sentences in a book, words, pictures, maps with intentional properties. A picture of Churchill refers to the historic figure. The French word 'cerise' means 'cherry'. My map of London is a correct representation of the city. In these cases intentionality is not ascribed metaphorically, but quite literally. However, these things do not themselves have intentionality; the property is the result of human agency, it is derived from human intentionality. Therefore, Searle calls this *derived* intentionality (Searle, 1992: 78 ff; cf. Dretske's classification). Mark his dis-agreement with Dretske and Dennett (1987, 1995), who believe in a continuum from mechanical or organismic representations to fully-fledged human meaning.

BOX 10.3 Different forms of intentionality (Searle)

Intrinsic intentionality is a phenomenon that humans and some other animals have as part of their biological nature.	*Derived* intentionality is a property ascribed to non-mental things (books, words, pictures); it is the result of human agency and derived from human intentionality.	*As-If* intentionality is a property ascribed metaphorically to arte-facts of human design (a 'thirsty' lawn); in fact this is not an intentional relation at all.

Only humans and certain other animals have the real thing, *intrinsic* intentionality, according to Searle. This is not something mysterious, nor is it beyond the reach of scientific study; it is a property that those creatures have because of their biological nature. Searle's biological approach to intentionality is that he sees it as a product of the brain, just as real and intrinsic and part of nature as the weight of a stone is. Intentionality and consciousness are **emergent** products of the brain in roughly the [glossary] same way as temperature regulation is a product of the circulation. (See Chapter 7.4 for Searle's rejection of intentionality in syntactic machines.)

What makes it a complicated property is that it cannot be reduced to just a property of propositional attitudes or propositions with content. An intentional state is, firstly, related to a complete network of other beliefs, desires, hopes, fears, anticipations, feelings of satisfaction and so on. This is what is called the holistic network. When you want to borrow John Searle's book *Intentionality* it is, say, because you want to write a paper on that subject, you know that you can find the book in the library, you also know that you have to show your library pass, that you have to walk about five minutes, so that you don't need your bike, that you have to cross the market square etc. Much of the network you are unconscious of. Secondly, there is the **background**, defined by Searle as a 'set of nonrepresentational mental capacities that enable all representing to take place' (Searle, 1983: 143). These capacities are not themselves intentional states, but they are preconditions of intentionality. You could not form the intention to go to the library without opening doors, running up and down stairs, crossing streets etc. If little Peter is learning how to cycle, he does not have to learn that he cannot go through the tree, nor that he has to go around it anyhow. Background capacities come with the biological and physiological make-up, such as the bodies we have. They are inevitable and belong to our 'know-how'.

glossary

Intentionality as 'being in the world'

With the biological turn, in general, the conception of intentionality has broadened. It is not so much the property of sentences, mental states, not even of mind alone; it is the property of a complete being, cognitive and active in the world. Cognitive activities work in the interaction between organism and environment. Intentionality gets a kind of ecological interpretation, an organism's situatedness in the world. This is also what the second generation of phenomenologists had in mind. They sometimes called themselves 'existential' phenomenologists, like Heidegger and Merleau-Ponty. Intentionality expresses the property of human engagement with the world. It characterizes human existence, human living and acting in the world; 'Dasein', 'être au monde', as continental philosophers called this 'being-in-the-world' (see Chapter 9).

We don't have to return to philosophical speculation, however. The programme of finding a natural solution to the problem of intentionality does not stop here. The phenomenon is not an exclusive philosophical problem. There is much to win when it is approached from biological, neurological and psychological perspectives as well. This was expressed aptly by the cognitive philosopher Andy Clark who called one of his books (1997): *Being There: Putting Brain, Body, and World Together Again* (see Chapter 9 on the extended mind).

Since intentionality has many features in common with consciousness we will encounter some of the same problems in the last section of this chapter.

10.2 Folk Psychology

As we have seen in previous chapters, the relation between scientific psychology and folk psychology is one of the hot issues of philosophy of mind. Looking closer, folk psychology is a hybrid affair. At first sight it is common-sense psychology, understanding, explaining, and predicting one's fellow's beliefs and desires, as we do in everyday life. Second, it is the philosophical reconstruction of commons sense in terms of intentionality, aboutness (see previous section), and mental objects. Reconstruction of common sense as **belief-desire** explanation, and forging beliefs and glossary desires in terms of propositional attitudes, has sparked the debate on reduction or vindication of folk psychology by scientific psychology discussed in Chapter 8, among others. Third, there is the questions of how these skills of empathy and prediction ('mind-reading') work. Two accounts have been given of mind-reading: on the first, it is a matter of applying an information-rich theoretical framework; on the second, it is using one's own decision mechanisms as a model of the other's mind ('simulation').

We will first discuss some additional arguments from both sides on the reduction of folk psychology, and in the last section offer a brief discussion of the simulation theory.

Folk psychology and reduction (1): syntactic reductionism

Fodor thinks that folk psychology is *vindicated* by the computational theory of mind (CTM, see Chapter 7). **Propositional attitudes** tally with the language of thought, and glossary support explanations in terms of beliefs and desires: we have discrete, causally active symbol structures in our heads that produce our behaviour, and we are literally right in invoking these as explanations.

It should be mentioned that at least one proposal turns CTM's syntactic psychology against folk psychology. Stephen Stich (1983) suggests that all semantic and folk-psychological idiom should be deleted from cognitive science, so that a purely syntactic (computational) theory of mind can exist without folk psychology. The difference with Fodor is that the latter wants to keep intentional explanation, in a naturalized form, tied up with computation. Fodor would consider it a major cultural disaster if we had to abandon folk-psychological discourse, and considers the conjunction of computational implementation and intentional explanation the essence of his work (Fodor, 1994).

Stich (1983), on the other hand, happily sacrifices the intentional, meaningful idiom of folk psychology. The explanation in terms of beliefs ('She goes to university to get a degree because she wants to be rich and famous, and thinks a degree helps to achieve that') has no place in cognitive explanations. Stich's 'case against belief' (the subtitle of his book) is that cognitive psychology should only refer to formal and syntactic processes, since the intentional and semantic idiom of belief talk is hopelessly vague and full of connotations and ambiguities, and is dependent on context. It misses relevant generalizations; and too many fine-grained distinctions get in the way of useful explanations. Furthermore, as Churchland argued, folk psychology cannot explain the behaviour of the mentally retarded and disturbed, but is limited to the psychology of 'people like us'. Cognitive science has, in order to be rigorous and respectable science, to get rid of all the vague connotations; has to restrict itself to formulae; and has to generalize and explain on the basis solely of syntactic relations, without reference to content, but only to uninterpreted symbols.

Interestingly, this programme seems to come close to Churchland's eliminativism, with syntactic rather than neurophysiological replacements for beliefs and desires. Stich (1992) argues that Churchland's eliminativism is less revolutionary than it seems. Science has always adjusted its theories to fit new discoveries about its referents and it is not obvious that this really means the dramatic massacre of common sense that Churchland suggests. As to the alternative, Stich (1992) deems Fodor's project – to make the mind respectable within the framework of natural science by reducing mind to computation – quite hopeless. We do have reliable intersubjective concepts for behavioural and mental phenomena, and there is no need either to naturalize them or eliminate them. Common sense and sciences such as ethology can work with broad functional descriptions (see Chapter 1) of behaviour, which are difficult or impossible to translate into some physical language, but which are good enough as they are.

To sum up then, Stich (1992) deflates the notion of representation as the foundation of cognitive science, and concludes with a kind *of pluralism*. This is consistent with his pragmatic view of cognition: there is no single best way of going about the business of cognition (Stich, 1990). There is nothing intrinsic or special about beliefs and truth, it is just that they are instrumentally useful.

Folk psychology and reduction (2): pragmatists dismantling folk psychology

From a historical perspective, Richard Rorty arrives at an even more radical conclusion. He thinks that the concept of mind is a turbid mixture of two concerns, the knowing subject and the moral agent (Rorty, 1982b). Rorty thinks that philosophy of mind has been the victim of seventeenth- to nineteenth-century ideas, which consider consciousness and intentionality as irreducible, and mind as a kind of substance. He has sympathy for the Ryle-Dennett tradition that dismantles the notions of inner theatre of which we, supposedly, have intuitive direct knowledge. He suggests that we should abandon these ideas of mind as a thing, and be content to let 'the subjective realm float out of ken'. We may forget about intractable consciousness and keep only what can be accounted for in science. In his view Searle and Nagel (cf. previous section; and 10.5) are like medieval essentialists who think that the mind has an intrinsic essence, in more or less the same way as medieval philosophers were interested in the essence of material things.

Rorty thinks that philosophers have now all but dispensed with consciousness – they may now start to sacrifice intentionality and meaning. Fodor's intentional realism (representations and intentionality, the beliefs and desires of folk psychology, it all really exists) is now 'fading out', he thinks, as consciousness has faded out before. Connectionist modelling is the first sign that all things psychological become the subject of physiology, and that there is little left for philosophers to do here. The idea of mind will 'float out of ken', disappear as medieval substances have disappeared from our conceptual framework. Consciousness, and subsequently intentionality, will become untractable, philosophy of mind shrinks to nothingness, and psychology itself, the study of consciousness and rationality, disappears in biology. Mind as an entity does not exist, and psychology may become a pseudo-discipline.

Rorty compares this sorry story of the demise of consciousness and intentionality with the Galilean outlook on science: explanation is about useful terms, not about intrinsic natures. Searle and Fodor are partisans of an intrinsic view of intentionality, Dennett and Ryle have seen the pragmatic Galilean light. Mental concepts are not about 'what there really is', but depend on the context of the questioner, on the needs of the current empirical inquiry, on the uses to which we put them. Mind is not, or has not, an intrinsic, internal structure, but is a set of concepts whose cash value has something to do with describing and relating a kind of behaviour – namely, that kind of behaviour which has a certain freedom from the direct coupling of behaviour and environment. It is not some independent inner place.

Thus, the whole philosophical debate about representations and intentionality is dissolved in pragmatic considerations; how to describe the brain in action in the most useful way. Mind, intrinsic intentionality, beliefs and desires, representations and consciousness are unfortunate residuals of outdated philosophies according to Rorty's radical disavowal of the central notions of the philosophy of mind.

Folk psychology and reduction (3): if connectionism wins, folk psychology loses?

In the debate on connectionism and folk psychology Churchland just seems to assume that connectionism will replace folk psychology. Why exactly the two cannot coexist is explained by Ramsey, Stich and Garon (1991). The key is the idea of 'functional discreteness', which is a built-in assumption of the classical (CTM) reconstruction of folk psychology. If beliefs and desires can figure in psychological laws as causes (he acts so-and-so because he believes such-and-such) they have to be identifiable, having a discrete causal role. But if connectionism is right, beliefs are fuzzy and distributed across many nodes, they are produced by input activation, and are therefore context-dependent (slightly different recognition vectors (representations) will emerge at different inputs). Since a network has no such identifiable beliefs and desires, no discrete states that can be identified with propositions and attitudes, it has no functionally discrete causes of behaviour.

So, if folk psychology presupposes functionally discrete belief-desire states, causing behaviour, and connectionism implies distributed representations, then the realist view of folk psychology is incompatible with connectionism. To the extent that neural networks are a good simulation of our cognitive life, we do not have beliefs and desires, and explaining our fellow beings in these terms cannot be literally correct.

Different job descriptions

However, there is a way of keeping apart cognitive and neuroscience on the one hand, from common-sense psychology on the other. Folk psychology has just a different job description (Bechtel and Abrahamsen, 1993). It gives a coarse-grained account of global adaptive behaviour, whereas neuroscience (or classical symbolic theories) gives a fine-grained account of the underlying mechanisms. Scientific psychology is about *subpersonal* level underlying mechanisms, folk psychology is about *personal* level global behaviour (Clark, 1996a). It is the domain of Dennett's *intentional stance* (Dennett, 1978; see Chapter 6 and the previous section), and roughly describes what people can and should do in a normal environment, not what the inner structure and causes of that behaviour are.

Andy Clark (1989, see also 1993, 1996a) wants to preserve folk psychology as a practical utility, but not as a description of a causal mechanism. His main argument is that folk psychology is not a scientific theory at all. If one understood the nature of folk psychology in the right perspective, then it should not, according to Clark, be sought as the opponent of connectionism or any neurophysiological theory. Original folk psychology does not seek to model cognitive processes *at all*. It is the classical cognitivist approach which contends that concepts and relations spoken of in natural language are mapped neatly on computationally operated and syntactically specified internal states. The mapping, the idea that there are in-the-head analogues to propositional attitudes, is in the eye of the orthodox cognitivist who endorses a language of thought.

Churchland (1989d), therefore, is wrong in attacking folk psychology as a bad *theory*. Remember that Churchland thinks that folk psychology is stagnant and infertile and hopelessly backward compared to the sophisticated science we now have; and because it does not 'carve up nature at neurophysiologically respectable joints'. According to Clark, this is not its purpose at all, folk psychology is not playing the same game as scientific psychology; it is not a scientific theory. It should not be identified with classical cognitivism, nor with any other physical theory of cognition. The primary purpose of folk-psychological talk is to make intelligible and predictable in a convenient way *to us* the behaviour of fellow agents acting in the world. If I have a forged rail ticket to Scotland, is his example, and I want to sell it, I am not interested in the fine-grained details of anyone's neurophysiology. 'All I want to know is where to find a likely sucker', irrespective of his neurophysiological make-up. 'Folk psychology is *designed* to be insensitive to any differences in states of the head that do not issue in differences of quite coarse-grained behaviour' (Clark, 1989: 48).

But what is more, because of its purpose, folk psychology defines what cognitive science has to explain in the end: people's behaviour and not simply mechanisms and bodily movements. Therefore cognitive science '*must*, of course, rely on a folk-psychological understanding at every stage, for we need to see how the mechanisms we study are relevant ... to our performance in various cognitive tasks' (ibid.: 53, original emphasis). And these tasks have to be specified in folk-psychological terms. Psychology, Clark seems to say, is more than a theory about the brain (cf. 'the extended mind' in the previous chapter). He pleads for the autonomy of psychology in its full-blown intentional idiom.

BOX 10.4 Folk psychology

1. Folk psychology is *common-sense psychology*, understanding, explaining, and predicting behaviour as on the basis of one's fellows' beliefs, reasons, and desires, like we do *in everyday life*. That behaviour is thus guided by goals, knowledge and reasons, and is an assumption of most clinical and social-psychological explanations, as well as in economics ('fear and greed') and sociology.
2. Folk psychology is a *philosophical reconstruction* of common sense in terms of *intentionality* – mental states represent some state of affairs; they have content and aboutness.

In this sense, the computational theory of mind (Chapter 7) aims to vindicate folk psychology, assuming that intentional representational states are an *internal symbol system* of mental propositions plus attitudes, such as believing and desiring.

What is mind-reading? Theory theory and simulation theory

The view assumed by both Churchland and Fodor is the 'theory theory': folk psychology is a theory, and judging behaviour in terms of beliefs and desires is applying theoretical notions to phenomena, assuming that they refer to (presumed) laws (like: when someone desires a drink, she will go to the fridge). Such laws explain acts as caused by mental contents (thoughts). This is not to say that application of such generalizations occurs explicitly or must be conscious; on the contrary, we know them only tacitly and implicitly. Nor is it assumed that these laws are interesting as new discoveries in physics are – mostly they sound like platitudes. Nevertheless, Fodor thinks, it is a major cultural feat of the CTM to vindicate such laws, and Churchland is equally eager to eliminate them.

The 'theory theory' has generated much research. One interesting development is that we may have an inborn specialized capacity to reason about others' thoughts and feelings, a theory of mind module (ToMM), more or less isolated from other aspects of intelligence. Baron-Cohen (1995) suggests that autists, who have problems in understanding other people's feelings, lack that module (but may be as intelligent as everybody else).

The information about others that the 'theory theory' consists in is not necessarily the same as a set of truisms, proverbs, and clichés on human behaviour ('smooth words make smooth ways', 'boys will be boys', that sort of thing). As Nichols and Stich (2003) argue, it is very plausible that the theory of mind that underlies empathy is richer than the platitudes that we could consciously come up with. We know more than we can tell, and the information we use in understanding others is likely to be richer than what we can explicitly phrase.

However, there is another possible interpretation of our predicting and explaining other people's behaviour than the 'theory theory'. Folk psychology might be a kind *of simulation*; we might just put ourselves in other people's shoes and imagine, 'simulate' what we would do, think or feel ourselves if we were in their situation. This is a kind of imaginative or dramatic *skill*, not the application of a *theory* of what causes behaviour. Compare: we causally explain the behaviour of falling stones as according to the laws of gravity (the analogy of the 'theory theory'), not from dramatizing our own experiences when diving (as in the 'simulation theory').

A useful analogy is the following. The simulation theory is like building a scale model of, for example, an aeroplane and seeing how it behaves in the air. The theory theory, in contrast, is like trying to predict its behaviour according to the laws of gravity and aerodynamics. In the former case, the 'model' is our own decision-making mechanisms and we run these to simulate the 'target' (the other whose mind we are trying to read). According to the simulation theory, 'pretend beliefs' that the target is hypothesized to have are fed into these mechanisms, and the output of the belief generator is sent 'off-line': the resulting belief is not acted upon but stored in a belief-predicting system. So, you use your own decision-making as a model to simulate the target, more or less like the model airplane is a model of the real one. The point is that you don't need theories or common-sense laws, as the theory theory would require, just your own cognitive mechanisms.

Plausibly, mind-reading is a multifaceted skill, with both theory- and simulation-like components (Nichols and Stich, 2003). Very roughly, predicting others' beliefs is usually very accurate, which suggests simulation by the same kind of cognitive inference-making machinery. In contrast, attributing desires is often inaccurate, going against our intuitions. That cannot be explained by the simulation theory.

Although Churchland has built his attack on folk psychology on the theory theory, the simulation theory is also compatible with eliminativism: if we abandon appealing to beliefs and desires, we can also forget about the mental realm as a really existing entity. Talk of beliefs and desires requires in that case no more than assumptions about our behavioural dramatic simulating skills, not about inner causes (Crane, 1995).

Folk psychology and reduction (4): naturalizing mind?

For most of the 1970s and the 1980s, the cognitive revolution in psychology and its philosophical vehicle, the computational model of mind, seemed to promise an explanation of all these soft and hugely important properties of the human mind like meaning, consciousness, feeling, experience, and rationality. Before, these were considered glossary inaccessible to hard science. As we saw in Chapter 2, the domain of **hermeneutics** (*Verstehen*) that was concerned with understanding those higher properties of humans was set sharply apart from explanation in the sciences (*Erklären*). And as we saw in Chapters 7 and 8, both CTM and connectionism are projects to naturalize mind, by showing how rationality might be mechanically possible (Fodor, 1987b), and how folk psychology could be legitimized and explained within a computational model of mental processes. Attributing beliefs and desires to others, 'mind-reading' or empathy is of course closely related to hermeneutic understanding, and if cognitive psychology can provide a mechanical explanation in terms of information processing mechanisms, elimination lies around the corner. The 'theory theory' fits smoothly in the **naturalization** `glossary` project, reducing mind-reading to symbol manipulation (Fodor, Stich) or neural network activation (Churchland).

The 'simulation theory' seems less reductionist; the imaginative or dramatic skill to impersonate the mental life of the target looks like the subjective prejudice that the hermeneuticist brings to understanding. However, the approach sketched above, in terms of decision mechanisms and 'off-line beliefs', the terminology of the simulationist, comes very close to the 'boxology', the flow diagrams and information processing subroutines of mainstream cognitive science. Some think that mainstream philosophy of mind mistakenly tries to assimilate psychology, in particular beliefs, desires, intentionality and empathy, to the model of the hard sciences, and tries to predict and control our fellow human beings like physical objects. The faculty of imagination as access to other people's minds, making judgements about others' thoughts, and judging their rationality, does not fit in the natural science model (cf. discussions in Chapter 9).

BOX 10.5   Mind-reading and how it works

Folk psychology, as common sense, gives rise to the cognitive psychological question of *how* '*mind-reading*', these everyday skills of empathy and prediction, *works*.
Two naturalistic and 'hard-science' accounts of mind-reading have been given:

- the *theory theory*: a matter of applying unconsciously a tacit and implicit information-rich theoretical framework;
- the *simulation theory*: using one's own decision mechanisms as a model of the other's mind.

From a more continental philosophical perspective, mind-reading is much like *Verstehen*, understanding, where we recreate from our own subjectivity a state of mind like the mind of the other.

Heal (2003) proposes a contrasting view of simulation (which she also calls reproduction or co-cognition) that is more like the *Verstehen* tradition. The contrast is most obvious in the treatment of rationality. The classical cognitive approach aims at a mechanical account of rationality, in terms of algorithms that can (ideally) be empirically tested. Heal emphasizes the holistic aspect of rationality: it is not exhausted by a complete specification of the rules to be followed. Treating the other as a rational and responsible person is different from the objective scientific method that rests upon the causal-explanatory role of a mental state.

Heal's alternative is, like *Verstehen*, where we recreate from our own subjectivity a state of mind like the mind of the other. It involves thinking about the same reality, the same subject matter, that the other thinks about, with (as far as possible) the same reasoning abilities and background beliefs. The term 'co-cognition' is coined for this variety of mind-reading.

As mentioned above, the 'cognitivist' approach to simulation engages in empirical investigations trying to specify the cognitive machinery that produces psychological judgements. Heal's 'hermeneutic' variety does not consider one's fellow beings as machines whose internal mechanisms one must know and manipulate to predict and control. Rather it tries to understand from the inside, from our own person, recreating the way others construct their view of the world. The other person must be supposed rational, in the same way as one takes oneself to be rational. The presumption of shared rationality does not allow us to see persons as objects. This hermeneutic version of mind-reading (co-cognition) is a personal-level view, whereas the cognitivist version (the boxology of off-line simulation etc.) can be seen as a subpersonal claim about the way co-cognition is realised. Rationality then is a kind of 'framework principle' at the personal level: I cannot act rationally or cognitively if I don't assume a priori that I am a subject, a cognitively competent thinker whose thoughts lead to (an above-chance probability of) success, and I have to assume the same about others. This intersubjective principle is missing in the subpersonal cognitivist view. We can debate on the correctness of our reasoning against a background practice that we can and should give reasons for and ask the other for reasons.

To sum up

The issue that runs through this section is whether psychology should take its basic concepts from natural sciences, and aim for a mechanistic account of rationality, understanding and empathy/mind-reading. Obviously, most of the action and the excitement is in research and development in cognitive and neurosciences, and the new explanations of the skills we bring to understanding other minds. One controversial line of thought is that mind, mental content, rationality, intentionality is an obsolete and confused way of talking, a philosopher's fine conceptual mess that is best eliminated and forgotten (Churchland). The other extreme is that rationality is beyond the reach of empirical science and lies at the personal level.

Probably the most sophisticated view recognizes that there is a multiplicity of ways of understanding human behaviour (see Chapter 2), and that the views discussed above serve different explanatory purposes. The ideas of Clark (1996a) and Bechtel and Abrahamsen (1993) fit in the general framework sketched in Chapter 6 and elsewhere, where personal/intentional and subpersonal/mechanical/design explanations can coexist.

10.3 Mental Causation

The problem of mental causation: the place of mind in the physical universe

Recall that functionalism held that mind is multiply realized in physical systems, and that **supervenience** suggested that somehow mind can be dependent on matter (blocking dualism) but is not reducible to matter (blocking reductionism) (see Chapter 2.5, Box 2.6). It seems that on these views, we can have our cake and eat it: we can be materialists without being reductionists. In Chapter 2 we have defended explanatory pluralism, the legitimacy of causal, functional, hermeneutic explanations as different perspectives, and co-evolving theories at different levels. This is a position on the value of distinct types of explanation. However, philosophy has a branch called **metaphysics**, where the coherence of our world view and the compatibility of our different commitments are scrutinized. Kim (1998) argues that we need such a discipline to avoid 'free lunches' (1998: 59), all too easy solutions to deep problems. And in this rigorous metaphysical analysis, the commitments on the nature and explanation of mind and brain mentioned above are an unstable mix. Metaphysically-minded philosophers try to find a place for the mind in a physical world (Kim, 1998), and they suspect that the causal role of mind is incompatible with physics.

glossary

glossary

Thinking causes?

Mental causation means that the mind causes physical events to happen. On the one hand, the idea of 'thinking causes' (Davidson, 1993) is problematic. How can thinking cause bodily changes? Is it possible that thoughts, will, intentions and plans literally cause muscle contractions? Is itching the cause of scratching? Does the desire to praise God really cause lots of stone to be dragged around and Gothic cathedrals to be built?

This is a very old metaphysical problem. It haunted dualists like Descartes, who never found a solution to the question of how a thinking substance could make causal contact with the material substance – the famous pineal gland was supposed to be the place of contact, but how does the immaterial mind impress the nerves?

One answer is that thinking just is a physical process, and so-called mental causes are really brain processes. That leaves little to do for the mind. It means than thinking is causally inert, mental processes do not really exist, or are no more than epiphenomena, by-products. Mental processes then are like the whistle of the steam engine that has no causal impact at all on the way the engine (the brain and the body) works: mind makes no difference at all (see also Chapter 6.2).

Agency

The above picture, that the mind is causally inert, is also unattractive. It would undermine most of our intuitions on persons, morals and responsibility. Common sense has held for ages that attributing beliefs and desires does explain behaviour: your reading this book can be explained by a desire for knowledge or at least for getting a degree (folk psychology, see previous section; and Chapter 7). The notion of agency and free will underlies much of our culture (see Chapter 10.4). Some philosophers argue that unless we take **reasons** literally as **causes** that move the physical world, we have to give up the idea of ourselves as free, responsible agents. Brain mechanisms cannot be blamed for anything. It makes a big difference in court whether you killed your rich uncle in a car crash intentionally, to get the inheritance, or hit him by accident – the first involves intentions, the second may be a matter of just brain mechanisms. You cannot sue an avalanche: but what if a person is not qualitatively different? It makes no sense to demand that someone observes the conditions of a contract unless he has understood it. If cogitation and desiring do not make a real causal difference, then agency, responsibility, crime and punishment have to be given up, and the foundations of society are shaken. We need mental causation as part of our view of persons, society and law, since we can blame only intentional persons, whose thoughts have effects in the world – not machines, or brains. Therefore, metaphysically-minded philosophers argue, we need *mental realism*: thoughts must be real, and have causal powers. There must be some place for mind in the physical world.

glossary

Anomalous monism: mental events are physical events

However, we also feel intuitively that the world is a causally closed physical system, and physical causality must be complete – otherwise things would happen for no reason at all, or spooky causes could interfere with physical things; energy could emerge out of nothing. Most of us would think that there are no such gaps in the causal nexus of the world. Kim (1998) proposes the principle of *causal-explanatory exclusion*: you cannot have two causes for one event. If we agree that the physical world is causally closed, that is, every event has one or more physical causes, and that nothing happens without a physical cause, then obviously bodily behaviour is completely physically determined, and a role for mental causation is excluded. It would be strange if an immaterial mind could overrule the laws of force and energy – 'causal overdetermination' would be the result, which would be bizarre. The mind cannot be pulling the same muscles as the motor cortex.

When there is no causal gap to fill for thought, we are left then with *epiphenomenalism* (Chapter 6.2): think of a train. The locomotive, pulling a string of carriages, is casting a shadow, so that it seems as if the shadow-loc causes the shadow carriages to move. The shadows are the epiphenomena, and the shadow locomotive seems to pull the shadow-carriages 'epiphenomenally'. In the same way, mental processes are causally irrelevant shadowy by-products not doing any work – just shadows of the physical processes in the brain.

So, the dilemma is to reconcile a causally closed world with *agency*, that is, some room for mind, freedom, etc. Davidson (1963, 1993) suggested a now famous solution to combine a role for the mind with materialism: *anomalous monism*. Monism means that there is only one kind of substance, physical matter, and anomalous means that there are no laws, in this case no laws between mental and physical (brain) events.

Recall the standard solution reconciling **materialism** with methodological dualism: glossary **functionalism** (Chapters 3 and 7) and multiple realization. It precludes identification of mind and brain because mental states are functional states and functions can be multiply realized. On the other hand, mental states are realized in material processes, such as the brain. **Dualism** is thus avoided, and no non-material processes are glossary assumed: mind is the way the brain works (is programmed).

Furthermore, in Fodor's view (Chapter 7) mental states are real: beliefs and desires exist, as real as stones and clouds, and they figure as genuinely causal processes in intentional laws. The desire to get a degree in psychology is a hard fact of the mind and causes all sorts of late night reading and keyboard punching behaviour.

Anomalous monism is roughly compatible with these ideas: we have a *token* identity of mental and physical events, but not *type* identity. Mental processes are brain processes, but the natural kinds (categories, laws) of psychology and physics do not map. According to Davidson, reasons are genuine causes, and mind has a place in nature. Only, there are no laws that can serve to make nomological connections between mental and physical events. So, this position combines materialism with anti-reductionism.

However, anomalous monism has been criticized, most forcefully by Jaegwon Kim (1998). He and other philosophers believe that anomalous monism does not save agency. They argue that on this account mental events have causal powers only *qua* or *via* the physical, that is, because and insofar as they are physical. Mind as such must be causally inert since it has no lawful relations with physical events. These philosophers seem to find it obvious that physical events are causal, and that the problem only lies with mental causes. Davidson (1993: 12) disagrees: mental events are not causally inert. He believes that in principle all events are causes, whether they are described as mental or physical. There may even be regularities between the mind and the brain; it is just that there are no strict laws to be found. So, Davidson's opinion is that mental events do make a difference. He does not seem to mind that they do so indirectly *via* the physical properties on which they supervene.

Mental causation, metaphysics, and explanation

Debates among metaphysical philosophers are here as elsewhere often convoluted and seldom conclusive. The outcome of the above is that in a causally closed physical world mental events have no place – in the end, mind, rationality, intentionality and agency survive only as a property of the brain. Mental processes just come along for the ride. Think of the following analogy (Burge, 1993): phenotypical traits (e.g. blue eyes) in parents seem to produce the same traits in children (as parents have known for millennia). However, in reality it is the gene causing the trait in parents that is passed on to the offspring and then causes the same trait there – eye colour by itself is causally inert (as far as genetic inheritance is concerned.), a by-product of the gene. On the epiphenomenalist picture, mind is like this: pain does not cause wincing, but nerve excitation causes wincing. There is no such thing as mental causation.

BOX 10.6 Mental causation and anomalous monism

Mental causation: mental processes like thinking and willing cause behaviour. Thoughts must be real, and have causal powers, and there must be some place for mind in the physical world for our most basic convictions about persons, society and law to be true: we can blame only intentional persons, whose thoughts have effects in the world, not machines, or brains.

Anomalous monism: Mental processes are brain processes, mental events have *causal powers* only *qua* or *via* the physical, i.e. because and insofar as they are physical.

   However, mental processes cannot be reduced to brains since there are no laws that can serve to make nomological connections between mental and physical events. This position combines materialism with anti-reductionism, and seems to make some kind of mental causes (*qua* brain causes) possible.

Problem: anomalous monism does not really save agency and free will; mind as such does not really in itself cause behaviour – the brain does. Mind is *epiphenomenal*, an inert byproduct of brain processes, in this conception.

---

glossary However, other philosophers are not impressed. They note that **explanations** in terms of agency and mental causation are obviously useful: attributing agency, will, and goals to our fellow beings works well in practice in explaining their behaviour, it provides insight indispensable in psychology and ordinary life (a politician's desire to be re-elected explains silly laws, wars, budget deficits and baby-kissing; fear and greed explain the stock exchange; and so on). They believe that causal power is a very unclear notion, and that the whole problem of mental causation disappears when we simply focus on explanations (Burge, 1993).

   Metaphysicists' worries about causation look far-fetched and not very credible in view of the robust explanatory powers of agency explanations. A much more sensible approach seems to call causes whatever enters into explanatory practices, and then there seems nothing wrong with the notion of mental causes. Whatever works as explanation in respectable science (biology, psychology, neuroscience) may be called a cause (Looren de Jong, 2003; Hardcastle, 1998).

10.4 Free Will

Reasons and causes revisited

In Chapter 2.6 we discussed the tension between reasons and causes, between explaining human action as goal-directed, reason-guided, motivated by intentions on the one hand, and causal mechanical explanations in terms of neurotransmitters, muscle contractions, brain processes on the other. The historical controversy between natural and social sciences (Chapter 2.3) and correspondingly between explaining and understanding (*Verstehen*) was another expression of the same tension.

Above, the solution provided by computational theory of mind (Chapter 7) and its idea of mechanical rationality, reconciling intentional regularities with nomological explanations, was described (Pylyshyn, 1984). We may also note that the mentalist discourse works in daily life: we do describe our fellow beings as desiring and choosing. It can be argued that this is the basis for social sciences and economics (which assumes rational choice by more or less rational individuals). Functional and intentional terms may yield good predictions and reliable regularities, and in this way we could get psychological laws of some sort. Fodor (1990) would be perfectly satisfied with such laws and explanations.

However, one might still doubt whether beliefs and desires are genuine causes, or just placeholders, no more than labels. Remember, how even the lowly thermostat could be described in terms of beliefs and desires ('It's cold here, we must turn up the heat'), while no one would say that the thermostat is in reality a reason-guided being. So, we still have to answer the question whether humans are rational beings, or just machines; maybe they can be described loosely and metaphorically as rational, but in essence are driven by cogs and wheels, neurotransmitters and neuronal impulses, not by thoughts. Perhaps reasons are just metaphors. In the previous section (10.3) the problem of mental causation and the status of reasons as causes were discussed; the analysis by Davidson (1963) and Kim (1998) that mental events are really physical events was not comfortable for believers in genuine irreducible human reason. The same problems surface in the question of free will: if beliefs and desires, thoughts and intentions are just physical events, free will makes no difference in a causally closed world, and as Tom Wolfe (2000) has put it in a famous essay, our soul has just died.

Free will

Freedom of will is one of the venerable problems of philosophy. It is closely related to questions of reduction and naturalism: if reason can be naturalized, if we can see how rationality is mechanically possible, if the mind is a computer or a neural network, then it is difficult to see how man can have free choice. You cannot be blamed for breaking the china if someone pushed you – but if it is true that all your behaviour is caused (pushed) by neural causes, then you are not responsible for anything. Being caused seems to be the same as having no control, and having no free choice. The contrast is suspect however. Hume argued that if actions 'proceed not from some cause in the characters and dispositions of the person who perform'd them' (Hume, 1739/1969, p. 458/Book II, Part III section ii), that is, if they are random and unpredictable, they cannot be said to be good or bad, and the actor cannot be held responsible either. Freedom of choice must be more than the absence of causes for choosing.

So the dilemma (also known as Hume's fork) is that, on the one hand, someone cannot be held responsible, be praised or blamed for her decisions, which are mechanical and pre-programmed – these cannot be rational and free. If reasons are really causes, if intentions are ultimately physical processes, then we can be no more held responsible for them than a stone for falling or a desk calculator for truncating numbers. On the other hand, actions that are entirely unconstrained, that seem produced by some sort of random generator, have little to do with free will in a morally interesting sense either.

Three conditions

There is general agreement that for ascribing free will, genuine freedom to choose, real responsibility for one's actions, to an agent, three conditions must be fulfilled (Walter, 2001):

1   The agent must have been able to do otherwise. This is obvious at first sight, but it turns out to be very difficult to spell out what it means to have an alternative. External constraints are reasonably straightforward: you are not free to jump over the moon. But there seems to be something like internal constraints. You don't take the stairs out of free choice when the elevator has broken down, but could someone with severe claustrophobia be said to be free to take the elevator rather than the stairs? Do internal constraints, the blind impress that all our behavings bear (Philip Larkin, 1988: 94), leave any freedom to do otherwise than we do? When exactly can we claim that someone could have been done otherwise?

2   The act must originate in the agent, not in external forces. You are not free to win at roulette, or that you cannot be blamed for (the favourite thought experiments of philosophers in this trade often involve malign scientists implanting a remote control in your brain) hypnosis and post-hypnotic suggestion is a similar case of behaviour that is not free because originating outside the person. The interesting question is of course how much of our behaviour is externally induced.

3   The action must be rational, or understandable as the outcome of rational deliberation. Someone making decisions in an entirely random fashion would be considered loony, not free. As David Hume (1739/1969, Book. II, Part III sect. ii) realized long ago, there is something deeply paradoxical about free will. If behaviour is determined by internal and external causes, it is not free. If it is entirely undetermined, random, unreasonable and unpredictable, it is not free either.

BOX 10.7 Three conditions for ascribing free will and responsibility

1 The agent must have been able to do otherwise.
2 The act must originate in the agent, not in external forces.
3 The action must be rational, or understandable as the outcome of rational deliberation.

The Big Metaphysical Question is, now, whether freedom is possible in a natural world. It seems a reasonable assumption that every event has a cause, that is, nothing happens without cause. Then every event is determined by previous events, and whatever we think, reason, or decide has a cause (or more plausibly a host of causes).

The alternative to a causally closed world is an even less attractive picture: unexplainable random unruly happenings, and anarchy let loose upon the world. Naturalism, the assumption that all there is can ultimately be explained by science, seems to involve determinism: nothing happens randomly or unexplainably. (There is some debate in quantum indeterminacy, the idea that at subatomic levels reality is not deterministic, and some philosophers have tried to relate quantum indeterminacy to free will, with rather implausible results, see McFee, 2000). How can agents be free if they are part of the closed causal chain that makes up the natural world? Recall the contrast between reasons and causes, actions and events, doings and happenings that was characteristic for setting social sciences apart from natural sciences, and that distinguish agents from mechanisms. Machines don't act.

Compatibilism and incompatibilism

There are roughly two answers to the question of whether freedom is possible in a material causally closed world: compatibilism (somewhat confusingly sometimes called 'soft determinism'), which holds that some kind of free will is compatible with determinism; and incompatibilism or libertarianism, which holds that free will requires some kind of metaphysical freedom, that breaks through the causal chain of natural events. The difference between these positions is in fact a difference in the 'could have done otherwise' condition. Libertarians take this criterion categorically: the agent could in the same internal and external conditions have done something else; compatibilists interpret it conditionally, as 'could have done otherwise in the same external conditions, if the internal conditions had been different'. You could have done otherwise, if you had wanted. Freedom in this view is freedom from external force, but the willings of humans are part and parcel of the causal chains of the natural world, determined by an individual's history, genes, nervous system, and the rest. If no external circumstance forces him to do otherwise, the claustrophobic is free to take the elevator, and if he had had therapy, he might have done so. Thus, on the compatibilist view, free will is compatible with determinism.

BOX 10.8 Freedom and materialism (determinism)

Compatibilism: some kind of free will is compatible with determinism.

The agent could have done otherwise in the same *external* conditions, if the *internal* conditions had been different. He *could have done otherwise*, if he had wanted, but what he wants is still *determined* by internal causes.

Free will is freedom from external force, but the willings of humans are part and parcel of the causal chains of the natural world, determined by an individual's history, genes, nervous system, and the rest.

Incompatibilism or libertarianism: free will is incompatible with determinism; it requires some kind of metaphysical freedom, which breaks through the causal chain of natural events. It takes the 'could have done otherwise' condition categorically: the agent could have done something else in the same *internal and external* conditions.

In a classic paper Frankfurt (1971) introduces the idea of 'second order desires'. These are characteristic of persons, and suggest how free will and personhood can exist in a causally closed world. Persons, unlikes brutes and machines, can have second-order desires about their (first-order) desires; for example, the claustrophobic can desire (second-order) to get rid of his phobia (first-order desire to avoid closed spaces) and go into therapy; the addict can (second-order) want to fight his habit, his (first-order) desire for illegal substances. Freedom and personhood lie in the possibility of reflection on one's first-order desires and in the possibility of second-order desires; it is not some metaphysical freedom, outside the causally closed world of nature.

In assigning responsibility, we appeal to freedom in the sense of second-order desires, the capacity to will oneself to will something, and that does not require libertarian

glossary freedom of causal determination. **Actions** are free when the intentions behind them correspond to the intentions we have chosen, that is, when we have the desires that we want to have. Free will is willing in accordance with second-order volition.

Dennett's naturalistic account

Dennett (1984, 2003a) gives a good sketch of freedom worth wanting in a deterministic universe, freedom that organisms like us, evolved through natural selection and supported by cognitive tools and cultural props, can achieve.

Dennett's naturalistic account of free will attempts to break the spell of anti-reductionism. Determinism is compatible with some sort of free will. The tricks that Mother Nature has put in organismic design enable complex and sophisticated kinds of behaviour, that enable (most importantly in evolution) avoidance of harm. These make the organism free in the sense that it can act to prevent itself from being annihilated. This involves foresight, discrimination, recognition, preemptive strike, retaliation, and so on.

Such actions can be ascribed to genes, bacteria, and on the evolutionary ladder in a seamless ascending sequence to organisms and finally humans. Dennett's evolutionary approach exploits the elements of scaffolding, luck and gradualism (2003a: 273). There is no clear-cut division between intelligence and mechanism, doings and happenings, but some complex organisms are more adroit at avoiding harm than other more simple ones. The former's behaviour is also caused, in a deterministic way, by their evolved apparatus to dodge enemies. The intentional stance (see Chapters 6, and 10.1) shows their behaviour in terms of doings, not happenings, as actions, not physical movements, as rational and goal directed activities, not as mechanical causes. This can happen in a deterministic world. 'Evitability' is not incompatible with determinism.

Determinism does not restrict possibilities. Chess programs are deterministic, for example, but the better program can exploit opportunities. An intentional (macro) perspective in terms of means, goals, strategies, brief, an agent-perspective showing actions/doings, not happenings, is indispensable in explaining their behaviour. Deterministic worlds thus offer opportunities, in the macro-trained eye. Even when causally closed, the world is subjectively open: evolved organisms seek information about the unknown, explore and invent, and in that sense, create new behaviours.

In *Kind of Minds* (1996) Dennett describes four levels of sophistication in generating and testing new behaviours of organisms, the most developed minds having some kind of internal world picture, and exploiting cultural tools such as language. Organisms don't have a fixed nature, but have changed and adapted to changing environments and opportunities. This takes, in Dennett's view, the sting out of determinism. We have a degree of freedom that is compatible with a deterministic universe. We have a kind of self-created selves.

Agents have a degree of freedom unlike static fixed objects, because they have a flexible nature and can anticipate disaster and plan for escape. Thus, free will is an natural skill, developed in evolution and through cultural learning.

To sum up

In conclusion, we could say that determinism and the problem of free will have been and still are typical philosophers' problems (McFee, 2000). They are global theses and in a certain sense metaphysical because they pertain to the universe and humans in a very general way. However, asserting that every event has a cause or many causes, and defending determinism is one thing, it is quite another to explain or describe exactly and exhaustively which causes preceded a particular event. Shortsighted as we are, we can never know the complete state of the world before the onset of an event, and we have to mobilize 'Natural Laws' with a cautious *ceteris paribus*. If it is impossible to give a complete explanation of a particular natural event (pinpointing all its causal circumstances), this must be more than hopeless when trying to explain daily human actions. In taking the intentional stance, folk psychology has already 'provided for' these situations of accounting, explaining or understanding behaviour. The 'normal' why-questions are not meant to ask for (neuro)physi(ologic)cal details, they work in a social environment. This was the drift of the section about reasons and causes (Chapter 2.6). We can uphold the general ontological idea of determinism, and at the same time accept that, epistemologically speaking, we cannot know all causal details; that in certain situations we even do not need to know them, depending on what we are interested in. The question about responsibility, say in the juridical sphere, may change continuously according to growing insight into the causes of human conduct. It will remain (often painfully) difficult to decide upon what we can accept as a reason or have to acknowledge as a cause; how somebody could have done otherwise, or how he was driven beyond his will.

10.5 Consciousness

As we have seen throughout this book, cognitive scientists equipped with powerful theories and ideas from philosophy, linguistics, biology and neurology have tried very hard to demonstrate that we now have less and less reason to accept an essentially autonomous mental domain detached from the world of material phenomena. Their conviction is that cognitive, mental or psychological functions such as thinking, perceiving, remembering, talking, loving, hoping, intending, acting etc. have to be the outcome of (or are the same as) material processes. Just as it can be demonstrated that life has once been developed out of non-living material, it must be possible to establish scientifically that the human mind is the result of natural evolution. This is what the programme of naturalism intends to offer. Although naturalism can mean different things (from eliminativism and physicalistic reductionism to explanatory pluralism, see Chapter 2) the common ideal is to debunk myths and unveil mysteries – although there remain, of course, many deep and nearly unsurmountable problems and many unsatisfactory or partial answers.

BOX 10.9   Naturalism

Naturalism is the approach in cognitive science and philosophy of mind that tries to demonstrate:

- that we now have less and less reason to accept an essentially autonomous mental domain detached from the world of material phenomena;
- that we do not need to answer difficult questions in the light of a priori metaphysical convictions;

BOX 10.9   Naturalism (Continued)

- that cognitive, mental or psychological functions have to be the outcome of (or are the same as) material processes;
- and that it must be possible to establish scientifically that the human mind is the result of natural evolution.

It does not mean that all cognitive problems can be solved only by natural science (this is called *physicalism*).

Nor does it mean that all problems can be solved by science (this is called *scientism*).

Confronted with the naturalistic assaults, some philosophers consider consciousness as the castle keep of the true human mind. Maybe many mental capacities can be analysed as cognitive features to be studied by cognitive science, but consciousness, they think, is an elusive property. It may be described in a circumvential way, but it cannot be scientifically objectified. Choosing from an abundant field of theories, approaches and arguments, we will present a highly selective number of proposals for dealing with consciousness.

Consciousness and qualia

Among the toughest issues and most debated attributes of consciousness are **qualia** `glossary` (singular: a quale). These are the phenomenal or qualitative features of being conscious, like feeling pain, seeing red, tasting wine, hearing music, feeling the warmth of the sun, suffering a pang of jealousy. Some philosophers argue that these highly subjective, feeling-like features are, in principle, irrespective of any future development in neuroscience, irreducible to brain events or information processing.

The idea, put more formally, is that first-person descriptions, knowledge by acquaintance cannot be translated into third-person knowledge by description; how I feel is not exhaustively describable in intersubjective terms (Russell, 1988). This intuitively plausible idea that you cannot explain how it feels to watch the stained-glass windows of Chartres Cathedral at sunrise to someone who is colour blind, or why Chardonnay goes well with *suprême de volaille* to someone who subsists on pizza and hamburgers, or how it is to be depressive, has been exploited by some philosophers to demonstrate that consciousness is essentially private and ineffable, and that qualia are directly experienced by the subject, the mind, consciousness, or whatever.

These experiences then are supposed to appear in a private mental space, called after Descartes the 'Cartesian theatre'. Hence, this mental theatre is populated by subjective self-transparent things called qualia; and, as some philosophers go on to argue, the mind knows the contents of consciousness directly, infallibly. If you take this last step, however, claiming that these subjective experiences deliver infallible knowledge, you fall prey to what Sellars has called the 'myth of the given' (see Chapters 3.4, and 4.5). It is this view that has been rejected in naturalist approaches to consciousness.

Thomas Nagel on the irreducibility of first-person experience

A well-known attempt to shield first-person experience, qualia, from reduction to third-person talk, for example, neuroscience, is Thomas Nagel's (1980) bat story: 'What is it like to be a bat?' His argument is in essence that no amount of descriptive knowledge could possibly add up to experiencing how it feels to be a bat, and what it is like to perceive by sonar (as bats do: lacking sight, they navigate by echo). Conscious experience is 'what it is like' to be an organism to the organism itself. Proposals for reduction of that subjective experience must be considered unsuccessful as long as the reducing theory (for instance: the standard example used in Chapter 6.2: pain is the firing of neurons in some brain centre) is logically possible without consciousness. This is known as the *zombie problem*. A zombie is supposedly one of the walking dead, who behaves more or less normally, but without conscious experience. It seems fair to demand that a theory of consciousness should be able to distinguish us from zombies.

Nagel argues that subjective experience is connected with a single subjective point of view, a 'pour-soi' (a 'for-yourself') as the French philosopher Sartre called it, which is not accessible from an objective physical point of view. Feeling what it is like to be a bat is not the same as imagining, by extrapolating from our own experience, how we would feel hanging from a beam. We may never be able to know animals' or other people's minds, and we may never have an adequate language to describe subjective experience. That does not mean that the latter is not real, complex, rich and highly specific in nature.

The facts of experience are accessible only to a subjective, single, first-person point of view, and not to objective third-person points of view. Nagel admits that in the latter case there is a multiplicity of viewpoints, tending to greater objectivity, less dependence on subjective and individual impressions, and hence the possibility of *reduction* to more basal physical mechanisms. In the former case, however, reduction fails. Moving from subjective 'appearance' to objective 'reality' does not work; more objectivity (e.g. focusing on the working of the brain) means losing touch with subjective experience. Nagel ends with a rather desperate call for an objective phenomenology that develops concepts dealing with descriptions of subjective experiences. He argues that any solution to the mind–body problem is dependent on such an attempt to gauge, and span, the subjective–objective gap.

Jackson's story about Mary, the colour-blind scientist

In the early 1980s the Australian philosopher Frank Jackson (1990) came up with another thought-experiment. A (hypothetical) neurophysiologist, Mary, who knows everything about colour perception, but having been raised in a black and white environment, has never experienced colours herself. Though she has (*ex hypothesi*) all the physical information there is to obtain about what goes on when we see ripe tomatoes, Mary does not know what it is like to have the sensation of seeing red. When given a colour television set instead of her black and white one, will she learn something new? It seems obvious, according to Jackson, that she does learn something about the world. But then her previous knowledge was incomplete; and the thesis that all (correct) information is physical information is false. This is what he calls his 'knowledge-argument' for the peculiar existence of qualitative experiences.

Again, a slightly different example. Assume someone who can make colour discriminations nobody else can see; assume neuroscientists know everything about her nervous system, and can completely explain this extraordinary ability. Nevertheless, in a sense they would know more if they themselves could, through some brain transplant, actually experience the colour differences. Hence, the argument goes, physics or neurophysiology is incomplete; there is a limit to what science can teach us about our private experiences, about real consciousness – there must be something non-physical to it.

McGinn and the mysterious property *P*

Another fundamental argument against the possibility of explaining consciousness is given by Colin McGinn (1991a), who introduced the idea of 'cognitive closure'. Minds have evolved in biological history, just like bodies; and therefore they differ as to their capacities. Different species are capable of perceiving different properties of the world. 'What is closed to the mind of a rat may be open to the mind of a monkey, and what is open to us may be closed to the monkey' (McGinn, 1991a: 3). A type of mind is cognitively closed to a certain property or a certain theory if the cognitive powers at that mind's disposal are inept for grasping the property or understanding the theory.

Therefore, he thinks that there are problems which human minds are in principle equipped to solve, but there are also 'mysteries' which elude our understanding. In his study McGinn tries to show that the mind-body problem is not cognitively accessible to humans; that the nature of the connection between consciousness and the brain is and will remain a mystery to us. However, it is not a mystery because it is somehow supernatural – the property of the brain that accounts for consciousness is a *natural* phenomenon. Like life, consciousness is a biological development; we avoid vitalism and 'the magic touch of God's finger' as explanations of life, because we think there must be some natural account of how life comes from matter. Likewise there *has* to be some naturalistic explanation for how brains cause minds, but we are cognitively closed to that natural property, *P* for short, which therefore remains a mystery to us.

Why can't we grasp *P*?

Now, what reasons does McGinn have for asserting that our minds are closed to the correct theory of the psychophysical connection and that we cannot grasp this property *P* which is responsible for the nexus?

If we want to identify P, there seem, according to McGinn, to be two avenues open to us: 'we could try to get to P by investigating consciousness directly; or we could look to the study of the brain for P' (ibid.: 7).

As to the first avenue, we know what it is to be conscious; we have direct cognitive access to properties of consciousness by introspection. We know it when we taste something bitter or when we feel sad. But in these autophenomenological, first-person ascriptions we never catch the mind-brain relation, we never get a glimpse of P. Introspection of consciousness reveals only its surface, not 'the inner constitution' (ibid.: 80). The problem of the consciousness-brain connection lies outside consciousness and cannot be solved by simply being conscious.

Will neuroscience, then, be the place to look for P? Negative. All our empirical investigations to understand the workings of the brain do not lead to consciousness. The property of consciousness itself is not an observable property of the brain and cannot be found by empirically investigating the brain. You can stare into a living conscious brain and see there a variety of brain properties – shape, colour, texture, etc. – 'but you will not thereby *see* what the subject is experiencing, the conscious state itself' (ibid.: 11, original emphasis). The senses can only present things in space with spatially defined properties, and while the brain is a spatial object, consciousness is not. But, you would say, neither are the properties of quantum theory; many theories contain unobservables; without concepts about hidden structures, we could not achieve successful theories in many domains (ibid.: 89). McGinn maintains, however, that explanations of brain data will never disclose consciousness; we cannot know which property of the brain accounts for consciousness. 'Consciousness is as natural as anything else in nature, but it is not given to us to understand the nature of this naturalness' (ibid.: 88).

Dennett's multiple drafts model of consciousness

Dennett has put forward a theory of consciousness (Dennett, 1991a) which in essence tries to explain it in terms of information processing. A design made from subpersonal components can yield consciousness, in the same way as simple subsystems can make up complex rational behaviour, as, for example, in a chess computer. Dennett's proposal is that the mind is a jumble of parallel information-processing sequences, a kind of text fragments or narratives, which he calls 'multiple drafts', distributed throughout the brain and continuously revised and updated. The mind is a pandemonium of narrative fragments and goals, which compete for resources, attention and priority, dominance and influence over the rest of the brain. Being conscious is gaining 'cerebral celebrity' (Dennett, 1994); it occurs when a winning draft is known throughout the brain and attracts attention from all over the system. Think of a toothache: it will monopolize your mind, to the exclusion of less pressing concerns, or a neon sign proclaiming that the end of the world is near – these are surely conscious.

In Dennett's multiple drafts model, there is no central executive, no central agent or 'Cartesian theatre' where it all comes together. Thus, he tries to defuse the

Cartesian heritage of a thinking substance, self-transparent, populated with ghostly mental events, a kind of inner mental theatre as immaterial counterpart to the material world.

As explained above, in the view of philosophers like Nagel, McGinn and Jackson, a major obstacle to explaining consciousness is the intuition that it is essentially private and subjective, only accessible in first-person mode (by acquaintance), and that it eludes objective third-person descriptions. How pain feels, or what it is like to win the lottery, is difficult to describe.

Mentalist philosophers concluded that mind was essentially private, subjectively experienced, and therefore beyond the grasp of objective explanations. Furthermore, mentalists thought that the furniture of the Cartesian theatre was open to observation by its owner, who had privileged access. Introspection, the observation of mental events, was the method of psychology for the last half of the twentieth century. Dennett argues that what is reported is not a view of one's inner screen; he tries to deconstruct the idea of private access to one's own mental theatre. For once, he argues, there are no definite and ready-made thoughts and ideas in our heads, but a messy lot of half-finished narratives. Thoughts are in fact produced when uttered, as in response to an external probe, when someone asks us something. Many of us only know precisely what we feel when we have put it into words, and we sometimes hear ourselves expressing opinions that we did not know we had. Put somewhat provocatively, we only know what we think when we hear ourselves pronounce it. So, there is no inner Cartesian realm where mental events exist before the mind's eye – there is just a tangle of narratives.

No qualia and no self

Thus, Dennett (1988, 1991a) tried to provide a convincing argument that the philosophical notion of qualia, as observable private entities in the mind, is a bad habit of thought, a metaphysical muddle that cannot be solved, but should be dissolved – a knot to be cut rather than disentangled. He concentrates on the philosophical definition and tries to demonstrate that such a thing as a quale does not exist. In his reconstruction, qualia are complex dispositions that have the property of producing certain effects on their owners. They are dispositions to react in certain ways to sensory stimuli: for example, the quale of a red colour leads to pronouncing 'red', stepping on the brake pedal, adding a little tomato paste to the sauce, appreciating Schongauer's *Rosenmadonna*, etc. No intrinsic properties are required to explain the behaviour of a system that has the power of discriminating colours, smells, and so on. Qualia as private ineffable intrinsically conscious properties simply do not exist. And Dennett is not impressed by philosophers' intuitions about the unbridgeable gap between subjective and objective. In the case of the bat and the colour-blind scientist, we simply cannot tell what it means to have all the information about the nervous system, and this 'lack of imagination' (Dennett's, and also Churchland's, cherished reproach at their opponents) should not be confused with a metaphysical necessity. Mysterians like McGinn trade on our ignorance of neuroscience: who can be sure that, if we *really* knew *all* about colour perception, we could not predict from the neuroscientific facts how it feels to see red? Furthermore, Dennett is not impressed by introspective evidence: it is an error to think that there is an exact point in time where perception or recognition or a thought occurs in the mind. Seeing or recognizing or thinking something is a kind of horse race between competing drafts (Dennett and Kinsbourne, 1992): we cannot pinpoint mental events in time. There is no such thing as private, privileged and infallible access to mental events. This, of course, applies to introspection: we do not observe our thoughts, but we construct a narrative from bits and pieces of self-observed behaviour; we sometimes confabulate and invent inner precesses as reasons for our own behaviour, more or less the way fiction is created: the story has to make sense. It should be added that there is some evidence for this counterintuitive view. Nisbett and Wilson (1977) showed that people have little insight into their own decision making, and when asked about it, tend to make something up.

Thus, Dennett thinks that he has effectively destroyed the mentalist claim that there is something in the mind that is seen and reported in introspection. Having demolished the Cartesian theatre, Dennett can also make short shrift of its principal tenant: the self or the I or the subject. The self is only virtual, not substantial. Just as the centre of gravity of the earth is only an imaginary point, not something substantial that draws falling objects towards it, the self is only the virtual centre around which multiple drafts gravitate, it is not the central controller of the mind. The brain spins a web of words and deeds, but there is no central subject to oversee it: 'tales spin us'.

Churchland: it is nothing but a special pathway of knowing

Churchland (1985a) places his proposal for reducing qualia within a neurocomputational perspective against the background of his (1979) ideas on reduction and elimination of scientific theories. Thus, he challenges Nagel's claim that the qualitative experience exists before its conceptualization and description: that we know exactly what it is like to see a red tomato or smell coffee, even if we cannot put it into words. Like the bat, each one of us has a 'peculiar access, to exactly one's own sensations, that no other creature has'. This is because each one of us 'enjoys a unique set of intimate causal connections to the sensory activity of one's own brain and nervous system', by way of, for instance, the axonal network of our proprioceptive system (Churchland, 1995: 196–7). But the existence of this unique way of our knowing about our own internal states does not show that there is a non-physical aspect to conscious states. 'Auto-connected' ways of knowing have as objects the same physical things and circumstances as are occasionally known through 'heteroconnected' ways of knowing. My knowledge of my facial blush differs from your knowledge of my blush, but the blush itself is as physical as you please (Churchland, 1995: 198–9). Both are knowledge of the same fact, to wit, a neural process; it is only the mode of knowing, the kind of access to that fact that is different. And there is nothing mysterious about that:

children know Santa Claus as a bringer of gifts, parents know the same Santa Claus as a neighbour in a rented suit: same object, different ways of knowing.

And thus, the fact that we have here two different 'epistemic access-relations', the subjective first-person and the objective, scientific third-person access, does not undermine 'the naturalist's hope of isolating the specific properties that subserve first-person experience', writes Owen Flanagan optimistically in his (1992: 118) book on consciousness.

But is a private experience the same as a knowledge-claim?

Damasio and the neurobiology of consciousness and emotions

Among other philosophically-minded neurobiologists who have dealt with problems of mind and consciousness, Antonio Damasio has proposed a coherent neurobiological theory of the structure and development of consciousness (1999). Though he does not take part in the philosophical discussion about qualia, he implicitly defends the thesis that becoming conscious is, indeed, getting in certain neurological states; consciousness is a complex system of happenings in the life of organisms in interaction with their environment.

It begins early in the life of an organism, and it is regulated deep down in its evolutionary old brain structures. The organism encounters something in the world and must react: can it be eaten, is it dangerous, is hiding necessary? These early confrontations and reactions are in fact 'emotions' in a literal sense of the word: elicitations to make a move. Emotions are part of a hierarchy of life-regulation mechanisms beginning with devices such as metabolism and reflexes, and constituting the organism's early sense of 'self'. This is what consciousness is about: the sense of self facing the world. Damasio calls this early fundamental stage 'core-consciousness', in connection with 'core-self'. In evolutionarily more complex organisms with much more capacity it develops into more sophisticated states of consciousness; in us humans it reaches the stage of 'extended consciousness'. Extended consciousness is the feeling and knowing of what happens bodily and cognitively in interaction with the world. At this point language enters the stage, enabling the telling of stories and constructing our 'autobiographical self'; it comprises the capacity of reasoning and planning; it makes going beyond the here and now possible. Thus, in contrast to the traditional idea that consciousness is dependent on language, Damasio maintains that the earlier state of consciousness comes before language and description. Only when consciousness becomes extended do the stories about self and the world need these means of reflection and communication.

For all the stages of consciousness Damasio refers to brain structures and neural patterns. There is no one central headquarters, no homunculus in a Cartesian theatre, many regions are involved; numerous functions are formed in a highly distributed manner, fundamental functions for life-management in evolutionary older parts, deep in the brain.

Damasio's book gives us a picture of the complexity of the matter. He weaves his story going from neurology and biology to clinical cases and conceptual issues. Once again the message is that we cannot solve problems about cognition and consciousness in a one-dimensional way.

To sum up

Apparently consciousness is not a 'ghost in the machine', nor a region in our heads, not a kind of manager who oversees what's going on, who gathers the data and who by the exercise of his will makes the decisions about what to do next. It is no Self or I residing in the boardroom where the 'buck stops'. It is not concealed inside the organism and working secretly deep in the interior. It is rather an integrated whole of interactive functions beginning with the first contact of an organism confronting the environment and resulting in a change in the organism and the situation. The interaction develops into awareness and movements, then into attention and purposeful activity, and in the end into a human individual communicating and acting in a cultural exchange. In between there is a very complex ensemble of lower- and higher-order functions of a biological and physiological nature; of brain, body and world, developing into psychological activities and reactions.

From this perspective a quale is just the tip of the iceberg; there is a lot more to explain about consciousness. But because they are vital in being conscious, it is important to know what they are and what they are not. A quale is a *happening*, it is a first-person experience, and not a piece of private *knowledge*, by privileged access of the individual. Because a person (or an organism) has them, they are unique to that person; they are really first-person experiences. We can try to describe or explain them, try to amass knowledge about them, but descriptions or explanations, knowledge in general, are not the experiences themselves. We can have knowledge about qualia, but knowledge about them is never the qualia themselves. The individual who has an experience, say tasting chocolate, can try to describe what he savours, but his first-person description of it is not his first-person experience itself. The first-person experiences do not, and logically cannot concur with scientific explanations. Therefore, they are not private and privileged knowledge.

Now, *having* these first-person experiences is very important for *being* conscious. But just having them does not, by itself, *explain how* we can have qualia, how we become conscious, how 'it' works. Cognitive scientists interested in these latter questions have to explain qualia, and not to explain them away. Again, qualia are among many other phenomena of consciousness; and depending on what we want to know we have to choose among different levels of explanation.

10.6 Conclusion: Mind and Science

In this chapter we have revisited a number of issues and debates which we already more or less discussed or alluded to in previous chapters. In this way this last chapter has been a concluding chapter of the book and of its two themes: mind and science. In the book we have examined many different ideas about science put forward during the twentieth century. And we have come to the conclusion that science is not a metaphysical or supra-human treasure-house of knowledge, available only to the scientist with the unique and proper methods, but that it is a human endeavour and therefore liable to human conditions. The time when philosophers of science could cherish the ideal of being able to demarcate science from quasi-knowledge and of prescribing how science had to be done according to absolute criteria has had its day. It appears that science is not altogether non-historical and non-social but to a large extent a human enterprise, as we wanted to demonstrate in the first part of the book.

Though science is about the world and the world is represented in a certain sense by scientific knowledge, it is also moulded by the historical and social circumstances of the scientists. This intricate interplay of humans and the world is a moment in the evolution of the coupling of organisms and their environment. Organisms have to know things about the world in order to cope with it; and this knowledge, generating actions, becomes more and more complex when produced by humans. This emphasis on knowledge for action is characteristic for pragmatism and the pragmatic conception of science that we advocated in the book.

Psychology has become more and more important within studies of science, because science is about knowledge and knowledge is a result of cognitive functions such as observing, thinking, inferring, conceptualizing, etc. Cognitive (neuro)psychology and its philosophical sparring partner, philosophy of mind, help us to understand how the human mind works, how knowledge is acquired, how perception, thinking and other cognitive functions take part in the scientific process.

Seen in the context of science studies the cognitive turn in the second part of the book is, thus, a quite natural sequel to the first part on science. It is at the same time an intellectual domain in its own right that is of theoretical importance for the student of psychology.

The question, what is science, is not an exclusive philosophical problem anymore. Epistemology, the branch of philosophy once supposed to lay the foundations of the true scientific method, has been naturalized; that is, the study of knowledge acquisition and of its limits can be successfully supported by (cognitive) psychology.

And in the same way as conceptions of science have been naturalized, we have tried throughout the book to strip notions of mind of their mystery. Thus the study (or philosophy) of science and cognitive psychology (or the philosophy of mind) have come closer to each other.

Central issues and perennial problems in the philosophy of science and the philosophy of mind – reduction, levels of explanation, naturalism, causality, free will and human actions, scientific and folk psychology, intentionality and consciousness – are discussed in an integrated way in this last chapter. So, this chapter can be seen as a collection of 'case studies', bringing together the different approaches of science and the nature of mind, and concluding the themes of the book – mind and science.

Further Reading

10.1 Intentionality

Lyons, W. (1995) *Approaches to Intentionality*. Oxford: Oxford University Press.
A clear overview of different approaches and an interesting viewpoint of its own.

10.3 Mental causation

Heil, J. and Mele, A. (eds) (1993) *Mental Causation*. Oxford: Clarendon Press.
A useful reader.

10.4 Free will

Dennett, D.C. (2003) *Freedom Evolves*. London: Allen Lane.
A well-written and interesting discussion.

McFee, G. (2000) *Free Will*. Teddington: Acumen Publishing.
A clear introduction to the debates and different approaches.

10.5 Consciousness

Block, N., Flanagan, O. and Güzeldere, G. (eds) (1997) *The Nature of Consciousness: Philosophical Debates*. Cambridge, MA: MIT Press.
An extensive reader of influential articles.

GLOSSARY[1]

Abduction   Or *inference to the best explanation*. The art (or logic) governing the principles by which we arrive at hypotheses for subsequent testing. Unlike induction,* abduction goes beyond generalizing from empirical evidence; compare: all swans are white (induction), and: insufficient hygiene must be the cause of the epidemic (inference to the best explanation). Like induction, and unlike deduction,* it is non-demonstrative. Thus, abduction is usually considered to belong to the context* of discovery, although some tried to develop a logic of prescriptive rules for hypothesis construction – with little success.

Action   What a human agent does. It should be distinguished from mere movement, and also from behaviour, in the technical sense of behaviourism (observable responses). Action involves intentionality* and rationality. However, not every action is done on purpose and it might be that a person cannot be held responsible for it. In this sense the problem of free will is related. To explain or to account for an action is asking/giving reasons* for it, rather than causes.*

Artificial Intelligence Making machines (computers, or better: computer programs) do things that would require intelligence, if done by men (in Minsky's definition), for example, playing chess, constructing mathematical proofs, answering insight questions about a story, etc. *Weak AI* aims at nothing more than a working program. *Strong AI* aims, in addition, at producing programs that do essentially the same as, and are 'equivalent' to, a human thinker. Strong AI thus entails the claim that mental activity is in essence computation,* be it symbol manipulation, or simulation of spreading activation in networks (see Connectionism).* There seem to be fewer believers in strong AI nowadays than there used to be; weak AI is a booming business.

Background   A concept in the philosophy of mind meaning the general and implicit *know-how* and capacities that enable a person to function in, or to understand her environment. The background operates implicitly, implying that it need not, and even cannot, be explicitly formulated or reflected upon. Background know-how is opposed to *knowing-that* or declarative knowledge.

Belief   A mental state, a thought, by which a proposition is held to be true, and upon which one is prepared to act: which guides action,* as pragmatism* would add. Beliefs, together with desires, are taken as the paradigms of mental states – particularly of propositional attitudes* – in philosophy of mind. See also: Belief-desire psychology.

Belief-Desire Psychology   A theory in the philosophy of mind (main exponent: Jerry Fodor) that takes beliefs and desires, as used in folk psychology,* as the paradigms of mental states. According to Fodor, these mental categories from folk psychology do really exist as cognitive states and have causal efficacy, i.e. they cause behaviour and other mental states. The theory thus takes folk psychology seriously as the point of departure for scientific cognitive psychology.

Cause, Causality, Causation   A relation between two events, such that the first can be said to bring about or to necessitate the second event, so that it *must* occur. It is a notorious philosophical problem how this can ever be empirically* established, and whether causes are not subjective constructions, rather than elements of reality. Hume held that we can say only that events occur with some regularity one *after* the other, not that one occurs *because* of the other. What is the difference between the going together of two events (the 'constant conjunction'), and the claim that one causes the other (e.g. smoking and cancer)? *Causal laws* describe an invariant relation between two events, where the cause is a necessary condition for the effect, i.e. the latter does not occur without the first. In this context, what counts as a cause is also dependent on explanatory* interests, since an event may have a number of causes, only some of which are relevant. Causal laws are contrasted with teleological* laws. See also: Reasons.

Coherence Theory of Truth   See: Truth.

Common-Sense Psychology   See: Folk psychology.

Computation   In the most general sense: manipulating symbols. The idea of a general-purpose computer was traditionally that it executes symbol manipulation according to formal mechanic procedures. One should distinguish between this classical symbolic view, as described, and the recent connectionist view on computation, as the spreading of numerical activation through a (neural) network. The computational theory of mind* holds that mental processes are essentially computation.

Computational Theory of Mind   The theory that mental processes essentially consist in computation, i.e. symbol manipulation. CTM in its classical version, associated with Jerry Fodor, assumes that mental states are symbol states, strings in a formal language (imagine a computer language, or predicate calculus in logic) in the head, and mental processes are transformations of these symbol strings. Churchland's alternative, that mental processes are activation patterns in a multidimensional vector space, could also be called a computational view of mind, although a completely different kind of computation (numerical versus logical). See also: Language of Thought; Connectionism.

Confirmation   Showing a statement to be supported by empirical* evidence (see also: Verification). Carnap thought he could develop a logic in which the degree of inductive* support could be assessed. Popper showed that a theory can only be corroborated, but can never be confirmed conclusively; it can, however, be proved wrong with absolute certainty (falsification).*

Connectionism   An approach in cognitive psychology and Artificial Intelligence* that uses self-organizing networks (modelled on neural networks) of interconnected nodes, in which the changing of weights of the connections underlies the network's learning of a discriminating response. In this model of information-processing the network is supposed to tune itself to the environment, rather than following a programme of pre-set rules and commands. See also: Representation.

Consciousness   The state of awareness, of being conscious. Also: the whole set of higher-order mental states and psychological functions that the subject can be aware of, such as thoughts, beliefs, desires, feelings, intentions. Consciousness is a much-debated topic in modern philosophy of mind. Some philosophers think that it is essentially a private, first-person experience. Others try to demystify and to naturalize* consciousness, to make it available for third-person objective explanation (e.g. that it emerges from brain processes). Consciousness involves the problems of intentionality* and qualia.*

Consensus Theory of Truth   See: Truth.

Constructionism, Social   A position in (social) psychology and in the philosophy of science that considers all the products of knowledge and (social) science, such as categories, concepts, facts, data, measurements, to be completely a matter of social artefacts, since all knowledge is conveyed only by language and communication. The role of language is not to refer to an extralinguistic world, but to contribute to mutual understanding and to sustain social relations. Truth* is defined by consensus, i.e. nothing more than what happens to be agreed upon. The position leans strongly towards relativism.*

Context of Discovery   In this context the focus is on a reliable description of the historical, social and even psychological circumstances and influences that were relevant to the discovery of a scientific theory. It is the subject of a methodological programme for a contextual historiography of science, in opposition to the positivistic* programme of the context of justification* of theories.

Context of Justification   In this context the focus is on the methodological requirements of a scientific theory, its logical argument, i.e. the degree to which the conclusions are supported by factual premises (induction),* or are inferred from general lawlike premises (deduction).* In this positivistic* programme it is maintained that it is not the business of science to pay attention to the social or psychological circumstances of the problem-solving situation.

Correspondence Theory of Truth   See: Truth.

Deduction   The reasoning process or argument in which a conclusion is logically drawn, or deduced from a set of premises. Induction* and abduction* are non-demonstrative, whereas deduction is demonstrative: its conclusions follow with logical certainty, on pain of contradiction. It is also seen as the argument that takes you from general statements (e.g. All birds are …) to particular conclusions (This bird is …).

Deductive-Nomological Model of Explanation   The view that explaining is deriving a proposition describing the event to be explained (the *explanandum*) from a general law or set of laws (the *explanans*): for example, all plants containing chlorophyll are green, grass contains chlorophyll, therefore grass is green. Subsuming an event under a 'covering law' is considered tantamount to answering the question why it happened. The positivist* ideal of a theory as an axiomatic formal system accounts for the element of (logical, demonstrative) deduction; 'nomological' means lawful. See also: Explanation.

Demarcation   Since the logical positivists,* philosophers of science have tried to find an unfailing criterion separating rational scientific knowledge from metaphysical speculation, irrationality, superstition and pseudo-science. The logical positivists proposed as such verifiability,* Popper falsifiability.* Neither works.

Dualism   A position in the mind-body problem, associated with the seventeenth-century French philosopher Descartes, and part of the whole tradition called 'Cartesianism'. Dualism divides human existence into having a mind and having a body. Mind and body are completely different substances, though they interact in a mysterious way. Mind is associated with a private inner mental world (theatre), to which the owner by a kind of inner eye has privileged access, whereas the body is part of the external observable world. See also: Consciousness.

Dynamical Systems Theory   A general formalism for describing complex systems, using the notions of an abstract space of possible states of the system (state space), and of a trajectory through it, governed by laws that can be described mathematically For psychological purposes, behaviour (like approach–avoidance, or walking) can be described, in a more or less geometrical way, as evolution (or 'flow') through state space. Important assets are its conceptualization of the agent-environment coupling and the evolution over time.

Eliminativism   The claim that folk psychological* categories like beliefs* and desires eventually can, and should, be eliminated and replaced by neuroscientific terms: we will talk about the firing of our neurons rather than about pain when hitting our thumb. In contrast, reductionism* allows us to keep our common-sense concepts (like 'water') even when they are identified with scientific concepts (water is 'really' H_2O).

Emergence   When a system has new properties that are not present in the constituents, these are called emergent: the system is more than the sum of its parts. Sometimes a system's emergent properties can be explained and predicted from the properties of the parts and their interactions (as in chemistry, where a molecule can be predicted from the way the atoms are put together). However, some authors prefer to restrict the term emergence to those systemic properties that are entirely unpredictable from the lower-level parts.

Empiricism   A doctrine in philosophy and, in particular, a position in epistemology* which says that all knowledge comes from the senses, and that only those expressions have a claim to knowledge and to truth* that can be translated, directly or indirectly, into sense impressions. These impressions, or *sense-data*, form the *given* content of our mental states of which we have direct awareness. This view was taken as the rock bottom of positivism.* See also: Theory-laden; Rationalism; Foundationalism.

Epistemology   The theory of knowledge, a main branch of philosophy. Its central problems are the origin and legitimacy of knowledge. This relates to questions about the credentials of the senses and of reason; about the nature of truth, of meaning, etc. The main historical positions in the field are rationalism* and empiricism.*

Explanation   In normal discourse, to make something easier to understand, to elucidate, or to answer a why-question. In the theory of science, especially when logical positivism* held sway over the field, it was considered as a strictly logical relation between the *explanandum* (that which has to be explained) and the *explanans* (that which explains). This ideal was found in the *covering-law model of explanation*: an event is explained when it can be deduced from a natural law plus initial conditions. Accordingly, the model was also called *deductive-nomological** (D-N model; Greek *nomos* is law). This model has been challenged: the notion of law and the ideal of the logical relation were disputed as requirements for explanation, in particular in the human/social sciences, where sometimes the *context* is seen as useful circumstantial evidence for interpretation/explanation (see also: Reasons). The *inference to the best explanation* is the idea that one sometimes opts for the best among a set of possible explanations (see also: Abduction; Teleology).

Falsification   Showing a statement to be false. According to Popper, a theory is to be rejected when predictions derived from it turn out to be false. Thus, whereas a theory can never be verified,* it can conclusively be falsified.

Folk Psychology   *Common-sense psychology*, the kind of explanation of everyday behaviour in terms of the goals, desires, beliefs, opinions and plans that supposedly drive one's fellow beings' behaviour. Fodor and others consider folk psychology as belief-desire psychology,* the kind of psychology that uses intentional* language, and requires representations* as explanatory concepts. Beliefs and desires, construed as propositional attitudes,* are, in this view, literally causes and lawful explanations, and can and should be preserved in a computational theory of mind.*

Foundationalism   A (usually dismissive) label for those normative positions in epistemology or the philosophy of science, like positivism,* which demand that true knowledge and science should be demarcated* from irrationality or pseudo-science by building upon secure epistemological* foundations, such as empiricism,* rationalism* or other views which call upon universal, ahistoric principles or postulates of rationality.

Functionalism   The thesis that mental states are functional states of a machine or a brain, implying that the actual physical make-up of the machine (the *implementation*) is irrelevant to the functional *role* it realizes. As a simple example of a functional description consider a carburettor: it can be made in infinitely many different materials and designs, all with the function of providing fuel to an engine. Analogously, mental states are functional roles: they have causal relations with input, with other mental states, and with behaviour, that can be described irrespective of the physical make-up of the system. An important consequence of functionalism in the philosophy of mind is that the same mental process (functional state) can be realized in brains as well as in computers (or in a contraption made of empty beer cans, for that matter); this is called *multiple realizability*. *Narrow (or machine) functionalism* considers a function solely in terms of the internal economy of the system. *Wide functionalism* is more like the biological notion of function: it includes the role a function has in the system's environment; for example, a rattlesnake has a heat detector and a movement detector: this has the function of detecting mice only in an environment where the snake can feed on mice.

Hermeneutics   Originally (since the seventeenth century) the art or the method for the exegesis of classical, theological and juridical texts. At the end of the nineteenth century hermeneutics was made into a general methodology for understanding (*Verstehen*) and interpretation in the human sciences, in contrast with the objective method of explanation in the physical sciences. *Philosophical hermeneutics* was developed in the twentieth century; it became a philosophical theory of the fundamental historical and linguistic situation of human experiences. It is one of the main epistemological convictions in modern hermeneutics, that since in the human sciences *meaning* is the central concept, the knowing subject and the known object share a common background. Hence, to understand the sometimes subtle meanings in these sciences, subject and object confront each other, are partners in a discussion, so to say. To understand the meaning of social, historical or psychological concepts and actions, it is essential to understand the context; and to understand the context, it is essential to understand the parts; this is the *hermeneutic circle* (see also: Holism).

Holism   The idea that the whole has priority over its parts. Holism is encountered in different domains. In contrast with the empiricist*/associationist account of perception, Gestalt psychology contends that perception should not be analysed in atomistic sensations, since in normal perception a gestalt is predominant: perception is organized by certain configurations. *Epistemological holism* is the (Quine–Duhem) thesis that the meaning of a term or a sentence can only be understood in the context of a whole body of sentences, a theory, or even a worldview. This also means that observational data can only be appreciated within or in the context of a theory. See also: Theory-laden.

Homunculus   Literally: little man. Refers to the kinds of explanation where intelligent behaviour is explained by intelligent processes (the little man) inside the agent – which is a pseudo-explanation when the intelligent processes themselves remain unexplained. Dennett made a variety of the homunculus explanation respectable under the label of *intentional stance:* the prediction or description of intelligent behaviour (of, say, a chess computer) in terms of the goals and knowledge it has. This is legitimate as long as it yields adequate descriptions and successful predictions (it is perfectly OK if it helps you to win a game of chess), and if it can in the end be explained by specifying the *design* (e.g. the chess computer's program). This consists in decomposing the intelligent 'little man' inside, with its complex function, into an 'army of idiots', each with a much more simple function.

Idealism   A philosophical doctrine holding that reality is essentially mental, consisting in something like the World Spirit (Hegel); this is called objective idealism. Idealism is usually considered as a subjective epistemology, implying that knowledge is first and foremost a product of the activity of the knowing subject, and that there is no way of finding out whether knowledge corresponds with, or refers to, something like an external reality. The idealist view of truth* is coherence, being consistent with the rest of knowledge. See also: Realism; Relativism.

Identity Theory   A materialistic solution to the mind-body problem, which says that mental events are identical with physical events. The *mind-brain identity theory* identifies mental events with brain events. This is a strong conception of materialism,* type-materialism, saying that a type of mental state (e.g. being angry) is identical with a certain type of brain state (say, the firing of specific neurons x, y, z). Functionalism* (token-materialism) opposes it.

Ideology   According to the Marxist interpretation, ideology is the production of ideas, the set of beliefs, conceptions, categories, moral standards, etc. of a social class, reflecting the material basis, the socio-economic conditions of the group. Since in this view all groups, except the proletariat, have the wrong ideas or 'false consciousness', ideologies are deceptive. In later interpretations ideology has lost the connotation of 'false consciousness', though the ideas of a group are still supposed to be influenced by the socio-economic circumstances and to guide the group's social and political action.

Idiographic   The method leading to the understanding of individual, unique events (Greek *idios* – unique, individual), as in the human sciences and history; it is opposed to the nomothetic* method.

Incommensurability   Literally: having no common yardstick. When two theories do not refer to a common set of facts, they are incommensurable. Since a paradigm* produces, according to Kuhn, its own evidence, and facts are theory-laden, there is no neutral ground for comparing one paradigm with another and they make sense of the world in terms of completely different categories, concepts and meanings. This notion can be criticized for leading to relativism.*

Individualism   A thesis in the philosophy of mind holding that for purposes of psychological explanation, only the internal features of an organism are relevant, i.e. that 'psychology ends at the skin'. What someone believes can be described without reference to the things in his or her environment. Almost the same as internalism;* see also: Solipsism; Functionalism, narrow.

Induction   The reasoning process or argument in which an empirical conclusion (a generalization) is inferred from empirical premises, that is observation statements. Unlike deduction,* induction is non-demonstrative: its conclusions are not logically certain. The conclusion of an inductive argument is *probable, supported by* the premises. It is also seen as the argument that takes you from particular statements to generalizations. See also: Abduction; Confirmation.

Inference to the Best Explanation   See: Abduction; Explanation.

Instrumentalism   The view that scientific theories, concepts and entities are instruments or convenient tools that help us to understand the world and facilitate our thinking, but do not convey literal truths and do not have ontological* import.

Intentionality   The distinguishing property of mental states or psychological phenomena, implying that they have a content, are directed at, about, or involved with objects, whereas physical things lack this property. Words, or books, are directed at, are about objects, have meaning, but they take the intentionality from mental states; they have *derived intentionality*, not *intrinsic intentionality*. Intentionality in this technical sense has little to do with being intended or on purpose; to intend to do something is one among the many manifestations of intentionality. Materialist* theories aim at naturalizing* intentionality.

Language Game   A pattern of practices, a 'form of life', which explains the meaning of interconnected expressions and concepts. It is associated with the later Wittgenstein, who compared the use of language with a game and rules. The message that the meaning of a word or an expression can never be isolated from its practical context – *meaning is use* – can also be taken to imply the relativistic* notion that expressions or beliefs derive their meanings only from the social context of language games, and that language games are a matter of (arbitrary) consensus. See also: Truth.

Language of Thought   Fodor's hypothesis that mental activity has a structure like a formal, or logical, language. Mental representations* are strings of symbols that are characterized by their syntactical* structure (see also: Solipsism, methodological). Thinking is manipulating these symbols in more or less the same way as constructing logical proofs is. The LOT hypothesis explains the *systematicity* and *productivity* of thinking: you can think infinitely many thoughts by combining a finite number of mental elements, and these thoughts cohere with each other.

Laws   A much-debated concept in the philosophy of science. Historically it suggests a lawgiver, and during the seventeenth and eighteenth centuries it was the idea that the Creator had dictated that nature should progress according to His will, and that the scientist could discover its laws. Nowadays, laws are seen as rather lawlike, empirical generalizations. Some laws are causal (e.g. Frustration leads to aggression); others are not (e.g. All swans are white). Laws may contain *unobservables*: theoretical terms that cannot be directly seen, but from which testable predictions can be derived (e.g. the unconscious; genes). See also: Cause.

Logical Positivism   See: Postivism, Logical.

Materialism   A metaphysical doctrine in philosophy that the world and all its entities and phenomena, including psychological phenomena, are manifestations of spatiotemporal matter. There are strong and more or less weak versions. The strong versions imply reductionism:* mental phenomena have to be seen as manifestations of body or brain processes and must, scientifically, be reduced to these processes. The identity theory,* physicalism* and eliminativism* are strong versions. Naturalism* might be seen as a weaker version of materialism, allowing for the non-reducibility of mental phenomena. Non-reductive materialism is also called *emergent materialism:* it holds that some objects or processes, while entirely dependent on matter, nevertheless have properties that transcend the vocabulary of physics (for example consciousness as a product of the brain). See also: Supervenience.

Metaphysics   A branch of philosophy that tries to answer questions about the general or abstract nature of reality, also about a reality that is supposed to lie behind the world and that is not accessible by scientific method. In psychology and the philosophy of mind, metaphysics includes questions about mind, consciousness,* intentionality,* qualia;* in the philosophy of science it involves questions about causality,* matter, rationalism,* etc. Metaphysics is challenged, in a sense, by positivism,* materialism,* and naturalism,* though these positions themselves are supported by metaphysical presuppositions.

Methodological Solipsism   See: Solipsism.

Model   A model is sometimes used as a synonym for a theory (as in: a model of the brain); it is mostly, however, a kind of mini-theory, usually in a more or less visual or metaphorical form.

Modularity   The idea that the mind consists of a set of more or less separate skills or special purpose processors. Fodor demands that to count as modules, processors must be informationally encapsulated, stimulus-driven and automatic, insensitive to higher cognitive processes, and probably innate and hardwired. He assumes that we also have a holistic central cognitive system operating on the symbolic inputs from the modules. The sensory systems are examples of encapsulated modules, independent of higher level cognition, translating sensory input into a symbolic code fit for the central system.

   Evolutionary psychologists propose modularity in a far looser sense, as specialized skills or cognitive tools (stereovision, cheater detection) tailored to adaptive problems, with some coordination between these skills.

   Brain imaging in neuropsychology sometimes assumes some weak sort of modularity, such that areas of the brain are interpreted as specializing for certain cognitive functions.

Multiple Realizability   See: Functionalism.

Naturalism   A claim that the methods of natural science can be applied to all phenomena, including mental processes. This can be construed as physicalism,* which holds that the concepts and methods of current physics can in the end explain everything. However, it can also mean that some phenomena, although beyond the realm of physics, can and should be investigated and explained in an objective, scientific way, i.e. not necessarily in terms of physics, though at least not contradicting physics. In psychology this suggests a broadly biological approach, considering mind as a capacity for survival, developed from animal patterns of reactivity. By extension, naturalism may imply a rejection of solipsism:* minds are capacities for coping with the environment and mental functions should be considered in relation to the organism's world. *Naturalizing*, therefore, is the name of the programme that aims at demystifying, stripping a concept or a theory of its metaphysical* content, and using for its explanation objective, scientific methods, as in naturalizing epistemology,* or naturalizing intentionality.*

Natural Kinds   The ontological* view that natural kinds are the categories that divide things in natural classes, 'carve nature at the joints' (such as gold, water, animals). Some philosophers try to relate the notion of natural kinds to essences and necessary properties (like, 'Gold has necessarily the atomic number 79'). The issue of what natural kinds are is closely related to questions of taxonomy: what should the classification of science be? For example, consider the question of whether a whale should be classified as a fish or a mammal. Some opponents of the natural kind view hold that classifications are human-made and theory-laden.*

Nomothetic   The method for finding general laws (Greek *nomos* – law), as in the positivistic* notion of explanation.* It is the opposite of the idiographic* method.

Objectivism   The view in the philosophy of science that the scientific method should be objective, that is, based on observables, empirical matters of fact; and that science is a realistic enterprise. It is a dismissive label, affiliated to positivism* and opposed to subjectivism/relativism.*

Ontology   A main branch of philosophy, concerned with the question: what kinds of things, properties and events exist (fundamentally), as furniture of the world? A traditional and popular position is materialism:* only spatiotemporal matter exists. The Cartesian position, important in psychology, is dualism,* which presupposes two principal substances: mind and matter (body). See also: Natural Kinds.

Paradigm   A concept in the philosophy of science, introduced by Kuhn. It is a whole complex of methods, concepts and theories; techniques and laboratory apparatus; social processes and institutional structures, which determine what are legitimate problems and solutions in a field of scientific research. See also: Incommensurability.

Physicalism   A reductive materialist* doctrine in the philosophy of science saying that all the sciences or scientific theories should be reduced to physics, and that only the language and methods of physics are scientifically respectable. See also: Reductionism.

Positivism, Logical   Positivism in general refers to philosophical positions that emphasize empirical data and scientific methods. Logical positivism (or neo-positivism) is mostly associated with the so-called Wiener Kreis (1920s–1930s), a group of philosophers, physicists and logicians who claimed that legitimate knowledge consists exclusively of observation sentences and logical connections between them. Statements that are not (empirically) verifiable* are meaningless nonsense or metaphysics.

Pragmatic Theory of Truth   See: Truth; Pragmatism.

Pragmatism   The philosophical view that knowledge should primarily be considered as guiding our actions in coping with the world, rather than as a theoretical set of beliefs, or a picture corresponding in some way with the world. See also: Truth; Realism.

Propositional Attitude   A mental state consisting of an attitude ('He believes', 'She expects') and a proposition ('that it is/will be raining'). Propositional attitudes make up folk psychology* (belief-desire psychology),* in the sense that mental states, such as beliefs and desires, figure as explanations of behaviour ('She buys an umbrella because she expects …') and specify mental content in the form of propositions (which happen to fit nicely in a language of thought* theory). Hence, they are closely related to issues of intentionality* and mental representation.*

Qualia   (Singular: quale) The *first-person* phenomenal qualities, experiences or feelings, such as feeling pain, seeing red wine, tasting a truffle, hearing 'God save the Queen'. Friends of qualia think that they exist, that humans/living beings do experience them, but that they are not accessible to objective, *third-person*, scientific means. Some materialists* deny the existence of qualia; others suggest they can be reduced to brain processes.

Rationalism   An answer to the epistemological* question about the origin of knowledge. Rationalists believe that knowledge is based on naturally given, *innate ideas*. The opposite position is empiricism* (or empirism).

Realism   The view that our knowledge, or scientific theories, correspond to reality. Specifying what 'correspondence' means is difficult. In the *naive* version it means something like 'mirroring' or 'copying'. *Scientific realism* holds that theories correspond to reality; that, for example, elementary particles cited in the laws of physics really exist. *Convergent realism* claims that the increased agreement between, and wider applicability of, the scientific laws (e.g. elementary physics, or evolution) indicate that they somehow approach reality. Realism is less obvious than it seems: patently false theories can be useful, and may produce correct predictions. *Internal realism* (Putnam) rejects the naive copy-theory of truth and holds that knowledge is a human creation, without being subjective. In the *pragmatic* view it is claimed that the epistemological relation to the world should not be seen as exclusively linguistic or theoretical (intellectualistic), but that in the subsequent practice of intervention, manipulation and action the world makes a difference: replies, so to say. See also: Idealism; Relativism; Truth.

Reasons   The means by which we explain, or account for, actions.* Reasons can be distinguished from causes* because actions have meanings, to be interpreted in the light of (social) contexts, that cannot be traced in the physical/physiological events and processes that cause the movements of the action. Some philosophers maintain that reasons are causes.

Reductionism   See: Eliminativism; Materialism; Physicalism.

Relativism   Holds that theories, concepts and categories are not absolutely true or valid, but are irredeemably dependent on subjective views, social contexts and historical processes: there is no such thing as objective knowledge, no knowable world independent from knowing subjects; neither are there objective criteria to assess whether one of the many possible perspectives is more warranted than another. Informally speaking, truth* is in the eye of the beholder; it all depends on how you see things. Relativists challenge realism* and the correspondence theory of truth. Relativism is related to idealism.*

Representation   Mental representation is a crucial but problematic concept in cognitive psychology. Mental states supposedly mean, refer to or stand for something else: they have mental content. The concept of mental representation is thus burdened with many of the problems of meaning and intentionality* (see also: Semantics; Propositional Attitudes). One of the problems is that mental representation runs the risk of a homunculus* pseudo-explanation. Fodor assumes that mental representations have a symbolic format, as sentences in the language of thought.* Connectionists* consider them as activation patterns in neural networks. These theories one might call a *representational theory of mind*: thinking is essentially having and manipulating representations. This constitutes an attempt to exorcize the homunculus pseudo-explanation by naturalizing* representations. Some recent developments (such as dynamic systems theory*) question the usefulness of representation as an explanatory construct in cognitive psychology.

Semantics   Concerning the *meaning* of linguistic representations* (utterances) and by extension of mental representations (thoughts). It is a deep philosophical question how words or thoughts can mean a thing in the external world; even more, how they can mean things that do not exist (e.g. how one can think of a unicorn). Some proposals suggest relations of causation or covariation between representation and referent. See also: Language Game.

Sense Data   Experiences that are, supposedly, directly *given* in the senses, such as colour or sound, and which are thus evident, indubitable, unadulterated by cognitive processing. Some empiricists* thought that sense data could and should be the foundation* of knowledge. It is doubtful whether there is such a thing as pure sense data, and even more dubitable whether they can carry the epistemological* burden that empiricism requires. See also: Theory-laden.

Social Constructionism   See: Constructionism, Social.

Solipsism   The view that only oneself and one's experiences exist and that, accordingly, one can only know what is in one's own mind. *Methodological solipsism* is associated with Fodor's philosophy of mind, implying that only the syntactical (formal) structure of mental states is of psychological importance and that their semantics, such as the reference to the world, is not relevant for explaining mental states and how they affect behaviour and other mental states: Claire's *belief* can be about an extraterrestrial and cause her *desire* to meet him, her *visiting* a secret place in a cave, and her *waiting* for what is to come; though it might well be that the creature *does not exist*. So, we should approach mental states as if they were solipsistic states. See also: Language of Thought.

Supervenience   A relation between two epistemological domains. The notion of supervenience holds that no changes can occur at the mental level without some changes at the physiological level. This means that there is no such thing as a disembodied mind (mental processes without accompanying neurophysiological processes). Supervenience nicely fits with non-reductive materialism:* it only entails a rejection of metaphysical dualism,* but does not require lawful correspondences between mind and brain; it is therefore entirely compatible with functionalism.*

Syntactical   Refers to the *form* of statements, that is, the logical or formal linguistic relations between sentences or parts thereof. See also: Semantics.

Teleology   Goal-directedness. Teleological explanations invoke *functions, goals, purposes* or *end-states* as explanations* of behaviour (e.g. a thermostat has the goal of keeping the room temperature constant; the function of the heart is to pump blood; the purpose of their making so much noise was to scare off the animals). This poses a problem for classical physics, where only causes* (events preceding the effect in time) are recognized: in teleological explanations, the effect follows the goal.

Theory   A coherent (and non-contradictory) set of statements (concepts, ideas) that organizes, predicts and explains phenomena, events, behaviour, etc. Ideally, hypotheses (testable predictions) can be derived from a theory. Theoretical terms should be unambiguously defined. A formal-logical axiomatic structure is the ideal of clarity and coherence for theories; this can be seen in mathematical theories in physics, but is almost never realized in psychology. See also Theory-Laden.

Theory-Laden   An epistemological characteristic of observations, statements, etc., meaning that they only make sense in a system or context of other beliefs, a theory, or a worldview. The idea of theory-ladenness was mainly developed in contrast to the empiricist* doctrine of neutral, objective sense data;* this doctrine was criticized for implying the 'myth of the given'. Since the idea of the 'given' proved to be untenable, the relation between the knowing subject and the known object became an issue in epistemology* and the philosophy of science, especially in the debate between relativism* on the one hand, and scientific realism* and pragmatism* on the other.

Truth   The term for the abstract concept *the* truth, as in 'The truth and nothing but the truth', as well as for the epistemological* quality of theories, beliefs, propositions, statements: 'What she says is true' or 'Which statement is true?' Realists* distinguish truth from *reality:* only conceptions, beliefs, statements, etc. *about* the reality or *about* the world can be true (or false). This realistic distinction, however, is in conflict with the relativistic* notion that thought and world are interconnected. A particular version of the abstract concept is the philosophical/epistemological problem of truth: 'What is truth, anyway?' There are different theories of truth. The *correspondence theory of truth*, which states that truth consists in the correspondence between thought and reality, is associated with realism. Critics of this theory contest the nature of the concept of correspondence, taken as a kind of *mirroring*, and they dispute the distinction between subject and object. Idealism* and relativism, therefore, adhere to the *coherence theory of truth:* the more beliefs in a system are coherent, the truer they are. Relativism also adheres to another theory, the *consensus theory of truth:* truth is what is agreed upon by common consent. Both theories of truth are criticized by realists, because the world does not play any role in the theories, and, as to the latter theory, realists do not like the idea that truth is dependent on group-think. The *pragmatic theory of truth* claims that the truth, or better the *reliability* (because truth is never absolute) of a belief cannot be conceived apart from its practical consequences, but is demonstrated in subsequent experiment, test or action. This theory is sometimes ridiculed in the phrase, 'True is what works.'

Turing Machine   The prototype of a symbol manipulator, a Turing machine can read a symbol from tape, perform an elementary operation on it, and write the result back. The English mathematician Alan Turing proved that every task that can be written as a set of elementary operations (an algorithm) can be executed on a *universal* Turing machine. This is the basis for the claim of strong AI (see: Artificial Intelligence).

Understanding/Verstehen   See: Hermeneutics.

Verification   Assessing the fit between a theory (better, the prediction generated by the theory) and empirical facts. Logical positivists* proposed *verifiability* (specification of how to find empirical facts that make rejection or acceptance of the statement possible) as the criterion for a meaningful theory (see: Demarcation).* However, it is impossible to verify general laws: they can only be confirmed or falsified.*

1 Very useful dictionaries are: Blackburn, 1996 for philosophy; Reber, 2001 for psychology.

BIBLIOGRAPHY

Ackermann, R. (1985) *Data, Instruments, and Theory: A Dialectical Approach to Understanding Science*. Princeton, NJ: Princeton University Press.

Allen, G. (1976) 'Genetics, eugenics and society: internalists and externalists in contemporary history of science', *Social Studies of Science*, 6: 105–22.

Amabile, T. (1983) *The Social Psychology of Creativity*. New York: Springer Verlag.

Amundson, R. and Lauder, G.V. (1994) 'Function without purpose: the uses of causal role function in evolutionary biology', *Biology and Philosophy*, 9: 443–69.

Anderson, J.R. (1983) *The Architecture of Cognition*. Cambridge, MA: Harvard University Press.

Anderson, R.I., Hughes, I.A. and Sharrock, W.W. (1986) *Philosophy and the Human Sciences*. London: Routledge.

Apel, K.O. (1982) 'The Erklären–Verstehen controversy in the philosophy of the natural and human sciences', in G. Fløistad (ed.), *Contemporary Philosophy, Volume 2: Philosophy of Science*. Dordrecht: Martinus Nijhoff. pp. 19–49.

Ayer, A.J. (ed.) (1959) *Logical Positivism*. New York: The Free Press.

Baker, G.P. and Hacker, R.M.S. (1984) *Language, Sense and Nonsense: A Critical Investigation into Modern Theories of Language*. Oxford: Blackwell.

Baker, L. Rudder (1987) *Saving Belief: A Critique of Physicalism*. Princeton, NJ: Princeton University Press.

Baker, L. Rudder (1995) *Explaining Attitudes*. Cambridge: Cambridge University Press.

Baritz, L. (1960) *The Servants of Power: A History of the Use of Social Science in American Industry*. Middletown, CT: Wesleyan University Press.

Barnes, B. (1977) *Interest and the Growth of Knowledge*. London: Routledge & Kegan Paul.

Barnes, B. and Bloor, D. (1982) 'Relativism, rationalism and the sociology of knowledge', in M. Hollis and S. Lukes (eds), *Rationality and Relativism*. Oxford: Blackwell. pp. 21–47.

Barnes, B., Bloor, D. and Henry, J. (1996) *Scientific Knowledge: A Sociological Analysis*. London: Athlone.

Baron-Cohen, S. (1995) *Mind-blindness*. Cambridge, MA: MIT Press.

Bates, A. and Elman, I.L. (1993) 'Connectionism and the study of change', in M.H. Johnson (ed.), *Brain Development and Cognition*. Oxford: Blackwell. pp. 625–42.

Beakley, B. and Ludlow, P. (eds) (1992) *The Philosophy of Mind*. Cambridge, MA: MIT Press.

Bechtel, W. (1985) 'Realism, instrumentalism and the intentional stance', *Cognitive Science*, 9: 473–97.

Bechtel, W. (1986) 'Teleological functional analysis and the hierarchical organization of nature', in N. Rescher (ed.), *Current Issues in Teleology*. Lanham, MD: University Press of America. pp. 26–48.

Bechtel, W. (1988a) *Philosophy of Science: An Overview for Cognitive Science*. Hillsdale, NJ: Erlbaum.

Bechtel, W. (1988b) *Philosophy of Mind: An Overview for Cognitive Science*. Hillsdale, NJ: Erlbaum.

Bechtel, W. (1990) 'Connectionism and the philosophy of mind: an overview', in W.G. Lycan (ed.), *Mind and Cognition: A Reader*. Oxford: Blackwell. pp. 252–73.

Bechtel, W. (1993) 'Decomposing intentionality: perspectives on intentionality drawn from language research with two species of chimpanzees', *Biology and Philosophy*, 8: 1–32.

Bechtel, W. (1998) 'Representations and cognitive explanations: assessing the dynamicist's challenge to cognitive science', *Cognitive Science*, 22: 295–318.

Bechtel, W. and Abrahamsen, A. (1993) 'Connectionism and folk psychology', in S.M. Christensen and D.R. Turner (eds), *Folk Psychology and the Philosophy of Mind*. Hillsdale, NJ: Erlbaum. pp. 341–67.

Bechtel, W. and Abrahamsen, A. (2002) *Connectionism and the Mind*, 2nd edn. Oxford: Blackwell.

Bechtel, W.B. and Graham, G. (eds) (1998) *A Companion to Cognitive Science*. Oxford: Blackwell.

Bechtel, W. and Mundale, J. (1999) 'Multiple realisability revisited: linking cognitive and neural sciences', *Philosophy of Science*, 66: 175–207.

Bechtel, W. and Richardson, R.C. (1993) *Discovering Complexity: Decomposition and Localization as Strategies in Scientific Research*. Princeton: Princeton University Press.

Bedau, M. (1990) 'Against mentalism in teleology', *American Philosophical Quarterly*, 27: 61–70.

Bedau, M. (2003) 'Artificial life: organisation, adaptation and complexity from the bottom up', *Trends in Cognitive Sciences*, 7: 505–12.

Beer, R.D. (1995a) 'Computational and dynamical languages for autonomous agents', in R.F. Port and T. Van Gelder (eds), *Mind as Motion*. Cambridge, MA: MIT Press. pp. 121–47.

Beer, R.D. (1995b) 'A dynamical-systems perspective on agent-environment interaction', *Artifical Intelligence*, 72: 173–216.

Beer, R.D. (2000) 'Dynamical approaches to cognitive science', *Trends in Cognitive Sciences*, 4: 91–9.

Bem, S. (1989) 'Denken om te doen. Een studie over cognitie en werkelijkheid' (Thought for action. A study of cognition and reality). Dissertation, University of Leiden.

Bem, S. and Keijzer, F. (1996) 'Recent changes in the concept of cognition', *Theory & Psychology*, 6: 449–69.

Bennett, M.R. and Hacker, P.M.S. (2003) *Philosophical Foundations of Neuroscience*. Oxford: Blackwell.

Berger, P.L. and Luckmann, T. (1967) *The Social Construction of Reality*. Harmondsworth: Penguin Books.

Bernstein, R.I. (1983) *Beyond Objectivism and Relativism: Science, Hermeneutics, and Praxis*. Oxford: Blackwell.

Bickhard, M.H. and Terveen, L. (1995) *Foundational Issues in Artificial Intelligence and Cognitive Science: Impasse and Solution*. Amsterdam: Elsevier.

Bickle, J. (1998) *Psychoneural Reduction: The New Wave*. Cambridge, MA: MIT Press.

Bickle, J. (2001) 'Understanding neural complexity: a role for reduction', *Minds and Machines*, 11: 467–81.

Bickle, J. (2002) 'Concepts structured through reductions', *Synthese*, 130: 123–33.

Bickle, J. (2003) *Philosophy and Neuroscience: A Ruthlessly Reductive Account*. Deventer: Kluwer.

Bigelow, J. and Pargetter, R. (1987) 'Functions', *Journal of Philosophy*, 84: 181–96.

Billig, M. (1987) *Arguing and Thinking: A Rhetorical Approach to Social Psychology*. Cambridge: Cambridge University Press.

Billig, M. (1990) 'Rhetoric of social psychology', in J. Parker and J. Shotter (eds), *Deconstructing Social Psychology*. London: Routledge. pp. 47–60.

Blackburn, S. (1996) *Oxford Dictionary of Philosophy*. Oxford: Oxford University Press.

Bleicher, J. (1980) *Contemporary Hermeneutics: Hermeneutics as Method, Philosophy and Critique*. London: Routledge & Kegan Paul.

Block, N. (1978) 'Troubles with functionalism', in W. Savage (ed.), *Perception and Cognition: Minnesota Studies in the Philosophy of Science*, Vol. 9. Minneapolis: University of Minnesota Press. pp. 61–325. Excerpts reprinted in Lycan (1990) and Rosenthal (1991).

Block, N. (1995) 'The mind as the software of the brain', in E. Smith and D.N. Osherson (eds), *Thinking: An Invitation to Cognitive Science*. Cambridge, MA: MIT Press. pp. 377–425.

Block, N. (1997) 'Anti-reductionism slaps back', *Philosophical Perspectives*, 11: 107–32.

Block, N., Flanagan, O. and Güzeldere, G. (eds) (1997) *The Nature of Consciousness: Philosophical Debates*. Cambridge, MA: MIT Press.

Bloom, P. and Keil, F.C. (2001) 'Thinking through language', *Mind and Language*, 16: 351–67.

Bloor, D. (1976) *Knowledge and Social Imagery*. London: Routledge & Kegan Paul. (1991, 2nd edn). Chicago: University of Chicago Press.

Blumer, H. (1969) *Symbolic Interactionism: Perspective and Method*. Englewood Cliffs, NJ: Prentice-Hall.

Bochenski, I.M. (1973) *Die zeitgenössischen Denkmethoden*, 6th edn. Bern: Francke.

Boden, M. (1972) *Purposive Explanation in Psychology*. Cambridge, MA: Harvard University Press.

Boden, M. (ed.) (1990) *The Philosophy of Artificial Intelligence*. Oxford: Oxford University Press.

Bolton, N. (1991) 'Cognitivism: a phenomenological critique', in A. Still and A. Costall (eds), *Against Cognitivism: Alternative Foundations for Cognitive Psychology*. Hemel Hempstead: Harvester Wheatsheaf. pp. 103–21.

Boorse, C. (1984) 'Wright on functions', in E. Sober (ed.), *Conceptual Issues in Evolutionary Biology: An Anthology*. Cambridge, MA: MIT Press. pp. 367–85.

Borst, C.V. (ed.) (1970) *The Mind–Brain Identity Theory*. London: Macmillan.

Boyd, R. (1984) 'On the current status of scientific realism', in I. Leplin (ed.), *Scientific Realism*. Berkeley: University of California Press. pp. 41–82. Also in Boyd et al. (1991) *The Philosophy of Science*, pp. 195–222.

Boyd, R., Gasper, P. and Trout, J.D. (eds) (1991) *The Philosophy of Science*. Cambridge, MA: MIT Press/Bradford Books.

Brandon, R.N. (1990) *Adaption and Environment*. Princeton, NJ: Princeton University Press.

Brannigan, A. (1981) *The Social Basis of Scientific Discoveries*. Cambridge: Cambridge University Press.

Brentano, F. (1924) *Psychologie vom empirischen Standpunkt*, 3 vols. Ed. Oskar Kraus. Hamburg: Meiner. Originally published 1874.

Brooks, R.A. (1991) 'Intelligence without reason', in *Proceedings of the Twelfth International Joint Conference on Artificial Intelligence*. San Mateo, CA: Kaufmann. pp. 569–95.

Brooks, R.A. (1995) 'Intelligence without representation', in G.F. Luger (ed.), *Computation and Intelligence*. Cambridge, MA: MIT Press. pp. 343–362.

Brown, H.I. (1977) *Perception, Theory and Commitment: The New Philosophy of Science*. Chicago: University of Chicago Press.

Bruner, I. (1990) *Acts of Meaning*. Cambridge, MA: Harvard University Press.

Buller, D.J. and Hardcastle, V.G. (2000) 'Evolutionary psychology, meet developmental neuro-biology: against promiscuous modularity', *Brain and Mind*, 1: 307–25.

Bunge, M. (1991–92) 'A critical examination of the new sociology of science, parts 1 and 2', *Philosophy of the Social Sciences*, 21: 524–60; 22: 46–76.

Burge, T. (1986) 'Individualism and psychology', *Philosophical Review*, 95: 3–46.

Burge, T. (1993) 'Mind–body causation and explanatory practice', in J. Heil and A. Mele (eds), *Mental Causation*. Oxford: Clarendon Press. pp. 121–36.

Burr, Vivien (1995) *An Introduction to Social Constructionism*. London: Routledge.

Buss, D.M. (1995) 'Evolutionary psychology: a new paradigm for social science', *Psychological Inquiry*, 6: 1–30.

Buss, D.M. (2000) 'The evolution of happiness', *American Psychologist*, 55: 15–23.

Buss, D.M., Hasselton, M.G., Shackelford, T.K., Bleske, A.L. and Wakefield, J.C. (1998) 'Adaptations, exaptations, and spandrels', *American Psychologist*, 53: 533–48.

Byrne, A. and Hilbert, D.R. (2003) 'Color realism and color science', *Behavioral and Brain Sciences*, 26(1): 3–63.

Cain, M.J. (2002) *Fodor: Language, Mind and Philosophy*. Cambridge: Polity.

Callebaut, W. (1993) *Taking the Naturalistic Turn: How Real Philosophy of Science is Done*. Chicago: University of Chicago Press.

Cantor, G.N. (1975) 'Phrenology in early nineteenth-century Edinburgh: an historiographical discussion', *Annals of Science*, 32: 195–208.

Carnap, R. (1931) 'Die physikalische Sprache als Universalsprache der Wissenschaft', *Erkenntnis*, 2: 432–65.

Carnap, R. (1932/1933) 'Psychologie in physikalischer Sprache', *Erkenntnis*, 3: 107–42.

Carruthers, P., Stich, S. and Siegal, M. (eds) (2002) *The Cognitive Basis of Science*. Cambridge: Cambridge University Press.

Chalmers, A. (1990) *Science and Its Fabrication*. Milton Keynes: Open University Press.

Chalmers, A.F. (2003) *What Is This Thing Called Science?* Maidenhead: OUP/McGraw-Hill.

Chalmers, D.J. (1996) *The Conscious Mind: In Search of a Fundamental Theory*. Oxford: Oxford University Press.

Chemero, A. (2000) 'Anti-representationalism and the dynamical stance', *Philosophy of Science*, 67: 466–89.

Chomsky, N. (1990) 'Linguistics and Descartes', in J.-C. Smith (ed.), *Historical Foundations of Cognitive Science*. Dordrecht: Kluwer, pp. 71–9.

Churchland, P.M. (1979) *Scientific Realism and the Plasticity of Mind*. Cambridge: Cambridge University Press.

Churchland, P.M. (1981) 'Eliminative materialism and the propositional attitudes', *Journal of Philosophy*, 78: 67–90.

Churchland, P.M. (1985a) 'Reduction, qualia, and the direct introspection of brain states', *Journal of Philosophy*, 82: 8–28.

Churchland, P.M. (1985b) 'The ontological status of observables: in praise of the superempirical virtues', in P.M. Churchland and C.A. Hooker (eds), *Images of Science: Essays on Realism and Empiricism*. Chicago: University of Chicago Press. pp. 35–47. Also in Churchland (1989a) pp. 139–51.

Churchland, P.M. (1988) *Matter and Consciousness*, 2nd edn. Cambridge, MA: MIT Press.

Churchland, P.M. (1989a) *A Neurocomputational Perspective: The Nature of Mind and the Structure of Science*. Cambridge, MA: MIT Press.

Churchland, P.M. (1989b) 'On the nature of explanation: A PDP approach', in P.M. Churchland (ed.), *A Neurocomputational Perspective: The Nature of Mind and the Structure of Science*. Cambridge, MA: MIT Press. pp. 197–253.

Churchland, P.M. (1989c) 'On the nature of theories: a neurocomputational perspective', in P.M. Churchland (ed.), *A Neurocomputational Perspective: The Nature of Mind and the Structure of Science*. Cambridge, MA: MIT Press. pp. 155–196.

Churchland, P.M. (1989d) 'Folk psychology and the explanation of human behavior', in P.M. Churchland (ed.), *A Neurocomputational Perspective: The Nature of Mind and the Structure of Science*. Cambridge, MA: MIT Press, pp. 111–127.

Churchland, P.M. (1992) 'Activation vectors versus propositional attitudes: how the brain represents reality', *Philosophy and Phenomenological Research*, 52: 419–24.

Churchland, P.M. (1995) *The Engine of Reason, the Seat of the Soul*. Cambridge, MA: MIT Press.

Churchland, P.M. (1996) 'The rediscovery of light', *Journal of Philosophy*, 93: 211–28.

Churchland, P.M. (1998) 'Conceptual similarity across sensory and neural diversity: the Fodor/LePore challenge answered', *Journal of Philosophy*, 95: 5–32.

Churchland, P.M. (2001) 'Toward a cognitive neurobiology of the moral virtues', in J. Branquinho (ed.), *The Foundations of Cognitive Science*. Oxford: Oxford University Press. pp. 77–98.

Churchland, P.M. and Churchland, P.S. (1990) 'Stalking the wild epistemic engine', in W.G. Lycan (ed.), *Mind and Cognition: A Reader*. Oxford: Blackwell. pp. 300–11.

Churchland, P.M. and Churchland, P.S. (1994) 'Intertheoretic reduction: a neuroscientist's field guide', in R. Warner and T. Szubka (eds), *The Mind-body Problem*. Oxford: Blackwell. pp. 41–54.

Churchland, P.S. (1986) *Neurophilosophy*. Cambridge, MA: MIT Press.

Churchland, P.S. (2002a) *Brain-Wise: Studies in Neurophilosophy*. Cambridge, MA: MIT Press.

Churchland, P.S. (2002b) 'Self-representation in nervous systems', *Science*, 296: 308–310.

Churchland, P.S. and Churchland, P.M. (2002) 'Neural worlds and real worlds', *Nature Reviews Neuroscience*, 3: 903–7.

Churchland, P.S. and Sejnowski, T.J. (1990) 'Neural representation and neural computation', in W.G. Lycan (ed.), *Mind and Cognition: A Reader*. Oxford: Blackwell. pp. 224–52.

Churchland, P.S. and Sejnowski, T.J. (1992) *The Computational Brain*. Cambridge, MA: MIT Press.

Clark, A. (1989) *Microcognition: Philosophy, Cognitive Science, and Parallel Distributed Processing*. Cambridge, MA: MIT Press.

Clark, A. (1993) *Associative Engines*. Cambridge, MA: MIT Press.

Clark, A. (1996a) 'Dealing in futures', in R.N. McCauley (ed.), *The Churchlands and Their Critics*, Oxford: Blackwell. pp. 86–103.

Clark, A. (1996b) 'Happy couplings: emergence and explanatory interlock', in M. Boden (ed.), *The Philosophy of Artificial Life*. Oxford: Oxford University Press. pp. 262–81.

Clark, A. (1997) *Being There: Putting Brain, Body, and World Together Again*. Cambridge, MA: Bradford/MIT Press.

Clark, A. (2001a) *Mindware: An Introduction to the Philosophy of Cognitive Science*. Oxford: Oxford University Press.

Clark, A. (2001b) 'Reasons, robots and the extended mind', *Mind and Language*, 16: 121–45.

Clark, A. and Chalmers, D. (1998) 'The extended mind', *Analysis*, 58: 7–19.

Clark, A. and Karmiloff-Smith, A. (1993) 'The cognizer's innards: a psychological and philosophical perspective on the development of thought', *Mind and Language*, 8: 487–519.

Clark, A. and Toribio, J. (1994) 'Doing without representing?', *Synthese*, 101: 401–31.

Copeland, J. (1993) *Artificial Intelligence: A Philosophical Introduction*. Oxford: Blackwell.

Copi, I.M. (1961) *Introduction to Logic*, 2nd edn. New York: Macmillan.

Cosmides, L. (1989) 'The logic of social exchange: has natural selection shaped how humans reason? Studies with the Wason selection task', *Cognition*, 31: 187–276.

Cosmides, L. and Tooby, J. (1994) 'Beyond intuition and instinct blindness: toward an evolutionary rigorous cognitive science', *Cognition*, 50: 41–77.

Cosmides, L. and Tooby, J. (1995) 'From function to structure: the role of evolutionary biology and computational theories in cognitive neuroscience', in M.S. Gazzaniga (ed.), *The Cognitive Neurosciences*. Cambridge, MA: MIT Press. pp. 1199–1210.

Costall, A. and Still, A. (1987) *Cognitive Psychology in Question*. New York: St Martin's Press.

Crane, T. (1995) *The Mechanical Mind*. Harmondsworth: Penguin Books.

Craver, C.F. (2001) 'Role functions, mechanisms and hierarchy', *Philosophy of Science*, 68: 53–74.

Crick, F. (1989) 'The recent excitement about neural networks', *Nature*, 337: 129–33.

Cummins, R. (1980) 'Functional analysis', in N. Block (ed.), *Readings in the Philosophy of Psychology*. Cambridge, MA: Harvard University Press. pp. 185–90.

Cummins, R. (1983) *The Nature of Psychological Explanation*. Cambridge, MA: MIT Press.

Cummins, R. (1989) *Meaning and Mental Representation*. Cambridge, MA: MIT Press.

Cummins, R. (2000) '"How does it work" versus "What are the laws": two conceptions of psychological explanation', in F.C. Keil and R.A. Wilson (eds), *Explanation and Cognition*. Cambridge, MA: MIT Press. pp. 117–144.

Dahlbom, B. (ed.) (1993) *Dennett and His Critics*. Oxford: Blackwell.

Damasio, A. (1994) *Descartes' Error*. New York: Putnam.

Damasio, A. (1999) *The Feeling of What Happens: Body and Emotion in the Making of Consciousness*. Orlando, FL: Harcourt Brace & Company.

Damasio, A. (2003) *Looking for Spinoza*. New York: Harcourt.

Dancy, J. (1985) *Introduction to Contemporary Epistemology*. Oxford: Blackwell.

Darnton, R. (1968) *Mesmerism and the End of Enlightenment in France*. Cambridge, MA: Harvard University Press.

Dasgupta, S. (2003) 'Multidisciplinary creativity: the case of Herbert Simon', *Cognitive Science*, 2: 683–707.

Davidson, D. (1963) 'Actions, reasons, and causes', *Journal of Philosophy*, 60: 685–700. Reprinted in Davidson (1980a).

Davidson, D. (1980a) *Essays on Actions and Events*. Oxford: Clarendon Press.

Davidson, D. (1980b) 'Mental events', in D. Davidson, *Essays on Actions and Events*. Oxford: Clarendon Press. pp. 207–27.

Davidson, D. (1981) 'The material mind', in J. Haugeland (ed.), *Mind Design*. Montgomery: Bradford. pp. 339–68.

Davidson, D. (1993) 'Thinking causes', in J. Heil and A. Mele (eds), *Mental Causation*. Oxford: Clarendon Press. pp. 3–17.

Davies, M. and Stone, T. (eds) (1995a) *Folk Psychology*. Oxford: Blackwell.

Davies, M. and Stone, T. (eds) (1995b) *Mental Simulation*. Oxford: Blackwell.

Dawkins, R. (1985) *The Blind Watchmaker*. New York: Norton.

Dawkins, R. (1989) *The Selfish Gene*, new edn. Oxford: Oxford University Press.

De Groot, A.D. (1969) *Methodology*. The Hague: Mouton.

Delanty, G. and Strydom, P. (eds) (2003) *Philosophies of Social Science: The Classic and Contemporary Readings*. Maidenhead: McGraw-Hill.

De Mey, M. (1982) *The Cognitive Paradigm*. Dordrecht: Reidel.

Demopoulos, W. (1990) 'Critical notice: Hilary Putnam's *Representation and Reality*', *Philosophy of Science*, 57: 325–33.

Dennett, D.C. (1978) *Brainstorms: Philosophical Essays on Mind and Psychology*. Brighton: Harvester.

Dennett, D.C. (1984) *Elbow Room: The Varieties of Free Will Worth Wanting*. Oxford: Oxford University Press.

Dennett, D.C. (1987) *The Intentional Stance*. Cambridge, MA: MIT Press.

Dennett, D.C. (1988) 'Quining qualia', in A. Marcel and E. Bisiach (eds), *Consciousness in Contemporary Science*. Oxford: Clarendon Press. pp. 44–62.

Dennett, D.C. (1990a) 'The myth of original intentionality', in K.A. Mohyeldin Said, W.H. Newton-Smith, R. Viale and K.V. Wilkes (eds), *Modelling the Mind*. Oxford: Clarendon Press. pp. 45–62.

Dennett, D.C. (1990b) 'Cognitive wheels', in M. Boden (ed.), *The Philosophy of Artificial Intelligence*. Oxford: Oxford University Press. pp. 147–70.

Dennett, D.C. (1990c) 'The interpretation of texts, people and other artifacts', *Philosophy and Phenomenological Research*, 50: 177–94.

Dennett, D.C. (1991a) *Consciousness Explained*. Harmondsworth: Penguin Books.

Dennett, D.C. (1991b) 'Real patterns', *Journal of Philosophy*, 88: 27–51.

Dennett, D.C. (1994) 'Real consciousness', in A. Revonsuo and M. Kappinen (eds), *Consciousness in Philosophy and Cognitive Neuroscience*. Hillsdale, NJ: Erlbaum. pp. 55–63.

Dennett, D.C. (1995) *Darwin's Dangerous Idea: Evolution and the Meaning of Life*. London: Allen Lane.

Dennett, D.C. (1996) *Kinds of Minds*. London: Weidenfeld & Nicolson.

Dennett, D.C. (2003a) *Freedom Evolves*. London: Allen Lane.

Dennett, D.C. (2003b) 'Who's on first? Heterophenomenology explained', *Journal of Consciousness Studies*, 10: 30–40.

Dennett, D.C. and Kinsbourne, M. (1992) 'Time and the observer: the where and when of consciousness in the brain', *Behavioral and Brain Sciences*, 15: 183–247.

Derksen, A.A. (1985) *Wetenschap of Willekeur: Wat is Wetenschap?* ('Science or caprice: what is science?'). Muiderberg: Coutinho.

Devitt, M. (1997) *Realism and Truth*, 2nd edn. Princeton, NJ: Princeton University Press.

Devitt, M. and Sterelny, K. (1987) *Language and Reality*. Oxford: Blackwell.

Dewey, J. (1896) 'The reflex arc concept in psychology', *Psychological Review*, 3: 357–70.

Dewey, John (1929/1988) *The Quest for Certainty: A Study of the Relation of Knowledge and Action*. Vol. 4 of *The Later Works 1925–1953*. Ed. Jo Ann Boydston. Carbondale: Southern Illinois University Press.

Diggins, J.P. (1994) *The Promise of Pragmatism: Modernism and the Crisis of Knowledge and Authority*. Chicago: University of Chicago Press.

Donald, M.S. (1991) *Origins of the Modern Mind*. Cambridge, MA: Harvard University Press.

Dretske, F. (1981) *Knowledge and the Flow of Information*. Cambridge, MA: MIT Press/Bradford Book.

Dretske, F. (1988) *Explaining Behavior: Reasons in a World of Causes*. Cambridge, MA: MIT Press.

Dretske, F. (1991) 'The intentionality of cognitive states', in D.M. Rosenthal (ed.), *The Nature of Mind*. New York/Oxford: Oxford University Press. pp. 354–62.

Dretske, F. (1993) 'Conscious experience', *Mind*, 104: 263–83.

Dretske, F. (1995) *Naturalizing the Mind*. Cambridge, MA: MIT Press.

Dreyfus, H.L. (1979) *What Computers Can't Do*, 2nd edn. New York: Harper & Row.

Dreyfus, H.L. (1980) 'Holism and hermeneutics', *Review of Metaphysics*, 34: 3–23.

Dreyfus, H.L. (2001) *On the Internet*. London: Routledge.

Dreyfus, H.L. and Dreyfus, S.E. (1987) 'How to stop worrying about the frame problem even though it is computationally insoluable', in Z.W. Pylyshyn (ed.), *The Robot's Dilemma: The Frame Problem in Artificial Intelligence*. Norwood, NJ: Ablex. pp. 95–112.

Dreyfus, H.L. and Dreyfus, S.E. (1990) 'Making a mind versus modelling the brain: artificial intelligence back at a branch-point', in M.A. Boden (ed.), *The Philosophy of Artificial Intelligence*. Oxford: Oxford University Press. pp. 309–33.

Elias, N., Martins, H. and Whitley, R. (eds) (1982) *Scientific Establishments and Hierarchies*. Dordrecht: Reidel.

Eliasmith, C. (1996) 'The third contender: a critical examination of the dynamicist theory of cognition', *Philosophical Psychology*, 9: 441–63.

Eliasmith, C. (1997) 'Computation and dynamical models of mind', *Minds and Machines*, 7: 531–41.

Eliasmith, C. (2001) 'Attractive and in-discrete', *Minds and Machines*, 11: 417–26.

Elman, J.L. (1992) 'Grammatical structure and distributed representations', in S. Davis (ed.), *Connectionism: Theory and Practice*. New York: Oxford University Press. pp. 139–78.

Elman, J.L., Bates, E.A., Johnson, M.H., Karmiloff-Smith, A., Parisi, D. and Plunkett, K. (1996) *Rethinking Innateness*. Cambridge, MA: MIT Press.

Enc, B. and Adams, F. (1992) 'Functions and goal directedness', *Philosophy of Science*, 59: 635–54.

Farr, R.M. and Moscovici, S. (eds) (1984) *Social Representations*. Cambridge: Cambridge University Press.

Faust, D. (1984) *The Limits of Scientific Reasoning*. Minneapolis: University of Minnesota Press.

Feigl, H. (1967) *The 'Mental' and the 'Physical'*. Minneapolis: University of Minnesota Press. Originally published 1958.

Feyerabend, P. (1968) 'How to be a good empiricist – a plea for tolerance in matters epistemological', in P.H. Nidditch (ed.), *The Philosophy of Science*. Oxford: Oxford University Press. pp. 12–39.

Feyerabend, P. (1975) *Against Method*. London: Verso.

Feyerabend, P. (1978) *Science in a Free Society*. London: NLB.

Feyerabend, P. (1980) *Erkenntnis für freie Menschen*. Frankfurt am Main: Suhrkamp.

Fisch, R. (1977) 'Psychology of science', in I. Spiegel-Rösing and D. de Solla Price (eds), *Science, Technology and Society: A Cross-disciplinary Perspective*. London: Sage.

Fiske, S.T. and Taylor, S.E. (1984) *Social Cognition*. New York: Random House.

Flanagan, O. (1991) *The Science of the Mind*, 2nd edn. Cambridge, MA: MIT Press.

Flanagan, O. (1992) *Consciousness Reconsidered*. Cambridge, MA: MIT Press.

Fleck, L. (1979) *Genesis and Development of a Scientific Fact*. Chicago: University of Chicago Press. Originally: *Entstehung und Entwicklung einer wissenschaftlichen Tatsache*, 1935; new edn, 1980, Frankfurt am Main: Suhrkamp.

Fodor, J. (1968) *Psychological Explanation: An Introduction to the Philosophy of Psychology*. New York: Random House.

Fodor, J. (1975) *The Language of Thought*. New York: Crowell.

Fodor, J. (1980) 'Methodological solipsism considered as a research strategy in cognitive psychology', *Behavioral and Brain Sciences*, 3: 63–109.

Fodor, J. (1981a) 'Introduction', in J. Fodor, *Representations: Philosophical Essays on the Foundations of Cognitive Science*. Hassocks: Harvester. pp. 1–21.

Fodor, J. (1981b) 'Special sciences', in J. Fodor, *Representations: Philosophical Essays on the Foundations of Cognitive Science*. Hassocks: Harvester. pp. 127–45.

Fodor, J. (1981c) 'Computation and reduction', in J. Fodor, *Representations: Philosophical Essays on the Foundations of Cognitive Science*. Hassocks: Harvester. pp. 146–74.

Fodor, J. (1981d) 'Propositional attitudes', in J. Fodor, *Representations: Philosophical Essays on the Foundations of Cognitive Science*. Hassocks: Harvester. pp. 177–203.

Fodor, J. (1981e) 'The mind–body problem', *Scientific American*, 244(1): 124–32.

Fodor, J. (1984) *The Modularity of Mind*. Cambridge, MA: MIT Press.

Fodor, J. (1987a) 'Modules, fridgeons, sleeping dogs, and the music of the spheres', in Z.W. Pylyshyn (ed.), *The Robot's Dilemma: The Frame Problem in Artificial Intelligence*. Norwood, NJ: Ablex. pp. 139–49.

Fodor, J. (1987b) *Psychosemantics*. Cambridge, MA: MIT Press.

Fodor, J. (1990a) 'Making mind matter more', in J. Fodor, *A Theory of Content and Other Essays*. Cambridge, MA: MIT Press. pp. 137–59.

Fodor, J. (1990b) 'Why there still has to be a language of thought', in W.G. Lycan (ed.), *Mind and Cognition: A Reader*. Oxford: Blackwell. pp. 282–99.

Fodor, J. (1991) 'A modal argument for narrow content', *Journal of Philosophy*, 88: 2–26.

Fodor, J. (1994) *The Elm and the Expert*. Cambridge, MA: MIT Press.

Fodor, J. (1997a) 'Connectionism and the problem of systematicity (continued): why Smolensky's solution still doesn't work', *Cognition*, 62: 109–19.

Fodor, J. (1997b) 'Special sciences: still autonomous after all these years', *Philosophical Perspectives*, 11: 149–63.

Fodor, J. (2000a) *The Mind Doesn't Work That Way*. Cambridge, MA: MIT Press.

Fodor, J. (2000b) 'Why we are so good at catching cheaters', *Cognition*, 75: 29–32.

Fodor, J. (2001) 'Language, thought and compositionality', *Mind and Language*, 16: 1–15.

Fodor, J. and McLaughlin, B. (1990) 'Connectionism and the problem of systematicity: why Smolensky's solution does not work', *Cognition*, 35: 183–204.

Fodor, J. and Pylyshyn, Z.W. (1988) 'Connectionism and cognitive architecture', *Cognition*, 28: 3–71.

Frank, R.H. (1990) 'A theory of moral sentiments', in J.J. Mansbridge (ed.), *Beyond Self-interest*. Chicago: Unversity of Chicago Press. pp. 71–98.

Frankfurt, H.G. (1971) 'Freedom of the will and the concept of a person', *Journal of Philosophy*, 68: 5–20.

Franklin, S. (1995) *Artificial Minds*. Cambridge, MA: MIT Press.

Frawley, W. (1997) *Vygotsky and Cognitive Science*. Cambridge, MA: Harvard University Press.

Friedman, M. (1991) 'The re-evaluation of logical positivism', *Journal of Philosophy*, 88: 505–19.

Fuller, S. (1989) *Philosophy of Science and its Discontents*. Boulder, CO: Westview Press.

Fuller, S., De Mey, M., Shinn, T. and Woolgar, S. (eds) (1983) *The Cognitive Turn: Sociological and Psychological Perspectives on Science*. Dordrecht: Kluwer.

Gadamer, H.G. (1960) *Wahrheit und Methode*. Tübingen: Mohr. Trans. and ed. G. Barden and J. Cumming as *Truth and Method* (1975). New York: Seabury.

Gallagher, S. (2000) 'Philosophical conceptions of the self: implications for cognitive science', *Trends in Cognitive Sciences*, 4: 14–21.

Gardner, H. (1987) *The Mind's New Science: A History of the Cognitive Revolution*, 2nd edn. New York: Basic Books.

Geertz, C. (1973) *The Interpretation of Cultures*. New York: Basic Books.

Gellner, E. (1974) *Legitimation of Belief*. Cambridge: Cambridge University Press.

Gellner, E. (1982) 'Relativism and universals', in M. Hollis and S. Lukes (eds), *Rationality and Relativism*. Oxford: Basil Blackwell. pp. 181–200.

Gergen, K.J. (1980) 'Towards intellectual audacity in social psychology', in R. Gilmour and S. Duck (eds), *The Development of Social Psychology*. London: Academic Press. pp. 239–70.

Gergen, K.J. (1985a) 'The social constructionist movement in modern psychology', *American Psychologist*, 40: 266–75.

Gergen, K.J. (1985b) 'Social constructionist inquiry: context and implications', in K.J. Gergen and K.E. Davis, *The Social Construction of the Person*. New York: Springer Verlag. pp. 3–18.

Gergen, K.J. (1989) 'Social psychology and the wrong revolution', *European Journal of Social Psychology*, 19: 463–84.

Gergen, K.J. (1997) 'The place of the psyche in a constructed world', *Theory & Psychology*, 7: 723–46.

Gergen, K.J. (1999) *An Invitation to Social Construction*. London: Sage.

Geuter, U. (1992) *The Professionalization of Psychology in Nazi Germany*. Cambridge: Cambridge University Press. Originally, *Die Professionalisierung der deutschen Psychologie im Nationalsozialismus*. Frankfurt: Suhrkamp, 1984.

Gholson, B., Shadish, W.R., Neimeyer, R.A. and Houts, A.C. (eds) (1989) *Psychology of Science: Contributions to Metascience*. Cambridge: Cambridge University Press.

Gibson, J.J. (1979) *The Ecological Approach to Visual Perception*. Boston, MA: Houghton Mifflin.

Goldman, A.I. (ed.) (1993) *Readings in Philosophy and Cognitive Science*. Cambridge, MA: MIT Press.

Goodale, M.A. (2000) 'Perception and action in the human visual system', in M.S. Gazzaniga (ed.), *The Cognitive Neurosciences*, 2nd edn. Cambridge: MIT Press. pp. 365–77.

Gooding, D., Pinch, T.J. and Schaffer, S. (eds) (1989) *The Uses of Experiment: Studies in the Natural Sciences*. Cambridge: Cambridge University Press.

Gopnik, A. and Wellman, H. (1994) 'The theory theory', in L.A. Hirschfeld and S.A. Gelman (eds), *Mapping the Mind: Domain Specificity in Cognition and Culture*. Cambridge: Cambridge University Press. pp. 257–93.

Gould, S. and Lewontin, R. (1979) 'The spandrels of San Marco and the Panglossian paradigm: critique of the adaptationist programme', *Proceedings of the Royal Society of London*, B205: 581–98.

Gower, B. (1997) *Scientific Method*. London: Routledge.

Greenwood, J.D. (1991a) *The Future of Folk Psychology*. Cambridge: Cambridge University Press.

Greenwood, J.D. (1991b) *Relations and Representation: An Introduction to the Philosophy of Social Psychological Science*. London: Routledge.

Greenwood, J.D. (1994) *Realism, Identity and Emotion: Reclaiming Social Psychology*. London: Sage.

Gross, Paul R. and Levitt, Norman (1994) *Higher Superstition: The Academic Left and its Quarrels with Science*. Baltimore, MD: Johns Hopkins University Press.

Gross, Paul R., Levitt, Norman and Lewis, Martin W. (eds) (1996) *The Flight from Science and Reason*. New York: Academy of Sciences.

Gruber, H.E. (1974) *Darwin on Man: A Psychological Study of Scientific Creativity*. New York: Dutton.

Grush, R. and Churchland, P.S. (1995) 'Gaps in Penrose's toilings', *Journal of Consciousness Studies*, 2: 10–29.

Guttenplan, S. (ed.) (1994) *A Companion to the Philosophy of Mind*. Oxford: Blackwell.

Habermas, J. (1971) *Toward a Rational Society: Student Protest, Science, and Politics*. Trans. J.J. Shapiro. London: Heinemann (includes the essay 'Technik und Wissenschaft als "Ideologie"').

Habermas, J. (1984) *The Theory of Communicative Action*, 2 Vols. Cambridge: Cambridge University Press. Originally *Theorie des kommunikativen Handelns*, 2 Vols. Frankfurt am Main: Suhrkamp, 1981.

Hacking, I. (ed.) (1981) *Scientific Revolutions*. Oxford: Oxford University Press.

Hacking, I. (1983) *Representing and Intervening: Introductory Topics in the Philosophy of Natural Science*. Cambridge: Cambridge University Press.

Hacking, I. (1992) 'The self-vindication of the laboratory sciences', in A. Pickering (ed.), *Science as Practice and Culture*. Chicago: University of Chicago Press. pp. 29–64.

Hacking, I. (1999) *The Social Construction of What?* Cambridge, MA: Harvard University Press.

Hahn, R. (1971) *The Anatomy of a Scientific Institution: The Paris Academy of Sciences, 1666–1803*. Berkeley and Los Angeles: University of California Press.

Hameroff, S. and Penrose, R. (1996) 'Conscious events as orchestrated space-time selections', *Journal of Consciousness Studies*, 3: 36–53.

Hanson, N.R. (1958) *Patterns of Discovery: An Inquiry into the Conceptual Foundations of Science*. Cambridge: Cambridge University Press.

Hardcastle, V.G. (1998) 'On the matter of minds and mental causation', *Philosophy and Phenomenological Research*, 58: 1–25.

Harman, G. (1988) 'Wide functionalism', in S. Schiffer and S. Steele (eds), *Cognition and Representation*. Boulder, CO: Westview Press. pp. 11–20.

Harnish, R.M. (ed.) (1994) *Basic Topics in the Philosophy of Language*. New York: Harvester.

Haselager, W.F.G. (1995) 'The right frame of mind: cognitive science, folk psychology and the frame problem'. Dissertation, Free University of Amsterdam.

Haugeland, J. (ed.) (1981) *Mind Design*. Montgomery, VT: Bradford Books.

Haugeland, J. (1991) 'Representational genera', in W. Ramsey, S.P. Stich and D.E. Rumelhart (eds), *Philosophy and Connectionist Theory*. Hillsdale, NJ: Erlbaum. pp. 61–89.

Hawking, S. (1988) *A Brief History of Time*. Toronto: Bantam.

Heil, J. (1992) *The Nature of True Minds*. Cambridge: Cambridge University Press.

Heil, J. and Mele, A. (eds) (1993) *Mental Causation*. Oxford: Clarendon Press.

Heal, J. (2003) *Mind, Reason and Imagination*. Cambridge: Cambridge University Press.

Held, D. (1980) *Introduction to Critical Theory: Horkheimer to Habermas*. London: Hutchinson.

Hempel, C.G. (1965) 'Aspects of scientific explanation', in C.G. Hempel (ed.), *Aspects of Scientific Explanation*. New York: The Free Press. pp. 331–496.

Hempel, C.G. (1966) *Philosophy of Natural Science*. Englewood Cliffs, NJ: Prentice-Hall.

Hempel, C.G. and Oppenheim, P. (1948/1965) 'Studies in the logic of explanation', in C.G. Hempel (ed.), *Aspects of Scientific Explanation*. New York: The Free Press. pp. 245–90.

Hesse, M. (1980) *Revolutions and Reconstructions in the Philosophy of Science*. Brighton: Harvester Press.

Hobbes, Thomas (1651/1968) *Leviathan*. Edited by C.B. Macpherson. Harmondsworth: Penguin Books.

Holland, J.H., Holyoak, K.J., Nisbet, R.E. and Thagard, P.R. (1986) *Induction*. Cambridge, MA: MIT Press.

Hollinger, R. (ed.) (1985) *Hermeneutics and Praxis*. Notre Dame, IN: University of Notre Dame Press.

Hollis, M. and Lukes, S. (1982) *Rationality and Relativism*. Oxford: Blackwell.

Horgan, T. and Tienson, J. (1996) *Connectionism and the Philosophy of Psychology*. Cambridge, MA: MIT Press.

Houts, A.C. (1989) 'Contributions of the psychology of science to metascience: a call for explorers', in B. Gholson, W.R. Shadish, R.A. Neimeyer and A.C. Houts (eds), *Psychology of Science: Contributions to Metascience*. Cambridge: Cambridge University Press. pp. 47–88.

Hughes, J. (1990) *The Philosophy of Social Research*, 2nd edn. London: Longman.

Hume, D. (1748/1963) *Enquiry Concerning the Human Understanding*. Ed. L.A. Selby-Bigge. London: Oxford University Press.

Hume, D. (1739–40/1969) *A Treatise of Human Nature*. Ed. E.C. Mossner. Harmondsworth: Penguin.

Husserl, E. (1970) *The Crisis of European Sciences and Transcendental Phenomenology*. Evanston, IL: Northwestern University Press.

Hutchins, E. (1995) *Cognition in the Wild*. Cambridge, MA: MIT Press.

Hyland, M. (1981) *Introduction to Theoretical Psychology*. London: Macmillan.

Irzik, G. and Grunberg, T. (1995) 'Carnap and Kuhn: arch enemies or close allies?', *British Journal for the Philosophy of Science*, 46: 285–307.

Jackson, F. (1990) 'Epiphenomenal qualia', in W.G. Lycan (ed.), *Mind and Cognition: A Reader*. Oxford: Blackwell. pp. 469–77.

Jacob, F. (1977) 'Evolution and tinkering', *Science*, 196: 1161–6.

Jacob, P. (1997) *What Minds Can Do: Intentionality in a Non-intentional World*. Cambridge: Cambridge University Press.

James, William (1907/1975) *Pragmatism and the Meaning of Truth*. Introduction by A.J. Ayer. Cambridge, MA: Harvard University Press.

Janik, A. and Toulmin, S. (1973) *Wittgenstein's Vienna*. New York: Simon and Schuster.

Jarvie, I.C. (1993) 'Relativism yet again', *Philosophy of the Social Sciences*, 23: 537–47.

Jay, M. (1973) *The Dialectical Imagination: A History of the Frankfurt School and the Institute of Social Research, 1923–1950*. Boston, MA: Little, Brown.

Jeannerod, M. (2001) 'Neural simulation of action: a unifying mechanism for motor cognition', *NeuroImage*, 14: S103–S109.

Jeannerod, M. (2003) 'The mechanism of self-recognition in humans', *Behavioral Brain Research*, 142: 1–15.

Johnson, M. (1987) *The Body in the Mind: The Bodily Basis of Meaning, Imagination, and Reason*. Chicago: University of Chicago Press.

Joravski, D. (1989) *Soviet Psychology*. Oxford: Blackwell.

Kantorovich, A. (1993) *Scientific Discovery: Logic and Tinkering*. Albany, NY: State University of New York Press.

Kearns, J.T. (1997) 'Thinking machines: some fundamental confusions', *Minds and Machines*, 7: 269–87.

Keijzer, F.A. (2001) *Representation and Behaviour*. Cambridge, MA: MIT Press.

Keijzer, F.A. and Bem, S. (1996) 'Behavioral systems interpreted as autonomous agents and as coupled dynamical systems: a criticism', *Philosophical Psychology*, 9: 323–46.

Kettler, D., Meja, V. and Stehr, N. (1984) *Karl Mannheim*. Chichester: Ellis Horwood.

Kim, J. (1992) '"Downward causation" in emergentism and nonreductive physicalism', in A. Beckermann, H. Flohr and J. Kim (eds), *Emergence or Reduction? Essays on the Prospects of Nonreductive Physicalism*. Berlin: De Gruyter. pp. 119–38.

Kim, J. (1993) *Supervenience and Mind*. Cambridge: Cambridge University Press.

Kim, J. (1996) *Philosophy of Mind*. Boulder, CO: Westview.

Kim, J. (1998) *Mind in a Physical World*. Cambridge, MA: MIT Press.

Kim, J. (1999) 'Making sense of emergence', *Philosophical Studies*, 95: 3–36.

Kindi, V.P. (1995) 'Kuhn's *The Structure of Scientific Revolutions* revisited', *Journal for General Philosophy of Science*, 26: 75–92.

Kirsh, D. (1991) 'Today the earwig, tomorrow man?', in M. Boden (ed.), *The Philosophy of Artificial Life*. Oxford: Oxford University Press. pp. 237–61.

Kirshner, D. and Whitson, J.A. (eds) (1997) *Situated Cognition: Social, Semiotic, and Psychological Perspectives*. Mahwah, NJ: Erlbaum.

Kitcher, P.S. (1993) *The Advancement of Science*. Oxford: Oxford University Press.

Klahr, D. and Dunbar, K. (1988) 'Dual space search during scientific reasoning', *Cognitive Science*, 12: 1–48.

Klee, R. (1997) *Introduction to the Philosophy of Science*. Oxford: Oxford University Press.

Knorr-Cetina, K.D. (1981) *The Manufacture of Knowledge: An Essay on the Constructivist and Contextual Nature of Science*. Oxford: Pergamon Press.

Knorr-Cetina, K.D. (1983) 'The ethnographic study of scientific work: towards a constructivist interpretation of science', in K.D. Knorr-Cetina and M. Mulkay (eds), *Science Observed: Perspectives on the Social Study of Science*. London: Sage. pp. 115–40.

Knorr-Cetina, K.D. and Mulkay, M. (eds) (1983) *Science Observed: Perspectives on the Social Study of Science*. London: Sage.

Kornblith, H. (ed.) (1994) *Naturalizing Epistemology*, 2nd edn. Cambridge, MA: MIT Press/Bradford.

Kripke, S. (1980) *Naming and Necessity*, revised edn. Oxford: Blackwell. Originally published 1972.

Krohn, W., Layton, E.T. and Weingart, P. (eds) (1978) *The Dynamics of Science and Technology: Social Values, Technical Norms and Scientific Criteria in the Development of Knowledge: Sociology of the Sciences Yearbook*, Vol. II. Dordrecht: Reidel.

Kruglanski, A.W. (1991) 'Social science-based understandings of science: reflections on Fuller', *Philosophy of the Social Sciences*, 21: 223–31.

Kuhn, T.S. (1962) *The Structure of Scientific Revolutions*, (1970) 2nd, enlarged edn. Chicago: University of Chicago Press.

Kulkarni, D. and Simon, H.A. (1988) 'The process of scientific discovery: the strategy of experimentation', *Cognitive Science*, 12: 139–75.

Kukla, A. (2001) *Methods of Theoretical Psychology*. Cambridge, MA: MIT Press.

Laland, K.N. and Brown, G.R. (2002) *Sense and Nonsense: Evolutionary Perspectives on Human Behaviour*. Oxford: Oxford University Press.

Lakatos, I. (1970) 'Falsification and the methodology of scientific research programmes', in I. Lakatos and A. Musgrave (eds), *Criticism and the Growth of Knowledge*. Cambridge: Cambridge University Press. pp. 91–196.

Lakoff, G. (1987) *Women, Fire, and Dangerous Things: What Categories Reveal about the Mind.* Chicago: University of Chicago Press.

Lakoff, G. and Johnson, M. (1980) *Metaphors We Live By.* Chicago: University of Chicago Press.

Lakoff, G. and Johnson, M. (1999) *Philosophy in the Flesh: The Embodied Mind and Its Challenge to Western Thought.* New York: Basic Books.

Langton, C.A. (1989) 'Artificial life', in C.A. Langton (ed.), *Artificial Life: Proceedings of an Interdisciplinary Workshop on the Synthesis and Simulation of Living Systems.* Redwood City, CA: Addison-Wesley. pp. 1–47.

Langton, C.A. (1996) 'Artificial Life', in M. Boden (ed.), *The Philosophy of Artificial Life.* Oxford: Oxford University Press (an updated version of Langton, 1989). pp. 39–94.

Larkin, P. (1988) 'Continuing to live', in P. Larkin, *Collected Poems.* London: Faber & Faber.

Latour, B. (1987) *Science in Action: How to Follow Scientists and Engineers through Society.* Milton Keynes: Open University Press.

Latour, B. and Woolgar, S. (1979) *Laboratory Life: The Social Construction of Scientific Facts.* London: Sage.

Laudan, L. (1981) 'The pseudo-science of science?', *Philosophy of the Social Sciences*, 11: 173–98.

Laudan, L. (1990) *Science and Relativism.* Chicago: University of Chicago Press.

Laudan, L. (1991) 'A confutation of convergent realism', in R. Boyd, P. Gasper and J.D. Trout (eds), *The Philosophy of Science.* Cambridge, MA: MIT/Bradford Books. pp. 223–45.

Laudan, L. (1996) *Beyond Positivism and Relativism.* Boulder, CO: Westview Press.

Lave, J. (1988) *Cognition in Practice: Mind, Mathematics and Culture in Everyday Life.* Cambridge: Cambridge University Press.

Leahey, T.H. (2001) *A History of Modern Psychology.* Upper Saddle River, NJ: Prentice-Hall.

Leahey, T.H. (2004) *A History of Psychology*, 6th edn. Englewood Cliffs, NJ: Prentice-Hall.

Leplin, J. (ed.) (1984) *Scientific Realism.* Berkeley: University of California Press.

LePore, E. and Van Gulick, R. (eds) (1991) *John Searle and His Critics.* Oxford: Blackwell.

Leslie, A. (1994) 'ToMM, ToBY, and agency: core architecture and domain specificity', in L.A. Hirschfeld and S.A. Gelman (eds), *Mapping the Mind: Domain Specificity in Cognition and Culture.* Cambridge: Cambridge University Press. pp. 119–48.

Lessnof, M. (1974) *The Structure of Social Science.* London: Allen & Unwin.

Lewontin, R.C. (1998) 'The evolution of cognition: questions we will never answer', in D. Scarborough and S. Sternberg (eds), *An Invitation to Cognitive Science. Vol. 4: Methods, Models and Conceptual Issues.* Cambridge, MA: MIT Press. pp. 107–32.

Lloyd, E.A. (1999) 'Evolutionary psychology: the burdens of proof', *Biology and Philosophy*, 14: 211–33.

Locke, John (1690/1959) *An Essay Concerning Human Understanding.* Ed. A.C. Fraser. New York: Dover Publications.

Loewer, B. and Rey, G. (eds) (1991) *Meaning in Mind: Fodor and His Critics.* Oxford: Blackwell.

Looren de Jong, H. (1991) 'Intentionality and the ecological approach', *Journal for the Theory of Social Behavior*, 21: 91–110.

Looren de Jong, H. (1995) 'Ecological psychology and naturalism: Heider, Gibson and Marr', *Theory & Psychology*, 5: 251–69.

Looren de Jong, H. (2003) 'Causal and functional explanations', *Theory & Psychology*, 13: 311–37.

Looren de Jong, H. and Steen, W.J. Van der (1998) 'Biological thinking in evolutionary psychology: rockbottom or quicksand?', *Philosophical Psychology*, 11: 183–205.

Losee, J. (2001) *A Historical Introduction to the Philosophy of Science*, 4th edn. Oxford: Oxford University Press.

Lycan, W.G. (1987) *Consciousness.* Cambridge, MA: MIT Press.

Lycan, W.G. (ed.) (1990) *Mind and Cognition: A Reader.* Oxford: Blackwell.

Lyons, W. (1995) *Approaches to Intentionality.* Oxford: Oxford University Press.

McCauley, R.N. (ed.) (1996) *The Churchlands and Their Critics*. Oxford: Blackwell.

McDonough, R. (1989) 'Towards a non-mechanistic theory of meaning', *Mind*, 98: 1–21.

McDowell, John (1994) *Mind and World*. Cambridge, MA: Harvard University Press.

McFee, G. (2000) *Free Will*. Teddington: Acumen Publishing.

McGinn, C. (1991a) *The Problem of Consciousness*. Oxford: Blackwell.

McGinn, C. (1991b) 'Consciousness and content', in R.J. Bogdan (ed.), *Mind and Common Sense*. Cambridge: Cambridge University Press. pp. 71–92.

McGinn, C. (1999) *The Mysterious Flame*. New York: Basic Books.

Magnani, L., Nersessian, N.J. and Thagard, P. (eds) (1999) *Model-based Reasoning in Scientific Discovery*. New York/Dordrecht: Kluwer Academic/Plenum Publishers.

Mahoney, M. (1976) *Scientist as Subject: The Psychological Imperative*. Cambridge, MA: Ballinger.

Malcolm, N. (1971) *Problems of Mind*. London: Allen & Unwin.

Mannheim, K. (1936) *Ideology and Utopia*. London: Routledge & Kegan Paul.

Manuel, F. (1968) *A Portrait of Isaac Newton*. Cambridge, MA: Harvard University Press.

Marcus, G.F. (1998) 'Can connectionism save constructivism?', *Cognition*, 66: 153–82.

Marcuse, H. (1964) *One Dimensional Man: Studies in the Ideology of Advanced Industrial Society*. Boston, MA: Beacon Press.

Margolis, J. (1986) *Pragmatism without Foundations: Reconciling Realism and Relativism*. New York: Blackwell.

Margolis, H. (1987) *Patterns, Thinking and Cognition*. Chicago: University of Chicago Press.

Marr, D. (1982) *Vision*. San Francisco: Freeman.

Masterman, M. (1970) 'The nature of a paradigm', in I. Lakatos and A. Musgrave (eds), *Criticism and the Growth of Knowledge*. Cambridge: Cambridge University Press. pp. 59–89.

Maynard-Smith, J. (2000) 'The concept of information in biology', *Philosophy and Science*, 67: 177–94.

Mayr, E. (1988) 'How to carry out the adaptationist program', in E. Mayr, *Toward a New Philosophy of Biology*. Cambridge: Belknap. pp. 148–59.

Mayr, E. (1992) 'The idea of teleology', *Journal of the History of Ideas*, 55: 117–35.

Mead, G.H. (1934) *Mind, Self, and Society*. Chicago: University of Chicago Press.

Meijering, T.C. (2000) 'Physicalism and downward causation in psychology and the special sciences', *Inquiry*, 43: 181–202.

Meja, V. and Stehr, N. (eds) (1984) *The Sociology of Knowledge Dispute*. London: Routledge & Kegan Paul. Originally *Der Streit um die Wissenssoziologie*. Frankfurt: Suhrkamp, 1982.

Mendelsohn, E., Weingart, R. and Whitley, R. (eds) (1977) *The Social Production of Scientific Knowledge: Sociology of the Sciences Yearbook*, Vol. I. Dordrecht: Reidel.

Merleau-Ponty, M. (1945) *Phénoménologie de la perception*. Paris: Gallimard. English trans. *The Phenomenology of Perception*. London: Routledge & Kegan Paul, 1962.

Merton, R.K. (1970) 'Science, technology and society in seventeenth-century England', *Osiris*, 4(2). Reprinted with new preface, New York: Harper & Row.

Metzinger, T. (ed.) (1995) *Conscious Experience*. Paderborn: Schöningh.

Millikan, R.G. (1989) 'Biosemantics', *Journal of Philosophy*, 86: 281–97.

Mitchell, S.D. (1995) 'Function, fitness and disposition', *Biology and Philosophy*, 10: 39–54.

Moya, C.J. (1990) *The Philosophy of Action*. Cambridge: Polity Press.

Mulkay, M., Potter, J. and Yearly, S. (1983) 'Why an analysis of scientific discourse is needed', in K.D. Knorr-Cetina and M. Mulkay (eds), *Science Observed: Perspectives on the Social Study of Science*. London: Sage. pp. 171–204.

Nagel, E. (1961) *The Structure of Science*. London: Routledge & Kegan Paul.

Nagel, E. (1984) 'The structure of teleological explanations', in E. Sober (ed.), *Conceptual Issues in Evolutionary Biology*. Cambridge, MA: MIT Press. pp. 319–46.

Nagel, T. (1980) 'What is it like to be a bat?', in N. Block (ed.), *Readings in the Philosophy of Psychology*, Vol. 1. London: Methuen. pp. 159–68.

Napoli, D.S. (1981) *Architects of Adjustment: The History of the Psychological Profession in the United States*. Port Washington, NY: Kennikat Press.

Nersessian, N.J. (1992) 'How do scientists think? Capturing the dynamics of conceptual change in science', in R. Giere (ed.), *Cognitive Models of Science: Minnesota Studies in the Philosophy of Science*, Vol. 15. Minneapolis, MN: University of Minnesota Press.

Newell, A. (1980) 'Physical symbol systems', *Cognitive Science*, 4: 135–83.

Newell, A. (1992) 'Precis of Unified theories of cognition', *The Behavioral and Brain Sciences*, 15: 425–92.

Newell, A. and Simon, H.A. (1981) 'Computer science as an empirical enquiry: symbols and search', in J. Haugeland (ed.), *Mind Design*. Montgomery: Bradford. pp. 35–66.

Newton-Smith, W. (1982) 'Relativism and the possibility of interpretation', in M. Hollis and S. Lukes (eds), *Rationality and Relativism*. Oxford: Blackwell.

Newton-Smith, W.H. (ed.) (2000) *A Companion to the Philosophy of Science*. Oxford: Blackwell.

Nichols, S. and Stich, S.P. (2003) *Mindreading*. Oxford: Clarendon Press.

Nickles, T. (1980) 'Scientific discovery and the future of philosophy of science: introductory essay', in T. Nickles, *Scientific Discovery, Logic, and Rationality*. Dordrecht: Reidel. pp. 1–59.

Nisbett, R.E. and Wilson, D. (1977) 'Telling more than we can know: verbal reports on mental processes', *Psychological Review*, 84: 231–59.

Noble, D. (1990) 'Biological explanation and intentional behaviour', in K.A. Mohyeldin Said, W.H. Newton-Smith, R. Viale and K.V Wilkes (eds), *Modelling the Mind*. Oxford: Clarendon Press. pp. 97–112.

O'Grady, P. (2002) *Relativism*. Chesham, UK: Acumen Publishing.

O'Hear, A. (1989) *An Introduction to the Philosophy of Science*. Oxford: Clarendon Press.

Oppenheim, P. and Putnam, H. (1958/1991) 'Unity of science as a working hypothesis', in R. Boyd, P. Gasper and J.D. Trout (eds), *The Philosophy of Science*. Cambridge, MA: MIT Press. pp. 405–28.

Palmer, S.E. (1978) 'Fundamental aspects of cognitive representation', in E. Rosch and B.B. Lloyd (eds), *Cognition and Categorization*. Hillsdale, NJ: Erlbaum. pp. 259–303.

Papineau, D. (1993) *Philosophical Naturalism*. Oxford: Blackwell.

Parsons, Keith (ed.) (2003) *The Science Wars: Debating Scientific Knowledge and Technology*. Amherst, NY: Prometheus Books.

Penrose, R. (1989) *The Emperor's New Mind*. Oxford: Oxford University Press.

Penrose, R. (1990) 'Precis of *The Emperor's New Mind*: concerning computers, minds, and the laws of physics', *The Behavioral and Brain Sciences*, 13: 643–705.

Penrose, R. (1994) *Shadows of the Mind*. Oxford: Oxford University Press.

Pickering, A. (1984) *Constructing Quarks*. Edinburgh: Edinburgh University Press.

Pickering, A. (1989) 'Living in the material world: on realism and experimental practice', in D. Gooding, T.J. Pinch and S. Schaffer (eds), *The Uses of Experiment: Studies in the Natural Sciences*. Cambridge: Cambridge University Press. pp. 257–97.

Pickering, A. (ed.) (1992) *Science as Practice and Culture*. Chicago: University of Chicago Press.

Pickering, A. (1995) *The Mangle of Practice*. Chicago: University of Chicago Press.

Pickering, J. and Skinner, M. (eds) (1990) *From Sentience to Symbols: Readings on Consciousness*. Hemel Hempstead: Harvester Wheatsheaf.

Pinker, S. (1994) *The Language Instinct*. Harmondsworth: Penguin Books.

Pinker, S. (1997) *How the Mind Works*. London: Allen Lane.

Pinker, S. (1999) *Words and Rules*. New York: Basic Books.

Pinker, S. (2002) *The Blank Slate*. Harmondsworth: Penguin.

Pinker, S. and Bloom, P. (1990) 'Natural language and natural selection', *The Behavioral and Brain Sciences*, 13: 707–84.

Place, U.T. (1956/1970) 'Is consciousness a brain process?', in C.V. Borst (ed.), *The Mind–Brain Identity Theory*. London: Macmillan. pp. 42–51.

Pollack, J.B. (1990) 'Recursive distributed representations', *Artificial Intelligence*, 46: 77–105.

Popper, K. (1961) *The Poverty of Historicism*. London: Routledge.

Popper, K. (1966) *The Open Society and its Enemies*, 2 Vols, 5th edn. London: Routledge & Kegan Paul.

Popper, K. (1974) *Conjectures and Refutations: The Growth of Scientific Knowledge*, 4th edn. London: Routledge.

Popper, K. (1976) *Unended Quest: An Intellectual Autobiography*. Glasgow: Collins.

Popper, K. (1979) *Objective Knowledge: An Evolutionary Approach*, rev. edn. Oxford: Oxford University Press.

Popper, K. (1994) *The Myth of the Framework: In Defence of Science and Rationality*. London: Routledge.

Popper, K. and Eccles, J.C. (1977) *The Self and its Brain*. New York: Springer Verlag.

Port, R.F. and Van Gelder, T. (eds) (1995) *Mind as Motion: Exploration in the Dynamics of Cognition*. Cambridge, MA: MIT Press/Bradford Books.

Preston, J. and Bishop, M. (2002) *Views into the Chinese Room: New essays on Searle and Artificial Intelligence*. Oxford: Clarendon Press.

Priest, S. (1991) *Theories of the Mind*. Harmondsworth: Penguin.

Putnam, H. (1961) 'Minds and machines', in S. Hook (ed.), *Dimensions of Mind*. New York: Collier. pp. 221–31.

Putnam, H. (1975) 'The meaning of meaning', in *Mind, Language and Reality: Philosophical Papers*, Vol. 2. Cambridge: Cambridge University Press.

Putnam, H. (1980) 'Reductionism and the nature of psychology', in J. Haugeland (ed.), *Mind Design*. Cambridge, MA: MIT Press. pp. 205–19.

Putnam, H. (1981) *Reason, Truth and History*. Cambridge: Cambridge University Press.

Putnam, H. (1987) *The Many Faces of Realism*. La Salle, IL: Open Court.

Putnam, H. (1988) *Representation and Reality*. Cambridge, MA: MIT Press/Bradford Books.

Putnam, H. (1990) *Realism with a Human Face*. Cambridge, MA: Harvard University Press.

Putnam, H. (1994) 'Artificial intelligence: much ado about not very much', in H. Putnam, *Words and Life*. Cambridge, MA: Harvard University Press. pp. 391–402.

Putnam, H. (1999) *The Threefold Cord: Mind, Body, and World*. New York: Columbia University Press.

Pylyshyn, Z. (1984) *Computation and Cognition: Toward a Foundation for Cognitive Science*. Cambridge, MA: MIT Press/Bradford Books.

Pylyshyn, Z.W. (1987) 'What is in a mind?', *Synthese*, 70: 97–122.

Pylyshyn, Z. (1989) 'Computing in cognitive science', in M. Posner (ed.), *Foundations of Cognitive Science*. Cambridge, MA: MIT Press. pp. 49–91.

Pylyshyn, Z.W. (1991) 'The role of cognitive architecture in theories of cognition', in K. Van Lehn (ed.), *Architectures for intelligence*. Hillsdale, NJ: Erlbaum. pp. 189–223.

Quine, W.V.O. (1961) 'Two dogmas of empiricism', in W.V.O. Quine, *From a Logical Point of View*. New York: Harper & Row. pp. 20–46. Originally published in 1951.

Quine, W.V.O. (1969a) 'Epistemology naturalized', in W.V.O. Quine, *Ontological Relativity and Other Essays*. New York: Columbia University Press. pp. 69–90.

Quine, W.V.O. (1969b) 'Natural kinds', in W.V.O. Quine, *Ontological Relativity and Other Essays*. New York: Columbia University Press. pp. 114–38.

Quine, W.V.O. (1992) 'Two dogmas in retrospect', *Canadian Journal of Philosophy*, 21: 265–74.

Radder, H. (2001) 'Psychology, physicalism and real physics', *Theory and Psychology*, 11: 773–84.

Ramsey, W., Stich, S.P. and Garon, J. (1991) 'Connectionism, eliminativism, and the future of folk psychology', in W. Ramsey, S.P. Stich and D.E. Rumelhart (eds), *Philosophy and Connectionist Theory*. Hillsdale, NJ: Erlbaum. pp. 199–228.

Reber, A.S. (2001) *The Penguin Dictionary of Psychology*. Harmondsworth: Penguin.

Rescher, N. (1987) *Scientific Realism: A Critical Reappraisal*. Dordrecht: Reidel.

Ridley, M. (1996) *The Origins of Virtue*. London: Viking.

Rogoff, B. and Wertsch, J.V. (eds) (1984) *Children's Learning in the 'Zone of Proximal Development'*. San Francisco: Jossey-Bass.

Rorty, R. (1979) *Philosophy and the Mirror of Nature*. Princeton, NJ: Princeton University Press.

Rorty, R. (1980) 'A reply to Dreyfus and Taylor', *Review of Metaphysics*, 34: 39–46.

Rorty, R. (1982a) 'Comments on Dennett', *Synthese*, 53: 181–7.

Rorty, R. (1982b) 'Contemporary philosophy of mind', *Synthese*, 55: 323–48.

Rorty, R. (1993) 'Consciousness, intentionality and pragmatism', in S.M. Christensen and D.R. Turner (eds), *Folk Psychology and the Philosophy of Mind*. Hillsdale, NJ: Erlbaum. pp. 389–404.

Rorty, R. (1998) *Truth and Progress: Philosophical Papers*. Cambridge: Cambridge University Press.

Rosenberg, A. (1985) *The Structure of Biological Science*. Cambridge: Cambridge University Press.

Rosenberg, A. (2000) *Philosophy of Science*. London: Routledge.

Rosenthal, D.M. (ed.) (1991) *The Nature of Mind*. Oxford: Oxford University Press.

Ross, Andrew (ed.) (1996) *Science Wars*. Durham, NC: Duke University Press.

Rouse, J. (1987) *Knowledge and Power: Toward a Political Philosophy of Science*. Ithaca, NY: Cornell University Press.

Rouse, J. (1998) 'New philosophies of science in North America – twenty years later', *Journal for General Philosophy of Science*, 29:71–122.

Russell, B. (1988) 'Knowledge by acquaintance and knowledge by description', in N. Salmon and S. Soames (eds), *Propositions and Attitudes*. Oxford: Oxford University Press. pp. 16–32.

Ryan, A. (1970) *The Philosophy of the Social Sciences*. London: Macmillan.

Ryle, G. (1949) *The Concept of Mind*. London: Hutchinson.

Ryle, G. (1971) *Collected Papers*, 2 Vols. London: Hutchinson.

Salmon, W.C. (1990) *Four Decades of Scientific Explanation*. Minneapolis: University of Minnesota Press.

Samuels, R. (1998) 'Evolutionary psychology and the Massive Modularity hypothesis', *British Journal for the Philosophy of Science*, 49: 575–602.

Sanders, C., Van Eisenga, L.K.A. and van Rappard, J.F.H. (1976) *Inleiding in de grondslagen van de psychologie (Introduction to the Theoretical Foundations of Psychology)*. Deventer: Van Loghum Slaterus.

Schafer, W. (ed.) (1983) *Finalisation in Science*. Dordrecht: Reidel.

Schaffner, K. (1993) *Discovery and Explanation in Biology and Medicine*. Chicago: Chicago University Press.

Schouten, M.K.D. and Looren de Jong, H. (1998) 'Defusing eliminative materialism: reference and revision', *Philosophical Psychology*, 11: 489–509.

Schouten, M.K.D. and Looren de Jong, H. (1999) 'Reduction, elimination, and levels: The case of the LTP-learning link', *Philosophical Psychology*, 12: 239–64.

Schwartz, J. (1991) 'Reduction, elimination and the mental', *Philosophy of Science*, 58: 203–20.

Searle, J. (1980) 'Minds, brains and programs', *Behavioral and Brain Sciences*, 3: 417–57.

Searle, J. (1983) *Intentionality: An Essay in the Philosophy of Mind*. Cambridge: Cambridge University Press.

Searle, J. (1990a) 'Consciousness, explanatory inversion, and cognitive science', *Behavioral and Brain Sciences*, 13: 585–642.

Searle, J. (1990b) 'Minds, brains and programs', in M. Boden (ed.), *The Philosophy of Artificial Intelligence*. Oxford: Oxford University Press. pp. 67–88.

Searle, J. (1992) *The Rediscovery of Mind*. Cambridge, MA: MIT Press.

Searle, J. (1993) 'The problem of consciousness', *Consciousness and Cognition*, 2: 310–19.

Secord, P.F. (ed.) (1982) *Explaining Human Behavior. Consciousness, Human Action and Social Structure*. Beverly Hills, CA: Sage.

Seebass, G. and Tuomela, R. (eds) (1985) *Social Action*. Dordrecht: Reidel.

Segerstråle, Ullica (ed.) (2000) *Beyond the Science Wars: The Missing Discourse about Science and Society*. Albany, NY: State University of New York Press.

Sellars, W. (1963) *Science, Perception and Reality*. London: Routledge & Kegan Paul.

Shagrir, O. (1997) 'Two dogmas of computationalism', *Minds and Machines*, 7: 321–44.

Shanon, B. (1993) *The Representational and the Presentational: An Essay on Cognition and the Study of Mind*. Hemel Hempstead: Harvester Wheatsheaf.

Shapin, S. (1975) 'Phrenological knowledge and the social structure of early nineteenth-century Edinburgh', *Annals of Science*, 32: 219–43.

Shapin, S. and Shaffer, S. (1985) *Leviathan and the Air-Pump*. Princeton, NJ: Princeton University Press.

Shepherd, G.M. (1990) 'The significance of real neuron architectures for real network simulations', in E.L. Schwartz (ed.), *Computational Neuroscience*. Cambridge, MA: MIT Press. pp. 82–96.

Shieber, S. (ed.) (2004) *The Turing Test: Verbal Behavior as the Hallmark of Intelligence*. Cambridge: MIT Press.

Shotter, J. (1975) *Images of Man in Psychological Research*. London: Methuen.

Shotter, J. (1991) 'The rhetorical-responsive nature of mind: a social constructionist account', in A. Still and A. Costall (eds), *Against Cognitivism: Alternative Foundations for Cognitive Psychology*. Hemel Hempstead: Harvester Wheatsheaf. pp. 55–79.

Shotter, J. and Gergen, K.J. (eds) (1989) *Texts of Identity*. London: Sage.

Shrager, J. and Langley, P. (eds) (1989) *Computational Models of Discovery and Theory Formation*. San Francisco: Morgan Kaufmann.

Silvers, S. (ed.) (1989) *Rerepresentation: Readings in the Philosophy of Mental Representation*. Dordrecht: Kluwer.

Simonton, D.K. (1988) *Scientific Genius: A Psychology of Science*. Cambridge: Cambridge University Press.

Sklar, L. (1999) 'The reduction(?) of thermodynamics to statistical mechanics', *Philosophical Studies*, 95: 187–202.

Slezak, P. (1994) 'A second look at David Bloor's *Knowledge and Social Imagery*', *Philosophy of the Social Sciences*, 24: 336–61.

Smith, L.B. and Thelen, E. (2003) 'Development as a dynamic system', *Trends in Cognitive Sciences*, 7: 343–48.

Smolensky, P. (1988) 'On the proper treatment of connectionism', *Behavioral and Brain Sciences*, 11: 1–74.

Smolensky, P. (1989) 'Connectionism and constituent structure', in R. Pfeiffer, Z. Schreter, F. Fogelman-Soulie and L. Steels (eds), *Connectionism in Perspective*. Amsterdam: Elsevier. pp. 3–24.

Smolensky, P. (1990) 'Connectionism, constituency and the language of thought', in B. Loewer and G. Rey (eds), *Meaning in Mind: Fodor and His Critics*. Oxford: Blackwell. pp. 201–27.

Sober, E. (1985) 'Panglossian functionalism and the philosophy of mind', *Synthese*, 64: 165–93.

Sokal, Alan D. (1996a) 'Transgressing the boundaries: towards a transformative hermeneutics of quantum gravity', *Social Text*, 46/47 (Spring/Summer): 217–52. For this and other Sokal texts: http://www.physics.nyu.edu/faculty/sokal.

Sokal, Alan D. (1996b) 'A physicist experiments with cultural studies', Published as Sokal's Response in *Lingua Franca*, 6(4): 62–4. This and the *Social Text's* article and other material are reprinted in *The Sokal Hoax: The Sham that Shook the Academy*. Ed. *Lingua franca* (2000) Lincoln, NB: University of Nebraska Press.

Sosa, E. and Tooley, M. (eds) (1993) *Causation*. Oxford: Oxford University Press.

Sperry, R. W. (1969) 'A modified concept of consciousness', *Psychological Review*, 76: 532–36.

Sterelny, K. (1990) *The Representational Theory of Mind*. Oxford: Blackwell.

Sternberg, R.J. (ed.) (1999) *Handbook of Creativity*. New York: Cambridge University Press.

Stich, S. (1983) *From Folk Psychology to Cognitive Science: The Case Against Belief*. Cambridge, MA: MIT Press/Bradford Books.

Stich, S. (1990) *The Fragmentation of Reason*. Cambridge, MA: MIT Press.

Stich, S. (1992) 'What is a theory of mental representation?', *Mind*, 101: 243–61.

Stich, S. and Warfield, T.A. (eds) (1994) *Mental Representation*. Oxford: Blackwell.

Still, A. (1991) 'Mechanism and romanticism', in A. Still and A. Costall (eds), *Against Cognitivism: Alternative Foundations for Cognitive Psychology*. Hemel Hempstead: Harvester Wheatsheaf. pp. 7–26.

Still, A. and Costall, A. (eds) (1991) *Against Cognitivism: Alternative Foundations for Cognitive Psychology*. Hemel Hempstead: Harvester Wheatsheaf.

Still, A. and Good, J.M.M. (1998) 'The ontology of mutualism', *Ecological Psychology*, 10: 339–63.

Suppe, F. (1977) 'The search for philosophical understanding of scientific theories', in F. Suppe (ed.), *The Structure of Scientific Revolutions*, 2nd edn. Urbana: University of Illinois Press.

Taylor, C. (1971) 'Interpretation and the sciences of man', *Review of Metaphysics*, 25: 3–51.

Taylor, C. (1980) 'Understanding in human science', *Review of Metaphysics*, 34: 25–38.

Terwee, S. (1990) *Hermeneutics in Psychology and Psychoanalysis*. New York and Heidelberg: Springer Verlag.

Thagard, P. (1992) *Conceptual Revolutions*. Princeton, NJ: Princeton University Press.

Thelen, E. (1995) 'Motor development', *American Psychologist*, 50: 79–95.

Thelen, E. and Smith, L.B. (1994) *A Dynamic Systems Approach to the Development of Cognition and Action*. Cambridge, MA: MIT Press/Bradford Books.

Thompson, J.B. and Held, D. (eds) (1982) *Habermas: Critical Debates*. London: Macmillan.

Tomasello, M. (1999) *The Cultural Origins of Human Cognition*. Cambridge, MA: Harvard University Press.

Tooby, J. and Cosmides, L. (1995) 'Mapping the evolved functional organization of mind and brain', in M.S. Gazzaniga (ed.), *The Cognitive Neurosciences*. Cambridge, MA: MIT Press. pp. 1185–97.

Toulmin, S. (1990) *Cosmopolis: The Hidden Agenda of Modernity*. New York: The Free Press.

Trigg, R. (1973) *Reason and Commitment*. Cambridge: Cambridge University Press.

Trigg, R. (1985) *Understanding Social Science*. Oxford: Blackwell.

Trigg, R. (1993) *Rationality and Science: Can Science Explain Everything?* Oxford: Blackwell.

Turing, A.M. (1950) 'Computing machinery and intelligence', *Mind*, 59: 433–60.

Turvey, M.T. and Carello, C. (1995) 'Some dynamical themes in perception and action', in R.F. Port and T. van Gelder (eds), *Mind as motion*. Cambridge, MA: MIT Press. pp. 373–401.

Tweney, R.D. (1985) 'Faraday's discovery of induction: a cognitive approach', in D. Gooding and F.A.J.L. James (eds), *Faraday Rediscovered*. New York: Stockton. pp. 182–209.

Tweney, R.D. (1989) 'Fields of enterprise: on Michael Faraday's thought', in D.B. Wallace and H.E. Gruber (eds), *Creative People at Work*. Oxford: Oxford University Press.

Tweney, R., Doherty, M.E. and Mynatt C.R. (eds) (1981) *On Scientific Thinking*. New York: Columbia University Press.

Valentine, E.R. (1992) *Conceptual Issues in Psychology*, 2nd edn. London: Routledge.

Van der Steen, W.J. (2000) *Evolution as Natural History*. Westport, CT: Praeger.

Van der Veer, R. and Valsiner, J. (1991) *Understanding Vygotsky: A Quest for Synthesis*. Oxford: Blackwell.

Van Fraassen, B.C. (1980) *The Scientific Image*. Oxford: Clarendon Press.

Van Fraassen, B.C. (2002) *The Empirical Stance*. New Haven, CT: Yale University Press.

Van Geert, P. (1995) 'Growth dynamics in development', in R.F. Port and T. Van Gelder (eds), *Mind as Motion*. Cambridge, MA: MIT Press. pp. 315–37.

Van Gelder, T. (1990) 'Compositionality: a connectionist variation on a classical theme', *Cognitive Science*, 14: 355–84.

Van Gelder, T. (1995) 'What might cognition be, if not computation?', *Journal of Philosophy*, 91: 345–81.

Van Gelder, T. (1998) 'The dynamical hypothesis in cognitive science', *Behavioral and Brain Sciences*, 21: 615–65

Van Gelder, T. and Port, R.F. (1995) 'It's about time: an overview of the dynamical approach to cognition', in R.F. Port and T. van Gelder (eds), *Mind as Motion*. Cambridge, MA: MIT Press. pp. 1–43.

Van Gulick, R. (1989) 'Metaphysical arguments for internalism and why they don't work', in S. Silvers (ed.), *Rerepresentation*. Dordrecht: Kluwer. pp. 151–9.

Van Rappard, H. (1979) *Psychology as Self-knowledge: The Development of the Concept of the Mind in German Rationalistic Psychology and its Relevance Today*. Assen: Van Gorcum.

Varela, F.J., Thomson, E. and Rosch, E. (1991) *The Embodied Mind: Cognitive Science and Human Experience*. Cambridge, MA: MIT Press.

Von Wright, G.H. (1963) *Norm and Action*. London: Routledge & Kegan Paul.

Von Wright, G.H. (1971) *Explanation and Understanding*. Ithaca, NY: Cornell University Press.

Von Wright, G.H. (1993) 'On the logic and epistemology of the causal relation', in E. Sosa and M. Tooley (eds), *Causation*. Oxford: Oxford University Press. pp. 105–24.

Vygotsky, L. (1962) *Thought and Language*. Cambridge, MA: MIT Press.

Walter, H. (2001) *Neurophilosophy of Free Will*. Cambridge, MA: MIT Press.

Warner, R. and Szubka, T. (eds) (1994) *The Mind–Body Problem*. Oxford: Blackwell.

Weinberg, S. (1992) *Dreams of a Final Theory*. New York: Pantheon.

Weizenbaum, J. (1976) *Computer Power and Human Reason: From Judgment to Calculation*. San Francisco: Freeman.

Wertsch, J.V. (1985) *Vygotsky and the Social Formation of Mind*. Cambridge, MA: Harvard University Press.

Wheeler, M. (2001) 'Two threats to representation', *Synthese*, 129: 211–31.

Wheeler, M. and Clark, A. (1999) 'Genic representation: reconciling content and causal complexity', *British Journal for the Philosophy of Science*, 50: 103–35.

Wilkes, K.V. (1978) *Physicalism*. London: Routledge & Kegan Paul.

Wilkes, K.V. (1980) 'Brain states', *British Journal for the Philosophy of Science*, 31: 111–29.

Williams, M. (1999) *Wittgenstein, Mind and Meaning: Towards a Social Conception of Mind*. London: Routledge.

Wilson, T. (2002) *Strangers to Ourselves*. Cambridge, MA: Belknap.

Winch, P. (1958) *The Idea of a Social Science and its Relation to Philosophy*. London: Routledge & Kegan Paul.

Wittgenstein, L. (1953) *Philosophical Investigations*. Trans. G.E.M. Anscombe. Oxford: Blackwell.

Wittgenstein, L. (1961) *Tractatus Logico-Philosophicus*. Trans. D.F. Pears and B.F. McGuiness. London: Routledge & Kegan Paul. Originally published 1921.

Wittgenstein, L. (1981) *Zettel*, 2nd edn. Ed. G.E.M. Anscombe and G.H. von Wright. Oxford: Blackwell.

Wolfe, T. (2000) 'Sorry, but your soul just died', in T. Wolfe, *Hooking up*. London: Jonathan Cape. pp. 89–109.

Woolgar, S. (1988) *Science: The Very Idea*. Chichester: Ellis Horwood.

Wright, L. (1973) 'Functions', *Philosophical Review*, 82: 139–68.

Wright, L. (1976) *Teleological Explanations*. Berkeley: University of California Press.

Wright, R. (1994) *The Moral Animal*. New York: Pantheon.

Wyer, R.S. and Srull, T.K. (eds) (1984) *Handbook of Social Cognition*, 2 Vols. Hillsdale, NJ: Erlbaum.

Yates, F. (1964) *Giordano Bruno and the Hermetic Tradition*. London: Routledge & Kegan Paul.

Yates, F. (1972) *The Rosicrucian Enlightenment*. London: Routledge & Kegan Paul.

NAME INDEX

SUBJECT INDEX